The Parenting Journey

The Parenting Journey

From Conception through the Teen Years

GREGORY MOFFATT

Westport, Connecticut
London

Library of Congress Cataloging-in-Publication Data

Moffatt, Gregory K., 1961–
   The parenting journey : from conception through the teen years / Gregory Moffatt.
      p. cm.
   Includes bibliographical references and index.
   ISBN 0–275–97903–2 (alk. paper)
      1. Parenting. 2. Parent and child. 3. Child rearing. I. Title.
   HQ755.8.M627   2004
   649'.1—dc22   2003068727

British Library Cataloguing in Publication Data is available.

Library of Congress Catalog Card Number: 2003068727
ISBN: 0–275–97903–2

First published in 2004

Praeger Publishers, 88 Post Road West, Westport, CT 06881
An imprint of Greenwood Publishing Group, Inc.
www.praeger.com

Printed in the United States of America

The paper used in this book complies with the
Permanent Paper Standard issued by the National
Information Standards Organization (Z39.48–1984).

10 9 8 7 6 5 4 3 2 1

Contents

Acknowledgments

There is no higher calling than that of being a parent. The decisions and thoughts of the holders of many social positions affect more people than mine do. However, I know that there is no person in the world who has a greater influence on my own children than I do. No teacher, politician, doctor, minister, or friend will affect their lives as deeply as my own actions will. Therefore, I take my job as a father very seriously and I am grateful to those people who accept the responsibility of being a parent with the same level of respect and attention. To all of you who share this calling, I dedicate this work, that we might all be better at our jobs as mothers and fathers.

I wish to thank my parents, Mr. and Mrs. Carlys Moffatt, for their work and sacrifice as they raised my sisters and me. You not only cared for me, but through you I learned many of life's most important lessons and became what I am today.

Thank you to Christine Peters, Crissi Holzmann, Cal Beverly, the late Dave Hammrick, and others on the editorial staff at *The Citizen* newspaper in Fayette County, Georgia, for editing my work and allowing me to address your audience through my newspaper column on family and children since 1994 when I began writing this column.

Thank you to the many people who have inspired me through their examples to be a better parent. Each of you has taught me something important: Dr. and Mrs. R. Edwin Groover, Dr. and Mrs. Dennis Glenn, Dr. and Mrs. Tommy Oaks, Dr. Robert Woods, Mr. Earl Stuckenbruck, and Mr. Wye Huxford, just to name a few.

I am deeply grateful to Mr. and Mrs. Dale Mullins, my mother- and father-in-law, for setting such a tremendous example for me. By observing them,

I am learning how to be a grandparent and an in-law. It is my goal to be as gracious, loving, and accepting in both roles as they have always been for me and for my children.

To my wife, Stacey, who through more than 20 years of marriage has demonstrated true selflessness both as a wife and as a mother, thank you for your leadership and all that you do. Your example and leadership have made me a better man.

Finally, thank you to my three children, Megan, Kara, and Benjamin. It is from the three of you that I have learned the deepest and purest kind of love. Through the years you have made me laugh, introspect, and correct myself. You have made me work hard, but you also have given me the greatest joys of my life. I have learned more about the principles of growth and development from you than I ever learned from any book. Thank you for the many ways in which you have been my teachers. Through the stories about you that I share in this book, you have taught me, and you will also teach many others for years to come. I love you more than life itself, and you inspire me to be a better dad.

Author's Note

Many of the physical issues discussed in this book are complicated and have multiple causes. Often in the text I suggest that parents refer to their pediatrician or OB/GYN for advice. The developmental and physiological issues I address are meant to provide information on how the body works, but this book is not meant to be a medical text, nor should it substitute for professional advice from one's physician regarding physical and medical issues.

PART I

Conception through Delivery

CHAPTER 1

Introduction

Worrying is less work than doing something to fix the worry. Everybody
wants to save the earth; nobody wants to help mom with the dishes.
—P. J. O'Rourke, "All the Trouble in the World"

As a teenager and young adult I never really appreciated children. Young
children, especially babies, appeared to require constant attention; they made
unpleasant sounds and often produced noxious odors; and overall they just
seemed like a lot of work. Yet when I became a parent, I realized . . . I was
exactly right! But what I wasn't prepared for was the instantaneous love I
felt for my newborn and how insignificant those other things actually were.
Babies have the ability to evoke in a parent a caregiving response that
nonparents cannot fully understand.

Parenting is perhaps the most important job on the planet. There are few
things, if any, that we can do that have more impact on a person's present and
future than how we raise him, and yet for some reason the standard belief
seems to be that if we have the biological capability to reproduce, it is our right,
and we don't need any training. In other words, people seem to believe that
all that is required for being a parent is the ability to conceive a child. It is
only after people have children that they realize there are things they do not
know and that raising children is more confusing than they may have thought.
I've always been amazed at how many childless people have "corrected" me
about my views on parenting as compared to those who have children. There
are far more of the former. Being a parent is not an easy calling.

Many years ago I came home after finishing the last evening of a three-night seminar I had conducted on parenting for a community of parents and parents-to-be. I was excited about the seminar that I had just finished and I thought it had gone very well. When I arrived home, the telephone rang, and my sister was on the other end of the line. A worried tone in her voice caught my attention. I asked her what was wrong.

"I'm so discouraged," she told me. "I just got home from a parenting seminar at my church and I feel so inadequate. I'll never be able to be the kind of parent they talked about."

As I listened to my sister's words, I realized that in my attempt to present the ideal for parents, I might have sent participants home from my own seminar equally discouraged. I had tried to present the very best of what I knew, but easily a listener could have supposed, just like my sister, "I could never remember all of that." Those of us who teach parenting skills run the risk of:

Making parenting sound easy—it most definitely isn't.
Making parenting sound impossible—it most definitely isn't.
Sounding like we have all the answers—we definitely don't.
Sounding like we don't have struggles with our own kids—we definitely do.

Perhaps the biggest risk is unintentionally setting goals so high that people feel defeated to the point that they don't want to try. Since that telephone call more than 15 years ago, I have always tried to make sure that my readers, students, and seminar participants see me as one of them. Just like them, I get frustrated with my children, and I make mistakes. When I'm tired or distracted, I don't always practice what I preach. And even though it doesn't happen often, sometimes, as I'm trying to decide how to handle a given situation with my children, I find myself shrugging my shoulders, wondering what to try next. Parenting is difficult even for a child psychologist.

Even though these things are true, my many years of experience, clinical practice, and education have made parenting easier. I have always been frustrated with students who say to me, "I didn't study and I did better on the test than usual," as if *not* studying paves the way to brilliance. Learning about children and understanding how children develop physically, cognitively, emotionally, and socially can make you a better parent. This, combined with an understanding of behavioral principles, can make it easier to train your children, to achieve cooperation, and to anticipate their moods, struggles, and behavior. Recognition of their cognitive and physical limitations at any point in their development, and knowing their strengths as well as their social needs at various stages, have made me a better parent and it can do the same for you. This is what I hope to provide for you in this book and I am confident that when we work at parenting, we get better at it—as opposed to the philosophy of some of my students, who believe that they will be better if they just wing it.

I've spent my entire life preparing to be a parent. I apply everything that I do—my work, my education, and my daily experiences—to my role as a parent, so that I will improve. I make no decision in leisure or in my professional life without considering its effects on my family. I love my professional life and my leisure activities, but nothing comes before my children and their best interests—not my job, not my salary, not my personal desires. I carefully consider speaking engagements and I have established criteria for myself to avoid crowding my schedule with events away from home—an easy trap to fall into when one can earn thousands of dollars for each engagement. I decline many of these invitations because I know that I will have no more powerful influence on any human beings more than I will on my own children. Their productivity, their ability to face challenges, and their selection of a mate—as well as their emotional dysfunctions in adulthood—will in part be a product of what I create. My first responsibility is to them and I don't want to miss a thing.

I have written several books, lectured to thousands of people in hundreds of places, and written a newspaper column on family and children's issues for many years. I even tried out for the Olympics in soccer (*many* years ago!). Yet the highest compliment anyone can pay me is to call me a good dad. I know that my role as a father has an indelible influence on what my children become and how they choose to live their lives. By observing me, my son will learn how to be a father, how to discipline his children, and how to be responsible with his time and money. He will learn how to treat his wife, as well. By observing me, my daughters will learn how to interact with their children and how a man should treat a woman. By observing my relationship with my wife, they will learn what is expected of wives, what is acceptable and what is not—thus affecting their future choice of a spouse. These things they learn by watching, not by direct instruction from me. Even though my behaviors do not *determine* what they become, they have a significant influence on them. I am perpetuating who I am through my children. If I am rude to my spouse, selfish with my time and money, and uninvolved with my children, that is likely what their future families will experience. On the other hand, if I am loving to my children and my spouse, and if I demonstrate patience and acceptance with them through my actions, it is more likely that they will be patient and loving to their future families.

I am not mistake-free, but my efforts to invest in my family will be obvious to them over time.

Parenting is not a part-time job. It requires unparalleled commitment and devotion. There is nothing you will ever do that is any more frustrating and yet there is nothing you will ever do that is more rewarding. Every two years I teach a class to undergraduate students on prenatal and neonatal development. Most students in that class are single and have no children. When we study the birthing process and watch a number of videos on various birthing techniques—natural childbirth, cesarean, vaginal-unassisted, and so forth—my students try to comprehend such a large object (a full-term baby) passing through such a small space (a fully dilated birth canal). After watching these videos, many of them swear that they will never have children. What is difficult to communicate to them is what mothers all over the world have learned through experience. Even when delivery is painful (for some women it is easier than for others), the miracle of birth is so fantastic—the excitement of seeing your own healthy baby for the first time is so overpowering—the pain of childbirth is forgotten almost immediately. Parenting is both frustrating and rewarding—both anxiety-producing and liberating. Over the long term, the frustrations and pains our children cause us rarely overshadow the joy they bring. Being a parent is an adventure that I wouldn't trade for the world and my wish is that this book will communicate not only the nuts and bolts of parenting but also the excitement of the miracle of life.

I've talked a lot about how much children learn from us as parents, but I would be negligent if I didn't also address what we can learn from them. For close to two decades I have spent my days studying children, consulting with others about children, doing therapy with children, and raising my own. I coach little league soccer, I'm in a grade school at least once a week, and I regularly work with babies and toddlers at my church. I look for opportunities to be around children. I know some people consider my work with children as an altruistic act, but the truth is my motives are partially selfish. Children energize me. After a five-hour field trip with kindergarten children, I have more energy than I did when we started. Children not only give me energy, but when I pay close attention they remind me of some of life's most important lessons. These are some of those lessons.

I've learned to find pleasure in little things. While I'm busy worrying about balancing my checkbook, world events, or my job, my son is outside noticing the beauty of a beetle or a butterfly, the interesting way that water forms on a spider's web in the morning, or the pleasure of swinging on the playground and making up a song. On a bus ride while I'm thinking about reaching my destination, the children around me are enjoying each other, looking out the window counting cows or telling funny stories about each other. Children teach me to slow down, laugh more, and live in the moment.

Children remind me of the importance of touch. They have no understanding of personal space or privacy—lessons they will eventually learn— but the purity of closeness with children is powerful. They aren't afraid to hold hands, to give a hug to someone they like, or to kiss the forehead of someone who is feeling sad. They don't have to worry about lawyers, lawsuits, allegations, or innuendo. They simply act out what they feel. I can gauge my son's moods by how much energy he puts into a hug. When he is really excited and happy to see me, he makes a running start before he hugs me. This tells me how much he missed me. At bedtime he once told me that when I was gone he missed me "one thousand kisses." Children teach me how to be close to another human being.

Children constantly remind me how readily they accept the differences of others. Skin color, gender, size, birth defects, and language differences are easily overcome for children. They notice differences immediately, but they accept them almost as quickly. I have observed children on the playground helping a child in a wheelchair move from one area to another so the child could at least watch the other children play ball. They matter-of-factly accept situations as they are and go from there—no blame, no accusations, no condemnation, and no superior attitude. From children I've learned to look beyond the surface.

When I am around children, I remember how important it is to forget. Adults work hard at remembering things, but we fail to realize that some things should be forgotten. A child can quickly go from an embarrassing or hurtful situation back to "business as usual" when he or she is distracted by something more important. The memory of the bad experience can fade into oblivion when more important things are at hand. How many times have we all spent energy stewing over some embarrassing or hurtful event when it would have been much healthier just to let it go? From children I am reminded to forget.

From children I have learned the importance of forgiveness. When I have had to apologize to my children for a thoughtless remark I have made, they have always forgiven me. They take me at my word when I say, "I'm sorry." Their ready acceptance makes it much easier to forgive myself, and the good feeling that brings to me reminds me how important it is that I learn to forgive others when they have hurt me. Children teach me this important lesson.

When I play with children, they often see me as just another playmate. Even though I'm Kara's dad, or Benjamin's dad, I'm not too big to have fun and that is good enough for them. Even though I recognize that they have much to learn from me, it is I who feel like I'm getting the better end of the deal. Pay attention to your children and you will learn these things, too.

As I prepared this book, I had in mind as ideal readers both couples planning to have children and parents who already have them. New parents are at a distinct advantage because they can avoid many of the problems experienced by parents who establish dysfunctional patterns of interaction with their children over time, because these patterns of behavior are difficult, although not impossible, to change. For example, discipline of children involves a history of interaction, not a single behavior. As you will see in the coming chapters, when deciding how to deal with a toddler's or preschool child's behavior, one must consider not only how to discipline the child but also what the long-term effect of that interaction will be. For example, I work at home much of the year. Throughout the day, my children will come in and out of my office as I am trying to concentrate, asking me questions, wanting me to play, or wanting to show me something they have done. Even when I would prefer not to be bothered, I make myself think before I respond, "How will my response contribute to how they will remember me when they are adults and how they will treat their own children?" I want them to learn to respect my privacy and my need to work, but I also want them to remember me as a father who always communicated to them that they were important. When their children bother them in the future, I want them to think: "I remember how Dad always had time for me." With this in mind, I often find that my work can wait. My decision, therefore, reflects not only what I do at that time, but also how my children will see me, and themselves, many years down the road.

Once, while speaking to a group of parents on the issue of discipline, a woman in the audience asked me, "My 16-year-old daughter won't get off the telephone when I tell her to. What should I do?"

"Get a pair of scissors and cut the phone line," was my answer.

I went on to explain that I really didn't mean that, but I wanted to illustrate that her problem was much deeper than getting her child to hang up the phone. The woman's only problem wasn't that the child would not hang up the telephone—her real problem was that this teenage girl did not respect her mother. The mother's problem was one of respect, not compliance. That doesn't develop overnight. In some way, the woman had trained her daughter to believe that she did not have to obey or respect her mother. That kind of training takes just as much time as teaching respect and compliance. One of my students was a gentleman from Albania. He likened parenting to growing a tree. It is much easier to shape the tree, he said, when it is young and pliable. As the tree grows, it eventually becomes strong and firm and cannot be easily shaped. The early years of parenting are the years when shaping is most easily done. However, that doesn't mean you shouldn't try if you have erred along the way. I have seen some amazing healing take place between children and their parents, despite relationships that were seriously damaged by many years of bad decisions, because the parents were willing to change and were trying to do a better job of parenting.

An issue that I will address repeatedly in the coming chapters is day care. Many children grow up in day care and turn out fine. They don't have excessive health problems, emotional problems, or social difficulties. The research on day care is mixed. Some research has shown benefits for children in day care and some has shown problems. Most researchers agree that children do not benefit at all from day care prior to six months of age. After those six months, the professional community is divided regarding how to blend research findings with developmental theory. However, as you will see in my comments throughout the book, it is my belief that whenever possible, parents should avoid day care. Single parents, especially, have no choice but to use some form of day care. Many Americans, however, use day care because they choose a lifestyle that requires more money than a single income affords. My position is that there are very few drawbacks and many benefits to remaining home with your child and I will present this case throughout the book.

In this book, you will learn about shaping the tree. I will present a sketch, an outline, of the issues related to various stages in the parenting process, beginning with the decision to conceive a child and ending with launching your child into adulthood. Chapters 1 through 3 provide an overview of issues related to planning for a child, preparing for birth, and the birthing process. Chapters 4 through 9 and following are organized into three major sections: thinking, feeling, and doing. In these sections you will learn about what is happening in a child's mind and about his or her cognitive abilities and limitations. You will also learn about the child's emotions, what to expect, and how to prepare for and foster emotional development. Finally, you will learn about the child's physical body, what to expect at each stage of development, and what the child needs in order to develop normally. In each stage I also discuss issues that are generally of interest to parents of children in that particular stage of development. I would like this book to be exhaustive, but I know that is unrealistic. In a book of limited length, I could write either an extensive review of a few stages or a cursory overview of many stages. I wanted to prepare a book that answered the basic and most common questions about raising children. Therefore, this book presents the major issues and questions that arise in each stage of development.

There are many topics that appear in more than one chapter because they are important issues at more than one stage of life. For example, discipline is an issue at each stage of life, but the astute parent does not administer discipline the same way to children of different ages. Even though some readers may begin this book at chapter 1 and read through to the end, I recognize that many readers will use this book as a reference and read only topics pertinent to their interests at the moment. Therefore, I repeat myself in some places, anticipating this type of reader. It is also for this reason that in other places, I refer to previous sections or previous chapters. The index can be a helpful resource in locating topics that appear throughout the book. Finally, the detailed bibliography at the end of the book provides extensive resources related to parenting. Therefore, if you find that you need more information on a given topic than I have given you, use the bibliography to pursue further study.

Some of the many topics included in the following pages are the decision to conceive, conception, birth, adoption, birthing methods, discipline, health, development, education, recreation, social life, freedom, responsibility, and dating. How a child learns and how he or she acquires normal sexual responses, gay and lesbian issues, and sexual behaviors also are addressed in these pages, as are parenting styles, divorce, gay and lesbian parenting, and single parenting. The purpose in each of these sections is to provide enough information to answer direct questions, as well as enough of an overview of the issue so that the parent may have some foundation for further research.

Throughout this book I discuss methods of parenting, teaching, and decision making that have been used in my household. A healthy marriage and effective parenting are team efforts—a truth that I hope becomes evident as you read this book. Even though I am married and my wife and I make decisions together, I use the word "I" throughout the book. This does not mean that my wife was not a part of the process in each example. Rather it is descriptive of the fact that this book represents my perspective and I have chosen not to speak for my spouse by using the term "we," even though "we" is more often the correct word.

In our U.S. culture, many of us invest the majority of our lives into things that have no lasting value—jobs, cars, boats, games and toys. However, your children don't really care whether you are a bank president or a kindergarten teacher. They do care about the time you invest in them and they want you to be proud of them. Many times in my work as a therapist I have listened to adults, some in their fifties or sixties, who still cried when they talked about their parents and hurtful things that they did many years earlier. Never once have I worked with a client who complained that a parent's job wasn't prestigious enough. As P. J. O'Rourke said, we want to change the world, but often we don't want to do the work that is right in front of us. I believe we can change the world by doing the dishes. Being a better parent can affect generations of children.

Working to become a better parent can help you at any stage of life, even if your children are grown. You may find ways to heal damaged relationships with your adult children and this information may make you a better grandparent. For those of you who have children at home, do not deceive yourself into thinking that parenting ends when your children graduate from high school. It is a lifelong responsibility. I wish you the best as you embark on this entertaining, frustrating, and fantastic voyage—the hardest job you will ever love.

CHAPTER 2

Planning a Family: The Decision to Conceive or Adopt

Andy Griffith to six-year-old Opie: "If you married Karen, her name would become Taylor. And your children would be Taylors, too." "Oh, I don't think we'd have any children, Pa," replied Opie. "We already know plenty of kids to play with."

—*The Andy Griffith Show*

The baby was very close. Labor had been tolerable for my wife and reasonably short. At almost any minute the birth would be complete and our baby would arrive. I watched as his head, shoulders, and chest entered the outside world. His little eyes were closed; his body, pink and perfect. One last push from my wife and he was born, our third child and first son. I was the first to see him when his head was only crowning at the opening of the cervix; after he was delivered, I was the first to cradle his tiny body; and I was the first to know without question that our new baby was a boy. Three times I've been to the delivery room with my wife, and three times I've watched the miracle of birth. Having a baby is an experience that can be fully understood only by those who have lived it and it is like no other. But birth is not the beginning of raising a family. The beginning is the decision to conceive. The decision to have a child begins a life of frustration, fear, and hard work, but also one of joy, laughter, and elation. The decision to conceive is a lifelong commitment.

There are many things to consider when planning a family. How children change your life, how many children to have, when to have them, how far apart, and how to prepare financially are important considerations, as is one's marital status and the strength of that relationship. Adoption, birth-control methods, birth order, and the effect of a new baby on siblings are also important issues. Each of these issues is discussed in this chapter. as well as issues related to the age of parents-to-be, religion and its pertinence to child rearing, and many other topics of interest to prospective parents.

A CHANGE IN YOUR WAY OF LIFE

Whether one adopts, conceives naturally, or conceives through some assisted means, the decision to raise a child is a lifelong decision. No longer will you be able to go when and where you want. The child's schedule and needs will take priority. The decision to change your job, move to a new city, go on vacation, and so forth will not be made without first thinking about what is best for the child. Even after your children are grown, their influence remains. Where to live, for example, will be tempered by proximity to your children and grandchildren.

From the day your baby is born, your life will never be the same. You will sleep less, have less money for yourselves, and worry more than you ever did in the past. When your child is an infant, formerly simple tasks like running a quick errand to the grocery store become much more complicated. You can't leave the house without bottles, pacifiers, diapers, wipes, and a host of other items that make you feel like you're packing for a two-week trip every time you leave home.

Some couples are fortunate and have a child who begins sleeping through the night after a few weeks, but many parents aren't that lucky. Depending on the child's health, breast- or bottle-feeding, and a few other factors, the child may not sleep through the night for many months. In fact, your child may be up and down during the night for several years. Get used to living with less sleep.

As children get older, your schedule will be monopolized by registration for school, trips to the pediatrician, recitals, parent-teacher conferences, and programs at school. Your circle of friends will change to include parents of children who attend school with your child or who play on the same athletic team, and most of your travels will be to and from events that benefit your child. What adult would spend two days at Disneyworld if it wasn't for the entertainment of a child? As your children reach adolescence, your money will trickle out of your life—$25 for a field trip, $50 for a yearbook, $30 for new shoes. Sometimes your money will leave you en masse—$450 for a band instrument, $800 for summer camp, or $3,500 for new braces. Of course, a parent does not have to indulge each and every whim of the child, but regardless of one's intent, children are expensive.

Despite these changes, there is no joy like what you will experience when your child rolls over for the first time, or takes his first steps, or utters his first words. Get your camera and video recorder ready for capturing those moments. Other times will be important to you but hard to explain to others—like the joy of listening to your toddler sing to himself while he plays or watching your five-year-old ride a bike for the first time. Even taking a walk to the mailbox with your child will bring you happiness. Every night is a joy for me when my children put their hands on the back of my neck, hug me, and tell me they love me. What could be better?

THE DECISION TO CONCEIVE

Some women become pregnant by accident, because of ineffective birth control or lack of understanding about their own physiology. For example, some women falsely believe that they cannot get pregnant while they are lactating. While lactating women usually do not menstruate, they are still capable of conceiving. Other misconceptions are harder to believe but equally based on myth. For example, I once had a client who became pregnant because she believed that if she held her breath during her orgasm, she could not become pregnant.

Other couples plan their pregnancies. Their reasons for conceiving are varied. Some conceive to continue their family line and others choose to have children because they believe it is a natural part of life. They believe that if they do not have children, they are not complete. Unfortunately, the myth that a family is complete only with children leads parents to conceive children when they really don't want them and it also compounds the anguish of couples who are unable to conceive. The decision to conceive is a personal one that rests solely with the parents. Culture, tradition, and social pressure, while they may be considered in the decision, do not determine whether or not a couple should conceive. The responsibility of being a parent is too great for the decision to be based on these shallow reasons. The decision about whether or not to conceive should be based on a number of issues. For example, are you and your spouse prepared for the financial and emotional cost of parenting? Do you both want a child? Do you and your spouse agree that now is the right time? If the answer to these questions is yes, then it may be time to start a family.

Some couples are able to conceive the first month they try, while others, after months or years of trying, find it difficult or even impossible to conceive.

For couples who wish to have a child of their own but are having difficulty conceiving, there are many options available. In vitro fertilization, fertility drugs, and other medical interventions, while very expensive, can help the couple surmount biological difficulties.

ADOPTION

Many couples have wrestled with the question of having children. On the one hand, couples want a baby of their own—one who is a part of themselves and a physical representation of their union. Yet they may also believe that there are many children who are orphaned or in homes where they cannot receive proper care. Adoption can provide a couple with a child and a needy child with a home. Whether a couple adopts because of inability to conceive or for some other reason, adoptive parents usually find that they love their children as if they were biologically their own and don't even think of them as adopted. Adoption can be expensive and time-consuming, and there are risks for adoptive parents that do not exist with one's biological children.

Adopting through governmental organizations can take years. There is an elaborate process in place to ensure that prospective parents are competent and to ensure that the child will be well cared for. Adoption by this method can take up to ten years. It may be worth waiting ten years, but there are other options that are much faster. Private organizations, churches, and groups that care for unwed mothers can provide a child for a couple within months. These agencies provide prenatal care and ensure that the mother takes care of herself during her pregnancy. Sometimes these prebirth expenses are covered by the adoptive parents in exchange for custody of the child.

However, one potential problem with adoption agencies is that the birth mother can always change her mind. There have been a number of cases in the United States where a birth mother has signed away her rights to adoptive parents, but after the birth of the baby she changes her mind and sets in motion a very long and painful legal battle over custody of the child. Biological fathers have filed such suits as well. Sadly, the child may live with the adoptive parents for 12–24 months only to be wrenched away by social services agents when the court grants custody to a biological parent. This is extremely painful to the adoptive parents, not to mention its effect on the baby or toddler. In an attempt to avoid these problems, many couples have sought adoptions in foreign countries like Romania and Russia (the number-one foreign country for adoption of Caucasian babies). Foreign adoptions are expensive, costing $20,000 or more, and they are not without problems, but the likelihood of having to return the child to the birth mother is almost nonexistent.

I have worked with couples who have adopted a child from a relative, a choice that creates a potentially stressful dynamic within the family. In many cases, the mother of the child is young, unmarried, and incapable of raising the child herself. A well-intentioned relative offers to adopt the child and raise it as his or her own. The relative's love for this unborn child, however, often blinds him or her to the problems that this produces. If the birth mother remains involved, there is great potential for difficulties between her and the adoptive parents. Other complications in family dynamics are also possible. Grandparents, the birth mother, and other relatives may disapprove of the way the child is being raised and believe that they have the right to voice that opinion because they are the "real" relatives. For this reason, I do not recommend adoption within the family.

BABIES DO NOT FIX BROKEN MARRIAGES

As an intern I counseled married couples. Several of my clients had attempted to fix their damaged marriage by having a baby. Their belief was that if they had a common focus, a cute little baby, their differences could be overcome and their marriage would improve. Sadly, this is not the case. Even for healthy marriages, babies add stress; they don't remove stress. Babies require so much attention, time, and money that to believe they will fix a damaged marriage is naïve. Adding to the stressed relationship are more expenses, less personal time with the spouse, less privacy for oneself, and less sleep. These circumstances exacerbate marriage difficulties. Couples whose marriages are on shaky ground should repair their relationship before adopting or conceiving.

BIRTH CONTROL

It may seem odd to have a discussion of birth control and abortion in a parenting book, but over the years I have seen too many children who were neglected or abused by parents who really didn't want them. I must emphasize that the decision to conceive is a serious one, and a couple should not conceive until they are ready to accept the lifelong responsibility of raising children. For a couple who wishes to have children but wants to time the event, an understanding of birth control is imperative. Too many people either take their chances that they won't get pregnant or they assume that they can get an abortion if they conceive at an inconvenient time. Birth control is a more responsible way to ensure that one does not become pregnant until one is ready to be a parent.

There is only one way to prevent conception, and that is to prevent the fertilization of the ovum by the sperm. Even though abortions and intra-uterine devices (IUDs) are often considered methods of birth control, they do not prevent conception. I will discuss both of these issues later in the chapter. Anytime a healthy, mature sperm and healthy, mature egg come together, fertilization is likely. I once knew a religious couple who decided that they would let God decide whether or not they should have children. They considered prayer a form of birth control. While I appreciated their faith, I was quite certain that if both of them were sexually healthy, they would conceive a child within the first few months of their marriage. Sure enough, God decided within the first month of marriage that He wanted them to have children. The biology of reproduction is predictable. Myth, religion, and folklore are ineffective means of birth control. All of the methods of birth control discussed below prevent the egg and sperm from uniting or they prevent implantation of a fertilized egg into the wall of the uterus. My suggestion to abortion advocates who argue that a woman should have a right to choose what she does with her body is that they recognize that she can retain her right to choose by choosing to behave responsibly in regard to her decision to have sexual intercourse as well as selecting a method of birth control that will ensure she does not become pregnant. This is cheaper, easier, less physically and emotionally painful, and less controversial than abortion. A little more than half of all pregnancies are unplanned.[1] The most common reasons for unwanted pregnancies are the failure to use contraception or using contraceptives improperly, broken condoms, and misunderstanding of one's physiology. The following contraceptive methods vary in their effectiveness, and no method of contraception, except for abstinence, protects against sexually transmitted diseases.

Abstinence

Abstinence is one way to choose not to have children, and this method of birth control is 100 percent effective. Abstinence outside of a committed marital relationship is effective not only in preventing pregnancy but also in preventing the spread of sexually transmitted diseases. Within a marriage, periodic abstinence is effective in prevention of pregnancy. Abstinence during ovulation, menstrual periods, or times of physical discomfort is not uncommon among married couples, but long-term abstinence is not psychologically healthy for the marriage unless both partners agree and have little interest in sexual interaction—a rare situation in marriages.

Ovulation Timing

The timing of ovulation and abstaining or using another method during ovulation is also called the "rhythm" method. During ovulation one of the woman's two ovaries releases an *ovum*. Once the ovum is released from the ovary, it moves across a small space between the ovary and the fallopian tube. Once it is inside the fallopian tube, if the male gamete (*sperm*) is present, fertilization is likely and a zygote, the cellular beginnings of a human being, starts to take form. The ovum, however, is capable of being fertilized for only about 24–48 hours from the time of ovulation (therefore, a woman is only fertile about 24-48 hours each month). The other 26–27 days in the woman's menstrual cycle are either preparation for fertilization, preparation for menstruation, or menstruation itself. Therefore, if the woman could know when she ovulated, she could either abstain from intercourse for the next 48 hours or use another method to prevent pregnancy. The problem with this method is that many women have irregular cycles and identifying the point of ovulation is difficult and inexact, although it can be done by checking one's temperature. An increase of about half a degree occurs at ovulation. Thermometers are available at drugstores specifically for this purpose. The rhythm method is about 75 percent effective.

Hormone Pills

Many women today, both married and unmarried, choose to be sexually active. Birth-control pills are prescribed by a physician and, when taken as directed, are very effective in preventing pregnancy. They are made up of a combination of hormones that prevents the egg from being released from the ovary. The pill also causes the cervical mucus to thicken, making it difficult for sperm to survive, and it causes the uterus to thin, making implantation of a rare fertilized egg unlikely. Birth-control pills have other benefits as well. For women who have irregular or painful menstrual cycles, they can regulate their menstrual cycles, thus easing the difficulties they experience during menstruation. While some studies suggest a possible link between taking birth-control pills and some forms of cancer (cervical and ovarian tumors), there are no clear data that link the pill to breast cancer, and it may even reduce the risk of endometrial cancer. The greatest risk is for cardiovascular disease, but in all cases, only certain segments of the population seem to be at risk (women who smoke, are over age 35, or are obese, who have high blood pressure, and who are long-term users of the pill). The pill is about 95 percent effective.

Norplant®

This is a form of birth control in which thin plastic capsules are implanted under the skin on the woman's arm. The implant slowly releases a hormone that functions in the same way as birth-control pills. The advantage of Norplant® over the pill is twofold. First of all, it is extremely effective—99.9 percent. This implant is the most effective form of birth control available other than abstinence—statistically even more effective than sterilization. Second, because it is effective for five years, the woman does not have to remember to take a pill every day. The implant is effective within about a day of implantation and once it is removed, the woman is fertile within hours. The cost for this procedure and for the inserts is about the same as what a woman would spend on birth-control pills over five years. Neither Norplant® nor the pill should be used while a woman is nursing or pregnant.

Depo-Provera

Similar to Norplant® is a hormonal injection called Depo-Provera. A woman choosing this method receives an injection from a physician in the arm or the buttocks about every 12 weeks. Depo-Provera prevents the egg from being released from the ovary and is 99.7 percent effective. All chemical methods of birth control—the pill, implants, and Depo-Provera—have some risks, and the decision to use them should be made only after consultation with one's physician.

Condoms, Foams, Sponges, and Spermicides

These are among the least effective birth-control methods, varying between 60 and 80 percent in their effectiveness, but they are better than no birth control at all. All of these methods are meant to prevent sperm from reaching the ovum. Condoms, when used properly, prevent semen from entering the woman's cervix, although leakage and breakage may occur. Foams, sponges, and spermicides do not prevent the sperm from entering the cervix, but they either prevent the sperm from reaching the ovum (sponges and foams), or they kill the sperm in the cervix (spermicides), or they do both. Many women and their partners find these methods inconvenient and argue that they destroy the romantic mood during foreplay and intercourse. This seems a small sacrifice, however, when compared with the lifetime responsibility of raising a child. Talk about inconvenience!

Diaphragm

A diaphragm is a device that is inserted into the cervix and acts as a barrier to prevent the sperm from passing into the uterus and eventually to the fallopian tube, where fertilization usually occurs. Diaphragms must be fitted by a physician. The woman inserts the diaphragm prior to intercourse. Diaphragms require the use of a spermicidal jelly and must be properly fitted, or their effectiveness is decreased. Diaphragms are most effective when used in conjunction with other forms of birth control like the pill, a condom, or spermicides. By itself, a diaphragm is about 80 percent effective.

Withdrawal

Withdrawal is yet another form of birth control. Users of this method engage in unprotected intercourse. Just prior to ejaculation, the male withdraws from the woman's vagina, thereby preventing the introduction of sperm into the uterus. This method is among the least reliable forms of birth control for several reasons. Some men ejaculate quickly, before they can withdraw. Others intend to withdraw but lack the self-control to do so at the height of orgasm. Even assuming that the man withdraws prior to ejaculation, pregnancy is still possible. Pre-ejaculatory fluid that is emitted during foreplay and intercourse contains some sperm. Although pregnancy is unlikely from the minimal amount of sperm present in pre-ejaculatory fluid, it is possible. It is also a remote possibility that pregnancy could occur if the male ejaculates onto the surface of the vagina, even if he has withdrawn. At best, withdrawal is only about 80 percent reliable.

Intrauterine Device (IUD)

An IUD is a small device that comes in various sizes and shapes. It is inserted into the uterus by a gynecologist, and a small string runs from the IUD and out through the cervix. The string is used to withdraw the IUD. The device floats around inside the uterus, but it does not prevent pregnancy. The IUD acts as a form of early abortion. In the normal process of fertilization, the fertilized zygote moves down the fallopian tube and into the uterus. After about two weeks of rapid cell division, the zygote implants itself into the wall of the uterus, where it develops into an embryo and, eventually, a fetus. It is the implantation into the uterine wall which cues the woman's body that pregnancy has occurred and causes her to cease menstruation. The movement of the IUD in the uterus prevents the implantation of the zygote into the uterine wall, acting sort of as a no-loitering traffic cop. Since the zygote never implants into the uterine wall, the woman's body never knows that it is pregnant and the normal menstrual period occurs, expelling fluids including the zygote. The effectiveness of the IUD depends on the type that is used and ranges between 98 and 99 percent.

Abortion

Regardless of one's position on this most sensitive issue, powerful emotional reactions are expressed. Perhaps one of the greatest barriers to progress in the debate over the issue is the hateful rhetoric that tends to surround the issue. I debated on the inclusion of this section because I recognize that my position, regardless of what it is, may damage my credibility with readers who hold different opinions. I have attempted to present this discussion in a respectful manner and I acknowledge that in our country abortion is legal, and that unless that fact changes, abortions will continue. My position on abortion is pro-life. I respect the human life not only of the fetus but of all humans, including those who believe differently than I and those who have had abortions. My purpose for including this information is not to proselytize or condemn those who have chosen to have abortions, but rather to provide information so that individuals can reach an informed opinion regarding the life or death of an unborn child. This is not a biology book, so I will not go into a complicated discussion on when life begins. Therefore, my treatment of this topic will be relatively brief, given its social, religious, and political complexities.

Most of the abortions that are performed are convenience abortions. Abortion advocates argue that abortions should be allowed when the life of the mother is at stake, but this is an issue in only 1 percent or less of all abortions. For example, data provided by the government in Great Britain show that of the nearly 175,000 abortions performed in England and Wales in 1999, only one was performed to save the mother's life, and only 94 were performed because of risk to the mother's life.[2] Those two categories combined to only about .05 percent. Likewise, only a small fraction of pregnancies that ended in abortion were the result of incest or rape. One study of 1,000 women who had been raped showed not a single pregnancy.[3] There are no data on pregnancy resulting from incest. By far the majority of the women who have abortions simply do not want to be pregnant or to be a parent. According to the Centers for Disease Control and Prevention (CDC), most women who have abortions are younger than 25, Caucasian, and single, and abort within the first eight weeks of gestation.[4] Nearly all abortions nationwide (88 percent) are done within the first trimester.

The right to choose is one of the primary arguments by pro-choice advocates, but it is a weak argument. Pro-choice advocates call pro-life advocates "anti-choice." That is not the case at all. Women are free to choose what they do with their bodies. However, once the decision has been made to become pregnant, the woman's decision and her right to choose what she does with her body no longer affect her alone. The right to choose is the right to choose whether or not to engage in intercourse, whether or not to use effective contraception, and whether or not to choose to act responsibly with her body. To argue that a woman who has become pregnant because of irresponsible decisions should choose to abort the fetus is like saying a surgeon should have the right to walk out of open-heart surgery. Once he has made the decision to begin the process, taking another life into his hands, it is no longer his right to choose to do whatever he wants, because his decision can detrimentally affect another person.

In some states, abortion is legal even up to the time of delivery. A procedure called partial birth abortion allows a physician to deliver a healthy baby's feet and then insert a syringe at the base of the skull while the head is still in the birth canal. The skull is then crushed by a tool especially made for this procedure and the fetus is then delivered. The procedure usually kills the fetus by destroying brain tissue, although there are reports of babies surviving this barbaric procedure. Many states, however, do not allow abortions beyond the second trimester. Abortions early in pregnancy are done in a number of ways, but the relief that women feel from having terminated an unwanted pregnancy is often tempered by a sense of violation because of the cold and sterile procedure. As they visualize their unborn child in a garbage bag, they experience loss and remorse. I have had many adult clients who, even years after their abortion, still feel guilt and grief over the death of their child, Some women experience something called *postabortion syndrome,* which includes a number of physical symptoms and risks, such as hemorrhaging, cervical lacerations, and even various forms of cancer. Emotional and behavioral symptoms include increased risk for drug abuse, promiscuity, and eating disorders.[5] It should be noted that this syndrome does not exist in the *DSM IV-TR* and that there are no diagnostic criteria specifically for women who have experienced an abortion. Clinically, these symptoms would most likely be classified under some form of depression. Abortion clinics do not always adequately prepare women for these emotions. Immediate convenience of terminating a pregnancy is gained in exchange for long-term grief and potential physical problems. Not all women experience grief, remorse, or guilt, and some have had a very positive experience. But that positive experience is at the expense of the child.

To give some balance to my argument, it is important to note that religious conservatives have not helped the plight of those who find themselves pregnant and alone. Traditionally, churches, communities, and even family members have disowned young women who become pregnant out of wedlock. Males who have sired unwanted children have not helped when they have failed to live up to the financial and emotional responsibility of raising the child they helped create by believing the pregnancy is the woman's problem. These women, therefore, have been ostracized and alienated at a time when they need support the most. When abortion was illegal, many women believed they had no choice but to seek an illegal abortion in a filthy clinic by an unqualified abortionist. Some even tried to abort their babies by using wire hangers or other instruments. It is very easy to adamantly argue the pro-life cause when one is not pregnant, alone, and without financial backing, and when one does not see all dreams for the future fading away.

In summary, my words will not resolve the abortion issue. I prefer to suggest to women that they exercise their right to choose not to be pregnant by utilizing an effective means of birth control or abstaining until they are prepared for parenthood.

PARENTING OUT OF WEDLOCK AND
SINGLE PARENTING

It is difficult to discuss these issues without first recognizing the many religious and cultural mores that have historically governed views regarding these issues. I have attempted to avoid religious issues other than acknowledging their presence because that is not the focus of this work. Psychologically, however, young teens do not make very good parents. They are sometimes physically incapable of having children (the rate of stillbirths is higher among young teens than other age groups), but more likely they are emotionally and financially unprepared for the pressures and responsibilities of parenthood. Many times over the years I have had pregnant teenage girls as clients. I have discussed many issues with them, one of them being the possibility of giving the child up for adoption. This option allows the woman to get on with her life and pursue her personal goals and dreams. It is advantageous for the child because he or she is more likely to be raised in a two-parent home, to have his or her physical and emotional needs met, and, statistically, to be less likely to be abused or neglected. Testimonials by women who have gotten pregnant early in life and decided to keep their children rather than give them up for adoption proclaim how their children have become blessings to them over the years. However, I am not concerned about the mother being blessed. I'm concerned about what is best for the child and the child will more likely have its needs fully met with a mature couple who are ready for the responsibility of being parents.

Young pregnant women, especially teens, face a number of difficulties. Because of their age, they will have difficulty finding employment that will sustain a mother and child. They are less likely to have health insurance, and the culture, while it has relaxed its position on unwed mothers since the 1970s, still tends to shun pregnant teens. Their immaturity makes it harder to cope with the stresses of parenting and of being thrust into an adult world while their peers are still in high school or college. Males are more likely to abandon a pregnant teen than a woman who is older and married, meaning she is forced to face these difficulties alone. Regrets and resentment toward the father, family, society, and even the infant are normal reactions. For these reasons, the incidence of child abuse is greater among this population than any other group.

A further disadvantage of single motherhood is that there will be no male role model in the home. Children learn how to be mothers, fathers, spouses, girls, and boys by observing both their male and their female parent. When one gender is absent, the child is at a disadvantage. For this reason, it is best for the child of a single individual, regardless of age, for the parent to seek married adoptive parents.

It is an unfortunate truth, however, that many individuals become single parents unintentionally. A spouse may leave upon finding out the woman is pregnant. In other cases, divorce, jail, death, or military service may cause an individual to become a single parent. In these cases, I encourage the parent to find a member of the opposite sex who can be a mentor to the child, thus providing some of the role modeling that is done in a two-parent home.

DIVORCE AND ITS EFFECTS ON CHILDREN

Continuing the discussion of single parenting, one must also consider parenting in light of divorce. Many divorces in our country are not contested. Couples cite irreconcilable differences and go their separate ways. Divorce is almost always painful for adults and children alike, even at its very best. However, adults have experience and coping skills to help them work through many difficult issues that arise during and after a divorce. Children, on the other hand, have little experience and few, if any, effective coping skills. Research clearly shows that divorce has both short- and long-term effects on children. Therefore, divorce should be considered very carefully when children are involved. I encourage parents to work through their differences or endure their unhappy marriages as long as possible, for the good of their children.

Marriages fail in many cases not because the couple is incompatible, but because they stopped working at their relationship. My first year of college, I bought a used Ford Mustang. It was the nicest car I had ever owned. The first few months I had the car, I washed it diligently, waxed it several times, and kept the interior clean. I drove very carefully because I planned on keeping that car forever. However, after a year or so, the newness was gone. I didn't wash it as often and I almost never waxed it. I drove it as I had driven all my other cars, and I elected not to invest my energies in the car as I had thought I always would. The benefit of working on the car as I had in the beginning no longer outweighed the cost of my time and energy.

As I counsel engaged couples, they always express dreams and ideals about what their lives together will be like. The work of marriage is easiest in the beginning—when a couple is still enamored with the new relationship and the novelty of being married. As time goes on and the newness wears off, they choose to work at it with less vigor and often simply quit trying. The relationship is dinged and dented from wear, and the payoff no longer seems to outweigh the cost. We live in a culture that tells us we can get what we want now. "Don't wait" and "Don't work for it" are common mantras. Many marriages fail because one or both people are not willing to work at it. Perhaps this is why we who live in the most affluent culture in the history of mankind have one of the highest rates of depression of any nation and a divorce rate of about 50 percent.

Other relationships end because of serious problems, such as marital unfaithfulness. Even then, recovery is possible. Overcoming difficulties requires that the couple live up to the responsibility they accepted when they married. Controlling one's anger and sexual urges and focusing on the responsibility of developing the marriage and the children in that marriage are imperative. One of the keys to success in marriage is a realistic expectation that it requires work, endurance, training, and discipline—all the things that our culture seems to loathe. The first step in renewal of one's marriage is a determination to succeed.

Parenting is a team activity that requires commitment. I've been a soccer player all my life. Some of my teams have been very good, and many of them have not been so good. On every team I have ever played on, problems have arisen. Sometimes we would get irritated at each other and sometimes we just plain did not want to be around each other. But an interesting thing differentiated the poorer teams from the better ones. On the poorer teams, we carried our personal conflicts onto the field, and it showed in our performance. Bickering was not uncommon on the field. On my better teams, however, no matter what frustrations or personality conflicts may have been present, when we walked on the field, we were unified. We played together, knowing that if one of us did well, it was good for the team. We also knew that if one of us did poorly, it brought the entire team down. We accepted the fact that, like it or not, we were on the same team and we had to work with what we had.

Marriage works the same way. You select your mate. Once the vows have been said, your team selection is made. Conflicts arise in all marriages, but in weak marriages, couples air their differences in public, tear each other down, and do things that weaken the team. In mature relationships, people deal with conflicts when they come up but do not work to destroy their mate, for they know that tearing down a team member will weaken the team.

In more than a decade of counseling families, I have seen a pattern that is unmistakable. The weakest couples are the ones in which one or both members do not want the marriage to succeed. The permanence of marriage is weakened when one or both people decide to quit trying. Every soccer season starts with the hope of a championship, and marriages start with hopes and dreams of living happily ever after. The reality of marriage is that no matter how strong the team, one must learn to live with differences and frustrations. One must learn to endure the work of the relationship in order to benefit as a team. Ask any couple who has been married 25–30 years or more, and they will tell you there were times when it would have been easier to quit, but since they endured, they are stronger for it.

All that being said, there are some situations where separation or divorce is advisable, if not imperative. In situations where one spouse is physically abusive to the other, in cases of sexual abuse of the children, or when children are being neglected or physically abused, the risks of divorce far outweigh the risks of remaining in the home. Especially in the case of sexual abuse, the recovery rate for sexual abusers is not very good, and it is almost a given that a sexual abuser will repeat his actions as long as victims are available.

Custody

Almost all of the forensic work that I have done for children over the years has involved custody issues. When assisting parents and the court with custody decisions, I must consider many issues simultaneously. The child's age and gender, the issues that led to the divorce or separation, special needs of the child, and the emotional maturity of the child are just a few of those issues. For example, if a divorce happens when a child is under the age of 18–24 months, she will have almost no memory of the intact family. Even so, the separation will be painful for her. She has no ability to understand why one parent is no longer living at home. Over time, children of this age adjust as well as they do at any age—one of the few situations where "younger is better."

In divorced families, children, especially older children, will prefer to be with the parent who is more accommodating and has the less restrictive rules. It is an easy trap to fall into, if you are the noncustodial parent, not to want to waste visitation by arguing over rules. The problem is that the child learns he can manipulate the parent. Lack of discipline only leads to problems in middle and late adolescence. Creating home environments that have similar rules is helpful. Parents should not use their children as weapons against the former spouse, criticizing the other's weaknesses or airing differences in front of the child—regardless of the child's age. This is confusing to a child, whose loyalties are torn between both parents. Children know that they care about each parent, but when they hear bad things about one parent from the other, they don't know whom to believe. I once worked with a child whose parents were divorced. After several meetings with both parents and the child, I realized that this couple got along better than most married people. They were very accommodating regarding one another's visitation times. They discussed discipline and school problems, and sought solutions together. Disciplinary practices were similar in both homes in order to make the transition from one to the other easy for their daughter. In meetings with me, they always consulted with one another before answering any of my questions. They were so amicable that I eventually asked them why they divorced. They answered that they couldn't get along while married, but they were the best of friends as a divorced couple. I have never worked with a divorced couple who was any more accommodating to the children of the relationship, and because of the energy they invested in helping their child adjust to the divorce, she had very few problems outside of ordinary childhood issues.

WORKING MOTHERS OR FATHERS AND DAY CARE

It is best if one parent can stay home with the child at least until he or she enters school at age four or five. These early years are important for both parent and child. The child needs regular contact with a primary caregiver— it can be the mother or the father—and the parent needs the time to bond and grow emotionally with his or her infant. Either father or mother can be equally effective at meeting the child's physical and emotional needs as a stay-at-home parent. Many parents mistakenly believe that two incomes are needed in order to provide things that the child needs. However, more often what is perceived as a need is really a desire on the part of the parents.

Given a choice between extra toys, nicer clothes, and material things, or the presence of a parent, children will always choose the parent. If a couple has decided to conceive, it is a full-time job of one parent to stay home and raise that child. Instead of getting a second job to support an expensive lifestyle, adjust your spending to meet your single income. Critics of this position argue that it is easy to say this when one's salary is $50,000 or more a year, but impossible for people who make only $20,000 a year. However, I don't just talk about this position—I practice it. When my first child was born, both my wife and I worked full-time. We made very little money even with two incomes. We decided almost immediately to adjust our lifestyle to fit my income rather leaving the responsibility of raising our daughter to someone in a day-care center. Over a 12-month period, we paid off as many debts as possible and we avoided unneeded expenses. We rarely ate out and we did not take expensive vacations. After three children and 15 years of my wife's being a stay-at-home mom, neither my wife and I, nor my children, regret that decision.

One cannot replace the minutes in the early morning snuggling in bed with a toddler, walks in the park, teaching him or her to tie shoe laces, and reading books together in an overstuffed chair just before an afternoon nap. When those early years are past, no parent who has stayed home to raise children will regret it. However, many parents who missed those hours, first steps, and irreplaceable one-on-one times, trading them instead for business meetings and rushing to and from the office, will. Children of working parents are awakened at 5:30 or 6:00 in the morning, rushed through dressing and breakfast, and left at day care, where they stand by the window at 6:00 at night, when the parent rushes in. After racing home as quickly as possible, they eat dinner, bathe, and dress for bed. Then they have 15 minutes of "quality time" with their parents before ending the day, only to start it all over again the next day. Weekends are maddening because, since both parents are busy with work all week, there are dozens of chores and errands to tend to, thus removing weekends as time for picnics, bike riding, and playing together. It is an interesting paradox that parents can justify only a few minutes each day with their children by calling it quality time, and yet they argue that jobs, children, and responsibilities leave them with almost no time for one another. If 15 minutes of quality time is acceptable for raising children, then 15 minutes before bed with a spouse should be enough quality time for an adult relationship. Obviously, it takes more than 15 minutes a day to build and maintain quality relationships.

The results of research on the effects of day care are mixed, but what seems to be evident is, at the very least, that day care has a neutral effect. In other words, it doesn't help children, but it doesn't hurt them either. However, many studies show a number of negative effects of day care. Children in day care are more aggressive and more prone to illness. At the very least, day-care children miss their parents and look forward to being picked up at the end of the day. On the other hand, there are two fairly clear benefits of day care. First, children who are exposed to day care tend to socialize better and to adapt to new situations better than children who have not been in day care. Trading bonding time and the early years with the infant for the weak improvement in social skills, however, is a meager trade-off. Also, toddlers don't necessarily need that socialization. Even though day-care children socialize better, those children who are not exposed to day care socialize just fine when they enter their school years.

A second benefit of day care is that children exposed to day-care programs with an academic component are academically ahead of children who did not have that advantage when they start kindergarten. However, as with socialization, this is an unnecessary advance. The purpose of kindergarten is to prepare children for first grade—to socialize them to the school atmosphere and provide the basic academic tools for starting first grade. Children can be well prepared for first grade regardless of prior academic training through day care, and the academic advancement in day-care and preschool children disappears by the third grade. In other words, it helps in the first year or so, but otherwise does not. As with socialization, it is a bad trade—time with your children for a minimal improvement.

There are situations where some form of day care is necessary. In a marriage where both parents choose to remain employed outside the home or in a single-parent family, day care is required. The general rule about day care is that the facility should be clean and well-staffed. Staff should be trained to work with the ages for which they are responsible and the student–teacher ratio should be low. Ideally, having a relative care for the child is better than a day-care center. Private day care, in other words, homes where a person keeps four or five children, can be better than large day-care centers as long as the children are well monitored, the facility is clean and safe, and no potential perpetrators of crimes against children have access to them.

COHABITATION AND CONCEPTION

In the 1960s, the cultural taboo against men and women living together outside the bonds of a marriage relationship began to be questioned. Free-spirited young people rationalized that cohabitation provided a chance for couples to get to know one another and to see if they were compatible enough to marry. The logic sounds nice, but the research does not support it. Cohabitation does not give "practice for marriage," and people who co-habit are no more likely to have successful relationships than those who do not. In fact, the divorce rate is higher for couples who cohabit before marriage than for those who do not. It may be that the lack of commitment in the relationship while cohabiting weakens the relationship as opposed to a couple who commit through marriage. When a couple is not bound by matrimony, they are free to leave at the first sign of difficulty in the relationship, whereas people who have committed to one another through a marriage ceremony are more apt to work through problems. For these reasons, co-habiting couples should avoid conceiving until they are ready to commit to one another. The bond of marriage improves the likelihood that the child will be raised in a home with both parents present.

GAY AND LESBIAN PARENTING

The *Diagnostic and Statistical Manual for Mental Disorders* (*DSM*) *II* and previous editions of the DSM included homosexuality as a mental disorder under "sexual dysfunction." Upon publication of the *DSM III* (1973), homosexuality was no longer considered a mental disorder unless the individual was painfully uncomfortable with his or her homosexuality—a condition termed *ego-dystonic homosexuality*. Upon revision of the *DSM III*, even that classification was dropped, although in the current edition (*DSM IV-TR*), one who is uncomfortable with his or her sexuality can still be classified under the category "sexual disorders not otherwise specified." Homosexuality was removed from the DSM due to a vocal homosexual lobby, not because of research. However, it might also be noted that it was included in previous editions of the DSM because of cultural beliefs at the time, not because of research. In any case, whether it should or should not be deemed normal behavior is only a tangential issue here. Some members of the mental health community still consider homosexuality abnormal behavior, but the majority of the profession does not. Even though the culture at large has changed dramatically since the 1970s, becoming far more accepting of homosexuals and homosexual lifestyles, homosexuality remains a very controversial issue. Compounding that controversy is the issue of homosexual couples raising children. Female couples have chosen adoption, in vitro fertilization, sperm donors, or men willing to impregnate one of the women in order to have children. Male homosexuals have chosen surrogate mothers or adoption as ways to have children.

There is minimal research regarding the effects of homosexual parenting. Anecdotal information is available from various sources, but for every story where one finds homosexuals raising children with few problems, one might just as easily find stories to the contrary. My presentation here is based in part on the research that is available and in part on theory, but more research is necessary before any definitive conclusions can be drawn. There is no evidence that children raised by homosexual parents are any more likely to become homosexual themselves. Likewise, there is no evidence that homosexual parents are any more or less competent than heterosexual parents simply because of their sexual orientation. Lesbian and gay couples are perfectly capable of providing a loving, warm, and nurturing environment for infants and children. There is a growing body of literature which bears out that children raised by lesbian or gay couples are no worse or better off than children raised by heterosexual parents. Religious groups oppose homosexual parenting because of their faith, and homosexual advocacy groups propose that individuals who choose this lifestyle have a right to raise children.

However, there is an insurmountable problem with homosexual parenting. Theory posits that children adjust best when they have both a female and a male role model in the home. Years of research on divorce has demonstrated that adjustment problems are due, in part, to the lack of one gender as a role model. Both genders contribute to socialization of gender and model life skills, as I discussed in a previous section. One of the boldest statements in the literature in favor of same-sex parenting came from the American Academy of Pediatrics early in 2002. A committee of members of the American Academy of Pediatrics published a statement which suggested that children of same-sex parents were no worse off in their social or gender development than were children of heterosexual parents. However, the paper admitted in its opening statement that adequate research in this area did not exist.[6] Further, the report admitted the confounding variables between children raised by same-sex parents and the fact that the parents of many of these children were divorced. These children very possibly may have learned adaptive skills in their dysfunctional or troubled homes that allowed them to overcome deficits that exist because of same-sex parenting, but this research base makes it impossible to know. History and theory teach us that both male and female parents play a significant role in the socialization of the child and in far more areas than were addressed by this particular review of the literature.

It is unfair to knowingly bring a child into the world with any preventable deficit. For example, many years ago a couple consulted with me regarding their decision to have children. The father had cancer and was expected to live less than two years. The couple wanted to have a child before the husband died. I suggested it was unfair to the child to knowingly bring him or her into a world where the father would be dead by the child's birth or shortly thereafter. Even though the child would have brought satisfaction and joy to the mother as a memory of her late husband, the child would never know the father and would have to deal with life without a father. I find it odd that anyone would deliberately plan that kind of pain for a child. Likewise, knowingly bringing children into a relationship where one gender is missing is unfair to the child. Therefore, regardless of religious beliefs about homosexuality and as unpopular as my opinion may be, it is my opinion that homosexuals should not have children.

NEW BABY WITH OLDER SIBLINGS

If you already have children and you are considering having another child, you can expect some jealousy. There is little you can do to prepare a sibling who is 12 months of age or younger for the arrival of a new baby; at this age children are not old enough to be jealous or even to realize that there is another child in the house. Toddlers, however, will demonstrate jealousy, as will some older children. You can help alleviate jealousy by talking with your child about the things that he or she can do that the baby cannot. Finding ways to allow the sibling to assist in child care is also helpful. Do not be surprised if a sibling occasionally makes comments that imply he or she wishes the new child wasn't around any more. This is not abnormal, and reflects the child's fear that he or she is being replaced. Respond to such comments with reassurance that the child is important, will always be loved, and will never be replaced.

Most experts agree that the health of the newborn is least at risk if the woman waits approximately 18–24 months between children. Statistically, both mother and child have a greater risk of health problems if a woman conceives prior to 18–24 months after an earlier delivery. Some suggest that two to four years between children is ideal. Other experts suggest that siblings adjust the best to a new baby if they are over four years of age.[7] Either way, it appears that between two and four years is a good rule of thumb.

Having a new baby can be a wonderful opportunity to teach a child about biology. Some childbirth experts even suggest allowing children in the delivery room, although the pain, blood, and noise of a birth are traumatic even for adults. Therefore, this is not a very good idea for younger children. Information about conception, reproduction, pregnancy, and delivery can be conveyed to the child, varying in detail according to the child's age. Toddlers will have little interest in this information, but children age eight or nine and beyond can be given details about the biology of conception that can launch discussions about sexual issues pertinent to their development.

Siblings will have to be monitored to ensure they do not hurt a new baby. Toddlers and preschool children will see a new baby like a toy. They will try to pick the baby up, feed it things, and drop toys into the crib for the baby to play with—all behaviors that could easily result in injury to the infant. Never leave a baby alone with a toddler.

PREPARING FINANCIALLY FOR A BABY

Most estimates place the cost of feeding, clothing, and caring for an infant at around $9,000 per year (by 2003 cost of living standards), but regardless of the actual cost, babies are very expensive. When my first child was born in 1988, we had health insurance, but the delivery and related expenses still cost us over $3,000. Costs related to difficult deliveries or health complications can run to tens of thousands of dollars. And this is only the beginning. Lost wages due to maternity leave or health complications in the woman should be considered as possibilities. Diapers, bottles, day care, clothes, doctor bills, furniture, and other related items can be very expensive. As children get older, they may need orthodontic work, and they will need money for school supplies, educational trips, and birthday presents. My wife and I sometimes found ourselves buying presents for children three times each week because of all the birthday party invitations our children received.

Financial stress is especially difficult in young marriages. Newlyweds who are in their late teens or early twenties usually have less disposable income than older couples. Likewise, they can easily fall into a credit trap. Charging fuel for vehicles, clothing, and groceries is inadvisable, and this kind of debt increases monthly financial obligations. Newlyweds tend to believe they should have all the things their parents have (a nice vehicle, washer/dryer, furniture, stereo, etc.), but they forget that their parents accumulated those possessions over 20 or 30 years. Falling into a credit trap makes it much more difficult to raise babies because surprise expenses pop up on a regular basis. Doctor visits for ear infections, colds, and flu; medications; and expenses for clothes that the child soon outgrows take a huge bite out of one's regular income. Day care alone is easily $100+ per week for a single child. However, even though it is important to be prepared for the cost of having children, do not let the cost discourage you from doing so. These costs are minimal compared to the satisfaction of having children. Simply plan for the costs of child rearing and adjust your lifestyle to your income.

AGE AT WHICH TO BEGIN A FAMILY

How long to wait after marriage before having children is a personal preference. Each culture has expectations about producing children. Some cultures expect a couple to produce several children very quickly. In such cultures, siring offspring is a sign of virility and sometimes is considered a blessing from a deity. In the United States, the decision about when to have children generally lies in the hands of the couple, although pressure to have children both from family members and from friends can become quite intense. It is expected in the American culture that a married couple will have children. This social expectation is unfair to couples who either do not wish to have children or cannot conceive. Even though most married couples elect to have children, there is nothing wrong with choosing to remain childless.

Psychologically, if all things are equal, I advise couples in their late teens and early twenties to wait a few years to have children. The transition into marriage can be difficult, and finances for young newlyweds are usually tight. The first few years of marriage are among those of highest risk for divorce, and having a few years to get to know one another and to establish a life together lays a wonderful groundwork for raising children. Even for older couples, those who marry in their late twenties and early thirties, waiting is advisable because they still need time to get to know one another as married people. However, couples who marry in their late thirties or early forties are pushing the biological time limit for fertility. In these cases, seeking a gynecologist's opinion is advisable. The probability of birth defects like Down Syndrome increase greatly as a woman approaches menopause (often in her mid-forties).

There are advantages to having children early in the marriage. The primary advantage is that the couple will still be relatively young when the children are grown. Advantages of waiting a few years include more money, more maturity, and knowing one another better. Disadvantages to conceiving late in life include the fact that the children may still be at home as the couple approaches retirement years. The disadvantages of having children quickly include increased marital stress due to an immature relationship, less financial stability, and little time to be alone as newlyweds. Again, what is an advantage or a disadvantage is, in part, a personal preference.

HOW MANY CHILDREN ARE RIGHT FOR YOU?

There is no single answer to this question. Cultures vary in their expectations, and families have personal expectations and preferences as well. Any choice, from no children to many children, is up to the couple, and no one has the right to dictate a number. There are advantages to having few children. One or two children are obviously less expensive than a larger family. Yet in larger families, siblings enjoy growing up together and playing together, and the bonds between siblings are often as strong as, if not stronger than, than those between married couples.

Some couples continue having children until they have both a male and a female. They want the experience of raising both genders. Again, this is a personal preference. Throughout history, cultures have placed a higher value on male children than on female children. Even in the United States in 2003, the birth of a boy brings more praise, especially from adult males, than does the birth of a female. However, the only advantage of having a boy rather than a girl is the continuation of the family name. This is extremely important to some families. There is no psychological, sociological, or physical advantage to having a male other than those we create for ourselves.

BIRTH ORDER

Among the many things that have an effect on a child, his personality, and the behaviors he exhibits is birth order. The research on the effects of birth order is questionable, but it seems evident that there are some general differences between children stemming from their order of birth. Oldest children tend to be driven, academically successful, and eager to please. Research studies that show firstborn children are "smarter" than subsequent children are probably the result of the time, energy, and emphasis on parenting that new parents exhibit. After the first child, parents have less time with each child, but they also relax and do not place as much emphasis on the same issues they did with the first child. Middle children are competitive, and it is believed that they are especially challenged by older siblings. They vie for a parent's approval and are easily discouraged if they fear they have not lived up to the achievements of their older siblings. They are not as obsessed with control as firstborn children tend to be. Middle children often feel ignored. The older child has more freedom and the younger child gets more attention, making middle children feel isolated. Youngest children are more often treated as the baby of the family, making them more dependent than other siblings. Unless parents make a concerted effort to let the child grow up, he is likely to carry his dependency into adulthood. Youngest children are also more likely to rebel than middle or firstborn children.

Only children fare just as well as, and sometimes better than, children who are raised with siblings. They exhibit the characteristics of firstborn children, and because parents do not have other children demanding their time and money, they get more attention and privileges. They mature more quickly than other children. In his study of birth order, Alfred Adler said that when there is a gap of around seven years between children, the younger child tends to assume the characteristics of an only child.

RELIGION AND CHILD REARING

Parenting is easier if both the mother and the father are affiliated with the same religion or are unaffiliated with any religion. Religion is a very personal matter and people tend to have strong feelings about male and female roles, discipline, and participation in religious activities and rituals. Marriages where the couple holds different religious views or where they are affiliated with different faiths experience many conflicts when it comes to child rearing. Prior to the decision to adopt or conceive, the couple should discuss the role religion will play in the child's life and how they will raise the child in a given religion. Many couples minimize the importance of religious differences upon marriage, but then discover the complications of conflicting rituals and practices when children arrive.

There are religious issues that pertain to a child's development. Every faith has its own views of spirituality, sin, afterlife, judgment, and so forth, but my purpose here is to address the psychological and social benefits of a religious upbringing. First of all, involvement in a religious body provides social interaction for children of all ages. For preschool-age children, the church or synagogue may be the only place where they interact with other children of the same age. They learn to develop friendships, share toys, and interact in a group setting. If the child is not in day care or preschool, this interaction helps to prepare him or her socially for the school years. With older children and teens, parents can have a high level of confidence that their children are engaging in productive and safe behaviors when they are with their youth group or other religious groups. Camps, social activities, and mission trips allow these children to interact in an environment that is clean, safe, and productive physically, spiritually, and psychologically.

Religious involvement provides a safe environment for socialization. Whether on an outing at an amusement park or serving on a mission project, the child is with a responsible adult who is concerned about the child's physical and spiritual well-being. Of course, youth ministers and priests have molested children, but such incidents are relatively rare, and abuse by clergy is no more frequent than among any other professionals who work with children (for example, coaches, teachers, scout leaders).

Religious involvement teaches morality. I doubt that there are any two people on the planet who have perfectly identical views on morality, but common among nearly all religions are encouragement of prosocial behaviors and discouragement of antisocial ones. Problematic or risky behaviors like drinking, sexual promiscuity, and dishonesty are less likely among children who grow up in religious homes than among those in whose homes no religious teachings are encouraged. Teens who are active in a religious organization are less likely to steal, lie, become pregnant, or use illegal substances than teens who are not active in one.

Likewise, religious involvement teaches altruism. Altruism is selfless investment in the needs of others. People are naturally selfish and egocentric. We start life believing that everything about the world exists for our benefit. Some people never overcome this infantile handicap. Selfishness, in fact, is at the root of most interpersonal problems at home, school, and work. Most religions teach that there is something greater than oneself and that giving of self is an important part of maturation. This benefit is long-lasting. Religious individuals are more likely to be satisfied with their jobs, friendships, and family; their marriages last longer; and they report greater satisfaction with their partners than do people who are uninvolved with any religion.

Children tend to follow their religious teachings into their adult years, even if they slip away during late adolescence or early adulthood. Children who are not raised in any religious body are unlikely to pursue religion in their adult years. Therefore, as couples plan for children, they must decide well in advance what role, if any, religion will hold in the raising of their children.

SUMMARY

It is possible that after reading this chapter you may have decided that having a child is not for you. If you are not emotionally, financially, and physically ready for the responsibility of having a child, then wait. However, do not let the great responsibility of being a parent frighten you—just respect it. If you are adequately prepared for having a child, you will find it to be a joyous experience. You will find pleasure in watching your child sleep, hearing his first words, and watching him trying to eat spaghetti for the first time. Your vocabulary will change to include your child's mispronounced words—words you will adopt and use with your spouse even when the child is not around. You will learn not to smile while disciplining your child for something funny that she has done, but you don't want her to know how funny it is. If you decide to have a baby, you will find that within just a few weeks after the child's delivery, it is hard to remember life without your child and you will not want to go back for anything in the world.

CHAPTER 3

The Miracle of Life: Conception, Pregnancy, and Delivery

A seven-year-old boy asked his mother where he came from. She took a deep breath, unprepared for the "birds and the bees" discussion that she knew was inevitable but had not expected so soon. For several minutes she explained the biology of reproduction. When she stopped, her son looked at her quizzically and said, "That's weird, because Tommy said he was from Ohio."

Most adults know the basics of conception, but especially early in marriage, that knowledge may be limited. Limitations in one's knowledge exist because sex is a topic that makes people nervous and many people have religious qualms about discussing the subject. Not too many years ago, churches would have forbidden the use of the word "sex" within their walls. A lady who attended a conference where I spoke on sexuality told me that her very pious mother's attempt to explain sex to her came on the day of her wedding. "Your husband is going to want to do something to you that will hurt and you have to let him" were her only words of direction regarding the honeymoon. Even those who are sexually experienced may not know the intricacies of the biology of sex and fetal development. For example, you may not have known that all babies would be girls, regardless of genetic makeup, if it were not for one incredible event during the early development of the fetus called the "testosterone bath." In the following pages you will read about conception, fetal development and the events that occur at various stages of prenatal development, gender socialization, multiple births, and issues related to preparing for the arrival of your new baby. You will also learn about delivery methods and the many decisions that you have to make as an expectant parent, long before your child arrives.

CONCEPTION AND PREGNANCY

The Biology of Conception and Pregnancy

As I mentioned in chapter 2, if a healthy sperm and a healthy egg are together in the same space, conception is almost a certainty. Variability in fertility basically all boils down to how, when, where, and how often a sperm and an egg are in the same place at the same time, and how healthy they are. Our sexuality is a significant part of who we are, and pregnancy, the ultimate purpose of our reproductive selves, is a rewarding, frightening, and exciting experience.

The egg and the sperm are unique cells of the body called *gametes*. They are different from all other cells of the body in several ways, but the most notable difference is that they contain only half of the genetic material that all other cells contain. The woman is born with all the *ova* (the female gametes, also called eggs) she will ever have, and they are stored in immature form within her two ovaries (one on each side of the uterus)—about 400,000 of them. Beginning at puberty, one of the two ovaries releases one egg each month, around the 14th day of her menstrual cycle, in a process called *ovulation*. A mature egg is about the size of the head of a straight pin and is visible to the naked eye. The uterus has only one job: to prepare for pregnancy. Around the 23rd day after the end of her last menstrual period, if the woman's body is not notified through hormonal changes that conception has occurred, the uterus begins to contract, and cleanses itself of all the material it has stored in preparation for pregnancy. This expulsion of material is known as the *menstrual period*. For about five days, the uterus continues to drain, and by approximately the 28th day, the cycle is complete. The uterus then once again prepares itself for a fertilized egg, storing material along its walls. This process repeats itself throughout the woman's life until menopause, when the ovaries stop releasing eggs. At this point, the woman is no longer fertile. The unused eggs in her ovaries will remain there until she dies.

When the woman's ovary releases an ovum, it passes across a small gap between the ovary and the fallopian tube that runs from the ovary to the top of the uterus. As the ovum enters the fallopian tube, it begins its journey that will end either as a fertilized egg, called a *zygote*, or as an unfertilized ovum. If it is fertilized, it will eventually implant itself into the wall of the uterus, where it will be nourished and pass through several transitions that will eventually result in a fully developed baby. If it is not fertilized, it will be expelled during normal menstruation.

Unlike females, who are born with all of the gametes they will ever have, males produce sperm throughout their lives, to the tune of about 300 million per day. The testes produce sperm from puberty until death, barring some health complication. The epididymis surrounds the testes and contains billions of sperm. After they are produced, the sperm are stored in the epididymis, where they mature. Sperm are very small and cannot be seen without the aid of a microscope. From puberty until death, with each normal ejaculation, millions of sperm, in conjunction with fluid from the prostate, are emitted. The sperm and other components of seminal fluid are constantly being replaced as they are used. However, if the man does not ejaculate for a long period of time, this material would build up. Therefore, the man's body monitors its production of sperm, and if the stored sperm are not used, they are eventually absorbed by the body and new ones are created. This keeps the testes from swelling due to millions of unused sperm.

During intercourse, the male releases around 40 million sperm into the woman's vaginal region, but as you will see, most of these sperm never even come close to the ovum. The vaginal area is bathed in a natural chemical that protects it from invaders like bacteria and other foreign bodies. This chemical treats sperm as it would any other invader and attempts to destroy them. Even though most sperm die at this point, some survive and travel upward toward the uterus. The sperm that survive to this point still have only a very remote chance of finding the egg. Some sperm are defective— they have no tails (called *flagella*) or their tails cause them to swim in circles. Other sperm swim around aimlessly and never find the fallopian tube. Still other sperm will find stray cells within the uterus and try to penetrate them, thinking they have found the ovum.

For those few sperm that actually find a fallopian tube, statistically half of them will choose the wrong one, since only one ovary releases an egg into its respective fallopian tube during normal ovulation. Those that choose the wrong fallopian tube will swim aimlessly until they die. From the original millions of sperm, only a few hundred will find the ovum. At that point, they surround the ovum and furiously attempt to penetrate its cell wall. The instant that the head of a sperm penetrates the wall of the ovum, it loses its tail. The ovum also changes, making it impossible for another sperm to penetrate the cell wall. As the head of the sperm enters the cell, it releases its genetic material, 23 chromosomal strands, which combine with the ovum's 23 chromosomal strands.

These 46 strands, 23 from the male and 23 from the female, contain the genetic code that will provide instructions for the cells of the body from this point until death. Of the 23 strands in the ovum and in the sperm, 22 contain various genetic codes that will determine things like hair color and texture, height, intelligence, and personality, as well as disorders like color blindness and mental retardation and diseases such as Huntington's chorea and Parkinson's disease. The 23rd chromosome, however, is shaped differently than the other 22. It is either X-shaped or Y-shaped. This 23rd chromosomal pair determines the gender of the child. All ova have an X-shaped chromosome in the 23rd position. Spermatozoa have either an X-shaped or a Y-shaped chromosome in the 23rd position. When the sperm and egg join, the combined result on the 23rd pair will be either XX or XY. An XX combination is female, and an XY combination is a male. Therefore, the male will always be the partner who provides the X or Y chromosome, and hence determines the gender of the child. This genetic difference becomes very important about six to eight weeks after conception. (See the section "Gender Development and Socialization.")

After the sperm releases its genetic material into the ovum, the DNA material joins together, creating one cell made up of 23 pairs of chromosomes. The cell then begins to divide rapidly. For the next two weeks, the fertilized egg that began as a single cell will divide millions of times. As it divides, it first takes the shape of a ball of cells called a *blastocyst*. During this time of cell division, the blastocyst continues to migrate down the fallopian tube toward the uterus. Within two weeks, the ball of cells implants into the wall of the uterus, serving as the first announcement to the woman's body that she is pregnant. When implantation occurs, the woman's body changes its hormone production and notifies the uterus not to menstruate. It is this hormonal change, evident in a woman's urine and blood, that most pregnancy tests detect.

At the end of the two-week period and at about the time of implantation, the blastocyst begins to collapse upon itself, forming a tiny groove called a *neural tube* that will eventually become the brain and spinal cord, the very first thing to develop in a baby. When this change occurs, the structure is no longer called a blastocyst. It is now an *embryo*. Thus far, the cells of the blastocyst have been undifferentiated, that is, they are all the same and any cell can become any part of the body—bone, skin, heart, hair, or brain. These *stem cells*, as they are called, then begin to migrate to various places in the developing embryo where they will differentiate and begin to take on specific characteristics. Some cells are instructed to migrate toward the outside of the body, and begin to develop as arms or legs. Other cells migrate toward the inside of the body and begin to develop as heart muscle or other internal organs.

Stem cells hold great promise in many types of biological research. Unlike other cells of the body, nerve cells do not reproduce if they are damaged or destroyed. Therefore, spinal injuries and brain damage are permanent. Since stem cells have the potential to become any type of cell, scientists speculate that implanting these cells in areas where neurons are damaged due to injury, Parkinson's disease, Alzheimer's disease, stroke, and other illnesses will cause the cells to develop as new neural tissue, thus reversing damage or at least improving one's ability to function. This research is laden with ethical and moral dilemmas, and no consensus has been reached regarding the ethical issues as opposed to the advantages the research may bring to diseased or injured people. This controversial research tends to wax and wane based on the political party in power at any given time. For example, President George H. W. Bush banned stem cell research during his administration, but Bill Clinton lifted the ban almost as soon as he took office. After his election as president, George W. Bush reestablished limitations on stem cell research.

Once the blastocyst has become an embryo and is implanted in the wall of the uterus, it begins to take the shape of a baby. For the next six weeks, the developing embryo will grow to about an inch in length and will develop arms, legs, a brain, a spinal cord, a heart, bones, and a digestive tract. The embryo develops a sense of touch and has tiny fingers and toes. Yet even as all of this is happening, some women are not yet aware they are pregnant.

Pregnancy is divided into three equal parts, each approximately three months long. These divisions are called *trimesters*. Toward the end of the first trimester, the embryo begins to grow rapidly. At nine weeks, the developing embryo changes names again and is now called a *fetus*. At 12 weeks' gestation, the end of the first trimester, the fetus is about three to four inches in length and weighs approximately an ounce. The fetus sucks its thumb, and the function of the heart muscle is visible by means of ultrasound. Genitalia, eyes, nose, mouth, and even teeth have developed by the beginning of the fetal stage.

In the second trimester, the fetus begins to respond to sound and the mother may begin to feel movement in her abdomen. The child's external genitalia, formed in the first trimester, are big enough that a perceptive physician (with the help of a cooperative fetus) may be able to determine gender by ultrasound, although results are inexact. Because all cells in our bodies contain the same genetic content, it is also possible to determine the gender of a child, as well as genetic defects, through a procedure called *amniocentesis*.

In this invasive procedure, a needle is inserted into the woman's abdomen and a small amount of amniotic fluid is withdrawn. The cells in the fluid contain the baby's chromosomes. Because this is a potentially risky procedure to both the fetus and the mother, it is not usually recommended unless the health of the mother or the child is in question.

Also during the second trimester, the baby will be sensitive to touch and to light, and will develop functional taste buds. During this trimester, the baby will blink and develop fingernails and fingerprints; and by the end of this trimester, the fetus will have all of the neurons its brain will ever produce. By the 24th week, the baby can hear sounds from outside the womb, including the mother's and father's voices, which he will recognize at birth. Toward the end of the second trimester, a fetus reaches the age of viability. This is the point at which the child has a chance of surviving outside the womb. Currently, 22–24 weeks gestation is considered the absolute earliest age of viability. Prior to that time, the fetus is too small to be treated and its lungs are not yet developed to the point that they can process oxygen. Even though any delivery at less than 36 weeks is considered premature, after about 30 weeks gestation, baring other complications, the baby's chance of survival is very good.

By the beginning of the third trimester, the fetus starts to finalize its development and prepare for birth. The lungs mature, and the baby increases in length and weight. On the average, a full-term baby weighs about 7.5 pounds and is approximately 20 inches long.

During the pregnancy, there are various points of risk to the developing child. Caffeine, alcohol, some types of cleansers, radiation, birth-control pills, and a host of other common products can detrimentally affect the unborn child, as can stress and disease. Even a hot tub could cause problems with pregnancy. Therefore, a pregnant woman should maintain regular contact with her OB/GYN and avoid any activity, food, drink, or chemical that could interrupt normal development. A physician will likely give a woman prenatal vitamins and she should monitor her exercise habits. Exercise is almost always productive. The more important question about exercise is not whether you *should* or *shouldn't* exercise, but how much and *what type* of exercise is appropriate at a given stage of pregnancy. Many women worry about weight gain. Again, one should exercise and diet only after seeking the advice of one's physician.

Problems with Conception and Pregnancy

There are many problems that can inhibit a couple's ability to conceive. A low sperm count in the male and failure to ovulate in the female are two possibilities. Many problems like these can be overcome through fertility drugs or artificial insemination. Even when conception does occur, there are many things that can go wrong. On a rare occasion, the ovum misses the fallopian tube and ends up in the woman's abdomen. If a sperm finds it and fertilizes it in the abdomen, an extra-uterine pregnancy occurs. In such cases, the baby is unlikely to survive. Likewise, a fertilized egg may implant into the fallopian tube instead of migrating to the uterus. Called a *tubal* or *ectopic pregnancy*, this is a serious problem that puts both mother and fetus at risk. These situations are rare, but problems are common. In fact, about 75 percent of all pregnancies end in miscarriage. Many of these miscarriages happen before a woman knows that she is pregnant. If a woman continues taking birth-control pills after conception, the uterine wall may be too thin to sustain the developing cells of the embryo. Other problems, such as poor health in the mother, use of drugs, exposure to toxins, and genetic defects, can lead to miscarriage. It is imperative that a pregnant woman visit an obstetrician regularly to ensure that she is taking necessary vitamins, eating properly, and not doing anything to compromise her own health or the health of her developing baby.

GENDER DEVELOPMENT AND SOCIALIZATION

At the very beginning of development, the zygote has the capacity to develop as either a male or a female. Both males and females have the rudiments of the system that would have developed if they had been genetically the opposite sex. The structure that causes an embryo to develop as a male is called the *Wolffian system,* and the structure that causes the embryo to develop as a female is called the *Müllerian system*. At about six to eight weeks' gestation, the uterus is flooded with a hormone called testosterone. This event, called the *testosterone bath*, causes the Wolffian system to develop in genetic males instead of the Müllerian system. If it were not for this event, all babies would develop as if they were genetically coded to be females. You might say that "female" is the default mode for gender development.

As the fetus is literally bathed in testosterone, the genetic code in an XY embryo turns on the Wolffian system, instructing it to develop an epididymis, a prostate, and a penis. The instructions for this event come from the *bipotential gonad*. This is a structure that can develop into either testes or ovaries. In XY zygotes, the bipotential gonad develops into testes, and in XX zygotes, it develops into ovaries. In a genetic male, the bipotential gonad develops into the very beginning of what will become testes, which in turn produces the necessary chemical for the testosterone bath. If the embryo is genetically female, XX, the default mode remains in place because there are no testes present to produce the hormone for the testosterone bath, and the Müllerian system is allowed to develop ovaries, a uterus, and a vagina. The undeveloped system in both genders will remain dormant in the body forever. A rare abnormality occurs when testes begin to develop in a genetic female (XX). When they release testosterone, the Wolffian system believes the fetus is male and develops accordingly. Therefore, a baby could be born that externally appears to be a male but is genetically female. This type of abnormality is called *hermaphroditism.*

We can address gender in many ways. *Genetic* gender of the child relates to the 23rd pair of chromosomes as either XX or XY. We can also talk about *gonadal* gender—the presence of ovaries or testes. Likewise, we can address gender in terms of *hormonal* gender. Hormonal gender involves the preponderance of either male or female hormones. Even though both genders have both types of hormones in their bodies, males have far more male hormones than female hormones, and vice versa for females. *Genital* gender has to do with the presence of a penis or a vagina. Genital gender is what most people mean when they ask if a child is a boy or a girl, but it is only one of several issues related to the child's gender. All forms of gender are usually in harmony, but abnormalities are possible. A hermaphrodite, as I mentioned in the previous paragraph, has the genetic gender of a female but the hormonal, gonadal, and genital gender of a male.

Yet even though these four types of gender are important, there is one last aspect of gender that is by far the most important. This is called *gender identity.* Gender identity has to do with one's perception of one's own gender, and is the result of how parents, siblings, playmates, and the culture at large socialize a child in regard to gender and its meaning. Couples begin socializing a baby from the moment they know its gender. The most obvious forms of gender socialization are the names we choose and the way we dress our children. We have labeled certain names as "boy" names and other names as "girl" names. Likewise, blue is a "boy" color and pink is a "girl" color. This connection of names or colors with one gender or the other is purely socialized. Children are taught the meaning of maleness or femaleness in far more subtle ways, however, than their names.

My first two children were female, so for eight years I had no boys in the house. When my wife and I had a son, I was amazed at all the advice I got about raising a boy. I listened politely as people tried to explain to me how different boys are from girls. They told me that I "really had my work cut out for me" because a boy was in the house. But the fact is that there are only a few distinct differences between males and females. In adolescence and adulthood, males are typically stronger than females, and girls mature, on average, earlier than boys. Boys statistically perform better in math and spatial skills, and girls are generally stronger in verbal skills. The hormone testosterone is much more prevalent in males than in females. It is believed that this hormone accounts for the fact that boys (and men) are typically more aggressive than girls (women). Generally, males are more task oriented and females are more relationship oriented. With these few exceptions, by far most gender differences are socialized. We teach our children how to be boys and how to be girls. We tell them from their very earliest days which colors are "girl" colors and which ones are "boy" colors. We teach our children which games are gender-appropriate. Even in preschool, they learn about careers that the culture perceives as careers for girls, those that are for boys, and those that are open to either. Attempts are made in children's literature to avoid gender stereotyping, but the fact is that these stereotypes exist.

People don't know nearly as much about gender as they think they do. Research has demonstrated that adults who are exposed to children when gender cannot be clearly identified treat children differently based on social expectations of a given gender. For example, when children fall down, parents are more likely to tell their sons to get up and "shake it off" than they are their girls. Research also indicates that fathers show "negative reactions to any behavior by their sons that seems effeminate."[1] Parents respond more positively to children who pick gender-appropriate toys. Recent research has demonstrated that boys are much more sensitive than was once thought, but that over time they are taught that showing their feelings or expressing emotion is negative behavior. Therefore, they are less likely to demonstrate or talk about their feelings.

Gender socialization is not all bad. It is important that within any given culture, children learn what is expected of them as males or females. They must exist within the culture, and knowing its rules helps them to function effectively. Among other things, it is through gender socialization that we learn the rules for courtship. For example, imagine how awkward it would be if you did not have any idea who was supposed to ask whom out, who was to drive, who was to pay, and so on. Socialization provides us with guidelines in response to these questions.

Gender socialization is not all good, either. Through our culture we limit children in what they believe they can be or what they believe they can do, given their gender. For example, in very traditional homes, girls may be taught that they should not pursue any career; rather, they are taught that marrying and running a home is the appropriate role for them as women. Likewise, our culture has traditionally taught that a man must be the primary breadwinner in the family. There is nothing wrong with a woman being a housewife, nor is there anything wrong with the man being the primary breadwinner, unless the individual is led to believe that he or she has no choice simply because of his or her gender. In other words, when gender roles trap us into believing we can't do certain things, or we must do other things, simply because of our genetic makeup, we are unnecessarily limited. Nearly identical behaviors in girls and boys evoke different responses from caregivers. A rowdy girl is "unladylike," whereas a rowdy boy is "all boy." Parents who have given me advice about boys often explain away their own sons' impolite behavior by attributing it to his gender rather than to poor manners.

Boys will play with dolls and girls will play basketball. There is nothing genetic in these interests. Rather, there is a cultural emphasis which teaches that boys shouldn't play with dolls and girls should. Boys will play with dolls, but they are called action figures. Parents sometimes call me, concerned that their sons are playing with Barbie dolls with their sisters. There is nothing wrong with boys playing with Barbie dolls. Playing with dolls does not make a child effeminate and does not lead to homosexuality (suggestions I have actually heard people make). Dolls, doll houses, doll furniture, cars, and other such things are miniature representations of the adult world. This is what attracts children, both boys and girls, not the girl dolls. If given a choice, most boys will prefer action figures to Barbie dolls, but it is not abnormal for a child to play with either type of doll, or even both types of dolls at the same time.

Parents should be aware of how they communicate gender identity to their children. Parents may unconsciously alienate their child because of the child's decisions that violate social gender roles. For example, a father may inadvertently communicate his disappointment that his son prefers reading to outdoor sports by ignoring the child, or disengaging from him, or through facial expressions or hurtful comments about his choices. It is difficulty with gender identity that leads people to seek sex changes or struggle with homosexual issues, and it even leads to suicidal behaviors. It is important to recognize when we are socializing, how it is productive, and where it may be counterproductive.

SYMPTOMS OF PREGNANCY

Most women first suspect that they are pregnant when they miss a menstrual period. This is an unreliable indicator in some cases, because many women have irregular cycles. Likewise, there are many things that can cause a woman to miss a period. Diet, excessive exercise, eating disorders, and stress are just a few things that can interrupt normal menstruation. Over-the-counter pregnancy tests are fairly reliable about two weeks after conception.

These relatively inexpensive tests take only a few minutes and usually involve litmus paper and a urine sample. The color of the litmus paper indicates pregnancy or not. A home test is not an adequate substitute, however, for professional medical attention. As soon as a woman suspects or is certain she is pregnant, she should begin prenatal care under the direction of an obstetrician.

Morning sickness is another symptom of pregnancy and it affects about 60 percent of all pregnant women. A small percentage of these women experience serious nausea in the mornings, but most of them have minimal nausea that abates by the second trimester. Some breast changes, such as sensitivity, occur early in pregnancy, but the most noticeable changes in the breasts occur during labor as the body prepares for lactation.

Weight gain during pregnancy varies from woman to woman. Obstetricians differ in their opinions about what is appropriate and what is risky weight gain. Some doctors prefer their patients to limit weight gain to 30 pounds, while others are unconcerned about weight gain unless the woman has health problems that are exacerbated by weight gain. As you prepare for your pregnancy, consult with a physician. He or she can take into consideration your health, prior pregnancies, heart condition, diet, and other health issues in determining how much weight you should expect to gain.

Cravings are normal among men and women, regardless of pregnancy. We all crave various foods at various times for a variety of reasons. Pregnant women are infamous for craving unusual combinations of food (for example, pickles and ice cream), but much of this is folklore. Some cravings are the body's way of signaling a deficit in nutrients that the body needs. Other cravings are more directly related to situations, time, and place, rather than to biology. As long as the food doesn't make you sick, compromise your health, or violate your doctor's orders, eat what you want, even it if seems strange.

While it is extremely rare, some women experience full-term pregnancy without knowing they are pregnant. I have had clients to whom this has happened. They were all young, and I suspect they denied some of their symptoms, but it does happen that pregnancy is so easy and weight gain so minimal that the woman may not know she is pregnant.

MULTIPLE BIRTHS

Normal pregnancy in humans produces a single baby. One ovum is released and, if it is fertilized, results in one baby. However, variations can occur. Twins result in two ways. Dizygotic twins occur when more than one egg is released from the ovary. If sperm are present, both eggs can be fertilized, resulting in two babies. Assuming both zygotes implant into the uterine wall and develop normally, twins are the result. These twins are called *fraternal* or nonidentical twins. Triplets, quadruplets, or quintuplets can occur in the same way—multiple eggs are released and each is fertilized. These babies look no more alike or different than any other siblings and since they result from separate eggs, they can either be the same gender or different genders. They are simply two or more babies conceived and born at the same time. They tend to look alike only because they go through the same developmental stages at the same time and parents tend to dress them alike. Dizygotic twins are the more common type of twins.

Twins may also result from a single egg. Twins of this type are called monozygotic twins. On occasion, after the egg is fertilized but before it begins its rapid cell division into a blastocyst, it duplicates itself into two identical fertilized eggs. Those individual eggs then begin dividing independently into two separate blastocysts. These twins are called *maternal* or identical twins. They have exactly the same DNA, and therefore always will be the same gender and will be very hard to tell apart. Most people can most easily distinguish between identical twins by variations in their personalities or style of dress rather than their physical features. Research in many areas of psychology and medicine utilizes monozygotic twins as subjects because they are nearly identical. Their similarity controls for many variables that cannot be otherwise controlled, even among biological siblings. From this research we have discovered that many things—job preference, personal preferences, recreational interests, and so forth—appear to have a genetic link.

Both types of twins appear to result from a genetic trait, but many people who have twins have no recent history of twins in their family. Triplets, quadruplets, and quintuplets are most common among women who take fertility drugs. Some of these drugs cause ovulation resulting in the release of multiple eggs from the ovaries. Even though some women have been known to conceive eight or nine zygotes, quintuplets are usually the maximum number of children a woman can deliver. Her abdomen is too small to carry more than that and when five or more eggs are fertilized, some die, thus leaving room and nutritional resources for the surviving siblings. Tragically, in pregnancies of four or more children, some fetuses survive to delivery, but expire during labor or shortly after. Low birth weight and premature birth are quite possible with multiple births. An ultrasound in the first trimester can reveal if a woman is carrying more than one child, and in later pregnancy, multiple heartbeats indicate more than one fetus. When the woman has more than one child developing in her uterus, precautions can be taken to increase the probability of their survival by adjusting her diet, movement, and examination schedule—all of which increase the probability of a full-term pregnancy.

SELECTING A NAME

There are few things that occupy the minds of expectant parents as much as the name they will choose for their baby. Names are very personal, and often laden with meaning and honor for a namesake. In some cultures, names reflect a given time (April, June). Native American cultures often named children based on something in the environment (Running Bear, Peaceful Stream). Some parents in Western cultures do something similar, such as naming a child after a birthstone (Ruby, Opal). Many parents select names based on their cultural heritage (Greek, German, Scottish), while others choose names from religious history or names signifying some religious attribute (Faith, Grace). Some parents choose to take the mother's maiden name as the first or middle name of a child. Others prefer to name children after themselves or to take the name of a cherished relative. Still others select names that have no family connection, but that appeal to the parents. Books of names, web sites devoted to naming babies, and other resources provide expectant parents with ideas for naming their children. A child's name should reflect both parents' wishes. The baby will carry that name throughout life, and if one of the parents is not happy with the selection, it leads to frustration.

In some cultures, naming a baby involves selecting a unique name that does not exist in any baby name book, while in other cultures tradition dictates selection of a name from a limited number of choices. There is no right or wrong name, although many parents may wish to consider several issues when naming the child. Start the naming process by listing all the names that you might consider and then rank the names in order of your preference. Comparing your list with your spouse's list is one way to narrow the options. You can then eliminate names that either spouse is certain he or she does not like. Next, with the remaining names, consider how the name sounds in the combination of the first, middle, and last names. You may find that a name you like sounds awkward with the last or middle name. Many parents also consider what the baby's initials will be. You may change your mind if the initials on monogrammed possessions spell a word that you find unappealing.

Minor modifications of common names can help parents find just the right name. Jon instead of John, Traci instead of Tracey, and Kara instead of Cara are examples. Keep in mind, however, that an unusual spelling of a common name will mean both you and your child will have to spell the name every time someone wants to write it down. You have to decide now if it is worth the trouble.

You may also wish to consider your child's name in relation to other children in the family. For example, one of my friends has six children, and all of their names begin with J. My sister has three children and their names begin with A, B, and C, in order of birth. With my own three children, their names have nothing in common. We simply selected names by using the process that I have described.

Names that are difficult to spell or pronounce and names that require explanations as to how they came about are primary reasons why adults change their names. Even though the name might make great sense to you, think about what this name will be like for the child in adolescence and adulthood. Names that sound cute in childhood may not be appreciated by your child in adulthood. Names, like everything else, go in trends. Parents may wish to avoid a trendy name unless they are certain it will still hold meaning when the trend fades.

In most states, you will be required to complete a birth certificate for your child before you leave the hospital. Therefore, you will have to have a name by this point, but you do not have to name the baby before the completion of the birth certificate. Once that paperwork is done, however, the name is very hard to change. Keep your lists of options. As your children get older, both parents and child may be entertained by considering all of the names that might have been.

PREPARATIONS FOR A NEW BABY

Prenatal Care

Every parent experiences anxiety about the health of the baby. "We just want a healthy baby" is a phrase most parents utter at one time or another during pregnancy. The most important thing that a pregnant woman can do to prevent birth defects, miscarriage, and other prenatal problems is to ensure that she gets adequate prenatal care. Regular visits to an obstetrician provide an opportunity to monitor the baby's development and also to be educated on the important things one should do during pregnancy. Exercise, diet, rest, and prenatal vitamins are all issues that should be discussed with one's physician. Pregnant women should never smoke, expose themselves to high levels of stress, or use illegal drugs. Even many legal drugs have a detrimental effect on the developing fetus and should be avoided. Caffeine, birth-control pills, allergy medication, and other chemicals that are a part of a woman's normal daily life may cause miscarriage or birth defects. Consultation with her physician will allow the woman to be informed as to which medicines are safe and which are not.

Reading and Music

For several years there was a belief that reading to a child in the womb and listening to classical music somehow made the child more intelligent. In fact, in one southern state, the governor once dictated that every child born in the state was to be given a classical compact disc, in the hope that this would improve IQ. However, this belief was based on a misinterpretation of research. It is true that the same area of the brain that processes math also processes classical music. It is also true that stimulation of the brain in general is productive: it produces more connections, and it generates more cells (called *glial* cells) that act as the glue that holds the neural fibers together. The leap in logic, however, that listening to classical music leads to higher intelligence is mistaken. Does this mean that listening to classical music and reading to your child do no good? Of course not. Babies can hear while in the womb and soothing music can be calming. The baby's hearing is developed well before birth and voice recognition is part of the bonding process. Reading to the child, even in utero, is productive. The process of reading to the child, at the very least, can foster a nurturing attitude in the expectant parent. Parents who encourage learning are more likely to have children who succeed academically. But playing classical music for your baby, by itself, won't make your child smarter.

Preparing a Room

Prior to delivery, you may find it enjoyable to plan for your baby's arrival by decorating its room. Newborns have minimal visual skills. At birth they can see clearly only from 6 to 12 inches, but as they mature, their vision improves. Therefore, soft colors and large objects will be recognized most readily. You will need furniture for your new baby as well. A bed with sides or rails is a must. Newborns do not roll, but not long after their birth they can scoot or roll. A bed without rails increases the likelihood that the child will fall off of the bed. Crib bumper pads also protect the child's head and body when he scoots against the stiles of the crib. A changing table is not mandatory, but many parents find one helpful. It is high enough to allow easy access to the baby while changing, and shelves for storage of supplies—powder, diapers, pins, wipes, a change of clothes, and so forth—make for easy access to everything that the parent needs when changing the child.

Caution: A baby should never be left unattended on a changing table, even though these tables usually have low rails! In a flash, babies can roll off a changing table or, using the rails, push themselves over the edge and onto the floor.

Soft washcloths and towels, a plastic bathtub, sleepers, blankets, mobiles, bottles, pacifiers, and other such items will be needed. Many babies find windup or electric swings very soothing. It will be several months before you will need a high chair or a playpen. Most of these items are not expensive and if they are purchased throughout the pregnancy, the baby's room can be fully stocked by the baby's due date without a large outlay of cash.

An age- and weight-appropriate car seat is a requirement in many states. Even if it is not required by law, a baby should never travel in an automobile without being restrained in a car seat. The optimal location for a car seat is in the middle of the backseat. Infants should face the rear, while toddlers and older children can face forward. A car seat is advisable at least through age four.

Preparing Emotionally for a Baby

There is little you can do to prepare for the emotional response to having a baby. Labor, delivery, and recovery are emotionally draining. It is not uncommon for both parents to experience emotions ranging from elation to depression. During labor, neither parent gets much rest; it is sometimes painful for the mother, and seeing the mother in pain is difficult for the father. The joy of seeing one's healthy newborn is among the most incredible and exciting experiences on earth. Hospital stays are not conducive to rest when nurses, housekeepers, and guests file in and out of the room 24 hours a day. Coming home is exciting, but the house will never be the same as it was. You can't sleep when you want, and you can't expect the daily routine you once had. With everything changing, especially if parents are tired, slow in recovering, or dealing with personal problems unrelated to the pregnancy, depression or even resentment is not uncommon.

In the weeks following delivery, there will be trips to the OB/GYN to monitor the mother's recovery as well as trips to the pediatrician for well-baby care, checkups, and occasional illnesses. Financial stress due to illnesses, complications at birth, and medications can upset even the most easygoing parent. All of these issues are normal in uncomplicated deliveries. They are even more significant in premature birth, birth defects, or unforeseen complications in delivery (for example, cesarean section when one planned a vaginal birth), as well as for families who have no insurance and are financially responsible for huge hospital and doctor bills.

To prevent being overwhelmed by these emotions, prospective parents should make sure they are emotionally stable before having children. This may sound obvious, but many parents have killed their children and subsequent investigations have determined that the parent(s) was (were) mentally unstable before the child was conceived. Second, parents can prepare by resting as much as possible both before and after delivery. If possible, both parents should plan for time away from work after delivery. Even the father will need a few days of recovery time. Limiting visitors can also ease stress. A constant stream of visitors in the home can make one feel obliged to clean, entertain, and care for guests at the expense of one's rest. Don't be afraid to set visiting hours at home or to leave the answering machine on to screen calls. Finally, preparing for these mixed emotions and emotional reactions involves knowing they exist and not being surprised by them. As a new parent, if you find yourself overwhelmed by these emotions, seek help from your physician, midwife, or counselor.

BIRTHING METHODS

A comedian once said that calling childbirth without anesthesia "natural childbirth" was like calling a root canal without anesthesia "natural dentistry." While it may seem odd to some people, many women have found natural childbirth to be a rewarding experience. Fortunately for expectant mothers, barring health complications, there are many forms of childbirth from which one can choose. Options include a delivery by a midwife in a birthing center or at home, or a hospital delivery, and they can also select from several types of anesthesia or even plan to deliver without anesthesia. These decisions need to be made well in advance of the delivery date and should be made in consultation with the obstetrician so that the woman is fully informed of all the risks and advantages of her choices. Every woman is different in the length of her labor, in her pain threshold, and in the way she experiences pregnancy and delivery. In fact, many women's pregnancies differ from one child to the next. No one can tell you what is right for you, unless there is some physical complication that your doctor knows about. Therefore, it should be the woman's choice which method of delivery she believes will be most tolerable to her, rather than the choice of relatives, spouse, or friends.

Since the 1960s, alternative methods of delivery have become popular. Hospital deliveries, birthing centers, and Lamaze deliveries are widely used, while midwives and home delivery have been around for centuries. Both mother and father should participate in the choice of method.

Birthing centers and home deliveries with the assistance of a midwife allow the greatest flexibility. Mothers are able to move about, free from cords and tubes, in an environment that is soothing and comfortable. Friends, family members, and siblings can be present throughout labor and delivery. Water births (delivery in a pool of warm water) are sometimes used in these settings. The woman is free to walk, sit, or lie down during labor, and various birth positions (sitting, squatting, lying on one's side, etc.) are accepted. Minimal medication, if any, is employed, so that delivery is uninterrupted by numbed pelvic muscles. Likewise, the woman is fully awake and able to participate in the entire delivery.

Lamaze and similar natural childbirth methods take advantage of one's ability to control pain and participate in delivery via controlled breathing and the participation of a coach or birthing partner. Natural childbirth methods can be used in hospital settings as well as in birthing centers and home deliveries. Some women elect to begin labor using a natural childbirth method, but they also have an anesthesiologist on call in case they choose, midlabor, to receive anesthesia. The disadvantage to waiting is that if labor progresses quickly, there may not be time for the anesthesia to take effect.

Traditional hospital deliveries are more sterile and less flexible, but they also are very safe. Many parents select hospital deliveries because of the potential for complications. Hemorrhaging, toxemia (poisoning of mother and fetus from toxins), and anoxia (oxygen deprivation) are all possibilities. An OB/GYN once told me that delivering babies is a breeze until there are complications. Having the hospital staff and resources available in case of complications is comforting to many expectant parents.

Many hospitals have tried to create a homier atmosphere by providing birthing rooms in addition to the normal delivery rooms. These birthing rooms are furnished with recliners, wood paneling, and other homelike materials, giving the room a warmer feel, like a birthing center, yet still providing the medical facilities of the hospital. With hospital deliveries, drugs such as Pitocin can be employed to speed labor. Monitors keep track of the woman's labor as well as of the baby's heart rate and oxygen level. Monitoring these functions allows the physician and nursing staff to track labor and also ensures that the medical staff will be aware of any complications the fetus might encounter during delivery. Should complications occur, the woman can be whisked to an operating room where a cesarean delivery can be performed in minutes.

If a woman elects to have an epidural, anesthesia is administered during labor. The epidural is administered through a small tube inserted near the spinal column in the lower back. Anesthetic fluid then bathes the spinal cord, numbing everything from the pelvis to the toes. In layman's terms, this procedure is called a *saddle block*.

Complications

When problems during delivery arise, the life of both the mother and the child may be at risk. The normal position for the birth of the baby is with the baby's head toward the cervix and facing down. This is called the *occiput anterior* position. Abnormal positions, also called *malpresentation*, include *breech*, *occiput posterior*, and *transverse*. In the breech position the baby's buttocks precede the head during delivery. There are three variations of the breech position: the *frank breech*, the *incomplete breech*, and the *complete breech*. In the frank breech position, the buttocks are toward the cervix and the baby's feet are positioned toward head. In the incomplete breech, one or both of the baby's legs enter the birth canal before the buttocks. In the complete breech position, the baby's legs are crossed and the baby is in a sitting position. In this position, vaginal delivery is highly unlikely.

The occiput posterior position is similar to the normal position except that the baby is facing the mother's tummy instead of her back. This is the most common malpresentation, occurring in about one in 50 births. In the transverse position, the baby is positioned sideways. Most often, the baby's back covers the cervix. The transverse position is the rarest position, occurring in only about one in every 2,500 births. When a malpresentation exists, there are some exercises the mother can do that can move the child into the proper position, and external manipulation of the uterus is also sometimes successful. When the baby cannot be safely moved into the proper position for delivery, a cesarean delivery is usually required. Delivering a baby that is not in the occiput anterior position has been linked to a number of problems, including neurological damage and neurological soft signs (such as attention deficit disorder and dyslexia).

Other potential birth problems include difficulties with the umbilical cord. The umbilical cord, the baby's lifeline, can become entangled or wrapped around the baby's neck, causing suffocation, or it can be compressed between the baby's head and the pelvis, cutting off oxygen to the baby. Excessive bleeding during and after delivery can threaten the life of the mother. In fact, well into the 20th century, many women died during childbirth as a result of blood loss. If the baby suffers from any birth defects, immediate attention may correct some problems or arrest others. For all of these reasons, many women choose to deliver in a hospital where a wide variety of medical specialists are at their disposal.

DELIVERY

Labor

Braxton-Hicks contractions begin in the last two months of pregnancy. These contractions are sporadic and sometimes fool an expectant mother into thinking she is about to deliver. They are mild and are a normal part of the body's preparation for delivery. Several days before delivery, the baby moves into position in the pelvis in preparation for birth. This is called *lightening*. In the days prior to birth, the woman's cervix begins to dilate and efface. The cervix needs to be fully dilated and effaced for vaginal birth to occur. As the time of delivery nears, the sac of fluid around the fetus perforates or breaks. When this happens, a semiclear fluid flows from the vagina. If the flow is minimal, the woman may believe she has lost control of her bladder. In the last trimester of development, the growing fetus puts a great deal of pressure on the woman's bladder and small urinary accidents are not unusual. If the sac breaks fully, the flow of fluid is very noticeable and hard to confuse with anything else. When the sac either perforates or breaks, it is important to notify the midwife or physician. The baby is ready to be born. In some deliveries, the sac does not rupture on its own and must be ruptured by the attending physician in a quick and painless procedure. Using a tool that looks like a long crochet needle, the physician hooks the sac and perforates it, releasing the fluid inside.

Labor pains become regular, longer, and more frequent as delivery time nears. A monitor that is placed around the woman's abdomen allows the medical staff to monitor her contractions, how intense they are, their duration, and how frequently they occur. In hospital deliveries, a small wire may be inserted into the uterus and attached to the baby's head. This wire allows the physician to monitor the baby's vital signs—yet another way to watch for problems during delivery. The baby's heart rate may also be monitored using an external heart monitor placed on the woman's abdomen.

As the cervix approaches full effacement and dilation, the baby's head crowns. An episiotomy is sometimes performed at this point to avoid tearing of the vaginal walls. The episiotomy is a surgical procedure where incisions are made just below the vagina to widen the birth canal. During this part of labor, the woman pushes, much like trying to have a bowel movement, forcing the baby into the birth canal.

The most difficult part of a normal delivery is the delivery of the baby's head and shoulders. Once the head is exposed, the baby's airways are aspirated and the baby is prepared to take its first breath. The baby's shoulders and torso follow. The umbilical cord continues to pulsate even after delivery. Some natural childbirth methods recommend waiting to cut the umbilical cord until after it ceases to pulsate, but in hospital deliveries, the cord is cut very soon after the baby is delivered. Finally, the woman must also deliver the placenta. Necessary repairs are made to the birth canal and vaginal opening.

The length of labor varies from one woman to another and from baby to baby. Labor is usually longer for the first child than for subsequent children. It is not unusual for a woman to remain in labor for 15–20 hours with her first baby. Some women dilate and deliver very quickly, however, so being prepared for a quick trip to the hospital is a good idea.

Participation of the Father or Coach

Thirty or more years ago, fathers were usually bystanders during labor and delivery, stereotypically pacing in a waiting room while their wives were giving birth. Fortunately, this has changed dramatically. Fathers are present during delivery, lending support to their spouses, enjoying the excitement of a baby's first minutes, and even participating in the delivery by coaching their spouses through labor. I would not trade my time in the labor and delivery rooms for anything in this world. Those three trips not only were exciting for me, but I was happy to help my spouse endure the pains of labor, calming her, getting things for her, and helping her rest when she could.

Not all fathers have the stomach for delivery or want to be present. I encourage them to set their preferences aside. After all, the mother probably is not really looking forward to delivering a baby, either. However, when a father chooses not to participate, a surrogate *coach* can take his place. Ideally, the coach will go through childbirth training with the pregnant woman, learning breathing techniques and ways in which he or she can help ease the pain of labor and facilitate delivery. Coaches often are the mother, sister, or close friend of the pregnant woman. For single expectant mothers or for women whose husbands cannot or will not participate in delivery, selection of a coach well in advance of delivery can make the experience of having a baby more joyful, less painful, and less frightening.

Participation of Siblings during Delivery

The birth of a baby is one of the most fascinating, moving, and powerful events one can ever witness. Many parents want their children to share the birth of a sibling by allowing them to be present during delivery. It is also a good time to teach the child about the facts of life. However, even in the easiest deliveries, the process can be frightening to a child. The mother is bleeding, losing body fluids, and in pain. Some psychologists see nothing wrong with having siblings present for a birth, but I do not recommend it except for children who are ten years of age or older and have been desensitized to the pain and mess of a birth through videos or other educational materials. For example, children who grow up on a farm or who have been exposed to the birthing process may not find the experience frightening at all.

Documenting the Birth of Your Baby

Many parents elect to photograph or videotape the delivery of their children. Video cameras are small, easy to operate, and versatile. The decision to videotape should be made jointly by the father and the mother. The woman will have to contend with issues of privacy. Even though it is possible to videotape a birth without compromising a woman's modesty, it may be difficult to think about those issues in the intensity of delivery. If privacy is a concern, but you still want to document the birth, digital imaging may be the best choice. Editing of digital video images is easier than ever, so the graphic scenes can be removed or edited.

Videotaping allows the couple, relatives, and interested friends, and eventually the child, to see the event rather than just hear about it. However, focusing on videotaping makes it difficult or even impossible to enjoy the event as it happens. Likewise, if the person videotaping is supposed to be coaching or otherwise assisting in the delivery, he or she will be preoccupied and perhaps fail to perform well at either job. A tripod with the camera operating on its own may help, but during delivery, one cannot be sure who might be standing in the way of the camera.

Videotapes made during deliveries have been used as evidence in lawsuits in recent years, both to provide evidence of a physician's errors and to exonerate physicians or other hospital staff. Some physicians have banned their use. Whether one chooses to videotape the event for legal accountability or for personal pleasure in remembering the event, videotaping is something the prospective parents may want to consider. You can't go back and do it again later.

Circumcision

For centuries, male circumcision, the removal of the foreskin of the penis, has been a religious custom. Even among nonreligious individuals, for many decades it was believed that circumcision was helpful and promoted cleanliness. Today, the procedure is relatively quick and painless, and recovery takes only a few days. Circumcision is still practiced widely because circumcised boys have a 25-fold less incidence of urinary tract infections and fewer foreskin adhesion problems. Many people choose to have their sons circumcised for traditional reasons and, of course, the practice is still a part of some religions. The decision to circumcise or not should be made well in advance of delivery and only after the parents consider the reasons for and against the practice. One's physician can be helpful as one considers the benefits of this procedure.

Lactation

The breasts begin to produce milk on the day of delivery and lactation will continue as long as the milk is being removed, either by breast pump or by nursing. In the beginning, pain in the breasts is normal, but it should subside within a few days. Breast milk can be frozen and used at a later date. However, the woman should remember that the breasts accommodate to the baby's feeding schedule and will become engorged as feeding time nears. To avoid painful engorgement, a woman should either nurse regularly or express milk. Breast-feeding is discussed in detail in the next chapter.

Recovery

The mother's physical recovery from birthing depends on the difficulty of birth and the type of birth. A cesarean birth can require a week or more of hospitalization, whereas a normal, uncomplicated vaginal birth may require only one or two days. Abdominal muscles are disturbed during the cesarean delivery, thus requiring a much longer recovery period. A woman will most likely require a week or more of recuperation after any delivery. She will be limited in her mobility and at least for the first few days will be limited in what she can carry. Excessive blood loss or other birth complications will extend recovery time. For working mothers, six weeks is a minimum maternity leave. By the end of six weeks, they should be mobile and able to function quite well.

Birth Defects and Stillbirths

Little is more painful than discovering that one's baby is not healthy. Some babies live up to the point of delivery, but due to malpractice by the physician or an act of fate, the baby expires in the minutes or hours just before birth. When a stillbirth happens, many parents have found it comforting to spend a few minutes with the child in order to say goodbye. In retrospect, these parents value those minutes, the chance to see their child, and the chance to bond, if only briefly. Counseling is recommended to deal with grief, resentment, anger, and loss—all normal reactions after a stillbirth.

Birth defects, whether physical or cognitive, are sometimes apparent at birth. Other than gender, one of the first things that parents look for is "normalness." The disappointment at the discovery of a birth defect is immeasurable. Dealing with the pain, fear, disappointment, regret, embarrassment, shame, guilt, and other emotions that accompany such an event necessitates wise counsel. Counseling with a therapist, religious adviser, or other trusted individual can help one cope during this troubling time. Parents need not only to deal with their own emotions, but also to consult with physicians concerning the long-term prognosis of their child, the special needs of the child, and what they can do to mitigate the defect(s), giving the child the greatest chance for survival and a happy, healthy life.

Some birth defects will have a minimal effect on the child's development and productivity, while others are seriously debilitating and may lead to early death. Prior to consultation with medical staff, parents should not make any assumptions. It is easy to let one's mind run wild with exaggerated thoughts of the future. Patience, calm, and a dedication to the child will help parents in dealing with the difficulties that birth defects present for the family.

Birth defects can take a heavy toll on a marriage. In some cases, tragedy brings couples closer together, but more often it stresses relationships—even more than having a baby already does. The couple should seek counseling to deal with their individual emotions and fears, and the practical matters of raising a child with physical or cognitive limitations.

Bonding

Bonding occurs when parent and child develop a psychological connection with one another. Some animal species bond to the first thing they see. Ducks, for instance, will assume their mother is the first creature they see after they hatch. Konrad Lorenz demonstrated this phenomenon in a very famous photograph when he made sure he was the first thing ducklings saw, and from then on, they followed him anywhere he went.

People don't bond like this, but the attachment process is extremely important for both normal psychosocial development and survival. Bonding takes place over many months, but it begins with the first few hours of life when the mother or father and child engage in physical contact, shared sounds (babies obviously can't talk, but mothers can talk to them and listen to their cries and sighs), and face-to-face contact. At one time, once babies were born, they were whisked away to a neonatal nursery while the mother recovered in another room. The baby was brought into the mother's room for feeding but was otherwise monitored and cared for by medical staff in another room. Most hospitals today facilitate bonding by allowing the baby to stay in the room with the mother as much as the mother wants. Balancing the mother's recovery and time with the baby is now a decision left up to the mother rather than the hospital staff.

In the weeks following delivery, the mother and father will need to spend many hours holding, feeding, and snuggling with the child. These behaviors all help the child to view the world as a safe, comforting place where his needs will be met and also will strengthen the bond between caregiver and child. Bonding lays the emotional groundwork for all future relationships in adolescence and adulthood.

SUMMARY

The journey from conception through pregnancy and delivery is fascinating and exciting. You will see your baby growing, feel it rolling and kicking, and perhaps know its gender long before delivery. Careful attention to diet, rest, and exercise, as well as adequate prenatal care by a physician, can greatly increase the likelihood of a smooth pregnancy and a healthy baby. There is a lot to think about when preparing for a baby's arrival. Circumcision, whether to breast- or bottle-feed, and how much time to take off from work are issues that should be part of the prebirth planning. Understanding your role as a parent in teaching your child gender issues, gathering supplies, deciding upon sleeping arrangements, and lifestyle adjustment are just a few of the important things to plan. Naming your child and selecting a birthing method are also a part of the excitement of preparing for a new baby. Upon delivery, your journey as a parent begins.

PART II

Birth to Two Years

CHAPTER 4

First Weeks:
Neonates and Infants

Before you were conceived I wanted you
Before you were born I loved you
Before you were here an hour I would die for you
This is the miracle of life

—Maureen Hawkins

New parents bring their newborn to the church nursery for the first time. The infant is just a few weeks old and the proud mother and father hand their child over to the nursery worker. Almost immediately the child begins to cry. Guilt shows on the parents' faces. They want to take the child back, but the worker assures them that the child will be fine. With the baby screaming, the parents leave the nursery. Almost immediately the child stops crying. At this age, the baby is not old enough to "miss" anyone, including parents. The child will be fine until the parents peek in to check on their little beauty. As soon as the baby sees them, she begins to cry again, confirming in the parents' minds that the child desperately missed them. Not so. The baby cried the first time because of separation anxiety, and it will be several months before the child realizes that her parents exist when they are out of sight. The baby cried the second time because, when she recognized the face of her parents, she wanted to be with them. This chapter addresses cognitive changes as well as a host of other practical issues related to newborns and infants.

THINKING

During World War II, my wife's grandfather was sent to basic training while his wife was pregnant with my future mother-in-law. After finishing his basic training in Louisiana, he shipped out to Europe. More than two years later he returned to his daughter, who by then was a toddler. Our veterans sacrificed their lives and years of service for our country, but they also sacrificed something perhaps as great as my wife's grandfather did. He missed two of the most important years of his child's developmental life. He missed her first words, her first steps, and her first birthday party. He left a pregnant wife and returned to a wife and toddler. Children change faster in the first two years than they do at any other time of their lives. I can't imagine missing those events with my own children and I'm thankful for those who made this sacrifice. Watching my children as they grew physically, practiced using words, and seeing their faces when, for the first time, they recognized me and smiled created joy beyond measure. What we cannot see are the many changes that are taking place inside the baby's brain. Neural connections are made as the baby exercises his brain, learning about his surroundings, and he begins to build the foundation on which all of his future thinking about people and his environment will be based. Nearly everything in his future relationships, intellect, successes, and failures will, at least in part, reflect these first months of life.

Language Development

One of the most obvious signs of cognitive development is the ability of the child to communicate. Words, however, are only one way in which babies communicate and it will be months before your child uses words. But your baby can communicate with you from her first days. Typically, language development progresses from crying, to cooing, then babbling, and then first words.

Crying

Babies first communicate verbally by crying. A survey once showed that people identified a crying baby as the most unpleasant sound out of a series of choices. But one must remember that crying is a baby's main mode of communication. Consider how often you communicate with another person during your waking hours. Imagine that you could use no words. Your communications could differ only by tone and intensity. You would eventually develop a method of communication similar to what babies do when they cry. Their cries differ in pitch, intensity, and volume. Most parents can easily differentiate between the cries of their children. Babies cry when they are in pain or discomfort, when they are frightened, when they are fussy, and when they are lonely. Hunger, needing a diaper change, and being tired all create discomfort, but each cry is subtly different. Learning to identify these different cries will help you meet your baby's needs.

Cooing

Around two months of age, babies begin to make intentional sounds other than crying and grunting. The random use of vowel sounds is called cooing. These sounds are deliberate in the sense that the baby is deliberately using his vocal cords. They are not deliberate in the sense that the baby knows the sounds he is going to make. Therefore, these vowel combinations are random.

Babbling

Around six months of age, babies expand their repertoire of sounds by adding random consonant sounds to their cooing. Between 6 and 12 months, the child will increase his use of these random sounds. By accident, the child will occasionally say words that are recognizable to the listener, but during this stage, this is merely coincidence. It is believed that all children have an equal capacity to learn any language, but during the babbling stage, as parents hear random sounds that approximate words in their native language, they reward the child with positive feedback while ignoring sounds that do not exist in the native language. Therefore, as the baby interacts with parents, sounds (and eventually words) that are a part of their native language appear more frequently while nonnative sounds and words fall away. Eventually, the baby will lose the ability make some types of sounds altogether.

It is also during this time that babies begin to understand a parent's words. Around eight months of age, the child will begin to recognize single words.

First Words

Long before a child uses words, he will begin to understand a parent's words. Around eight months of age, the child will begin to recognize single words but will first use deliberate words between 12 and 15 months of age, on the average. However, some children use words sooner and some don't begin to talk until much later. Using words earlier than average is not necessarily a sign of exceptional intelligence, anymore than talking later than average is a sign of delayed development. Most children use words by 17 months of age, but even if a child is 20–24 months before she uses words, one does not necessarily have to worry that the child has a cognitive problem. Especially if the child has older siblings, delayed onset of speech is not unusual. When I evaluate a child who has not begun to use words by 20 months or so, I look for cooing and babbling. If the child is progressing normally through these stages, it may simply be that his language development is slower than normal. Child development involves physical, cognitive, and emotional development, but these areas do not necessarily have to progress in unison. If the child exhibits other signs of developmental delay, especially in another area (such as physical or emotional), I would definitely want the child evaluated by a physician. If, on the other hand, there are no symptoms of developmental delay in any area other than speech, and assuming the child does not fall into any high-risk category, I am not exceptionally concerned until the child approaches two years of age.

First words are usually unintentional words that occur during babbling. Saying "daddy" or some other simple word by accident because of random vowel-consonant combinations is not unlikely. First intentional words are usually one- or two-syllable words that utilize soft consonants like "d" or "n" in combination with vowels. Words that begin with hard consonants like "g" are harder to pronounce and usually show up later in development. Parents often want to document a child's first words. By the end of the second year, a child will have an average of 200 words in his vocabulary.

Duos, Sentences, and Motherese

When a child begins to use words, he will use single words to express an entire sentence or thought. For example, "Drink" will mean "I want a drink, please." As children develop their vocabularies, they begin to put words together into two-word sentences called "duos." "Mommy play," for example, will communicate that the child wants mommy to play with her. As the child's vocabulary expands, sentences increase in length. Nouns and verbs develop before articles, modifiers, and prepositions. *Telegraphic speech* is the term for sentences that contain only verbs and nouns, much as telegrams did in years past. The more a child is exposed to language, the faster he or she will learn to use language. As children begin to speak in sentences, the lack of clarity of their words and the incorrect usage of terms make it difficult to understand what they are trying to communicate, even though they are deliberately using language. Parents often can interpret what they mean. *Motherese* is the term for this language that develops between a caretaker and the child. Also called *caretaker speech*, this language involves the intentional use of words, but because of mispronunciation, missing articles or pronouns, or soft speech, caretakers often must interpret what the child is saying for listeners who are not accustomed to the child's use of language.

By age three, most children have a vocabulary of between 800 and 1,000 words. By age four, the child's vocabulary has increased to 1,500 words, and by age five, it is nearly 2,500 words. Few things are more important in a Western culture than learning to read and write. Development of vocabulary is a first step toward reading. Frequent interaction with the child, reading to the child, face-to-face contact, and play all assist in the child's speech development.

Object Permanence

When a baby is born, her immature brain is incapable of doing a number of things that adults take for granted. One of these things is *object permanence*. Object permanence describes the idea that we know things exist (they are permanent) even when we can't see them. For an infant, once an object leaves her field of view, it ceases to exist. It isn't that the child "thinks" about the fact that the object no longer exists. Rather, she ceases to think about it at all. For this reason parents of neonates don't have to worry that their child is missing them when they leave the room. Once the parents leave the child's field of vision, the child ceases to think about them. (Don't get too depressed. Parents are still extremely important to the child's development, even if the child doesn't think about them!)

Around eight months of age, the child begins to recognize that objects exist when they are out of sight. In a classic experiment, Jean Piaget demonstrated object permanence in children by using a toy and a blanket. He placed a toy in front of the child and then covered it with a blanket. In order to retrieve the toy, all the child had to do was remove the blanket. A child who had not achieved object permanence would simply look away or find something else to do. Conversely, a child who had achieved object permanence would quickly uncover the toy and pick it up. You can use lack of object permanence to your advantage when a child is upset. If a baby is distracted with a mobile or a book, or by looking out the window, she will quickly forget about whatever was upsetting her before (unless, of course, she is in pain).

You may have noticed that even though your child is not old enough to have achieved object permanence, he still cries when you leave him with a temporary caregiver. That cry reflects *separation anxiety,* which I will discuss in more detail in the "Feeling" section. Once you have left the house and the child has focused on something else, he will calm down and be fine. However, after about eight months of age when the child achieves object permanence, he may cry for an hour or more, especially if he is frightened, sick, or very tired. He knows you are out there somewhere, and he wants you to be home.

Repetitive Behaviors

Babies like to do the same things over and over. You could play peek-a-boo with a seven-month-old child for 15 minutes and the child would never get bored. Likewise, babies and toddlers may bang repeatedly with a rattle or a spoon until the parent can't take the noise anymore and takes the toy away. These behaviors are called *circular reactions*. The term "circular" represents the repetitious nature of the behavior. *Primary circular reactions* are repetitive behaviors that center around the child's own little world—mostly within his reach. For example, a child may repeatedly kick his legs or swing his hand up and down. Primary circular reactions begin to appear at one month. *Secondary circular reactions* appear around four months of age and represent an expanded view of the world. These reactions involve things outside the child's body, such as grasping a mobile, knocking a toy off a tray, or shaking a rattle. The child is learning that her behavior can have an effect on things apart from her own body. *Tertiary circular reactions* begin to appear around one year. During this stage, the child varies her behavior as she experiments on the world around her. For example, it is not until this stage that a baby can use shape toys—toys that require fitting shapes into matching openings. At this stage the child can alter her behavior, experimenting until she finds a way to make the shape fit into the opening.

Note that even though there is some intention in the child's behavior through tertiary reactions, this is very basic intention. In other words, the child does not do anything with a complicated plan or with malice. This becomes critical in understanding when to begin to use punishment with a child. Even in tertiary reactions, for example, a baby may drop his food on the floor, watching as you clean it up, only to repeat the behavior with some other object. The child is not deliberately trying to create work for you. Rather, he is experimenting on the world and he is fascinated that he can do something outside his body that causes something else to occur. Patience is the parent's best coping skill during this stage.

Brain Development

When a baby is born, she has all of the neurons in her brain that she will ever have. That does not mean, however, that her brain is fully developed.

Many changes take place in the baby's brain in the first years of life. First of all, at birth, nerve cells do not have the insulating coating that mature cells have. This coating, called *myelin*, serves to insulate the cell and ensure that the messages that enter the cell don't "leak out" as they pass through the cell and on to the next one. The jerky movements infants exhibit are due, in part, to the fact that even if they were cognitively capable of thinking about deliberately moving this way or that, they couldn't physically do it. As the chemical messages to and from their muscles pass through the uninsulated nerve cells, much of the information is lost and never reaches its destination. As he grows and myelin coats his nerve cells, the child will be able not only to think about picking up the rattle in front of him, he will also be physically able to do so.

Two other changes that are notable in an infant's brain are the development of cells that help nerve cells network, called *glial cells*, and the development of points of contact between cells, called *synapses*. In general, the more glial cells and the more synapses in the brain, the more efficiently the brain works. The development of these two parts of the brain are directly related to brain activity. Therefore, an environment that is stimulating to the child is preferable to one that has little or no stimulation. Yet again, this is why face-to-face contact, reading to your baby, and talking to your baby are so important. Mobiles, books, music, and physical contact literally help your baby's brain grow.

Facial Recognition

It is incredibly satisfying to parents when their baby recognizes them for the first time. Many animals recognize their parents at birth, but humans do not possess this skill. Even though babies may recognize voices, any caregiver can become the person to whom the baby bonds and sees as "mom" or "dad." Neonates do not discriminate between caregivers in their first days. As long as their needs are being met, they aren't too choosy about who is doing the feeding, cuddling, and so forth. By the second month, research demonstrates that babies begin to recognize faces. By six months, they show preference for faces that are novel compared to ones that they know. This indicates that they enjoy learning and exploring new things, not that they are bored with familiar people. They focus on faces more than anything else and they smile, laugh, and mimic the facial expressions of a parent as early as four months. They spend more time looking at a happy face than a sad face and as early as three months of age, babies can correctly match their mother's voice with her face.

FEELING

Almost from birth, a child has the capacity to demonstrate four basic emotions—sadness, disgust, fear, and anger—although it may be several weeks before these emotions exhibit themselves. Because babies sleep much of the time, their diet consists almost exclusively of milk, and they have minimal interaction with others, they don't have very many opportunities to exhibit these emotions. By the second month, your baby will begin to smile at you, and by four or five months of age, your baby will laugh. Before the end of the child's first year, he will regularly display these emotions as well as surprise, joy, and shyness.

Surprise is an interesting emotion because in order to be surprised, one has to have some level of expectation of a given event or situation. Prior to the development of expectation, babies can be startled or frightened, but not surprised. This is a cognitive skill that begins to develop around three to four months and continues throughout life. The more we learn about the world, the more expectations we develop in various situations.

Stranger anxiety begins to appear around six or seven months of age. Stranger anxiety is fear exhibited by the baby when confronted with a stranger. Depending on the personality of the child, he will exhibit at least some dissatisfaction when held by a new person. Even into the toddler years children will exhibit stranger anxiety, but infants can quickly warm to the new caregiver. When another caregiver tries to take the child, he will exhibit the same reaction to this new stranger as he did to the first one. Stranger anxiety results from transition and newness. It is also at this same time, about six to seven months of age, that separation anxiety appears, although it is most noticeable between 12 and 18 months of age.

Within just a few weeks of birth, your baby will mimic the expressions she sees on her mother's face. Likewise, babies as young as just a few weeks of age will mirror the mother's emotional state. Therefore, a mother who is frightened, stressed, or angry can pass these emotions on to the child. A tentative caregiver can inadvertently communicate insecurity to the child, increasing separation anxiety.

Can You Spoil a Baby?

It is not possible to spoil a baby. Babies need lots of love, attention, snuggling, and care. Without question, a parent can create more work for himself or herself by jumping at every whim and whimper of a child or carrying a child around every minute of the day. However, this is not synonymous with spoiling. Instead, the child is being taught a pattern of behavior. The child learns that the "normal" circumstances are when she is being held. When she is alone, she expects to be picked up and fusses until she is. There is nothing wrong with the child. She is only responding to what she has been taught and she will suffer no detrimental effects from the extra work by mother and father. In fact, she may benefit from the extra attention. For example, there has been some interesting research in recent years about sleeping with one's child. In Western cultures, common practice suggests that children should be encouraged to sleep on their own. However, there is no good reason that babies should learn to sleep on their own other than convenience for the parents. In many cultures, babies sleep with their parents for the first several years of life—in some cases even into their teen years. This causes no long-term problems for the child. In fact, when parents share the bed with their child, both mother and child sleep better, for longer periods at a time, and sleeping together increases bonding between parent and child. It is inconvenient for parents when they don't sleep as well as they might if the child were sleeping in a separate bed, and engagement in normal marital relationships is a challenge, but inconvenience is mistaken for spoiling. During the first two years of life, we cannot give our children too much attention.

Either my wife or I rocked each of our three children to sleep each night until they were about two years old. Some acquaintances told me I would be sorry. Indeed, it was frustrating sometimes, especially if we were away from home or very tired. We had to commit 15 to 30 minutes to putting our children to sleep, rather than a few minutes if they had been trained to go to sleep on their own, but I do not regret one single night of rocking, singing, and snuggling those babies. None of them has shown any dysfunction as a result, either. Just the opposite is true. They have developed very secure egos and are very confident children, just as theory would have suggested.

You will not spoil your child by rocking him when he is ready for sleep or by similar behaviors, but you must recognize the behavior patterns and expectations you are creating in your child. If you are willing to accept that the child will expect those behaviors and that it will be difficult to change the behavior once a pattern is established, go ahead and do it. If, on the other hand, you are unwilling to maintain those accommodating behaviors and unwilling to accept the fact that your child may not sleep, may not allow you to sleep, or may not calm down unless you accommodate him, do not start the practice.

Developing Self-Esteem

The first few years of a child's life are critical to how a child views himself. Over the years, my clients, both young and old, have described incidents from their childhoods where they were proud of something and looked to a significant adult for affirmation, only to be criticized or ignored. Words like "stupid," "ugly," and "idiot" are devastating to a child. We continue to seek our parents' approval long after childhood. Many of my graduate school colleagues, for example, admittedly were trying to prove their worth to a parent by pursuing their Ph.D.s. When my children look up to me and show me some work of art or some assignment from school, they are doing more than providing information. They are saying to me, "Am I OK?" and "Do I fit in?" They are not asking what I think about their work, they are asking, "What do you think about me?" There is no more important job than teaching my children that they are, indeed, OK and valuable. Even though a child's desire to be seen as worthy and accepted is most obvious in early childhood, the foundation for her esteem is laid during infancy.

Psychologist and theorist Erik Erikson proposed that the very first stage of a child's development was a conflict called *trust versus mistrust*. According to Erikson, in the first year of life caregivers meet a child's emotional and physical needs. By doing so, the child learns that the world is a safe and trustworthy place. He learns that when he is hungry, he will be fed; when he is in discomfort, he will be helped; and when he needs to be comforted, he will be snuggled. Many years ago, researchers compared the infant mortality rates in two environments. The first was a women's prison in the United States. These babies were born to women who had been incarcerated and were being raised in prison by their own mothers. The second environment was an orphanage run by nuns in Mexico. Stunned researchers discovered that the mortality rate was much higher among the children in the orphanage. The obvious question involved discovering what was missing from the orphanage that was being provided in the prison setting. None of the children in the orphanage died of starvation or physical neglect. They simply failed to thrive. The key ingredient that was missing in the orphanage was personal contact with a primary caregiver. The well-meaning nuns simply had too many children to care for and, consequently, met only their basic physical needs while unintentionally neglecting their emotional needs. This phenomenon is now called *failure to thrive*.

Babies often need to be snuggled and reassured that they will be cared for. Nursing, for example, provides more than sustenance for a baby. Being held close to a loving parent while hunger is being satisfied is part of the process of learning that someone is there to meet the baby's needs and that the world is safe. Babies also learn that the world is a safe place through the gentle, calming voices of their parents and siblings, which are reassuring as they learn about this world of noises, bright lights, and strange sensations. Even in the womb, babies respond to the emotional levels of the mother. Therefore, babies need a soothing environment created by soft sounds, singing, and quiet conversation. Talking with your child also lays the foundation for learning language. Development of trust in the world is necessary for developing self-confidence. Therefore, self-reliance, self-confidence, and self-efficacy in adulthood are directly related to the first 12 months of life. As you can see, it is the very behaviors which some critics call "spoiling" that, in fact, assist in fostering healthy and strong esteem in childhood and eventually in adulthood.

DOING

At birth, babies have very little control over their muscles. They cannot stand, sit, or hold their heads up, and they are even limited in how much they can turn their heads. They acquire some of these abilities within just weeks, and others within a few months, of birth. During their first two years, they need toys that develop their interest in the world and also are within the range of their physical abilities. Rattles, mobiles, and teething rings stimulate the child's environment yet are not beyond their developmental limitations for grasping and manipulating. Everything babies experience is new. They learn about their bodies in a very rudimentary way from their first hours. They first learn that their arms, legs, toes, and fingers are parts of themselves and can be used to make repetitious noises and (later) to manipulate objects. Having little muscle control, they explore the world with their mouths. They will even try to put a person's face in their mouths. Hold baby up to a mirror and he will open his mouth and lean toward the mirror. You will see your baby change from week to week as she grows, learns, and learns about her environment, and you are her primary teacher. From the moment of birth, there are many physical signs of normal development.

APGAR

Immediately after delivery, the physician makes a cursory evaluation of the baby's condition. There are several standards for this evaluation, one of which is called the *APGAR score*. Named for Dr. Virginia Apgar, a physician, it is also an acronym that represents five measures of a baby's condition: *A*ppearance, *P*ulse, *G*rimace/muscle tone, *A*ctivity and effort, and *R*espiration. Appearance refers to the baby's color. Ideally a white child is pinkish in color, indicative of proper blood flow. Pulse refers to heart rate. Grimace refers to muscle tone and structure. Activity refers to reflexes, and respiration refers to the baby's breathing. Each of the five measures is scored as 0, 1, or 2, with 0 representing an absence of the measure and 2 representing normal or ideal measure. Therefore, the total APGAR score ranges from 0 to 10. A score of 10 is perfect and a score of 0 would indicate a stillborn infant. The APGAR score is taken twice—once at one minute after birth and a second time five minutes after birth. Even in normal, uncomplicated births, the second score is often higher as the baby adjusts to its new surroundings. Normal APGAR scores are 7 or higher. The APGAR score does not indicate that there are no problems at all, nor does it necessarily indicate serious problems. The scoring system simply allows the physician to make a general evaluation of the baby's condition so that obvious problems can be addressed immediately.

Reflexes

At birth, babies are able to do a number of things reflexively. Reflexes are behaviors that we do not have to learn. For example, babies will blink when a puff of air is blown toward their eyes. They do not have to learn to blink their eyes. Some reflexes are permanent. For example, the blink reflex is permanent, as is the *patellar reflex* (the knee jerk when the patellar tendon is tapped with an object). Most neonatal reflexes, however, fade away within a few months of birth.

The *sucking reflex* occurs when an object enters the child's mouth. When the palate is touched, the child will suck. This behavior becomes voluntary around the second month of life. The *Babinski reflex* is also called the *fanning reflex*. When the sole of the baby's bare foot is stroked, the toes curl and then fan out. This reflex fades around the end of the first year. The *rooting reflex* helps the baby find food. If you stroke a baby's cheeks, the child will open her mouth and turn in the direction of the cheek that was touched. This reflex disappears by the third or fourth month. Also disappearing by the third or fourth month is the *Palmer reflex*, also called the *grasping reflex*. When an object is placed in the baby's palm, her fingers will close tightly around that object. Women with long hair, dangling jewelry, and men with beards, beware! The baby won't want to let go.

When babies are younger than two or three months, if they are supported upright and the soles of their feet touch a solid object, they will raise their legs in a manner similar to walking. This is called the *stepping reflex* and is often misinterpreted by parents as the child's attempt to walk. All normally developing babies do this and this reflex disappears around the third month. It will be several months before the child is ready to walk.

Several other reflexes are apparent at birth. It is easy to test for these reflexes and exciting to observe them as the baby progresses normally. When evaluating an infant, I always check for a series of these reflexes. Their absence is symptomatic of potential cognitive and/or physical abnormalities. In such cases, referral to a pediatrician is imperative.

Temperament

Temperament, a component of personality, appears to be a part of our genetic heritage. Any parent who has more than one child can attest to the distinct differences that are evident even during the first days of life of those children. There are three basic types of temperament in children. *Easy* babies are those who adapt quickly to changing environments and new people. They do not cry as often as other babies and they establish routines (sleeping, eating, etc.) fairly quickly. They smile and respond to face-to-face contact with caregivers in positive ways, thus eliciting more interaction with the caregivers. Every parent would choose a baby like this, but only about 40 percent of babies fit this category.

Difficult babies are just the opposite. They cry often, and even when their needs are met, these babies cannot be appeased. They have erratic sleeping and feeding schedules that make it difficult for parents to get rest or to plan their days. The lack of sleep and frustrations from listening to a crying baby increases tension in the home and exacerbates the baby's unhappiness. For obvious reasons, difficult babies are more likely to be physically abused than any other category, especially if the parents are very young or if they have poor coping skills. Fortunately, only about 10 percent of all children have this temperament. Parents sometimes incorrectly suppose their babies are difficult because they "cry a lot," but every baby cries. What seems like a lot may actually be quite normal. Babies who have colic, an ear infection, or some other common discomforting illness may cry much of the day, but once they have recovered from their illness, they cry far less and are more easily appeased. Even a diaper that is too tight can cause a baby to fuss.

Slow-to-warm-up babies have mixed traits. They are generally good-natured and accommodate to new situations fairly well, although not as quickly as easy babies. Babies with this temperament experience more distress when changing hands between one caregiver and another, but after a few minutes they adapt to the new caregiver (as opposed to difficult babies, who may not adapt to a baby-sitter or nursery worker for an hour or more—if at all). About half of all babies are slow-to-warm-up babies.

Hearing, Taste, and Smell

At birth, a baby's auditory sense, olfactory sense, and sense of taste are all fully functioning. I used to think that a baby surely couldn't smell because it seemed that babies who had smelly diapers weren't bothered by it, but my perception was incorrect. They can smell and taste, and will show preferences for foods based on these two variables. Babies also can hear very well, even in the womb. At birth, they show preference for voices they were exposed to in utero over novel voices. They also may show recognition of sounds (music, for example) that they were exposed to while in the womb.

Vision

For the first few weeks of life a neonate can see only about six or seven inches away. This is about the distance between a mother's and a baby's face while the child is nursing. Between one and three months of age, a baby can see several meters, and by four months he will be able to distinguish colors. By eight months to a year, a baby's vision is nearly fully developed: he can track objects across a room and he can easily recognize a familiar face or a toy when it enters the room. Parents who watch their newborn baby through a nursery window and believe that the child sees them are mistaken. The child may see movement, but from that distance he cannot focus on details enough to recognize a face.

Binocular vision refers to the fact that we have two eyes yet see a single object. Binocular vision is what keeps us from viewing things cross-eyed. Many babies are born somewhat cross-eyed because the muscles that control their eyes are not fully developed and they have not learned to work in unison. Between the third and fifth month of life, the baby's eyes should be working in harmony, making it easy for him to see things clearly, both up close and at a distance, as well as to focus on a single image.

Babies prefer to look at the edges of objects rather than the center. When exploring a face, they will trace the outside of the face with their eyes rather than focus on the nose, eyes, or mouth, as do older children and adults, but by their second month, they will view internal features. They prefer large, simple patterns as opposed to complex pictures or patterns, but long before their first birthday, they enjoy both complex patterns and novel patterns over simple and routine ones.

Motor Development

Motor development and locomotion refer to how a baby moves. Neonates have almost no muscle control and even the large muscles in their legs and arms are inadequate to support them. Their heads are largely out of proportion to their bodies, making it impossible for their weak neck muscles to hold their heads up by themselves. (For this reason, it is important to always support a newborn's head when moving him. Failure to do so could cause serious injury and even death of the child.) Babies develop control over their large muscles first and over their smaller muscles last. Large muscles in the arms and legs help them to crawl, reach, and walk. These are called *gross motor* movements. Smaller muscles and muscle groups allow the child to do things like pointing and grasping with two fingers. These are called *fine motor* skills. Fine motor skills take years to develop fully. For example, control of the sphincter muscle of the anus is a fine motor skill. Most children cannot control this small muscle until they are about two years of age. Likewise, most preschool children cannot play musical instruments very well because they have not developed the muscle control in their fingers that is necessary for playing instruments like the piano, flute, and violin.

Motor development is asynchronous but generally develops in the following order. Within a week or two of normal birth, the child should be able to turn her head, and by four weeks she will be able to hold her head up with assistance. However, it is not until the end of the second month that she will be able to lift and support her head by herself. At three months she should be able to sit up with some support; at three to four months she will roll over; and at six months she will crawl. Some children never crawl before they walk, while others may scoot or crawl backward but not forward. By eight months, your baby may be able to pull up to a standing position using a table, chair, or some other means of support. Around nine or ten months, your infant will be able to take some steps while holding on to a table or someone's hand, and by the end of her first year, she will be able to pull to a standing position and then stand alone. First unassisted steps follow shortly thereafter, between 12 and 15 months. When they are crawling, many babies are able to crawl up stairs, but negotiating stairs from a standing position with support occurs at around 16 months.

Once a child begins to move on her own, it is imperative that parents babyproof their home. Babies are fearless and have no understanding of their limitations. They will try to negotiate stairs long before they are physically capable of doing so. They will climb on tables, cabinets, other furniture, and anything else that catches their interest. Babies are sometimes killed when they attempt to climb on top of TV carts, only to have the top-heavy cart and TV crash down upon them. Sharp and breakable objects should be kept well out of the baby's reach, as should medications, poisons, and cleansers. Babies explore the world with their mouths, so it is a certainty that anything a child grabs hold of will end up in his mouth. Tablecloths and electrical cords present a danger to children because even infants can pull objects off a table or counter if they grasp a tablecloth, a lamp cord, or the cord of an iron. A babyproofed home is a safer home, plus it reduces a parent's frustration because sentimental objects are not broken when babies and toddlers get into them. Learning to live with the inconvenience of cabinet door latches and fewer decorations around the house is a small price to pay for ensuring the safety of your child.

Bone Structure

One of the most notable bone features of newborns is the "soft spot" on the top of the head. The skull is actually a series of platelike bones rather than one solid piece. These plates are separated by zigzag spaces called *sutures*. There are several places where sutures join together, but the most obvious one is at the very top of the head. If you watch closely, you can see the pulsations of the baby's brain at that spot. There is no bone tissue at that point. These spaces allow the baby's head to flex enough to pass through the birth canal and also accommodate the growth of the brain during infancy and childhood. By the end of the second or third year of life, the baby's brain will have grown as large as it will every get and the sutures will close. However, they will not fully seal until around age 40. Through the analysis of the width of sutures, anthropologists can approximate the age of a person based on the skull. In rare situations, a baby may be born with sutures that are closed. This presents a very dangerous situation, called *craniosynostosis*, that must be corrected. When this condition exists, parents will begin to notice that the child's head is misshapen. There are several types of craniosynostosis, depending on which sutures are closed. Most often only a single suture is closed, but multiple closed sutures are possible. In any case, if the condition is not corrected, usually through surgery, as the baby's brain continues to grow, it will be compressed by the skull, potentially causing blindness, brain damage, developmental delay, seizures, and mental retardation. At the very least, if left untreated, the malformation of the child's head will become more pronounced as the brain grows. Prognosis following surgical treatment of this disorder is very good and most children who are treated in early childhood go on to lead normal, healthy lives.

The bones of the arms and legs also are very flexible. Bones continue to harden over one's lifetime, but the soft bones of infants and children benefit them in two ways. First, they are less likely to break because they are softer, and second, they heal more quickly than adult bones if they are broken. The rigid bones in adulthood support the adult's weight but also make breakage more likely and healing slower.

Teeth

Teeth are the only exposed bones of the body and a baby's first teeth are beginning to form even before he is born. Around four or five months, the child will begin to salivate heavily as the teeth prepare to erupt through the gums. By six or seven months, the first teeth begin to show, usually the lower front teeth. As babies prepare for the eruption of teeth, they may experience discomfort and seem grumpier than usual. Refrigerated gel-filled teething rings can give relief, as can over-the-counter medications for teething. Babies will chew on anything while teething, so it is a good idea to have a teething ring or other sanitary object available at all times for a teething baby. It is frequently thought that diarrhea and fever are caused by teething, but current medical research discounts this belief. When these symptoms appear in conjunction with teething, they most likely have some other cause.

Even though first teeth normally appear around 6 months, some babies will not have their first tooth until 12 months. By 18 months, most children have both upper and lower teeth and by age three, all baby teeth are exposed.

Even before baby teeth appear, the baby's gums can be cleaned using a cool, soft washcloth. Baby teeth are susceptible to cavities and once a baby's teeth begin to protrude, consultation with a pediatrician or pediatric dentist is advisable concerning brushing, use of fluoride drops, flossing, and other routine oral hygiene practices.

Vaccinations and Immunizations

The medical profession has increased its knowledge of disease and disease prevention tremendously. Illnesses that were considered normal childhood diseases when I was a youngster are almost unheard-of in American children today. Most hospitals run simple blood tests on newborns that check for common, easily treatable diseases and illnesses such as phenylkenonuria (PKU). From the first week of life, parents should consult with a pediatrician and learn the recommended checkup and shot schedule for their child. Most pediatricians will see the child for the first time before mother and child leave the hospital. Any abnormalities that are evident will be noted and a plan for addressing them will be established. Likewise, parents can be assured by the pediatrician that all is well with their child and the physician can answer any questions about health care or parenting that they may have. A first office visit for the child will often be recommended sometime within the first month, after the mother has had time to physically recover from delivery— usually between two and four weeks. After that, checkups at 2, 4, 6, 9, 18, and 24 months are routine. Afterward, yearly checkups from ages four to ten are common. After age ten, some pediatricians recommend biyearly checkups. These schedules are common, but checkup schedules vary from doctor to doctor.

Sleep Patterns

Even in the womb, babies have a sleep-wake cycle. Mothers may be able to get an idea of the child's sleep cycle by the amount of activity they feel at various times of the day or night, especially as the delivery date approaches. Sleep cycles vary, but through the first year neonates sleep an average of two to four hours between feedings, and a total of about 18 hours out of 24. That means that during a normal night, a new mother or father can expect to be awakened by the neonate at least once or twice. There are no lights or clocks in the womb, so the "daytime" hours in the womb may actually be night. Therefore, the child may awaken for a 1:00 A.M. feeding and be ready to stay awake for an hour or two. Just as adults have to adjust to time changes and jet lag, it will take the infant several days, perhaps even two or three weeks, to adjust to a different sleep cycle. Parents can help with this adjustment by using dim lighting and quiet voices, and by not playing with the child in the middle of the night. Don't expect too much change too quickly. It is frustrating when you are tired and the baby won't go back to sleep, but this part of your baby's life won't last long and your tired days will soon be forgotten.

Pediatricians used to order feedings every four hours. If the baby was asleep, he was to be awakened. Today, unless there is some physical problem, it is assumed that babies will awaken when they are hungry and can be fed at that time. This is called *demand feeding*. Barring some health problem, babies will eat when they are hungry and sleep when they are tired. Waking your child every four hours for a feeding establishes a conditioned habit of waking every four hours. Once that habit is established in the child, it can be hard to break. Consultation with your pediatrician will provide further information on feeding schedules so that you can make an informed decision as to what is best for your child.

The older children get, the longer they sleep at a time, especially at night, and the longer they are awake during the day. During infancy, your child will probably take a long nap in the morning as well as a long nap in the afternoon. Even though the need for naps diminishes as the child gets older, through the first two or three years, your child will probably need at least one nap during the day. The number of hours most infants sleep per day declines from about 18 hours per 24-hour period at birth to around 12 hours per 24-hour period at one year of age. The need for sleep slowly declines throughout the life span, but on the average most children under age 12 need about ten hours of sleep per night compared to the average adult, who requires between seven and nine hours.

No parent enjoys being up all night long with a crying baby, but there are only a few things that cause a baby to cry—pain or discomfort, hunger, a wet or soiled diaper, and the need for attention. Your baby also will cry when she is startled, afraid, or tired. As an adult you recognize when you are tired and you know you need to lie down and rest. The bad feeling you get when you are really tired is the same feeling a baby experiences, but the baby does not know what to do. She only knows that she feels bad and wants the bad feeling to go away. This is why many babies cry themselves to sleep. They feel bad because they are tired, so they cry and fuss. Crying and fussing makes it difficult for them to sleep, so they fuss more, thus getting more tired and feeling worse. Eventually, exhaustion takes over and they fall asleep.

If your baby is fussy during the night, ensure that she is not hungry or in need of a diaper change. If this doesn't settle your child, rocking, gently cooing to her, and patting her back may soothe her, especially if she is in need of reassurance and attention. If she continues to cry, check to see if she is fevered. Nighttime crying could also be the result of colic, an ear infection, or teething—common problems in infancy that cause discomfort in the child. If you are certain your child is not sick, you have ensured she is fed and dry, and rocking or walking with her still does not comfort her, leave her alone for a while. It is hard for a parent to sleep when the baby is crying, but it won't hurt your child to cry herself to sleep on occasion.

Sleeping Positions

Current thinking among pediatricians is that babies should sleep on their backs. Crib mattresses should be firm and babies should not sleep on fluffy comforters or other soft material. Soft materials look cozy, but as the baby turns his head during sleep, his face could easily bury in a soft blanket, causing interruption in breathing or even suffocation. Other than bumper pads, there is no need for anything in the crib. Babies don't need pillows, stuffed animals, or toys while they sleep.

Sudden Infant Death Syndrome

Sudden infant death syndrome (SIDS), also called crib death, was first labeled in a paper published in the journal *Pediatrics* in 1972. Children were dying in their sleep for no apparent reason and it appeared that a sleep disorder called *sleep apnea* was to blame for many of the deaths. SIDS has also been called "crib death" in the United States and "cot death" in Great Britain. With this disorder, as the child sleeps, he or she stops breathing periodically. If the child's breathing pauses for an extended period of time, the child suffocates.

In the human body, the nervous system is divided into two major categories, the autonomic system and the somatic system. The somatic system rules our voluntary functions, such as walking, sitting, and standing. The autonomic system controls all of our functions that are reflexive or automatic. Heart rate, liver and kidney functions, and respiration are all controlled by the autonomic system. Fortunately, these functions operate on their own and we do not have to think about them. It is the autonomic nervous system that makes it impossible for you to hold your breath until you die, for as soon as you lose consciousness, your autonomic system will override the somatic system that was allowing you to hold your breath and you will start breathing again. In some neonates, especially in premature babies, the autonomic system does not function properly. As the infant sleeps, his or her respiration slows and periodically stops. In many children, even though breathing may become very slow or even stop, it eventually starts again on its own and the child is fine. In some neonates, however, the child does not start breathing again. He literally suffocates because his body forgets to breath.

Increased risk for SIDS occurs among children of very young mothers, children of mothers who smoke, babies who hold their breath or snore, and babies who wake frequently during the night. Many physicians question apnea as the cause of SIDS, and its actual cause remains controversial. Regardless, babies at risk for SIDS are easily treated either with a sleep monitor or by having them sleep on their back or side rather than on the stomach. This adjustment of sleep position alone reduced SIDS deaths by 30 percent between 1992 and 1996. Risk for SIDS dramatically declines after the child reaches 6 months of age, and it is statistically improbable after the child reaches 12 months of age.

Bottle- or Breast-feeding

In the 1950s and 1960s, bottle-feeding using formula grew in popularity. At that time, many women perceived breast-feeding as something common only among the poor. Baby food companies and even some physicians argued that manufactured baby formula was superior to breast milk. These claims turned out to be false. There is no relationship between breast-feeding and socioeconomic status, although poorer women may be less likely to afford formula. However, the social stigma of "only poor women breast-feed" is nearly nonexistent today. There are advantages and disadvantages to both breast- and bottle-feeding. Breast milk not only contains the nutrients that a baby needs, it also changes in composition as the child ages. *Colostrum*, the first thing the woman's breast produces after delivery of her baby, contains many nutrients that the baby needs. Some of these nutrients do not exist in baby formula. Breast milk is free and, unless the mother expresses milk for later use, does not require the use of bottles, nipples, or inserts; thus, there are fewer items to wash. Breast milk is always available. It is very frustrating for parents who bottle-feed their child when they are awakened by a hungry baby in the middle of the night, only to discover that they are out of formula. You can't tell the baby to wait until morning when you have time to go to the grocery store. Breast-feeding also provides a time of bonding for mother and child. The baby's face is within about six to eight inches of the mother, well within the range of the baby's vision, and since breast-feeding takes longer than bottle-feeding, the child and mother spend more time together. Breast milk can be expressed with the aid of a breast pump or by hand, and can be frozen and stored for later use.

On the other hand, women who breast-feed are saddled with the responsibility of feeding the baby or at least pumping milk several times a day. This can be oppressive, especially for women who are working outside the home or who have responsibilities that require them to be away from home several hours at a time each day. Women who breast-feed must be cautious about medications they take because chemicals can be delivered to the baby via breast milk. Women who bottle-feed are free from this responsibility and can use their normal medications without any risk to the infant.

Formula is heavier and tends to fill a baby's tummy faster than breast milk. This is an advantage when time constraints are an issue and may be especially important to mothers who need more sleep at night—fewer and faster feedings mean more sleep. Finally, there are some modesty issues present with breast-feeding. Many cultures around the world allow women to breast-feed in public, but in many places in the United States, breast-feeding and/or exposing a woman's breast is still taboo. At the very least, it can be socially awkward. A woman who breast-feeds may feel it necessary to do so in private, further restricting her freedom. A blanket over the shoulder covering the baby and the woman's breast is one common way of breast-feeding while in public and still maintaining one's modesty and respecting social customs.

As the breasts engorge in women who breast-feed, leakage is sometimes an embarrassing problem. Lactating women usually wear pads that absorb leakage and protect their modesty when their nipples swell in preparation for feeding. Saturated pads can stain clothing, and even though it is not a physical problem, it can create social embarrassment. Bottle-feeding, of course, avoids such social awkwardness altogether.

Expressing milk and storing it can be a way to take advantage of both forms of feeding. A father cannot breast-feed a baby, but expressing milk allows him to assist in feeding the baby and increase his time of bonding. A woman who both bottle-feeds and breast-feeds will produce less milk, thus reducing the number of times she has to express milk and yet still providing some of the benefits of breast-feeding.

In some cultures babies are breast-fed beyond two or three years of age. Breast-feeding toddlers is a cultural issue and has little bearing on the child's health as long as the child is eating other foods as well. There is no research which indicates that breast-feeding into the toddler years is in any way psychologically harmful. On the other hand, there is little reason for breast-feeding beyond 18–24 months of age except in cases of extreme poverty. Many women prefer to begin weaning their babies once teeth appear— especially when both upper and lower teeth are present. A nursing child can easily bite the mother's nipple. How long you choose to breast-feed your child should be determined by you, your spouse, and the advice you received from your pediatrician in regard to your baby's nutritional needs.

Pacifiers

Many babies suck on a pacifier for comfort, although some never do. Pacifiers come in various shapes. Some are long and balloon-shaped and they flatten out in the child's mouth when she sucks on it. Others are flat. The flat shape mimics a woman's nipple when the baby sucks on it. Pacifiers can be very helpful calming a child, especially in a confined space (in a car, at church, or in a restaurant) where other methods may be unavailable. Pacifiers should not substitute for parental interaction, feeding, or comforting a child who is afraid, in distress, sick, or in pain. Children should not be forced to use a pacifier. If the child spits it out several times, she most likely is not interested in having it in her mouth. I prefer that children use pacifiers rather than sucking their thumbs. It is easier to keep a pacifier clean than to keep fingers clean, especially as the child gets older, and giving up the habit is a little easier with a pacifier. It should not be assumed, however, that the child will want to suck either.

Cloth or Disposable Diapers

There are advantages and disadvantages to each type of diaper. Disposable diapers are, by far, easier to use. They are fitted to the child's legs, thus preventing leakage. Since they are absorbent and keep moisture away from the baby's skin, the child has far fewer rashes than with cloth diapers. Babies can easily wet a diaper just after it has been changed, though the parent may believe that it will be a while before another change is necessary. With cloth diapers, the moisture will stay against the baby's skin for a longer period of time than with disposable diapers, which are manufactured to keep moisture separate from the baby's skin. Disposable diapers have a plastic exterior that prevents moisture from reaching the baby's clothing, furniture, or the caregiver, whereas cloth diapers need additional plastic pants to serve this function. Disposable diapers use tape instead of pins. The tape can be easily affixed, allowing for a perfect fit, and is much simpler to use than diaper pins. Disposable diapers do not require any service and can be thrown in the trash. They are more expensive than cloth diapers because they cannot be reused, but many parents find the convenience worth the extra money.

Environmental concerns have led some parents to choose cloth diapers. Disposable diapers take decades to decompose and it is argued that they are an environmental hazard. Cloth diapers can be washed at home or by a diaper service. The cost of the diaper service is equivalent to the financial savings of using cloth diapers, but since cloth diapers are reused, they do not pose the same landfill problem. However, some environmentalists have argued that the energy used to clean cloth diapers actually poses an environmental problem itself. Cloth diapers also require pins that can stick a child or the parent's fingers. They do not fit as snugly as disposable diapers and babies who wear cloth diapers are prone to have diaper rashes more frequently unless the parent is diligent about checking the child for a wet or soiled diaper and changing the child quickly. My wife and I used a diaper service for one of our children and disposable diapers for the other two. Based on expense, environment, ease of use, and comfort for our child, our preference, by far, was disposable diapers.

MOMS AND DADS POST-DELIVERY

As parents make the adjustment to their new baby, there are several things for which they should be prepared. While some of these issues do not directly deal with parenting, they are practical issues that affect one's ability to care for children, both newborns and older children.

Postpartum Mood Disorders

After delivery, many women experience moodiness, crying, nervousness, and trouble sleeping. Feelings of melancholy, of being overwhelmed, and moodiness are due in part to normal hormonal changes that occur as the woman's body adjusts to the fact that there is no longer a baby in the womb. This is known as *postpartum blues* and it affects between 60 and 80 percent of all women who give birth. Other causes of mood disturbances are the physically demanding nature of delivery, blood loss during delivery, and lack of sleep. Life changes that accompany having a new baby in the house also can be depressing. For example, a woman who stays home with her child not only has to attend to her routine household chores, she also may feel as if she is constantly changing diapers, or rocking or feeding the baby. Trying to maintain a spotless home is nearly impossible with children present. Changes in diet and exercise habits because of child-care responsibilities make it difficult for some women to lose the weight they gained during pregnancy, further assaulting their self-image. Lack of adult companionship and conversation, frustration, and even resentment toward the baby and spouse are not unusual. A mother may feel torn between the love she has for her new baby and resentment for the loss of freedom. For most women, however, postpartum blues are short-lived and usually pass in a few days or weeks. Depressive symptoms and postpartum blues can be eased by exercise and eating properly. Both parents should take turns caring for the child, giving the mother private time to read, exercise, go to a movie, or to spend some time alone.

Postpartum Depression

Postpartum depression is a more serious disorder that affects between 10 and 20 percent of women. It may be temporary or it may last for months and even years. Symptoms usually appear within a few months of delivery but may not appear until up to a year after. Postpartum depression differs from postpartum blues not only in how long symptoms last but also in their intensity. Women suffering from postpartum depression experience inability to cope, suicidal thoughts, panic attacks, guilt, and anxiety. Attitudes toward the baby range from being over concerned to lack of any concern whatsoever. Children of mothers suffering from postpartum depression exhibit symptoms that reflect the mood disorder in the mother, and the family system is affected as well. Postpartum depression usually requires professional intervention, and treatment may include medication.

Even more serious is a relatively rare disorder called *postpartum psychosis*. This very serious disorder affects only about one in 1,000 women. With this disorder, women may envision harming themselves or their children, and some women follow through with these urges. Symptoms appear within the first two weeks after delivery. If you ever find yourself thinking about harming your child, seek a mental health consultation immediately. Postpartum psychosis always requires professional treatment. These symptoms do not pass on their own, and without treatment they intensify.

Child Maltreatment

Maltreatment is the general term for child abuse in its many forms. Sexual, physical, and emotional abuse, neglect, and child endangerment are serious problems that affect thousands of children each year. Not all maltreatment is intentional. Many parents physically abuse, neglect, or endanger their children out of ignorance or misinformation. Parents must understand that any behavior which causes bruising, scars, broken bones, lacerations, or burns is abusive. Parents may injure their children while disciplining them. Parents who choose to use corporal punishment should do so without causing injury. Using unkind words like "stupid" or "ugly" when referring to a child is emotionally abusive. It is never appropriate for parents to engage in any kind of sexual behavior with their children. An adult satisfying his or her personal sexual desires by preying on a child is not only breaking the law but also is scarring that child for life. Neglect involves failing to meet the child's emotional or physical needs. Failure to provide food, shelter, and clothing, or failure to provide comfort, to demonstrate love, and to provide a nurturing environment is neglectful. Endangerment involves placing the child in a situation that creates a risk for injury. Failure to properly use a child car seat is an example of endangerment.

Avoiding abuse involves self-awareness, patience, and self-discipline. Never displace your anger on your children, and always remember not only that your children are defenseless, but also that they will very likely treat their own children the way you treat them. Abuse or neglect that occurs due to ignorance is easily corrected with education and training. Abuse that is deliberate and cruel is inexcusable. Parents who cannot control their anger or urges should remove themselves from the child's environment until they learn the skills necessary to provide a safe and nurturing home. Seeking counsel from a trusted and qualified religious leader, social worker, or counselor can help parents learn how to cope with their anger and frustrations most effectively. If parents do not deal with their emotional difficulties that lead to abuse, they not only risk prison and the temporary or even permanent loss of custody of their children, they also perpetuate abuse that will exist down their family line, potentially for generations.

Day Care and Working Mothers

The media's portrayal of research studies in recent years has proclaimed that there are no long-term effects on children whose mothers are employed full-time. Some of these studies are very well executed, including one that followed 12,000 children over a period of several years. The author of this study attempted to control for race, age, socioeconomic status, and other variables. In fact, what researchers have found is that most effects of working mothers on their children seem to disappear after age 12 or so. However, the media's portrayal of research studies like this one has been misleading, giving the impression that there are no effects on esteem, cognition, behavior, and compliance in these children. There are two problems with this impression. First, the media's presentation of studies like this one imply that negative effects of working mothers on their young children are acceptable because they disappear after the child gets older. Negative effects in childhood, whether they disappear later in life or not, are unacceptable. Second, researchers generally tend to be much more cautious in their interpretation of these data than the media are. While some negative effects (like behavior problems, academic problems, and esteem problems) do appear to diminish over time, researchers almost always provide other possible reasons for this finding and they rarely assert that being a working mother is a good thing. All things considered, it is better in both the short and the long term that mothers (or fathers) stay home with their children if at all possible, especially in infancy.

Many parents assume that the financial benefit gained from two incomes is always a desirable thing for children and offsets the negative effects of day care. While more money may provide more material benefits for the child, the positive effects of additional income on academic and behavior measures is most seen in children who have only a single parent, but just the opposite is true of two-parent families. Therefore, children whose basic needs would have otherwise been unmet if a single parent were not working benefited from the mother working. But for those children whose basic needs are already being met, the extra income does not have a positive effect on these same measures. In short, more "stuff" doesn't necessarily make for a better life for children. They would rather have you than more toys.

As a footnote, some research studies, including the longitudinal study of 12,000 children mentioned above, have shown that not only do the negative effects on children of both parents working disappear over time, but the positive effects of an additional income also disappear. For some reason the media choose not to present this part of the research. We look for things to confirm what we want to hear and many people in our affluent society look for reasons to work and avoid the responsibility of raising children. It is easy to justify our behavior by saying we are providing luxuries our children would not have otherwise, but our children are a more important investment. Investing your energy as a stay-at-home parent, assuming the child's basic needs are being met, is far more advantageous than things an extra income could buy.

False Economy

Child care is very expensive. Unless you have a live-in sitter who works for free, much of a second income is lost to child care. Children in day care are ill more often than those who are not, thus increasing costs for prescriptions and doctor visits. Time away from work to take care of a sick child also reduces income. Costs associated with a job—travel expenses, dry-cleaning, uniforms, meals in restaurants, vehicle maintenance, and others—also reduce income. In the end, what a family actually gains from the second income may be insignificant, especially when considered in conjunction with the emotional toll on both baby and parent. Missing the child during the day, being missed by the child, rushing to and from work and day care, plus lost hours on weekends and days off doing chores and errands that could not be done during the workweek, is a very high price to pay.

The Pros and Cons of Day Care

Day care is a necessity in single-parent homes, and many two-parent homes elect to utilize day care as well, so here are the advantages and disadvantages. Among the advantages of day care are enhanced social interaction, learning of social skills, enhanced language skills, and leadership development. A significant issue for a developing child is the availability of an environment where a child is exposed to nurturance, guidance, and esteem-building activities and interactions. There is little research that supports full-time day care over a nurturing home environment. However, a home where the environment is not nurturing, or one in which the parents feel inadequate or incapable of meeting the child's needs may be one where day care is preferable. Even though children in day care have more frequent illness, some recent data suggest that these illnesses are actually beneficial in the long run. Exposure to illnesses at this age appears to help boost children's immune system, resulting in fewer illnesses later in childhood and even lessening the likelihood of diseases like asthma.

Disadvantages include more frequent illness, increased aggression, loss of bonding time with parents, and crowded and rushed schedules. Children in day care have very little one-to-one time with any adult, including the parent—something that is important to their development. Finally, children in day care miss their parents and it is nearly impossible for working parents to recoup the time with their children that they lose while working.

Day care does not have to be full-time. Whether the primary caregiver works part-time or simply needs some time for him- or herself during the week, part-time day care is a reasonable compromise in which a child from a nurturing home can perhaps receive the best of both worlds. One- or two-days-a-week day care programs or "mother's morning out" programs can be beneficial to the child in that these programs provide all of the benefits of day care, they provide a stay-at-home mom or dad with a break from full-time child care, and the negative effects of day care are lessened.

If a parent decides to utilize a day-care provider, there are several things that should be considered when looking for a good program. Most experts agree that a basic issue is child–caregiver ratio. This is regulated by state licensing agencies, but generally, the smaller the ratio, the better. For infant day care, four children to one caregiver is usually a maximum. The ratio is often higher for toddlers, and parents can be certain that any day-care program will pursue the maximum ratio allowed by state regulations. The more children in the program, the more money it makes. So if you visit a day-care facility and there are only two children in your child's class, don't assume it will stay that way if the management has any choice in the matter.

Certainly, a day-care facility must be clean. Children's possessions must be kept separate to avoid the spread of illness, and a thorough sanitizing process must be a standard part of the program for floor mats, toys, dishes and utensils, diapers and linens. A written program that outlines the procedure for dealing with children exhibiting symptoms of illness is imperative. Medications and potentially toxic materials (such as disinfectants and cleansers) must be secured well beyond the reach of toddlers. The parent should be allowed to observe anytime. Avoid a facility which requires you to call ahead and schedule an observation time. However, it is not unusual that you may not be allowed to make your child aware of your presence. This assists the teacher in keeping the child's attention and is an acceptable rule.

A structured academic program for older children that teaches shapes, colors, and numbers is a basic provision in many day-care facilities. Perhaps a more significant issue in day care is the nurturance, language development, and social skills that are provided through interaction with other children and adults through free play and structured games. A loving teacher will provide your child with appropriate attention and affection, giving him or her a sense of belonging and building esteem. Some day-care programs allow prospective clients to observe the teacher in action prior to registering.

Take advantage of such an offer and observe the teacher in action with your child. Certainly avoid a facility where it is apparent that the teacher is there simply for a paycheck. Find one where your child's teacher is there because he or she loves children and has *chosen* day-care work.

Premature Birth and Development

As you learned from the previous chapter, from the point of conception through delivery, babies develop various functions and body parts at various times. By the mother's due date, the baby should be fully developed and prepared for life outside the womb. However, when babies are born prematurely, they are developmentally lacking in many ways, depending on how many weeks premature they are. They will need the weeks following delivery to continue their development to what would have been their "correct" birthday. A baby who is born eight weeks premature, for example, will most likely be eight weeks behind in development. Therefore, things that I have said occur at 6 months in normal children may not appear until 10 or 12 months in a baby who was born 8 weeks early. Development will usually reflect the child's actual due date rather than the day he was born; however, children often begin to catch up after six months, and by two years of age, differences are negligible.

SUMMARY

When I had my first child, I was 28 years old, nearly finished with my doctoral program, and had spent years studying children and babies. However, I remember the first day we had our daughter at home. We excitedly loaded our baby into the car seat as smiling observers watched. As we drove home, both my wife and I privately wondered if we would be good parents. When we got home, we sat in the living room watching our beautiful child sleeping in her bassinette. We looked at one another and, after an awkward pause, I said, "What do we do now?" Nothing could have prepared me for the fear, excitement, and joy of being a parent. I immediately was fully in love with my new baby, but at the same time, even though I had years of formal training, I still feared I would not know how best to care for my child. I was extremely grateful that my mother-in-law spent that first week with my wife and me as we acclimated to a new family member and my wife recovered from her labor and delivery. My mother-in-law's practical experience changing diapers, feeding a baby, and other necessities was invaluable.

One of my professors in graduate school once told me that babies do only four things: cry, sleep, defecate, and cry. I humbly disagree with my teacher.

Perhaps the most significant events of life happen during the first two or three years of life, and many of these things happen in the first year. Children's development is a complex interaction of genetics, nutrition, stimulation, and social interaction. No individual is more important in these early days than the child's parents. When you stop and think about it, the responsibility of being a parent is overwhelming and frightening. Fortunately, with patience and practice, parenting is not impossible. Despite your best efforts, you will make mistakes, but your children will overcome most of your errors when you work hard to be a good parent. In nearly 20 years of clinical practice, the children and adults I have worked with who have harbored resentment had parents who were selfish with their time, money, and/or affections. Work hard at being a parent and you will succeed.

CHAPTER 5

I'll Do It Myself:
Toddlers (Ages 1–3)

Children have never been very good at listening to their elders, but they have never failed to imitate them.

—James Baldwin

As children leave infancy and become mobile, they enter a new stage of life. They are no longer dependent upon someone else for mobility or to determine what they can find within their grasp. They can crawl, scoot, climb, or walk almost anywhere they want. Cognitively, they perceive every object as existing for their personal enjoyment or examination. These two issues, combined with their natural desire to explore, means they will get into anything and everything within their reach. They will climb on furniture, open cabinets, and eat almost anything. During this stage almost everything goes into their mouths and they are beginning to develop willfulness. They must be watched constantly or they will break something, hurt themselves, or both. As their ability to talk begins to emerge, the word "no" is one of the first that many parents hear from their toddlers. Their mobility, development of will, constant demands on a parent's time, and use of language lead parents to call age two "the terrible twos." Research has shown that enjoyment of parenting declines between 12 months and 18 months, in part because of some of these developmental changes.

The phrase "terrible twos," however, is totally inappropriate. In fact, nearly all of the behaviors that two-year-olds do which create this impression are desirable and normal in the developmental process. Children who get into things are not being "terrible," they are simply doing what is a natural part of their development. In fact, the absence of these behaviors would cause some concern about their developmental progress. My wife summarized an appropriate viewpoint regarding toddlers one day when our son had been exceptionally active. "Isn't he perfect?" I said, somewhat tongue-in-cheek. "He's perfectly two," she answered.

The amazing changes during this period of development mark a dramatic transition. Children enter this stage with limited mobility and exit this stage fully capable of walking unassisted. In infancy, children have only the most rudimentary abilities to use their gross motor functions and they are incapable of controlling their bladder and bowels. By the end of their second year, they can manipulate objects with their fingers and they will have at least begun to control their bladder and bowels. They will grow several inches and gain several pounds during this period. Prior to this stage, children have very limited memory skills; but it will be some event that occurs during their toddler years that most likely will constitute their first permanent memory. Their sole means of communication in infancy is crying or cooing. Yet, by the time they leave toddlerhood, they will have full use of several hundred words, utter partial sentences, and be capable of understanding many more words than they can use. Perhaps as much as in any other age, the developmental changes during this stage of life are vivid.

THINKING

Toddlers are almost totally *egocentric*. This term literally means "centered around self." Children believe that everything happens either to them, for them, or is caused by them. In short, they believe that the world revolves around them. For example, once a man and his wife joined my wife and me for an evening as we played a board game on the living room floor. They had a toddler who repeatedly tried to sit in the center of the game board. The child chose this location because she assumed the game board and all the pieces were there for her enjoyment. From the middle of the game board, she could easily reach all of the pieces and access any adult she wanted. From this perspective, it was the most logical place to sit. While she didn't exactly make her decision in this way, in essence this is what was behind her decision. Because toddlers are egocentric, they will interrupt conversations, assuming their own needs should be met first. They become very frustrated if they are forced to wait for anything and they will not want to share their toys. Egocentrism will be an issue for children well into their teens. It could easily be argued that some adults never fully overcome egocentrism.

A toddler's attention span is longer than an infant's, but it is still brief. However, he can maintain attention for many minutes if he is interested in something. It is unlikely that a toddler will play by himself for very long, but he may play a game with a parent or sibling for 15 minutes or more if the game holds his interest. If he enjoys a game, he will play the same game over and over. Unlike adults, he will not get bored with the repetition. On the contrary, the toddler enjoys repetition and familiar activities.

Toddlers do not know how to solve problems. They will bring all their problems to the parent for help, even if it is something that the child can take care of. For example, the child may fall down on the floor. Even though she is unhurt, she may sit and wait for a parent to pick her up. Effective problem-solving skills are still two or three years away.

Repetitious Behaviors

Part of normal cognitive development between the ages of one and two is *circular reactions*. Circular reactions, as I discussed in the previous chapter, are repetitive behaviors. Throughout childhood there are several types of circular reactions, but generally what this means is that during the toddler years, the child will repeat behaviors because they fascinate him. For example, a child sitting in a high chair will take his spoon and deliberately drop it over the edge of the tray onto the floor. A parent will retrieve the spoon, wash it off, and give it back to the child, who will do the same thing again. He will repeat this behavior as many times as the parent will return the spoon. The child is not being mean or unkind to the parent. His behavior is perfectly normal—even desirable. These repetitious behaviors are part of the child's exploration of the world and set the stage for further cognitive development. Parents should expect these behaviors and know how to avoid playing into them when it is inconvenient. For instance, in the example of the child dropping the spoon, the parent should know that the child will continue to drop the spoon. The parent should either concede and play the game or put the spoon away.

Bigger Is Better

Prior to around age five or six, children believe things are what they look like. If something changes in its appearance, the thing itself is somehow changed. The ability to understand that things can change in their appearance but still be the same object is called *conservation*. Because children under age five have not acquired the cognitive skill of conservation, they think that

if things look different, they are different. This is why children get so upset
if their sandwich is cut the "wrong" way and also why they have special plates,
forks, or spoons. Even though adults recognize that any fork works, to the
toddler, only the special fork works properly. Inability to conserve leads children to observe only one variable or characteristic of an object at a time. In
a famous experiment, Jean Piaget used glasses of water, balls of clay, and other
objects to demonstrate conservation. For example, in one experiment, he
rolled up a lump of clay into a ball. Then, in the child's presence, he rolled
it out into a long, snakelike string. He asked the child if the clay rolled into
the string had more clay, less clay, or the same amount of clay. Before they
acquire the ability to conserve, children believed that there was more clay
because it covered more space, even when they were reminded that no clay
had been added. The inability to conserve is also why children like large
presents. In their minds, large presents are "more" presents. Interestingly,
it is this same cognitive issue that created problems for people on the old
game show *Let's Make a Deal*. Contestants were given the choice of trading
a small prize that they could see (like a diamond ring) for what was behind
"door number 1." Even if the contestant wanted the diamond ring, part of
the dilemma was juxtaposing the idea that something bigger was not necessarily better. Inability to conserve also will cause a child to be frightened if
her father shaves his mustache. To a toddler, he looks different, so he isn't
"the same person" anymore.

A parent can use the inability to conserve to his or her advantage. For
example, if a parent wants to give a child some ice cream, but doesn't want
the child to have very much, he should put the child's ice cream in a very
small bowl. In a small container, the ice cream takes up more space, making
the child think he got more ice cream than if he got the same amount of
ice cream in a larger container. Even though both bowls contain the same
amount of ice cream, the child thinks he has more ice cream because it "fills
his bowl up more." He cannot yet process two quantities together—amount
of ice cream and size of container.

Memory

One of the many amazing changes that occur between the ages of 12
months and 24 months is the ability to picture something in the mind—a
skill called *representational thinking*. Adults form mental pictures many times
every day. We do it so often that we take it for granted. However, prior to
two years of age, children cannot picture things in their minds. They have
difficulty remembering events because they cannot call up a mental picture

the way adults can. Therefore, they have minimal memory abilities. For most of us, our earliest memory is from around age two or three and is a picture—an image of an event like a vacation or a birthday party. Even though infants have a type of memory, it is very different from the more refined memory of adulthood. Representational thinking is the transition between these two types of memory. By age two, most children can begin to think about the past and can imagine things that they want because they can picture people, places, and things in their minds.

Magic

Until children reach age five or six, they do not understand cause-and-effect relationships. For them, the world is a magical place. Usually, children begin to fear the dark around age three, but they may begin even earlier. Fear of the dark parallels the development of representational thinking. When a child has the ability to picture something in his mind, he can imagine something that is not there, such as a monster in the closet. Nearly all children experience fear of the dark around this stage of development and create reasons in their minds for their anxiety. In order to cope with their fears, they use their magical view of the world to create magical ways to explain and deal with their fears. For example, many children believe monsters in the dark can't hurt them if they have their bed covers pulled up over their heads. They have, in essence, created a magical force field around themselves with the covers. Security blankets, teddy bears, and other security objects are magical in this way as well.

Explaining the irrationality of monsters to a toddler is futile. To her, the monsters are real and their presence makes great sense. Parents can pacify a child's fears by checking under the bed when asked, closing closet doors, and using a night-light. If the child needs extra encouragement, fill a spray bottle with clean water. Write on the outside of the bottle "Anti-Monster Spray." Draw a picture of a cartoon monster with a red "x" over it. Use the anti-monster spray like you would an air freshener, spraying it around the child's bedroom. In a child's magical world, he believes that the monster spray will keep monsters at bay in the same way pulling up the bed covers has done. Occasional use of the monster spray won't hurt the child and will not feed his or her fears. It will address the child's fear at the level where it exists—the magical world.

This same process explains why a parent's kiss makes a child feel better if he has fallen and hurt his knee. Kissing a child's wound is magical. Kisses hold no medicinal value, but they do make children feel better because they believe the kiss holds some healing power. Band-Aids can make a child's cut or scrape feel better because children perceive Band-Aids as medicine. They do not understand the real purpose of a Band-Aid, but since they believe Band-Aids will make them feel better, they do. You don't have to use a Band-Aid only when the child needs it. If the child is crying inconsolably, but is not really hurt, a Band-Aid may be the magic medicine she needs. You can also buy a small spray bottle at the drugstore. Write on the outside of the bottle in colored letters "Really Strong Medicine." If the child doesn't actually need medical attention, but wants it, get out the "Really Strong Medicine" and spray the hurt place once or twice with a puff of air. The air will feel cool on the bruise or hurt place. The child will be satisfied because he believes he has been healed. (Note: Of course, injuries such as broken bones, lacerations, and other serious injuries need appropriate medical attention, and this practice should never substitute for appropriate medical care.)

Another part of the magical world of a child is the belief that all things are living. In a toddler's mind, rocks, trees, stuffed animals, and houses all have personalities and intent. A child who hits his head on a tree branch might say that the tree was "being mean." This is called *personification*. Imbuing of intent on inanimate objects will continue through the preschool years. Children of this age also believe that inanimate objects can move. This is called *animism*. Therefore, a child believes a tree can "grab her" or clouds can "follow her." Because children believe that these objects are living and that the world is magical, they can easily be frightened by movies or television shows, even if the show is a cartoon. Therefore, a parent should use discretion when choosing programs, books, or movies for toddlers.

Language Development

Through the age of 15 months or so, parents can't wait for their children to start talking. By two and a half years, they wonder if their children will ever *stop* talking. Language develops through a process of progressively more difficult cognitive tasks that also involve progressively more difficult physical tasks. The forming of words involves a coordination of the many muscles of the tongue, lips, throat, jaws, and mouth. The first form language takes is crying, as I discussed in the previous chapter. Children then progress to *cooing*, repetitive vowel sounds like "ooo" and "aaah." Following cooing is *babbling*, which consists of repetitive vowel sounds that include random consonants. During the babbling stage of language development, children accidentally say words. Their use of words at this stage is accidental because they are randomly combining vowel and consonant pairs. Because the combinations are random, they accidentally say recognizable words like "mama" or "dada," but they will have had no intent to say them. First words follow the babbling stage. One can know the child has achieved first words when she clearly shows intent in the use of words, even if the words are not pronounced correctly. For example, a child's first word may be "dog." He may point to a dog and say "da." To an attentive observer, it is clear the child knows the term for dog and has used the term deliberately even though the word was mispronounced.

First words are usually terms for living creatures or action words (for example, "dog," "bye-bye"), and on average, children begin using first words around 15 months. However, there is a lot of variability. Children may begin talking earlier, but even if they are not talking by 20 months, as long as they have demonstrated cooing and babbling, their development may simply be slow in this area. If the child has not started babbling by 15 or 20 months, however, some developmental delay is evident and intervention is imperative to ensure that there are not deeper problems that have been manifested in the child's delayed speech.

By age two, children usually have begun to use two-word sentences called *duos*, and they may have progressed to *telegraphic speech*. Prior to the invention of the telephone, telegrams were short electronic messages sent by wire, using Morse code. Because every letter cost money, senders eliminated articles, conjunctions, and so forth, leaving only the most basic units of speech needed to communicate their message. In the same way, children using telegraphic speech may use two or three words to represent an entire thought. For example, the child might say "play outside" to mean "I want to go outside and play." During this stage of language development, and for the next many months, as children learn correct pronunciations and usages of words, they are often understood only by people who are around them all the time. For this reason, this period of language development is sometimes called *motherese*, because mothers or primary caregivers have to translate for others what the child has said. By age two, children should have more than 200 words in their verbal arsenal and they are able to understand many more words than that.

Bilingual Homes

Many children in the United States are raised in homes or environments where two or more languages are spoken. There is no evidence that children growing up in bilingual homes are in any way damaged or confused by two languages. On the contrary, when children are exposed equally to two different languages, and when they develop proficiency in those languages, such exposure is beneficial. There are several reasons why children learn languages more easily than adults. Perhaps most significant is the fact that they have not yet lost the ability to form sounds that are present in some languages and not others. For example, English-speaking adults have difficulty forming the sound that an umlaut represents in the German language. They have long since lost the ability to make that sound and can do so only with extensive practice. Children, on the other hand, have a much wider repertoire of available sounds because they have not abandoned those potential sounds as adults eventually do because the sounds are not required in their native language. Learning language is also easier for children because they have little or no fear of using words that are unfamiliar to them. In short, there is no reason to deliberately expose children to multiple languages, but children who are raised in bilingual homes suffer no disadvantage due to that exposure.

Reading

Reading to children assists them in the development of their verbal skills, so you should read to your toddler often. Reading is one of the most important ways to develop verbal skills. Teaching a child to enjoy reading begins long before she can read for herself. Regular trips to the library can allow a child access to a wide variety of books. A love for reading will be a tremendous benefit to your child throughout life, especially during her school years, and it begins in these very early years of life. Picture books with very few words are most appropriate for toddlers and they will want to look at the same books over and over. The repetition helps them learn labels for things and although parents will tire of looking at the same picture book, the child will find comfort in the familiar pages. Picture books for toddlers may be made of plastic, cloth, or cardboard. Keep in mind, however, that these children have little muscle control and they will want to put books in their mouths, so books with paper pages will quickly be torn or eaten if you are not careful.

FEELING

As you learned in chapter 4, a baby has four basic emotions at birth—sadness, disgust, fear, and anger. Between 18 and 24 months, children begin to experience shame, embarrassment, and pride. These emotions cannot occur until the child has at least a minimal understanding of right and wrong. The child has to have some ability to think about a behavior and its consequences. Therefore, the development of will goes hand in hand with the development of these emotions. Also emerging at this time is a sense of self. Prior to the development of the sense of self, when a child sees himself in the mirror, he perceives the reflection as another person. Around two years of age, the self begins to emerge and children recognize themselves in the mirror for the first time. They refer to themselves as "boy," "girl," or "baby." As they near three years of age, they refer to themselves as "I." Around this same time, they begin to develop empathy. This is a big step in their development. For the first time, children at this age can recognize someone else's pain or discomfort and imagine what they feel like. They also want to do something to help. For example, a toddler who has developed empathy might offer his favorite blanket or toy to another child who has fallen and hurt himself. All of these issues are a part of the development of the toddler's emotional self.

The Development of Willfulness

A toddler's thinking is just beginning to develop to the point where he has a sense of will. Around 15 to 24 months, toddlers use the word "no" and deliberately defy their parents. For example, a parent may clearly tell a child not to touch an object on the kitchen table. Prior to the development of will, the child may disobey the parent's command, but that behavior is not deliberate. This child disobeys because he doesn't understand words and simply wants to touch the object. The willful child, however, will disobey, sometimes even watching the parent as she touches the object, to see what will happen. The child knows what he wants to do. He knows that the parent has said no, and he understands the meaning of the word. He also has the cognitive ability to think about the future at least minimally, asking himself, "I wonder what will happen if . . ."

As the child's will develops, tantrums are inevitable. A child will resort to a tantrum when she has used all of her other options for getting her way, something that usually happens fairly quickly. The parent must never give in to a tantrum. Giving in teaches the child that the tantrum works and it is the beginning of the development of the child's problem-solving and coping skills. This can easily establish a lifelong pattern of behavior that is both annoying and unproductive. Once the child realizes the tantrum doesn't work, she will be less likely to use it. Endure brief tantrums in exchange for a more productive relationship. Excessive and extreme tantrums can be symptomatic of serious problems such as autism, but after nearly two decades of clinical work with children, I have found that serious problems are rarely the cause of tantrums. More often than not, excessive tantrums are the result of inconsistency in parental discipline.

With the development of will, a child begins to develop morality as well. However, because of a child's cognitive limitations, right and wrong can be understood only in concrete terms. A child believes that something is right or wrong based on two things: (1) what is taught at home, and (2) whether he will get in trouble if he does it. It will be several years before the child is capable of making moral decisions based on anything other than these two issues.

Part of the personality differences between children is the variability in their levels of willfulness. Strong-willed children are not necessarily abnormal, but they need more attention and will defy parents more often than other children. Strong-willed children will defy rules or orders for the sake of defying them. These children do not need harsher discipline. They need more rigid discipline. Flexibility with strong-willed children only leads them to believe that parents don't mean what they say. Therefore, even though all children need consistent discipline, strong-willed children, more than any others, need rigid and consistent discipline.

Perception of Self

Around age two, children begin to recognize their own reflections in a mirror. A simple test called the "rouge test" can easily demonstrate a child's recognition of his own reflection. Prior to the development of the concept of self, when a child sees his reflection in the mirror, he assumes it to be another person. In the rouge test, a blotch of rouge is placed on the child's nose. When the child sees the image in the mirror with rouge on his nose, the child who has not yet developed a sense of self will try to wipe the rouge off of the "other" child's nose. A child who recognizes himself in the mirror will move his hand to his own nose and try to wipe off the rouge. Recognition of self is necessary before the child can use "I" in language.

Empathy

Babies have no thoughts about how events affect other people. Their thoughts are occupied with their own needs and feelings. If a baby sees her mother cry, the baby may also cry, but not because she feels bad for her mother. She cries because she recognizes that something is not right, and her mood is a mirror of her mother's mood. By age two, children begin to develop an ability to think about what it is like to be in the other person's shoes. In order to do this, they must also have developed a sense of self. When they see another child crying or when they see a parent upset, they may offer something to the distressed person that they have found comforting themselves. Empathy will not be fully developed until adulthood, but it has its beginnings in these first few years of life.

Social Relationships and Interactions

Beyond infancy, children are just beginning to seek relationships outside their immediate families. They begin to have friends of their own at church, in the neighborhood, at day care, or among extended family members. Toddlers do not distinguish between children of their own age and adults. The only difference they notice is size. They are easily intimidated or frightened by bigger children, grown-ups, or loud individuals. Yet toddlers also can easily engage in play with older children and adults who are willing to play with them. Play is one of the most important components in forming relationships, so parents should play frequently with their toddler. When possible, play on the floor at the child's level. Toddlers will play alongside another toddler, but they do not cooperate in an activity. In other words, they will play in close proximity, but separately. This is called *parallel* play. Cooperating with another child to play a game is called *cooperative play*. Toddlers will play cooperatively with another person, but only an adult or a child who has developed beyond the parallel play stage. Two toddlers who have not developed cooperative play will not be able to maintain a mutual activity together. Toddlers will maintain a mutual activity with adults or older children because the older child or adult can easily accommodate to the interests of the child. As the toddler nears her third birthday, she will develop the ability to play cooperatively with another child.

Separation Anxiety

Separation anxiety, the fear of being separated from a caregiver, is most evident between 12 and 18 months. (See chapter 4 for more information on separation anxiety.) Children exhibit separation anxiety by crying whenever they are taken from a caregiver. Separation anxiety in the child can be seen even with people who are not primary caregivers. For example, a toddler in a nursery may spend much of the time with a given nursery worker. If another worker tries to hold the child, the toddler may cry or show fear of the stranger. Parents should not allow the child's tears to prohibit them from leaving the child with a sitter or nursery worker because the child will eventually learn that he can manipulate his parents with tears or tantrums. It will not hurt a toddler to leave him occasionally with a baby-sitter. In fact, parents need personal time together, especially when infants and toddlers are in the home. Occasional outings without the child are healthy for the marriage. Also, regular interaction with others helps the child develop social skills and social relationships and lessens the effects of separation anxiety.

DOING

Between the ages of one and three, children change dramatically in their motor abilities. During these two years, most children go from limited mobility to walking proficiently. Even though there is variability in what children can do and when they can do it, generally the order of development is something like this. Around the first birthday, most children can pull themselves to a standing position using a table, chair, or parental assistance. By 13 months the child should be able to climb stairs, and by 14 months, he should be able to maintain a standing position without help. On the average, children begin walking without assistance anywhere between one year and 15 or 16 months. The range of development is diverse, so parents shouldn't be worried if their child does not follow this order.

In a reasonably enriched environment, one where the child's development is encouraged and unobstructed, the child will naturally take on these skills. Other than spending lots of time interacting with the child and encouraging the child's natural instincts, there is little that parents need to do to promote the child's motor development. A parent cannot speed up the child's development, and there is no reason to do so. In other words, when the child is ready to walk, she will walk. When she shows the urge to do so, encourage the skill and help her practice, but don't force it. You will only frustrate yourself.

There is little evidence that there is any link between first steps and intelligence. Likewise, a child who takes his first steps later in development is not necessarily "behind." Each area of development is different. Usually, all areas of development—cognitive, social, emotional, and physical—progress at a similar rate, but that is not always the case. For example, a child may walk early but use first words late.

As the child approaches age two, she will begin to use table utensils, but will still prefer her hands. Sipper cups are a must if you want to avoid spills. The child will not be ready to use an open cup on a regular basis for several more months. By age three, the child will be able to use a fork, spoon, and open cup fairly well, but messy mealtimes are still to be expected.

Because children between 12 and 24 months have limited fine motor skills, toys for toddlers should be large enough that they can grasp them with their hands. Toys should be made of plastic or some other material that is easily sterilized because, as is true with infants, toys will regularly find their way into a toddler's mouth. A toddler will enjoy longer picture books than his infant counterpart. Toddlers will chew on any toy, including books, so cloth or paperback books should be kept from the child's reach when you are not reading to the child. You don't want to return library books with pages that have been chewed or eaten.

Safety

Because of children's mobility, their injuries as the result of accidents increase dramatically during the toddler years. The National Institute of Child Health and Human Development reported in 2001 that children between the ages of one and four are most likely to drown in swimming pools. Extreme care should be taken when a family has access to a swimming or wading pool, pond, or lake. Toddler's heads are large in proportion to their bodies, making them top-heavy. Thus, children can easily drown in a toilet or a bucket of water. They fall in headfirst and are not strong enough to pull themselves out, yet they may not weigh enough to knock over a bucket of water into which they have fallen. Therefore, even an open toilet or a mop bucket presents a hazard for toddlers.

Toddlers have no ability to see potential danger, which is why children climb on objects or eat poisons. Parents must watch their children closely to prevent serious injury or death. According to the Centers for Disease Control and Statistics (CDC), accidents are the leading cause of death from age 1 all the way to age 37! Electrical cords can cause strangulation, as can telephone cords. If the child can reach a long telephone cord on a wall-mounted telephone, he can easily pull the receiver off the hook and onto his head. Children will touch anything, including hot irons, hot pans, and open oven doors. They will quickly pull items with dangling cords from countertops onto their heads, not realizing what they are doing. Toxic substances should be locked away or well out of the reach of children.

Babyproofing

As children learn to crawl and eventually pull themselves up and walk, they will get into anything within their reach. They will open drawers and cabinets; they will explore objects left on tables, chairs, and on the floor; and they will push the buttons on clocks, stereo equipment, and televisions. Parents should put dangerous items or keepsakes out of the child's reach. Cabinet locks are very helpful, but don't forget that toddlers can reach into drawers. Knives and other sharp objects should be stored in a secure place. I guarantee that your child will eventually explore any item that is within his reach. If the object is fragile, it will get broken. Some parents have suggested that they want to teach children to obey, so they do not put some objects away; but unless you want that item to be destroyed, put it away. There are plenty of immobile objects such as outlets, televisions, and remote controls that the parent can use to teach obedience. If the parent leaves one-of-a-kind objects or heirlooms lying about, the child will eventually damage or break them. Better to put these items away and bring them back out when the child is older. Even worse, dangerous objects left within the child's reach could result in serious injury to the child or even death.

Sleep Patterns

As children leave infancy, their sleep patterns change. Most toddlers need about 12 hours of sleep a night, but unlike infants, they do not require naps as frequently. Infants nap two or three times a day, but toddlers may require only one nap in the afternoon, or perhaps no nap at all. Whether or not the child takes a nap should be determined by how well the child functions. Parents can usually tell when their children are sleepy and when their sleepiness is causing them to be grumpy. While it may be desirable at some point in the day for a child to nap, a child who requires little sleep may find it hard to get to sleep at bedtime if he takes a nap too late in the day. This can create frustration for both the child and the parents. Sleep patterns should be tailored to the individual child and his or her needs rather than a prescribed formula. Consistent routines for bedtimes and naptimes will help your child function best. Expect a grumpy child when vacations or other events cause an interruption in the routine.

Potty Training

Most children are not ready for potty training until age two or later. Even though a few children are ready as early as 18 months, this is uncommon. Other children will not be ready until age three. Potty training involves many skills. The child must be able to self-monitor—in other words, she must be able to recognize the need to defecate or urinate before it is imminent. Self-monitoring is a cognitive skill that most children do not have prior to age two. Second, controlling the sphincter muscles—the round muscles that control the openings to the anus and the urethra—is a fine motor skill. Children develop gross motor skills first. Gross motor skills involve the large muscles of the arms and legs. Fine motor control comes later. For example, the muscles of the fingers are fine muscles. Expecting a child to control his bladder or bowels too early is like asking a child to play the piano before she has developed fine motor skills of the fingers and hands.

Attempting potty training too early frustrates both the child and the parents, and creates extra laundry. Also, potty training takes longer if the child is not ready. A parent can know that a child is ready to begin potty training when the child recognizes the need to defecate or urinate. Children sometimes leave the room and hide, soiling their diapers in a quiet place like a closet or playroom. When children do this, they have demonstrated that they knew it was coming and they have at least minimal ability to control the sphincter muscles. Small rewards, like an M&M, when the child successfully uses the potty can be helpful in the training process. As a child gets more proficient, change the rate of reward. Instead of rewarding the child each time, reward the child for having a dry diaper for a longer period of time, such as through lunchtime or all day. Rewards will be unnecessary when the child has mastered potty training.

Every child is different, but boys are typically somewhat slower at potty training than girls. Some children are easy to potty train and others are resistant. Parents must be patient and allow the child's development to determine the speed at which she acquires bladder and bowel control, regardless of the experience they may have had with other children. If the parent tries for three or four weeks to potty train a child but sees no progress at all, it is most likely too soon for the child.

Some children are afraid of an adult-sized commode because they fear they will fall in; therefore, the use of a potty-chair that fits the child's small frame is helpful. There are several books available for teaching potty training, such as *Once upon a Potty*, by Alona Frankel. This book is available in two versions—one for boys and one for girls. It teaches the child about his or her anatomy and about the process of bladder and bowel control.

Daytime potty training is usually successful before overnight potty training. Limiting the child's fluid intake and snacks several hours before bedtime can help the child succeed in overnight potty training. Also, ensure that the child makes a habit of urinating just before going to bed. It is not uncommon for children who have succeeded in controlling their bladder and bowels during the day to continue having occasional accidents during the night for many months. The child who has accidents during the night is not being bad or lazy, or deliberately trying to create work for the mother or father. Therefore, a child should not be spanked or disciplined for an accident. It is the parent's job to adjust the child's schedule and fluid intake to help the child achieve dry nights. If necessary, get the child up once during the night to allow him or her to eliminate. This can cause disrupted sleep patterns, so it should be done only if the child is having consistent difficulty staying dry during the night.

Inability to maintain bladder or bowel control can be symptomatic of physical problems with your child. If your child has made little progress in potty training by 36–48 months, consult with your pediatrician. Enuresis that appears after the child has mastered potty training is potentially a symptom of physical and/or psychological problems. Consultation with a pediatrician in these cases is recommended in these cases.

Toddlers, Weather, and the Elements

Like infants, toddlers are sensitive to cold and heat, but toddlers are more likely to be out in the elements for longer periods of time than are infants. Therefore, they are more at risk for hypothermia and heat exhaustion. Adults lose about 30 percent of their body heat through their heads because the blood vessels in the neck do not constrict as they do in other parts of the body. This happens to ensure that the brain is constantly receiving adequate oxygen. Heat dissipation through the head is even more dramatic for infants and toddlers. Toddlers lose as much as 60 percent of their body heat through their heads.

Along with a warm coat, toddlers need mittens, hats, and scarves to keep their hands, heads, and faces covered when out in cold weather. In summer heat, they should be dressed in loose-fitting and light-colored clothing and they need to drink plenty of water. A toddler's skin is very thin and will sunburn very quickly. Therefore, sunscreen is a must if a child's skin is exposed to the sun. Ideally, children should not have much exposed skin when playing at the pool or the beach. A T-shirt, hat, and swimsuit will protect the child against sunburn more effectively than sunscreen.

Infants and toddlers should never be left alone in a vehicle. In summer heat, a car's temperature can soar to over 100 degrees in a matter of minutes. In such conditions, an infant or toddler can die of heat exhaustion in 30 minutes or less.

Toys

There is a joke that circulated some years ago about children and their possessiveness over toys. It went like this: "If it is my toy, it's mine. If I have one like it, it's mine. If I played with it anytime today, it is mine. If it is near me, it's mine." And so on. This is more evidence of a child's egocentricity. Children are possessive and have to be taught how to share. One reason toddlers have trouble sharing is their fear that if someone plays with something that belongs to them, they will lose it forever. Expect arguments over toys and be patient teaching them that sharing doesn't mean "giving away."

Between 12 and 24 months, children enjoy toys that make noise, especially pull-behind toys and musical toys. They are fascinated that they can push a button or pull a string and cause music or other noise to happen. They also enjoy toys that are imitations of the adult world. Toy dishes, telephones, cars and trucks, and cameras will be fun for them. Toys should be simple and made of plastic so that they can be easily cleaned and sterilized and they should not have parts that can be chewed off or pulled off. They should be large enough that they cannot be swallowed or put into body cavities like the nose or ears.

Toddlers enjoy puzzles with between four and six large pieces and toys on which they can ride, like wagons and scoot toys. They continue to enjoy peek-a-boo with a parent and with their newfound mobility, they enjoy playing hide-and-seek. Since toddlers cannot imagine the perspective of another person, they assume that if they cannot see the person "seeking" them, then the seeker cannot see them, either. Toddlers cover their heads with a blanket and think they are hidden.

Toddlers enjoy playing in sand and with sand toys. Don't forget they will put things in their mouth, so they need supervision. Sand in the mouth is no fun. They also enjoy wading in shallow pools and they will play with the same toys in the wading pool as they will in a sandbox. It is not too early to begin teaching a child to swim by acclimating him to a swimming pool. In fact, this is a perfect time to begin swimming lessons because babies and toddlers are buoyant and don't fear the water. Water temperature is important because children can quickly lose body heat. Infants and toddlers should never be exposed to frigid water or be allowed to play in Jacuzzi tubs. It is absolutely imperative that all children be carefully monitored around any body of water, even shallow pools. A toddler can drown in only six inches of water.

Transition from Crib to Bed

As infants become toddlers and begin to climb, they are in danger of climbing out of their cribs and falling to the floor. When a toddler is capable of climbing out of his or her crib, it is time to transition to a regular bed. Many children fall out of bed when they first begin sleeping without the security of crib rails. Transitional beds with rails help, but they do not teach the child to stay on the bed. Parents can lessen the risk of falls by starting their child out on a trundle bed or a mattress on the floor. Within a few weeks, the child will get used to sleeping in the bed and will be less likely to roll out of bed. Checking on the child after he is asleep and moving him or her to the center of the bed also can reduce risk of falling. Toddlers should not sleep on the top level of bunk beds, even though bunks usually have safety rails. Many toddlers and small children walk in their sleep and may climb over the safety rail in their sleep.

It is not uncommon to have difficulty getting children to stay in bed when they first move from the crib to a regular bed. Parents become frustrated when the child repeatedly gets up. The key to teaching children to stay in bed is patience and consistent instruction. A child who is put to bed too early in the evening will be especially frustrating, but even tired children occasionally get out of bed. Nighttime rituals like reading, a warm bath, bedtime story, saying prayers, giving the child a back rub, and singing "good night" songs can help the child transition from the activity of the day and prepare for sleeping. Do the same things in the same order as often as possible because consistency in bedtime rituals helps the child's body and mind prepare for sleeping. When traveling, maintain bedtime rituals as much as possible. The child should stay in bed fairly consistently after a few weeks of training.

Pacifiers and Security Blankets

Prior to age two, children are not yet afraid of the dark, but they have other fears. They find comfort in things that are familiar, such as a special toy or piece of cloth. The object can be almost anything, but it is usually something soft like a stuffed animal or blanket. Some children find the soft texture of a woman's slip to be comforting. If a child selects a slip as a security object, it is potentially embarrassing to the parents, but it is not unusual. I do not necessarily encourage security objects for young children, but I don't discourage them, either. Most children will find one on their own and it is quite normal. Never threaten to take away the child's security blanket as punishment. This won't cause any physical or psychological harm, but it will make for a very, very long night for both the child and parents.

Pacifiers are helpful to parents when a child is an infant because they help the child quiet down and sometimes assist the child in getting to sleep. As long as the child is not using a pacifier by four or five years of age, parents do not need to rush to stop its use. However, some pediatricians and pediatric dentists recommend eliminating pacifiers by age three because of an increased risk of dental problems. Pacifiers are preferable to thumb-sucking.

You can take a pacifier away, but you can't take a thumb away; fingers are unsanitary; and thumb-sucking can cause dental problems, just like pacifiers. Most children will give up their pacifiers when they are ready, but if the parent determines that it is time for the child to give up the use of the pacifier before the child is ready, replacing it with an object of the child's choosing is sometimes helpful.

Thumb-Sucking

Some children suck their thumbs and some do not. Other children suck one or two fingers other than the thumb. Physiologists suggest that children have an innate need to suck. If the child sucks his thumb, the parent should make sure the child's hands are washed several times a day. Eliminating the behavior can be frustrating. There are chemicals available over the counter at drugstores that a parent can put on the child's thumb. It causes the finger to taste bad and sometimes works to stop thumb-sucking. Smacking a child's hand for finger-sucking is inappropriate. Patience and gently removing the child's finger(s) from his mouth are all that is necessary to remind him. As with pacifiers, replacing the security of finger-sucking with another object can help. Children may suck their thumbs throughout their preschool years. Older children will suck their fingers most often when they are tired, afraid, or nervous. Finding other ways to comfort a child at these times can help reduce the need to suck on one's fingers. Hugs, sitting with the child and snuggling, or providing a favorite security object (blanket, stuffed animal) can replace finger-sucking. Consult a pediatrician, child psychologist, or pediatric dentist for assistance if the behavior continues beyond kindergarten.

Discipline

Prior to the development of willful behavior, infants should never be spanked. By around 18 to 24 months, a child begins to develop self-control and willfulness. As I discussed earlier in the chapter, when the will develops, children will deliberately test the parent. Parents need to begin disciplining the child at this time to establish clear boundaries. Spanking is only one of many disciplinary tools available to parents. Time out, holding the child, taking away objects, and even facial expressions that exhibit displeasure with the child's behavior are all effective. Every child is different, even within the same family, as to how he or she responds to punishment. Some children respond very well to a stern look, while other children may respond only to a spanking. The more disciplinary options a parent has, the more effectively she can tailor her choices to fit the child's personality, behavior, and circumstances.

Even though some parents find corporal punishment sometimes necessary, avoid spanking as much as possible. A mistake many parents make is assuming that spanking is the only thing that works before they have tried other means. You can play with a child and pat the child's bottom harder than you ever would spank the child, but he will laugh because he knows you are playing. Clearly, it is the intent of a spanking that upsets the child as much as the pain. Since the child is responding to the intent, not just the pain, creative parents can find other means to create the same intent without hitting their children.

For many parents, most of their disciplinary practices are based on telling a child what not to do. That is only half of the process. Telling a child what he or she should do—in other words, providing the correct behavior as well as identifying the inappropriate behavior—is also important. A parent can prevent the need to punish by encouraging the child to do a desired behavior. This is called *reinforcement*. Reinforcing the opposite behavior of the undesirable one (called *reinforcement of incompatible behaviors*) encourages the child to do the correct behavior and eliminates the need to punish. For example, when my eldest daughter was a toddler, she had a habit of getting up from the table during meals and wandering off. Instead of punishing her for getting up, my wife and I rewarded her for staying at the table. I whispered to my wife loud enough for my daughter to hear, "I'm noticing that Megan is staying at the table. That is amazing!" My wife played along, whispering back to me how amazing it truly was. We did this for two days. The third day Megan stayed at the table throughout the meal and we didn't say anything, but before we finished dinner, Megan said to us, "I'm noticing that I am staying at the table."

If the parent chooses to consider spanking as an option, he should reserve it as a last resort. If one does spank a toddler, inflicting pain is not necessary or desirable. A gentle swat on the behind is sufficient. The spanking lets the child know he is in trouble and he will respond to being in trouble as much as he will the spanking. Here are four rules for the use of discipline. **RULE 1**: If one can accomplish the goal without spanking, no matter what the age of the child, then don't spank. **RULE 2**: Spanking should be the last choice, not the first. Use it only when you have exhausted other possibilities. Spanking is easy and it is a method of discipline that every parent knows. Finding other options takes more work and patience on the part of the parent, but it is important. **RULE 3**: Parents need to be in agreement on the types of discipline they plan to use with their children and they must be unified in front of their children, even toddlers. Disagreements about the way one parent disciplines a child should be undertaken in private, out of the child's hearing. The forms of discipline that a couple chooses to use ideally should be decided upon during premarital counseling, long before children are present. **RULE 4**: The three most important words in disciplining children are consistency, consistency, and consistency. A parent must say what she means and do what she says she will do. If you don't mean it, don't say it. Idle threats only teach the child that you aren't serious. A child who learns that you sometimes don't follow through will assume you will never follow through, thus stealing your parental power and control.

It is the parents' responsibility to maintain control of their own anger when disciplining a child. Many parents have inadvertently injured or killed their children while trying to discipline them. Screaming, yelling, hitting, and other behaviors that demonstrate lack of control are inappropriate. For toddlers, the parent's rage is frightening. Toddlers need stability and security. Seeing a parent out of control threatens that security. For older children, the parent's lack of control teaches them that they can push the parent over the edge, hence making it harder for that parent to maintain control of the child.

Toddlers should never be screamed at, shaken, thrown, hit in the face, or struck with objects. The parent should never call a child stupid, idiot, dumb, or other unkind names. These very hurtful words leave emotional scars that affect the child's esteem and relationships well into adulthood. In many ways, hurtful words are as damaging to a child as physical abuse. The effects are just harder to see. The old adage "Sticks and stones may break my bones, but words will never hurt me" is not true.

Television and Computers

The television is both a very useful tool and potentially a very destructive tool. I can quickly and easily tell if a child I am seeing in my clinical practice watches a lot of television. Research studies as well as my clinical experience indicate that children who watch a lot of television are more lethargic, score more poorly in verbal tests, are more aggressive, have poorer social skills, and are in poorer physical health. It is easy to use the television as a baby-sitter, but it should not routinely be used that way. Toddlers need lots of human contact, especially from primary caregivers. I recommend that a child's television viewing be limited to one or two hours a day. Public broadcasting, educational programming, and educational videotapes/DVDs are most productive. Parents should supervise the programs their toddlers watch. Interaction with the child during the program solidifies the educational message of the program and ensures learning, and it also promotes bonding between parent and child.

Avoid cable stations that specialize in 24 hours of cartoons. Even though they are geared for children, they present a false impression to parents that they are good for kids. Cartoons are entertaining, but they are *passive* programs. Passive programs require minimal cognitive investment by the viewer. They may be entertaining, but they do not require any thinking by the viewer. *Active* programs require some involvement from the viewer. Educational programs and interactive programs are active programs that require the viewer to think, evaluate, and assess the material that he or she is watching. One of the most successful children's programs of all time (and in my opinion one of the best ever made) is *Mr. Rogers' Neighborhood*. This program relies exclusively on very simple sets and almost no technology (i.e., computers, technical changes, or computer generation), but requires involvement of the viewer.

Toddlers are not too young to begin using computers. There are many computer programs available that teach children colors, words, and shapes. Computers are a significant part of our world and exposure to the computer at an early age is helpful. The same rules suggested above for TV apply to the computer as well. Always supervise children when they use the computer. At this age, it will prevent damage to the computer and you will be available to help guide the child if there are problems with the program or if the child is unsure what to do. As they get older, supervision protects children from destructive things that are available on the computer, especially on the Internet.

Gender-Appropriate Development

There is nothing innate that causes boys to like baseball and girls to like dolls, but there are some innate differences. Boys are innately more aggressive than girls, and girls tend to take on nurturing roles in their play more than boys do. These differences become apparent as children reach their toddler years. Otherwise, much of what we observe as gender differences are taught by parents and the culture. Every culture has a set of behaviors, dress, toys, and activities that it considers appropriate for males or females. There is nothing wrong with boys playing with dolls. In fact, most boys do. Dolls for boys, however, are called action figures and are usually masculine in their appearance. There is also nothing wrong with girls playing sports. There are many advantages for children who play sports. They learn strategy, teamwork, and sportsmanship, and the exercise is good for them. It is up to parents to decide in which activities their children should or should not participate. Parents should allow the interests of the child to steer them rather than the expectations and gender norms of the culture.

Pets

Toddlers are too young to appreciate or care for pets. They can enjoy watching a cat, dog, or goldfish from a distance, but they will be afraid of animals if they get too close. Family pets, like dogs and cats, also can be a health hazard to toddlers. Pet dander irritates respiratory conditions such as asthma. Some reptiles carry salmonella that can make people sick. Cats can scratch the child and even passive family dogs can bite if they are cornered or hurt, or if they think their food may be taken away. Toddlers cannot think about how they might hurt an animal. They will readily try to pull a tail or an ear, not realizing the pet might be hurt. When a pet is being hurt, even when it is a gentle animal, it could easily nip or bite. Infants and toddlers can easily be hurt or killed by a dog. Parents should supervise their children whenever they are in the presence of a family pet.

Day Care

Day care is a controversial issue, but the research on its effects on children is becoming clearer every year. While this is not true for every age group, there are no clearly documented advantages of day care for infants and toddlers, except for children growing up in deprived or dangerous environments. Some toddlers appear to adapt to new social settings better if they are in day care, but this is of minimal importance. On the other hand, toddlers in day care are more susceptible to illnesses and are more aggressive than children who are not in regular day care. Some research indicates that poor-quality day care increases the likelihood of insecurely attached children. What is perhaps most discouraging is that if a child comes from a relatively nourishing home environment but is placed in poor-quality day care, detrimental effects to the child are measurable.

It is my opinion that a child should be at home full-time with a mother or father at least for the first two years, and preferably at least until the child starts kindergarten. Consistent interaction with a supportive, nurturing, and empathetic primary caregiver is imperative. One of the most important things the parent communicates to the child during the first two years is that the child is safe and important. Leaving the child in unfamiliar surroundings and/ or with varied caregivers compromises these two needs. When both parents work eight or more hours during the day, there is very little time left for play and relaxed social interaction with the child. There is no such thing as "quality time" with a toddler that is less than five or six hours every day.

Either parent can provide for these needs, so it does not matter whether it is the mother or father who stays home with the child. I recommend that parents adjust their spending needs so that they can exist on one income, allowing one parent to stay home. A second option is for a parent to work from home or to work part-time.

In the case of single parents, or if both parents choose to work, a single caregiver, ideally a responsible and mature relative, is most desirable. The child is more likely to have consistent one-on-one interaction when being cared for by a relative. If professional day care is required, the facility should be clean and safe for toddlers. Generally, the lower the child–caregiver ratio, the better. (See chapter 4 for more information on selection and evaluation of day-care facilities.)

Parenting Styles

Generally, there are three styles of parenting. Overly *permissive* parents regularly concede to their children's wishes and fail to provide appropriate discipline. Sometimes these parents are thoughtless or lazy and seek the path of least resistance for their own selfish interests. Other times, well-intentioned parents fear they will harm the child psychologically by being too strict or by withholding things that the child wants. Children of permissive parents predictably are more apt to become selfish and belligerent teenagers. In their teen and young adult years, they get into trouble at school and at their jobs because they expect to get their way, but their tantrums and manipulative behaviors are ineffective in these environments.

Authoritarian parents are at the opposite end of the spectrum. Authoritarian parents are overly rigid. Their rules are inflexible and they see their children as people to be controlled, rather than as children to be loved and nurtured. These parents are more apt to view their children as objects in the way rather than accepting them as people to be trained and mentored. Children of authoritarian parents are more likely to become bullies in their teenage years than are children who experience other parenting styles, and they more frequently develop resentment toward their parents than do children of authoritative parents.

Authoritative parents are sometimes called "democratic" parents. Authoritative parents blend appropriate permissiveness with appropriate discipline and rigidity. They have clear rules and expect them to be obeyed, but they are willing to examine their rules and consider exceptions when such exceptions are warranted by circumstances. Research indicates that children of authoritative parents are better adjusted in their teen and adult years than children of permissive or authoritarian parents.

Autonomy

Around age two, in conjunction with the development of willfulness, children begin to seek *autonomy*. Autonomy means to separate from the parent or caregiver and function alone. Of course, toddlers still need their parents' help and guidance in nearly every area of their lives, but their desire to be independent becomes clear. As they learn to walk, to talk, and how things work, they want to participate in activities they see others performing. If a parent is washing dishes in the sink, the child wants to help. If a sibling is coloring, the child wants to color. "Me do it" are words that one often hears from a two-year-old. It is important that the parent allow the child to explore and try new things. He won't be able to succeed at most of the things he tries, but the desire to be autonomous sets the stage for later competence. Children who are frustrated in their desire to be autonomous become adolescents and adults who are more likely to say "I can't" than "I can."

SUMMARY

One of the most important psychological needs of a toddler is consistent, nurturing, face-to-face interaction with a primary caregiver. Parents must stay involved with their toddler—reading, playing, and talking to the child. Children need time to play, sleep, and explore the world. They also need lots of supervision and reasonably clear and consistent rules as they learn to conform to the social expectations of their culture. Meeting these needs for the child prepares him or her for each subsequent stage of development.

PART III

Childhood

CHAPTER 6

Let Me Show You: Preschool (Ages 3–5)

Children are likely to live up to what you believe of them.

—Lady Bird Johnson

Men are generally more careful of the breed of their horses and dogs than of their children.

—William Penn

"See my picture," three-year-old Lasandra says to me. I look at the paper. A continuous blue crayon line zigzags about the middle of the page. The drawing took her less than ten seconds. "Tell me about your picture," I say. As we lie on the floor together in front of a drawing pad and a spilled box of crayons, she explains that it is a house with seven people in it, a cat is in the yard, and the family van is behind a tree, "but you can't see it." The more interest I show, the more explanations she has for her drawing. "I notice that you used a blue crayon," I say to her. "That is a beautiful color!" She beams at me. Between the ages of three and five, children actively participate in the development of their own esteem. They do things to test their value and they constantly want to be reminded that they are valuable, especially to primary caregivers. Lasandra was not as interested in whether or not I liked her picture as she was interested in whether or not I liked *her*. Her picture was her attempt to demonstrate her worthiness to me. Instead of asking, "Do you like me?", she asks, "Do you like what I have done?", but the former question is really the one that she wants me to answer.

At this stage of life, her behavior and her worth are one and the same, a problem with which even some adults struggle. Lasandra's cognitive development, language limitations, and emotional needs limit her ability to ask, or even to understand, her real question. More critical than any other, this period is one in which a child always seeks to be pleasing and acceptable. Toddlers and preschoolers are obsessed with *helping*. They want to prove to themselves and to the people they care about that they are able to do things—wash dishes, pick out clothes, and carry their plate to the sink. In this chapter you will read about esteem, preparations for schooling, developing friendships, and the importance of parental involvement, as well as the many other physical, emotional, and cognitive changes that occur between ages three and five.

THINKING

As a child moves toward her third year of life, she begins to develop a number of cognitive skills that were unavailable to her just a few months before. She is able to picture things in her head for the first time—something called *representational thinking*. Because of this skill, an event during the next few months of her life will become her earliest permanent memory. Her awareness of time is far from fully developed, but she will begin to expand her understanding of life in terms of past, present, and future. Her ability to use language will broaden and her vocabulary of a few hundred words prior to age three will explode into a vocabulary of several thousand words. Her ability to pronounce these words will improve as she moves toward age five. Yet with all these advances, her understanding of many things will still be limited. She will see the world as a magical place, and a full understanding of cause-and-effect relationships is still many years away.

Magic

Once when my mother-in-law was visiting my family, she tucked my four-year-old son into bed at the end of the day. As she was leaving the room, she turned to him and said a phrase that many of us have either heard or used during our lifetime. "Good night, sleep tight, don't let the bedbugs bite." My son got very quiet and sheepishly said, "Where are they?" He took her words literally and thought there were bugs in his bed.

This interchange is a perfect example of how differently small children see the world compared to older children and adults. Children under the age of five do not understand cause-and-effect relationships and they take things literally, as my son demonstrated in this interchange. For this reason they do not understand sarcasm or puns. In their minds, things happen by magic. They cannot comprehend what they cannot see. For example, water comes out of a faucet in the bathroom or kitchen. A young child cannot understand that there are pipes inside the walls that run from a well or a water system. In their minds, any faucet, anywhere, will produce water if you put it on a sink, even if there are no pipes connected to it.

When my daughter was three years old, she awakened me one night screaming. When I came into her bedroom, she was sitting up in the middle of the bed crying. When I asked what was wrong, she said there was a rhinoceros in her bed and it was poking her foot (obviously the result of a bad dream). When she awoke and found herself alone in the dark, she was afraid. Around age two or three, almost all children begin to experience fear of the dark and they believe in ghosts and monsters, which inhabit the dark space under the bed and the closet at night. Part of the development of these monsters is a set of rules children create, which protect them from these monsters. For example, many children believe that if they remain under the covers, monsters cannot hurt them. (See also "Magic" in chapter 5.)

As early as the child's first few days of life, she is beginning to construct a reality—an understanding of how the world operates. Prior to age three, children are not afraid of the dark because they have no reality that includes a fear of things unseen. The reason for this is that they cannot imagine things that are unseen. It is only when children begin to understand things symbolically that they fear what they cannot see. As this fear of the unknown develops, children create "reasons" for this fear. Fear of the monsters under the bed is one of these creations.

Children at this stage do not yet understand the logic, or lack of logic, in their thinking. For example, the logical impossibility of a rhinoceros entering our home and sneaking into my daughter's room without being detected was not something my daughter could comprehend. Almost anything is possible in the magical world of a three-year-old. Therefore, if I had tried to explain to my daughter how it was impossible for a rhinoceros to get into our home, it would not have altered her perception that it was there.

A simple solution for combating these monsters involves operating on the child's level. When my daughter explained the problem to me that night, I got out a broom and said, "Well, I better make sure he doesn't come back." I swept the broom around the room a few times and she watched me as I "magically" protected the room from any further disturbance from zoo animals and then I sat with her for a few minutes to comfort her. She soon was asleep and she had forgotten the incident by the next morning. Obviously, there was no logical connection between the broom and the monster, except that I used fantasy to beat fantasy. This type of fantasy is not a problem at this age and will not create a greater likelihood of the child believing in such things—she will believe in them anyway. I simply worked with her on her level until she was developmentally prepared for more logical explanations.

Movies with goblins and monsters, even when they appear playful to us, may easily frighten a child, and the more realistic these images are, the scarier they are to the child. It is disturbing to me to see very young children at movies that could frighten adults. Some "kids' movies" use real actors rather than animation, and the special effects make the "magic" appear especially real to a child who understands only what he sees. Therefore, when a child sees a witch on screen who turns into a cat (such as in a "Harry Potter" movie) or a giant spider chasing a little boy (such as in a "Lord of the Rings" movie), he believes such a thing actually happened and could happen again.

Even animated movies can be frightening to the child who cannot clearly distinguish between reality and make-believe. Prior to age four, children believe all things are living—rocks, clouds, and trees. This is why a child might say, "The sky is mad" if he sees lightning. Therefore, animated movies are just as real to them as movies with real people. In the 2002 movie *Monsters, Inc.*, for example, animated monsters enter children's bedrooms through the closet doors. Even though these animated characters are cute and funny, the possibility of a monster entering the room through the closet door is very real to a young child. In the entire movie, there are only two "bad" monsters, but it takes just one to make it hard for a preschool child to sleep at night.

I have always tried to be careful about what my children watch on TV, but sometimes I have made a bad choice. When my elder daughter was in kindergarten, I thought she might enjoy the first portion of *The Wizard of Oz*. I was sure she would like the Munchkins and I had planned to shut the TV off after that scene. However, I had forgotten about the brief entrance of the Wicked Witch of the West at the end of that scene. My daughter sat watching the witch with wide eyes. I explained that the witch was the same woman who rode the bicycle earlier in the show, just an actress, and that there are no real witches. When she was in bed that night, she cried out. I went to see what she needed and, of course, she was afraid of witches. Her words provided a clear summary of how children can process only what they see. "I know there are no such things as witches," she said as I sat on the edge of her bed, "but when I close my eyes, my head just tells me there are." Even at five years of age, the visual image was more powerful than her developing logic. She spent the night in bed with my wife and me.

If you don't want to fight such battles, think carefully about how your child will perceive the television shows and movies that you are considering allowing them to watch, as well as the books you read to them. Just because a movie is marketed to young children, that doesn't necessarily mean it is good for them.

Centration

Well into their grade school years, children will focus on a single factor to the exclusion of others. For example, if you ask a child to describe a person, he will say, "She is tall" or "She has long hair." A preschool child will never say, "She is tall and has long hair" because that requires the child to focus on two facets of one's appearance at the same time. While I was building a wall for a new room in our house, my daughter, six years old at the time, was helping me. She knew how to use a level and sometimes held it in position for me. I decided to test her abilities to decentrate. A wall must be both plumb (straight up and down) and square (not leaning side to side). Therefore, there are two ways it must be leveled. As I raised the wall, I held it clearly at a 45° angle (out of plumb). I asked my daughter if the wall was square and ready to nail into position. Even though she leveled the wall and found it to be in square, it clearly was out of plumb, but because of her inability to decentrate, she said the wall was ready to nail into position. Even when I asked her if she was sure, she said it was ready even though I still held the wall clearly at a 45° angle. Only when I pointed out that the wall was not yet plumb did she see what would have been obvious to a child just a year or two older.

Centration makes it likely that children will overlook many obvious things—clothes that need to be picked up, dishes on the table that need to be taken to the kitchen, and shoes or clothing that they want to wear. Centration will make it hard for them to find one toy in a room full of toys. They will focus on a single object or group of objects in the room and completely overlook what they are actually looking for.

Multiple Processing and Memory

By age three children can follow simple directions, but even through age five they will not be able to follow several directions at the same time. If you ask your child to go to his room, get his shoes, and take his laundry to the hamper, he can easily forget all three orders. On the way to his room, as he is trying to remember all three things, he gets confused and forgets them all. You will find him on the couch in the living room looking at a picture book. Instead, give your child a single direction, wait for him to comply, and then give him the next instruction. Not until your child is in first or second grade will he be able to remember more than one thing at a time. Some parents mistake this memory and concentration limitation as disobedience when in fact it is the parents' fault for assuming the child can perform a cognitive task that is developmentally beyond his ability.

Memory does not begin to take shape, as adults know it, until around age three. For most people, their earliest memories are of some event when they were around age three. Those memories are vague, still images rather than a clear, detailed understanding of the event. Even though memory begins to take shape around this time, unless a child is consistently reminded of a person, event, or place, she will easily forget it. For this reason, around age three or four children will, for the first time, anticipate special occasions like Christmas or their birthday. Younger children may get excited when the Christmas decorations go up, on Christmas Day, or when their presents are given to them on their birthday, but they cannot anticipate the event. Prior to this point in development they cannot think about something that hasn't yet happened, but by age three or four, children can remember a previous birthday or Christmas, they can recall the presents and excitement of that event, and they excitedly look forward to the next one.

Vocabulary

By age three, on the average a child's vocabulary includes between 250 and 300 words. That number increases fivefold in the next year, and by age five a child's vocabulary includes between 2,500 and 3,000 words. Children make common errors with language. They overgeneralize rules, such as adding "–ed" to words that do not follow the normal rules (for example, "runned" instead of "ran"), and they will continue to mispronounce many words and sounds. However, as children approach age five, their ability to articulate should improve noticeably as they acquire both an understanding of language rules and exceptions and as they practice making sounds common to their native language. (See chapter 4 for more information on language development.)

Conservation

The inability to conserve will continue to be an issue for children until first or second grade. Therefore, parents should be aware that appearances are significant to a child. To a child, anything that changes in appearance also changes in content. Therefore, children can easily get upset when foods look different than they expect, and they will believe that food will taste different if it is on a different kind of dish. (For example, it is this kind of thinking that makes children believe different-colored M&Ms taste different even though there is no difference in taste between colors.) Parents can save themselves a lot of frustration by anticipating these problems and by allowing the child to choose her own dishes, cup, and silverware. Let your child choose how you cut a sandwich, where you put the ketchup on the plate, and what color toothbrush you buy. (See chapter 5 for more information on conservation.)

Preschool

There is almost no issue more important to success in a Western culture than education. Even though some people become very successful in their careers without a college degree, statistically, education is highly correlated with happiness, job satisfaction, health, and success. We all want our children to talk the earliest, say the most words, walk sooner, and do things that make us believe they are brighter than normal children. This makes us proud. However, there is little correlation between genius and walking early or even using first words. Children who attend preschool tend to perform better on academic tasks through the first two or three grades, but those advantages disappear by the third grade. In other words, children who attend preschool do not differ academically from children who did not by the time they are all in the third grade. There is no need to prepare one's children for kindergarten by sending them to preschool. Many parents feel the need to push their children in an academic direction very early, caving in to social pressure to place their children in preschool on the basis of incorrect advice of friends who argue that preschool is necessary for academic success. These parents may also believe that there is something wrong with their children if they are not socialized early and if they do not like being away from home. In these early years, a child's social skills do not necessarily reflect either one's parenting abilities or the child's intellect or abilities.

Generally, I discourage parents from putting their children in preschool because parents who stay home with their children can do more for them educationally than preschool could ever accomplish, all without the negative effects of day care or preschool. Even so, many parents will choose to enroll their children in preschool. Here are some advantages and disadvantages of preschool.

Advantages

Perhaps the biggest and most obvious advantage of preschool is academic preparation. If the preschool program is well designed, the child should be more than ready to enter kindergarten after a year in preschool for four-year-olds. The child should know basic colors, shapes, and many if not all of the letters of the alphabet. He should be able to count to ten and he most likely will be able to write his name. He may even be able to read simple words. He may learn to tie his shoes, learn his telephone number, and learn how and when to dial 911 in emergencies. While all this is true, all of these skills will be taught in kindergarten. There is no relationship between learning the alphabet at age four (as opposed to age five) and future happiness or success.

A second often-cited advantage of preschool is that children who are in preschool programs are more prepared for the social environment of kindergarten. While they may be slightly more aggressive, they are more social and more easily accommodate to the structure of the classroom in kindergarten than children who have not been in a preschool or an academic day-care environment.

There are also advantages for the primary caregiver, often the mother. She has more time to herself once her children are in school and she can focus on household chores or a job without the trouble or expense of child care.

Disadvantages

The social and academic advantages described above are most evident in children from deprived backgrounds. However, in preschool children who are not underprivileged, the same gains can be achieved by providing educational toys and books at home. Investing time with one's child in one-to-one instruction is an advantage one will not likely find in any preschool and is actually more likely to provide long-term cognitive results than preschool. Likewise, exposing your child to varied environments (for example, church, clubs, play parks with other children) can help the child learn social skills. Preschool is simply unnecessary.

While the academic advantages of preschool linger through the first few grades, after the third grade there is no research that demonstrates any measurable academic difference between preschooled and nonpreschooled children (with the exception of underprivileged children). Likewise, many people seem to have forgotten that the purpose of kindergarten is to prepare children for first grade. Given the logic of some preschool advocates, one might suppose that eventually we will have pre-preschool so that toddlers will be prepared for preschool.

Prior to age five or six, children need lots of playtime, free time, and face-to-face interaction with parents. These needs are obviously compromised if the child is out of the house. Also, children develop at different rates and most four-year-olds are unprepared cognitively, emotionally, physically, and socially to sit in a classroom for five to seven hours. In fact, many children repeat kindergarten because they were not developmentally prepared. This doesn't mean they *can't* engage in proper social conduct in a school setting, but it is much more difficult for them. I have had many five-year-old children come through my practice who were emotionally unprepared for kindergarten. Their parents, teachers, and administrators did everything they could think of to force these children to cooperate at school when the simple fact was that they were too young and not yet ready for that environment. Forcing them only solidified in the child's mind that school was a bad place to be. This problem is even more likely for children younger than age five.

Perhaps the biggest disadvantage of preschool is that children are small only once. Those three short years between toddlerhood and kindergarten will have passed before you know it. Rushing around the house in the early morning, getting breakfast, dressing, brushing teeth, and rushing the child out of the house for several hours at school shortens the time parents and children have together. There is no need to rush them through their early years—enjoy them. You will never find any parent who looks back and says, "Boy, I wish I had spent *less* time with my child when she was a toddler."

In summary, there is no reason whatsoever for a child under the age of four to be enrolled in preschool unless the child resides in a home where his or her basic developmental needs are unmet. Except in these circumstances, the disadvantages by far outweigh the advantages.

A compromise would be to find three-hour programs rather than full-day programs, and three-day-a-week programs rather than five-day programs. Some children thrive on the company of other children and enjoy the challenges and entertainment of preschool, while other children are not ready to be in a structured environment or to be separated from their mother until they are five or six years of age. In such cases, forcing a child into a preschool setting may teach the child to dislike school—the very last thing that you want. The most important task a kindergarten or first-grade teacher has before her is to teach the children in her care to enjoy the school environment and to foster a love for learning. If she can accomplish this task, she has done well. At all levels of education, many, if not most, teachers take their jobs very seriously and work very hard to live up to their responsibilities and obligations. However, because some teachers are poorly trained, have bad attitudes, or have personalities and strengths that are not properly matched to the profession of teaching, a love of learning can help children overcome these deficits as well as a poor curriculum that they may encounter later in their educational careers.

Brain development is fostered in an active, stimulating environment much more than in an environment where there is no stimulation. It would be easy to misinterpret my suggestions and allow children to become couch potatoes.

If children do not attend preschool, they need a stimulating environment at home. Parents can provide the same benefits as preschool, if not better ones, without the disadvantages. Likewise, social interaction at church or other locations with other children can help a child develop social skills without the need for preschool. Finally, for caregivers who need some free time, a baby-sitter once or twice a week or part-time preschool can provide free time without the disadvantages I have discussed.

Preparing for Kindergarten

Children usually start kindergarten at age five, depending on when the child's birthday falls. Preparation for kindergarten, however, begins long before the child is registered for school. Reading to your children, working puzzles with them, and practicing shapes, colors, numbers, and letters, especially in the months immediately preceding their beginning school, can help them prepare for the school environment. Teaching your children to love learning and encouraging them to explore their environment also will help prepare them.

The biggest adjustment many children will have when they start kindergarten is being in a structured environment for several hours. They will have to adjust to sitting for extended periods of time and sharing with playmates. They will be tired, but many kindergarten programs have rest time after lunch. This adjustment could be eased by half-day, rather than full-day, kindergarten programs, but unfortunately half-day programs are fading away and most schools now have only full-day kindergarten programs. There is little reason for this other than the fact that many parents work and school serves as a replacement for day care. Little academic and social benefit is gained from the extra three hours in full-day programs over half-day programs. Earlier bedtimes, a proper diet, and plenty of exercise and playtime after school can help the child adjust.

FEELING

Esteem

A child's early years are vital to the development of esteem because after early childhood, children stop asking who they are. Instead, they spend their energy looking at things that confirm the perception they have already developed of themselves and ignore things which contradict that perception. They either find things to confirm their value or they find things to confirm that they are not valuable, depending upon their self-perception. Teens are especially prone to this behavior. For this reason, teenagers with low self-esteem will not believe the compliments they receive, but they will readily believe criticisms. Once one's perception of self is established, it is very hard to change it.

Esteem building involves more than compliments. Esteem building with your child involves lots of eye contact, laughing together, reading together, singing and playing together, sitting in a rocking chair, and going on walks. This is one of the reasons that it is nearly impossible to provide for this part of a child's development if both parents work full-time. Like many men, I have to check my behavior at home frequently. I have a tendency to spend a lot of home time working on things. I love my daughters and son to help me, but if I am not careful, I will interact with them only when they are doing things with me, rather than when I am doing things with them. Personal, patient interaction with one's children teaches them that they have value and encourages them to explore their environment. This time commitment is an investment in their future self-perceptions.

Emotions

Emotions in your child that develop during the years between ages three and five are empathy, shame, and guilt. Also during these years, children are very sensitive and can easily be embarrassed or humiliated. An immature version of love also begins to take shape during this time. Prior to age three, children "love" those who meet their needs or who give them things. Their love emotion is based on what they receive. Yet between ages three and five, children begin to develop an emotional attachment that is based on more than hedonistic desires.

Humiliation

When someone says something hurtful or embarrassing to an adult, the adult has the ability to recognize context and to consider the many reasons why the person may have made the hurtful comment. This knowledge allows the adult to cope with his emotional response to the comment. Children, however, do not have these skills. Therefore, inability to understand context, minimal ability to take another's perspective, and minimal coping skills leave the child vulnerable to hurt, embarrassment, and humiliation. It is never appropriate to humiliate anyone, adult or child, but it is especially damaging to a child's developing esteem to be humiliated. A child can be humiliated by public punishment, being hit in the face, and unkind words. One must carefully discipline in order to avoid humiliating a child.

Expression of Emotion

When my son was four years old, he and I were running an errand one day. As we made conversation, he said, "I love you and Mommy a lot." I asked him how he knew he loved us. "Because I draw you pictures," he said. "Do you feel anything inside your body that tells you that you love someone, Benjamin?" I asked him. "Yes," he said, "I feel happy."

This brief conversation with my son demonstrates two important principles in understanding emotion in children. First, his comment about drawing pictures indicates a child's understanding of emotion only as it pertains to behavior. From a child's perspective, his interpretation of emotion—either his own or someone else's—is directly related to action. Therefore, if the child feels a negative emotion, like anger, he will follow that emotion with an action, like hitting something or throwing an object. Not until the child is six or seven will he begin to think about and articulate his emotions and select an appropriate demonstration of them. It will be many years before he can hide his emotions. The child interprets the behavior of others in a similar way. For example, if a parent punishes the child, the child interprets the parent's behavior as anger, sadness, or dislike, and he will personalize those emotions, believing the parent dislikes him. Likewise, when parents of a preschool-age child divorce, the child assumes the divorce means that the parent who leaves does not love the child anymore. Young children cannot fully separate behavior from emotion, and even adults sometimes have difficulty distinguishing between the two.

As parents we must watch how we express our emotions around our children and must also recognize the emotion a child is trying to demonstrate through his behavior. When my son does something special for me, his purpose is not just to seek approval and acceptance; he is also attempting to express his emotional state. I once broke my leg and a number of times my son volunteered to hand me my crutches. By doing this simple task for me, he was demonstrating his affection for me. Once or twice, instead of saying thank you, I said, "Son, I can see how much you love me because you like to get my crutches for me." The look on his face told me that I was right.

The second thing of significance in this interchange with my son concerns his response to my second question. When asked if he had an internal feeling related to his emotion, his only word was "happy." A few days before this conversation he told me about a friend whose pet had died. I asked him how he would feel if his own dog died. "Sad" was his response. Prior to age five or six, children understand only the four most basic emotions—mad, sad, glad, and afraid. You will never hear a four-year-old say, "I'm frustrated" or "I'm depressed." The child cannot understand the combination of emotions that create frustration or depression—anger, sadness, irritation, fear, and others.

Parents must understand that children may often be unable to express themselves emotionally. Sometimes even adults experience a mixture of emotions to the extent that they are not sure how they feel. Children live with this sort of confusion on a regular basis. Helping a child recognize and deal with anger, hurt, frustration, confusion, or other emotions involves helping the child learn labels for those emotions. Paying close attention to the child's behavior can help the parent teach the child how to interpret his emotions. One very helpful tool I use in therapy is a poster composed of nearly 40 different cartoon faces. Each face expresses a different emotion and the label for the emotion is written beneath it. This feeling chart helps children identify with a face and then learn what that emotion is. It is interesting how quickly they can learn that they can experience several emotions at one time.

Watch your child's behavior carefully and occasionally respond to the emotion his or her actions imply. Doing so will help your child form labels, recognize his or her feelings, and give him or her the satisfaction of communicating his thoughts effectively.

Prejudice and Discrimination

Children begin to organize the world from their first minutes of life, but their organization of the world is most clear when their language skills begin to refine. Between ages three and five, children believe that the "right" way to do things is the way they are done at home and the "wrong" way is everything else. "Right and wrong" is based on what they know. Statements like "Mommies do this" or "Daddies do that" reflect early forms of prejudice, which are solidly based in what children have experienced. Likewise, children recognize racial, gender, and age differences in their playmates and they make assumptions about those differences as they try to fit them into their worldviews. Around age two, children first begin to show signs of distress when they find a toy that is broken. Distress regarding a broken toy indicates that the child recognizes what "ought to be."

People generally like to be around people who are like themselves and tend to fear or avoid those who are different. This is true of gender, race, and many other variables. Even when children grow up around children of various ethnic backgrounds, they will develop stereotypes. A child's system of right and wrong generally applies not only to the things he does, but also to the way he behaves and how he looks. If people wear different clothes, have unusual hairstyles, or talk with an unusual accent, children will find it odd and they possibly will believe that there is something "wrong" with the person who is different from themselves.

We cannot prevent biases in our children, nor are biases unavoidable even in our adult years. Bias is a by-product of socialization. Some prejudgments are necessary for survival. If we had no general rules of how the world operated, we would not know to be alarmed if we were being followed through a parking garage or if we saw a person with a firearm walk into a bank. In both cases, making assumptions about the person's motives, intentions, and character are important for protecting ourselves. We make a prejudgment about the person following us that he or she may intend to harm us, or that the person with the weapon is planning a bank robbery even though we cannot know for sure in either case. This form of prejudgment is helpful, but biases become problems when they are inflexible rules that operate in our subconscious and rule us rather than provide information for our discriminative use. Biases that are based on characteristics that do not logically go together, such as one's race and the likelihood of danger, are examples of detrimental biases.

A parent's job is not to prevent prejudgments entirely. That would be impossible even if you tried. Instead, a parent's job is to correct mistaken assumptions (for example, prejudice based on skin color), encourage productive generalizations (for example, don't talk to strangers), and help one's child know the difference between the two. Parents who are overtly prejudiced regarding race, gender, or religion will likely produce children who hold the same views. Likewise, parents who talk as if they have no prejudices but behave as if they do will produce children who hold negative prejudices. In a society where we must learn to live together, parents should teach their children, both verbally and through their behaviors, that even though differences exist, they are not necessarily bad. Even though adults have a difficult time setting their prejudgments aside, children don't have the disadvantage of experience and often can accept differences more readily than adults.

A Child's Concept of Death

At least until age six, children have great difficulty understanding anything abstract. Death, of course, is a very abstract concept. It is complicated by religious views that include life after death. How can one live and yet be dead? I would suppose that this is hard even for most adults to understand. When my younger daughter was two, I took her to the funeral home with me to visit the family of a friend whose aunt had died of cancer. The funeral home was so crowded that it was difficult to walk through, but I noticed that only one other youngster was present that evening. My daughter saw the deceased lying in the casket and noted that the lady was "very sleepy." She converted the idea of death, something abstract, into "sleep," something concrete that she knew.

Fear of the unknown and the finality of death make death frightening to adults, but both of these are abstract concepts. In fact, most religions reduce the anxiety associated with death by providing answers to these two questions. That is why many religious people do not fear death, but preschool-age children cannot contemplate these two issues because of developmental limitations. Therefore, death is not that scary to them, relatively speaking.

Parents can use this developmental limitation to their advantage in teaching children what it means to die. Children should be shielded from the details surrounding a tragic death, but they otherwise have nothing to fear unless someone tells them to be afraid. Attending the funeral or visiting a funeral home is not a good idea in the case of very sudden and tragic death, or if one could expect visitors to express uncontrolled grieving. The child will respond to the grieving, her lack of understanding will create fear, and that fear will then be associated with death. Otherwise, exposing children to the process during this developmental stage can ease the difficulty of attending a funeral or losing a loved one later in life. Children who are not exposed to cultural traditions surrounding death and dying during these earlier years will have to deal later with the normal emotions involved with loss, and these emotions will be compounded by anxiety associated with never having experienced the process before.

While we were at the funeral home, my daughter wanted to see the "sleeping lady." We walked to the casket briefly and she said the lady was very tired and that we should be quiet. I did not dwell on the issue or try to explain death to her at this point. She would learn more about this later. What she knows now is what a funeral home is and what happens when you go there. She learned that it was not painful and nothing scary happened. This knowledge will help ease her anxieties when she is older.

Death of a Pet

For most children, the death of a pet is their first experience with death. This was the case in our home when our dog was hit by a car and died. The death of our dog provided an opportunity for my children to experience for the first time the permanence of death and the deep sadness that one feels when something valuable is lost. Understanding death as part of our existence is a very important lesson.

Between the ages of three and five, a child is incapable of understanding death. The explanation "Doggy went bye-bye" is about all that most pre-school children can understand. They are young enough that they will soon forget about the animal. Unless they witness the pet's death, they will experience few long-term emotional effects of the loss, but they will experience temporary grief. Grief is normal and it is unfair to tell anyone who is experiencing a loss that they should not feel bad. You feel what you feel. Telling someone not to feel bad is often an attempt to deal with one's own discomfort. When our dog died, I explained to my crying children that I, too, felt bad and would miss our dog very much. I let them know there is nothing wrong with missing something that you have loved.

It is also helpful to help the child to say goodbye. As adults, we have elaborate rituals for saying goodbye to a loved one who has died. We have visitation, funerals, graveside services, and so forth. I buried our dog before my children could see his injuries, but we worked together to mark his grave with stones. Using a piece of wood, we constructed a small headstone for the dog and had a memorial service for him in our woods. At our service, we each said one thing we would miss about the dog. That validated our grief. However, in order not to dwell on our grief, we each said something about our dog that made us happy. We sang a song and we each said a short prayer. I let my children know they could visit our dog's grave anytime they liked. That was years ago and they still visit his grave.

Finally, teach your child to move ahead. Do not dwell on the death of the pet, but answer their questions succinctly and honestly. Don't be afraid to say "I don't know" and do your best to provide a positive outlook on the situation and teach them how to get beyond their grief. For example, my younger daughter was very inquisitive about the injuries our dog suffered. I told her that hearing about some details, like those regarding his injuries, would probably only make her feel bad, but that our dog had not suffered and that was really what mattered to her. Reminding her of the happy things we talked about at his memorial, I suggested that even though it was sad losing our dog, I was very glad we had him as long as we did. It was wonderful having a dog and I looked forward to another pet one day, even though we could never replace our beagle. Conversations like these teach your child that it is OK to be sad and to ask questions, as well as how to deal with grief.

Can You Spoil a Child?

"That is the most spoiled child I've ever seen." I've heard words like this since I was a child. I don't doubt that people are seeing inappropriate behaviors in children when they utter these words, but I do question their interpretation of the behaviors they see. It is not possible to spoil a child in the way most people think about it.

Traditional wisdom says that we should not give our children too much of anything—too many toys, too much coddling, too much affection—or we might spoil them. I disagree with many of these statements. Part of our cultural problems these days is that we don't give each other enough affection and attention, and there is no direct relationship between toys or affection and being "spoiled." The problem from which these children actually suffer is lack of discipline rather than being spoiled. Children who are given what they want in the absence of self-discipline often expect their immediate needs and wants to be addressed immediately. When their wants are not met immediately or they don't get their way, they throw tantrums, but it is the lack of discipline, not excessive attention, that creates their inappropriate behaviors. A child who is disciplined will learn to put his or her needs aside on occasion, regardless of how many toys he has.

Parents sometimes fail to realize that you can give a child frequent attention, but also teach the child discipline at the same time. If this were not so, all rich children would be spoiled and all underprivileged children would not be spoiled. The fact is, children from very affluent homes, when they are taught self-discipline, can exhibit exemplary behavior. Likewise, children in families of modest means can exhibit "spoiled" behavior when they are undisciplined.

Teaching restraint, patience, and self-control may involve *not* buying every toy, article of clothing, or video game for which a child asks. This may seem to contradict what I said in the previous paragraphs, but I did not say that buying everything a child wants is a good thing. You may have the money to buy something a child wants, but learning to wait is part of teaching self-discipline. Waiting also applies to attention and affection. I am willing to hold, hug, kiss, and snuggle with my children at almost any time. However, there are times when I can't because I am working on something or am busy with another child. Having the child wait doesn't mean that I won't snuggle at all. It means that he or she will have to wait a few minutes. Again, setting aside immediate gratification teaches self-discipline, but I'm not spoiling my children when I love them. I don't have my children wait just because I'm not interested in being with them at the moment. I keep them waiting if I think it will teach them something—manners, respect, or self-control.

Deservedly, psychologists got a bad reputation in the 1970s by suggesting that parents basically give children everything they want. This philosophy created a group of children who were selfish, obnoxious, and unwilling to consider the needs of others. While some may call this "spoiling," this more accurately describes lack of discipline. As a rule, we don't give our

children enough attention and affection. Showing affection and buying presents in the absence of standards of conduct creates undisciplined children.
Frequent affection in the presence of discipline creates altruistic, polite, and
well-rounded children. (See also "Can You Spoil A Baby?" in chapter 4.)

DOING

Between ages three and five, children will enjoy helping mom and dad.
Toddlers enjoy helping, but the new skill that emerges at this age is something called *initiative*. Initiative refers to the child's desire to think up activities by himself. While a toddler wants to do things once he sees someone
else doing them, preschool-age children want to create their own plans. "Let
me show you what I *did*" are words you will hear often. Even though children at this age, much like their toddler counterparts, will have difficulty
mastering the skills they want to perform, they will want to come up with
ideas on their own and perform those behaviors by themselves. For example,
at least by age four, a child will likely want you to come see her bed that
she made "without being asked!" Also during this stage, your child will
change dramatically in his or her physical abilities. She will grow several inches
and gain several pounds. Her muscle control will improve, and as it does,
she will greatly improve her competence in physical skills.

Fine and Gross Motor Skills

Even though these behaviors may be awkward, by age three or four, your
child should be able to cut with scissors, button and unbutton clothing, use
zippers, snap and unsnap clothing, and eat with a fork or spoon. Prior to
age four, no matter how slowly you toss a ball to a child and no matter how
close you are when you toss it, the child will not catch it. The ball will bounce
off her chest. By age four, however, she should be able both to catch and
to throw a ball.

Skipping is a task that many preschoolers do not master until age five. In
fact, even then only about 70 percent will be able to skip. By age three some
children can jump, but they won't be proficient at jumping until age five.
When three-year-olds try to jump, they bend their knees and spring upward,
but they will not leave the ground. By age five, most children (about 80
percent) can hop. At three years of age, children only have limited ability to
run. They frequently fall, but by age five, they are quite good at running,
although they often do not pay attention to where they are going, so falls
and injuries are not unlikely. Nearly all three-year-olds can climb stairs, but

they need a handrail. At age three, children negotiate stairs in a mark-time foot pattern. This means they step up with one foot and then, instead of stepping up to the next higher tread with the opposite foot, they bring the opposite foot to the same tread. Therefore, they negotiate stairs only one tread at a time. By age four, most children have abandoned the mark-time foot pattern.

Health Care and Vaccinations

Your child should have regular yearly checkups with a pediatrician, at which time the doctor can remind you of pending vaccinations—both recommended and required. Many illnesses that plague the majority of the countries around the world can be prevented with simple and inexpensive vaccinations. Unfortunately, many parents in America either do not know about vaccination schedules or do not take advantage of them, not only causing their children to needlessly suffer from illnesses but also perpetuating their existence. Even if vaccinations are cost-prohibitive, most large communities have public health services where they can be acquired either free of charge or at a greatly reduced cost. Prior to starting kindergarten, your child will have to have a shot record indicating that all vaccinations are up to date.

Teeth

On the average, children have a full set of baby teeth before their second birthday. Those teeth begin to loosen and prepare for mature teeth around age five. Losing the first tooth is frightening for children because they are afraid it will hurt. Parents can lessen the anxiety by not trying to pull loose teeth too soon. As baby teeth drop out, permanent teeth replace them within a few weeks. Incisors are usually the first permanent teeth to appear, followed by first molars, canines, and second molars. A child may have baby teeth as late as early pubescence. Wisdom teeth, if they ever erupt, usually do not appear until late adolescence or adulthood.

Crooked teeth are not unusual because the teeth move in the child's ever-changing gums; this does not necessarily mean a child will need braces. Consultation with a pediatric dentist can help establish proper dental hygiene and help a parent plan for long-term dental care that may be necessary. Some dental problems can be easily corrected if addressed early, which can decrease the likelihood of more significant problems later in development.

Sports, Dance, and Activities

Because of their limited physical abilities, children who participate in dance or athletic teams at age three or four should not be expected to perform tasks beyond their developmental abilities. Teachers and coaches should be aware of the limits to a child's abilities as well as the broad range of development during the preschool years. Even though they all may be the same age, some children will be able to perform a given task and others will not.

Preschool is an excellent time to introduce children to activities that help them practice using their bodies. Dance, baseball, martial arts, and soccer are good examples of activities that can be tailored to the child's developmental abilities. Parents should understand, however, that a child is limited not only by physical abilities but also by cognitive ones. He or she will be able to concentrate on an activity for only a limited period of time. Therefore, practices and rehearsals should be short—no more than an hour and preferably 30–45 minutes at the maximum. Any activity in which the child is required to physically disengage for any length of time will result in loss of the child's interest and attention. Therefore, children don't need long lectures during practice, rehearsals, or performances, and practices or rehearsals should involve all children. Children forced to sit by while other children participate will disengage, and their minds and bodies will wander.

Children should not be forced into any activity. Their interest in sports or other activities will ebb and flow with their moods; however, when it is clear that the child is consistently no longer interested in the activity, it is time to disengage. Finishing a season with the activity is fine, but at this age, once the season is over, parents shouldn't push their child to continue an activity he does not enjoy. The purpose of the activity is to provide physical exercise and develop social skills and an interest in the activity. It may be several years before the child finds a sport or other activity that he or she wishes to focus on for the long term.

Pets

Preschool children are still too young to be totally responsible for the care of a pet. Dogs and cats could easily injure them and they could easily injure a pet. Therefore, a child should always be supervised when family pets are present—especially dogs. Dozens of children are mauled or killed each year by family dogs even though some of these animals were not historically aggressive. In some cases, the child unintentionally threatened the animal's space or food, or the child injured the animal in some way. Children of this age are old enough to begin to learn the responsibility of caring for a pet, but they will need regular help feeding and caring for their dog, cat, goldfish, or other family pet. This is a good age for acquiring a pet, but only if the parent is willing to assume a primary role for the animal's care and to supervise the child while the pet is present.

Modesty

By age three children are fully aware of their bodies and body parts, but they will not learn modest behavior for many more months. It is not unusual for children to expose themselves, take their clothes off at inappropriate times, and comment about another person's body parts. Not doing these things is a social skill that must be taught in accordance with the parent's beliefs and the culture's mores. It is *abnormal* for children of this age to draw explicit sexual pictures, to engage in sexual activities, or to use overt sexual language. These behaviors are symptoms of sexual abuse or inappropriate exposure to sexual issues. Distinguishing between sexual behavior that is due to lack of socialization and sexual behavior that is abnormal can be tricky and requires a trained eye. If you are concerned about your child's behavior, consult with a psychologist or therapist who specializes in child development and abuse.

Children begin to develop modesty only when they have a sense of right and wrong. Morality doesn't begin to develop until age two and continues to be refined through adulthood. Between ages three and five, as parents teach children appropriate sexual behavior, children will begin to understand the social meaning assigned to the various parts of the body, how they differ by gender, and how those rules vary by social setting. Acquiring the various nuances of modesty in behavior and conversation will take several years, but by age five, children should know to keep their clothes on in public places, although they still may lack modesty at home. Parents need to understand this is a complex cognitive skill that takes time to teach. Children should not be spanked or otherwise punished for accidentally violating social constructs. As they begin to learn social rules governing modesty, clear instruction and reinforcement for appropriate behavior should be all that is necessary to teach these skills. Continually, willfully, and overtly violating social mores regarding modesty may be symptomatic of child abuse, and consultation with a child specialist is recommended in such cases.

Discipline

By far the most common questions I receive from parents have to do with discipline. Parents have been sensitized to issues of abuse and the potential harm in spanking or striking a child. More so than at any other time in history, parents invest thousands of dollars each year in self-help and parenting books (like this one) so they can learn how to deal with their children in the most effective way. I once read the following concerning a child's esteem: "Unfortunately, most of children's negative feelings about themselves are formed from evaluations placed on them by adults. Adults lecture, scold, moralize, nag, belittle, label, and criticize. Sometimes children decide they are worthless, stupid, and unlovable because of the continued judgments placed on them."[1] Such statements give parents the impression that one should never cause bad feelings in a child. However, punishment will almost always cause bad feelings. The $100,000 question involves "how" you should discipline. The next several paragraphs address the issue of discipline and how to maintain control of your child without damaging his esteem or causing injury.

Punishment is only one form of discipline, but it is one you will need on occasion. Appropriate punishment requires separating the child's worth from her behavior. Children will feel bad when they are in trouble and they should feel bad. Appropriate guilt is part of learning morality and ethical behavior, and an important part of the development of one's conscience. However, children need to attach the bad feelings to the behavior and not to themselves, but they will not do this on their own. They need to be taught that a person can do a bad thing and still be a good person. Reassure your child after discipline that you love her very much and you are trying to teach her to be a better person. It seems somewhat contradictory to punish a child and then hug her immediately after, but this is important for children who recognize emotion through behavior. The punishment says "you don't like me" while a hug reinforces that you do.

Parents must also set clear rules and boundaries up front and stick to them. Parents should remember these three principles: **ONE**: Say what you mean and do what you say. **TWO**: If you don't mean it, don't say it. **THREE**: If you do mean it, do it. Children will spend much of their time testing the boundaries you establish. If you set a meaningless boundary, children will suppose other boundaries are meaningless as well.

Avoiding assaulting the child's esteem or worse, assaulting the child physically, involves control of one's temper. Young children assume they are the cause of the parent's emotional state. If you are happy, the child assumes he made you happy. If you are angry, he assumes there is something about him that created your anger. Appropriate expression of emotions is acceptable, but it should never involve "belittling, nagging or labeling." If your anger at your child is out of control, take a few minutes in another room before dealing with the issue or, in a two-parent home, let the other parent deal with the discipline in this situation.

To discipline means to teach and many parents forget that they don't have to wait for a child to misbehave before they teach him. On the contrary, look for ways to praise children when they are behaving properly. It is too easy to ignore the good behavior and only give attention to the bad. Catch your child being good and recognize him for it. This builds feelings of worth and value in a child and teaches her she can succeed in pleasing you. Unfortunately, the intensity of feelings associated with punishment can be much stronger than the ones associated with praise. Therefore, you need to praise often to help counter the feelings of inadequacy associated with punishment.

Spanking

Parents should beware of anyone who suggests either "always spank" or "never spank." These ideas are equally problematic. When one should spank can be determined by answering five simple questions. First, can you accomplish the desired result without spanking your child? If so, don't spank. Second, will spanking at this time, in this place, or in this way be humiliating? Humiliation is never an appropriate disciplinary strategy, whether it involves spanking or not. Therefore, parents should never spank their children in public—public spanking is always humiliating.

Third, does the offense merit serious punishment like a spanking? Spanking tends to work very quickly as a deterrent and some behaviors must be terminated immediately for the child's safety. A child who is developing a habit of putting metal objects into an electrical receptacle must be deterred from this behavior immediately. However, spanking when one uses an inappropriate word, fails to remember a rule, or commits some other minor infraction is inappropriate and can be handled equally well with other forms of discipline or punishment. Fourth, is the child too old to spank? Many parents have said that their children are never too old to spank, but as children move into adolescence spanking is humiliating and should be avoided. Other forms of discipline should be practiced after age nine or ten. Finally, is spanking necessary? Parents must consider personality differences between children. One child may be deterred simply by a severe reprimand or stern look, but a sibling may require a spanking to achieve the same result. If you don't have to spank, don't do it.

Watch your own attitude. A parent is more likely to spank when he is tired, cranky, or out of ideas about how to deal with a child. In other words, simply not knowing what else to do is perhaps one reason parents spank too often. Never hit your child to satisfy your own anger. Spanking the child's rear end is acceptable, whereas hitting in other areas, such as the face or head, should be avoided. Always communicate to your child before, during, and after a spanking that you love him or her, but you cannot allow the specific behavior. This separates the behavior from the person.

What can you do if you don't spank? There are a number of possibilities. First, reinforce the child for what he or she does right. Catch your child being good and reinforce him or her for exhibiting the correct behavior. Second, time-out and loss of privileges (TV time, games, toys, snacks, etc.) are disciplinary strategies which tend to work well as alternatives to spanking. Third, using logical consequences also helps and it separates the person from the behavior. For example, if you want your child to clean his room before TV time, you can explain that you want the child to be able to watch the show, but the room must be cleaned up first. Therefore, if he fails to finish the job, both of you will be sad. Finally, pay attention to how much time you spend interacting with your children. Some misbehavior may simply be a request for attention.

Summary: Seven Rules for Control

The limitations of this chapter cannot address all possible issues in regard to discipline, but it is clearly much easier to spank children than it is to use other, perhaps even more effective, approaches. Working at knowing when to use which form of discipline takes much more energy than simply striking a child for any or all misbehaviors. There are no magic wands for controlling children, but there are a number of things that a parent can do to make obedience and good behavior more likely.

Rule 1: *Consistency*. Inconsistency in discipline teaches the child that the parent doesn't really mean what he or she says. Inconsistency teaches adults the same thing. Consider how you drive. Most people on the freeway drive faster than the speed limit. They know it is against the law and they know they could get a ticket. In fact, many of them have been cited for speeding, but the ticket doesn't significantly affect their driving behaviors because they know that sometimes they can speed and get away with it. Children will respond to parents the same way when discipline is inconsistent.

Rule 2: *Respect your child*. Some parents invest a lot of energy teaching children to respect others, but many times fail to return the favor. Respect does not mean that children should always get their way and it doesn't mean that they are not accountable for their behavior. It means you treat them as you would like to be treated—the "golden rule" applied to parenting. Teach your children, discipline them, and hold them accountable. Even though they should know you are the final authority, always try to think about how you would like to be treated if you were in their shoes. Of course, you have to adjust your words according to the child's age, but never speak or act disrespectfully to your children. If they are speaking, don't interrupt. If they are telling you about some event that is not all that interesting to you, listen politely, just as you would to a business associate who was telling you about an event in which you weren't really interested. You don't always have to cater to their requests, just as you don't with those people who work with you. If you have to decline a request, do it respectfully and with an appropriate explanation.

Rule 3: *Pick the right tool.* Many parents err in their disciplinary practices because they know how to do only one thing—spank. It isn't that spanking is bad in and of itself. Rather, it is a problem if you try to use it to fit every child and every situation. My father had a toolbox when I was little. He had only a few tools: a pair of pliers, a screwdriver, a hammer, and a few other odds and ends. Any work that he did around the house, on the lawn mower, or on his car was done with one of these few tools. Somehow he managed to make these limited tools meet his needs. I would guess that he often did a little damage trying to use the wrong tool. On the other hand, my garage is full of different tools. Some of the tools have only one use and I may have used them only once or twice. The right tool for the right job is a philosophy that not only makes most of my handyman chores easier, it also prevents me from causing damage by using the wrong tools.

Training our children works in a similar way. A reader of my newspaper column called me once and asked about an article I had written on discipline. "Spanking works for me," she said, "and my parents used spanking with me and my brothers and we turned out OK." She observed that spanking worked very well with her son and that he did not respond to other forms of discipline very well. It may be that spanking is the appropriate tool in many cases with her son, but it is unlikely that this is the only tool she will ever need. Like this reader, your children may seem to grow up fine if you use limited tools in their discipline. However, using less-than-appropriate tools for a given job risks causing problems when there is less risk with other forms of discipline. Learn some new approaches and invest a little more energy in training your children.

As with my father's literal tools, many parents only have one or two tools in their disciplinary toolbox and those are the only ones they know. They make them work even if they are not the best tools for the job. Adding tools to the toolbox makes for easier and more productive parenting. Perhaps some children need spankings. Certainly, all children need reinforcement. Some need time-out. Others need attention, grounding, withdrawal of privileges, extra work, conversation, lecture, or reprimand. Different children within the same family respond differently to various forms of discipline. As circumstances change, a child who normally is reprimanded easily by a stern look may require time-out, withdrawal of privileges, or some other punishment. The right tool for the right job is a great philosophy in circumstances besides mechanics and home repair!

Rule 4: *Natural consequences.* Teach your child that all behaviors have consequences and all choices have built-in rewards or punishments. For example, your child may take a long time to finish picking up his toys. A natural consequence can be that the TV stays off until the toys are picked up. A child who dawdles will have no time left for TV. You may find it helpful to remind your child several times that she may run out of time to watch TV, but the choice is still hers. You are not preventing her from watching TV. She is choosing not to if she doesn't finish her work. All behaviors have consequences—some good and some bad. Children will learn over time to correct their own behavior when they see that their choices have led to unpleasant consequences. Natural consequences also take some of the burden off the parent for having to be the bad guy.

Rule 5: *Reinforce positive behaviors.* "Discipline" does not always mean "punishment." Punishing wrong behaviors is just one method of discipline. Catching children when they are doing something right encourages them to repeat that behavior. It takes work to pay attention to a child's "good" behaviors and to reinforce them, but it is an important part of parenting. If a parent interacts with the child only when she is in trouble, the child will begin to believe that she can't do anything right. Simple words like "I noticed that you got ready for school right away and I didn't have to remind you. Thanks!" can have a very powerful effect on behavior.

Rule 6: *Work as a team.* Children learn very quickly how to play parents against one another. Parents who do not support one another end up fighting each other while the child gets what he wants. Parents must agree on their disciplinary practices, rules for the home, and so forth. Disagreements over the way one parent has handled a problem with a child must be conducted in private. The child must see his parents as 100 percent unified when it comes to discipline. This is especially critical when children reach their teenage years.

Rule 7: *Individual differences.* As I have mentioned above, there are no disciplinary practices that work universally. Some children respond very well to reinforcement. They almost never need to be punished because they are very cooperative and easygoing. Other children are more obstinate and difficult. Reinforcement may not work very well by itself and the parent finds herself always battling for control with a child like this. The parent then wonders what she is doing wrong because the other child was so easy. This is part of human variability. When I am working with teachers or parents to find a way to control a child whose behavior is out of control, it sometimes takes two or three tries before we find what combination of practices works best for that child. Every child is different, even within the same family, so don't expect the same disciplinary practices to work the same with each child. If a disciplinary practice is not working for a given child, find something else. Don't just do more of the same.

These ideas are general rules, but of course this is not all you have to know. If you are having trouble keeping your child under control, it may be necessary to seek professional assistance. Two or three sessions with a child psychologist or a therapist specializing in children's issues can often help parents see what they are doing right and what they could do differently. Parents who are motivated to improve things at home can see dramatic changes fairly quickly.

Abnormal Behaviors

The second most common question I receive from parents has to do with the normalcy of their children's behaviors. Parents want to know if the things their children can and cannot do, the way they behave, and the difficulties they face are normal. Generally speaking, there is a very broad range of what is "normal."

There is a normal curve for most behaviors. For example, a child at 15 months of age should have lost most of her neonatal reflexes, she should be walking, and she should be forming at least a few words. But there is variability in when these skills develop. A child who exhibits a behavior earlier than the average child is not necessarily exceptional. Likewise, a child who is later than average in exhibiting a certain behavior is not necessarily dysfunctional. For example, one child might easily skip at three years of age while another might not skip until age four and yet both could be seen as "normal." Likewise, parents may wonder if their children are normal because they appear more aggressive than other children, or because they seem to have disrupted sleep patterns. This is especially true for parents who have more than one child, with the child in question being the youngest, because the younger child is so visibly different from older siblings. Normal and abnormal behaviors must always be considered in the context of the child's environment, his age, his family dynamic, and the other parts of his development (social, emotional, cognitive, and behavioral). It takes practice and expertise to properly evaluate all of these factors simultaneously.

However, in children of any age, there are three specific behaviors that are almost never normal. These three behaviors are called the *terrible triad*. Their presence in a child, especially when the child exhibits all three behaviors together, is almost always symptomatic of serious problems. The first of these three behaviors is bed-wetting. All children, of course, wet the bed and how long it takes to train children to master bladder control varies. However, once the child has fully mastered both day and nighttime bladder control, a relapse several months or several years later is a troubling symptom. Even though there are several reasons why a child might begin to wet the bed after mastering the skill, trauma, such as sexual abuse, is included among them. I absolutely never draw any conclusion based on a single piece of evidence, but when this symptom is present, sexual abuse is something I would definitely investigate until I was satisfied that the relapse is due to some other cause.

The second symptom of the terrible triad is fire setting. Again, both children and adults have some level of fascination with fire. Curious children may occasionally experiment with fire or play with matches, but an obsession with fire and an apparent need to burn things is highly abnormal. This need to destroy is indicative of unresolved internal conflict and is often a precursor to more serious emotional and behavioral problems.

The final symptom of the triad is cruelty to animals. It is not unusual for children to hurt animals by accident, but harm to animals that is deliberate and cruel, especially if it is repeated, is abnormal. Normal children have compassion for animals and the absence of such compassion is a sign of a significant problem. I have always found significant disturbances in children who torture or kill pets, neighborhood animals, or wild animals that are caught for the purpose of torturing. Like fire setting, this is representative of a need to destroy and is a sign of serious emotional distress. Many years ago when I was beginning my practice, I worked with a child who delighted in killing frogs. He repetitiously found frogs and then threw them into trees or on the ground to kill them. In his case, killing these creatures was a symptom of significant rage that was the result of ongoing abuse that he was suffering. Many teenagers and young adults who rape, assault, or kill began their careers by torturing and/or killing animals. If there is no resolution to the internal conflict that drives this behavior, the child will eventually graduate to harming people.

Because every child is different, I am very careful in my developmental analyses and I look for a normal progression in development as much as for certain behaviors at a certain time. I also consider the wide variety of backgrounds and cultures that could contribute to behaviors that I see. However, a parent, teacher, or other concerned adult who sees any or all of the terrible triad should pursue clinical intervention for the child. These behaviors are not normal and the child should be referred to a psychologist or therapist for evaluation.

Parenting in a Divided Home

An unsettling reality in our society today is the fact that many children are being raised in broken homes. Caring for children is difficult. The added complication of managing a child's life between two homes makes the situation even more challenging. Living part-time in two homes can be confusing to a child. There are two sets of addresses, phone numbers, people, rules, and customs. The child has to adjust to two different beds and bedrooms. The transition from one setting to another will almost always create added difficulties. Divorced or separated parents should consider the following rules of thumb.

First, never use children as counselors or sounding boards for the difficulties that exist between you and your spouse or ex-spouse. Children should be concerned with books, toys, playing, and growing up. Relationship conflicts between parents are for the parents to work out. Venting personal frustrations about a spouse or former spouse with a child is never appropriate. Children will then experience torn loyalties between parents and will not know whom to believe. If you need to vent, use a counselor, friend, or other confidant. Even if your former partner is totally responsible for the divorce (a highly unlikely scenario), it still is inappropriate to discuss your former spouse's shortcomings with a child.

Second, regardless of the difficulties that may have existed between you and your mate, set your differences aside for the sake of your children. The transition will be easiest if both parents can agree on a similar set of rules that operate in both homes. They do not have to be identical, but the closer they are, the easier the move will be between homes. For example, common bedtimes and curfews, similar chores, table manners, appropriate and inappropriate language, and limits on TV time are rules that can easily be the same in both homes.

Third, be consistent in meeting your obligations. The party who is required to pay child support should be diligent in this responsibility. Not only will this help meet the child's needs, but it will also ease tensions with a former spouse. Also, set visitation times and keep them. Young children are especially vulnerable when it comes to visitation. Their understanding of time is very limited and the time from one Friday to the next can seem like an eternity. They expect Dad or Mom to be there at the scheduled visitation time. Missing one weekend may not seem like much for a parent, but to a child it is a lifetime. If the parent cancels or simply doesn't show up, the child's view of the world as a safe and predictable place will be compromised. If a weekly or daily phone call is promised, make it. Don't make promises you can't or don't intend to keep.

Finally, especially if you are the parent who does not have custody, avoid the temptation to "make it up" to your child by buying his or her approval through failure to discipline or with presents. Children are shrewd. They know how to take advantage of a parent and they will. Stick to your clearly defined rules. You will be tempted to let the rules slide because you think, "I see my child only two days a week and I don't want to spend my time fighting." However, you are still a parent and some discontent is part of the job. Presents are OK, but don't use them as substitutes for your presence—*presence is more important than presents.* The best present you can give is your time and a consistent, stable home life.

Pacifiers and Security Blankets

Pacifiers, security blankets, a soft piece of cloth, dolls, and stuffed animals all provide children with a sense of comfort and security. Children need reassurance and they soon discover they can find it in a familiar item. The world is frightening and unpredictable and these security items provide a sense of stability to a child.

We never outgrow the need for security. The things that give us security simply change in form. Grade school children are more apt to find security in a hug or comforting word than in a stuffed animal. Teenagers are more likely to find comfort in peer group acceptance. Adults do not carry security blankets, but we find comfort in relationships. Our car, our home, or even a favorite chair may provide us with a sense of security. We seek the familiar when we are afraid, lonely, or unsure of ourselves.

Children are rarely in control of their environment. When confronted with strange sounds, strange people, strange places, and other unfamiliar circumstances, children learn to cope through the familiar smell and feel of a well-worn T-shirt or blanket, the familiar feel of a pacifier, or the comforting weight of a favorite doll. (See also "Pacifiers and Security Blankets" in chapter 5.)

When Should a Child Abandon a Security Blanket?

Pacifiers can cause dental problems in older children and you should consult your dentist for a recommendation regarding when your child should give up the pacifier. However, with the exception of pacifiers, most security blankets are more of a social problem than a psychological or physical one. As children get older, they may be subjected to teasing or ridicule for carrying a security blanket or stuffed animal into social settings where the item is socially unacceptable. Don't rush your child to surrender his security item. Even though a child may keep a security blanket longer than the parent would like, he will eventually give it up on his own. There are not many adults still toting a pacifier or stuffed animal to work.

If you want to find out if your child is ready to surrender a security item, such as a pacifier, simply put it away. When the child asks for it, tell him he is big enough that he doesn't need it anymore. You can expect some resistance at first, but after a day or two, the child should get used to the idea that the pacifier is no longer available. Substitute another security item, especially at bedtime, if it helps the child adjust. A favorite toy or a stuffed animal can be a good substitute. If the child continues to ask for the item for several days and makes life miserable for mom and dad, give it back. He wasn't ready. Most children are ready to give up their pacifiers somewhere around two years of age. Depriving a child of his or her security blanket usually won't cause long-term problems, but if the child is not ready to give it up, he or she can certainly make your life difficult for several days. If you withdraw the security item too early, something will take its place. A potential drawback to removing a pacifier too early is that a child may take up thumb-sucking. This is a bad trade. You can also expect more reliance on security objects when the child's world is unsettled because of trauma, divorce, a move, or family disruption.

There is no magic age when children should no longer have their favorite blanket in bed with them or their favorite stuffed animal on a trip. In fact, many college-age young people still sleep with a teddy bear or favorite childhood toy. As a general rule, if it isn't harmful to the child physically, let it go until the child is ready to give it up.

Play

Play is an important part not only of child development but also of healthy living even for adults. The way we play changes from our early years, through school age, and eventually into adulthood, but it remains important at all stages of life. In infancy, when children first begin to play, they can entertain themselves for a few minutes at a time with a mobile, a rattle, or a similar object, but they will not play for an extended length of time unless they are engaged with an adult. As they reach toddlerhood, children engage in make-believe play, a type that predominates their playtime throughout early childhood. During these first few years, children will play side by side with another child, but they will not cooperate in a game or activity with that other child. Playing side by side is called *parallel play*. Most two- and three-year-old children prefer to play with an adult, but the adult must follow the child's interest. When young children try to play together, called *cooperative play*, they are quickly distracted by dissimilar interests, and fighting over toys is almost a certainty. By age three children will begin to play alone for longer periods of time, called *solitary play*, and as they reach four years of age, they engage in cooperative play with other children their own age. *Onlooker play* occurs when children watch others engaged in an activity but do not participate. It is not unusual for a shy child to engage frequently in onlooker play, but as the child gets older, this type of play will fade. Fantasy and pretend play is common in childhood and children tend to mimic things they see and know from the real world. You can learn a lot about what your child thinks about people and things in her environment by watching her fantasy play.

Young children need lots of time to play—one of the problems with organized day care. Even though play is included in such programs, a child does not have nearly as much freedom to move from one activity to another as he would if he were cared for at home. Naps, meals, and even playtime are structured and may not adequately meet the child's personal needs. Play helps children develop social skills and coping skills, it assists them in their physical development, and it helps them practice necessary life skills. Unless the child's play is dangerous, causes him to miss meals, or comes at the expense of needed rest, prior to age five children can't play too much.

SUMMARY

The years between ages three and five are my favorites. I prefer therapy with children this age and I am continually fascinated by the many changes and the broad range of abilities that I see in children during these years. During these years you will see your child grow from a toddler to a child stepping on the school bus for his first day of kindergarten. He will develop some mastery of language and he will go from playing by himself to regularly cooperating with playmates in games and activities. These are incredibly important years for the development of esteem, cognition, and a love for books and learning, and for developing a secure worldview. As much work as these years are for parents, they are perhaps the most rewarding.

CHAPTER 7

New Experiences:
Early Childhood (Ages 5–8)

Give me a child for the first seven years, and you may do what you like with him after.

—Anonymous

I love children's literature. For nearly a decade I have read to grade school children once a week. Stories about alligators searching for their mothers, green eggs and ham, an aardvark moving to a new neighborhood, a bear chasing a boy up a tree, and many other stories have made us laugh together and sometimes have provoked our thinking. Reading is one of the most important skills that children need to master in their academic careers, and a love for books helps draw them into the world of words. The most important thing a kindergarten teacher can do for children who are just beginning their formal education is to teach them to love learning. Teaching a love for learning involves reading, experimenting, and exploring. When children start formal schooling, their schedules change dramatically. They are no longer free to play anytime they choose and they are thrust, perhaps for the first time, into a setting where they must share toys and regularly interact with other children. It is an exciting time, but this transition is difficult for some children.

Each month during the years between age fives and eight, you will see differences in your child. He will grow several inches, gain weight, and begin losing his babyish appearance. His cognitive and social skills will improve dramatically during these years. His IQ will become a reliable measure by the end of this stage, his personality will be clearly defined, and his strengths and weaknesses (both social and cognitive) will be observable and measurable. These are but a few of the dramatic changes that you will see in the years between five and eight. This chapter addresses not only the social, cognitive, physical, and emotional development of children in early childhood, but also the many questions that surround the educational experience of young children.

THINKING

Between the ages of five and eight many obvious changes take place in your child and how he thinks. You will see a greater ability to follow directions as well as improved skills when it comes to solving problems. Your child will improve his understanding of distance and time. Also, your child will find it much easier to recognize the difference between real and make-believe. Even though appearances are always important, by first or second grade your child will understand that things are not living just because they move (*animism*). You will want to continue to encourage your child's natural creativity during this stage as she draws pictures, makes up stories and games, and tells you about her wishes and thoughts of the future. The significant events in your child's cognitive development during these years that are discussed below are mental operations, language skills, intelligence and testing, learning disabilities, and memory.

Mental Operations

Mental operations refer to a child's ability to manipulate ideas in his head. Prior to puberty, mental operations are very limited because children have difficulty thinking in abstract terms. Their thoughts are largely limited to what they can experience with one or more of their five senses. Even though their ability to think abstractly is limited, they develop several cognitive skills between the ages of five and eight. Among these skills are class inclusion, seriation, decentration, and conservation.

Class Inclusion

A class is a category in which an item can be classified. For example, dogs can be classified as animals. Before age seven or eight, a child cannot recognize that something can be a part of two classes at one time. For example, children can be classified by gender (boy or girl), but they also can be classified as people. When my son was five years old I was standing in a line with him and his classmates at school. Of the 15 children in his class, 9 were boys and 6 were girls. "We have more boys than girls," he told me. "Are there more boys or more people?" I asked him, testing for his ability to recognize that both boys and girls were also included in the class "people." As I expected, he replied, "There are more boys." However, by age seven or eight, he will readily classify objects in multiple classes and will no longer make this kind of mistake.

Class inclusion is an important part of organizing the world. Most things in life belong to many different classes. In fact, it is an understanding of class inclusion that helps a child understand seeming contradictions. For example, I am a therapist, a college professor, a writer, and a public speaker, as well as a dad, a son, a brother, and a husband. When my children were too young to understand class inclusion, they could not understand how I could be more than one thing at once. As they developed this skill, they were capable of understanding more clearly the nature of my work. The more a child understands classes and the objects that are included in them, the more efficient he will be in organizing his world. Most children will have acquired this skill between the ages of seven and ten.

Seriation

Seriation refers to the ability to organize objects in a series, such as biggest to smallest and vice versa. This skill develops around age six or seven, just prior to the ability to classify. Before this age, children can perform some organization based on size, but their efforts are ineffective and haphazard.

Decentration

As I discussed in the previous chapter, preschool children cannot focus on more than one item at a time. This is called centration. For example, when my older daughter was three, my wife and I were trying to decide how to tell her that we were expecting a second child. We realized we were sweating over nothing one Sunday morning as my daughter was dressing for church. I went into her room as she tried to get her clothes together and said, "Would you like to have a little brother or sister?" She looked thoughtful for a moment and then said, "No. I just need some socks." She was focused (centrated) on the task of dressing and could not think about the meaning of my words at the same time.

As children approach preadolescence, they greatly improve their ability to focus on numerous variables at the same time. Unlike a younger sibling, for example, who would describe a person based on a single feature (hair color, a piece of clothing, or gender), children who are seven or eight years of age can provide several descriptors of a person or place. At age five, a child who has misplaced an object will look in only one spot before complaining that she cannot find the object. Centration causes her to focus on only one variable—looking in the chosen spot for her lost item. By age eight, she can easily think about the fact that the lost item could be in many places. Therefore, she will look in several places, moving methodically from one spot to the next, before giving up.

Conservation

As discussed in the previous chapter, prior to age eight, children do not understand that as things change in their appearance. they do not necessarily change in their volume, mass, or number. At age five, if a child has five crayons and you place them together on the table and then, as the child watches, spread the same five crayons out across the table, he will think he now has more crayons. Appearances matter. Yet by eight years of age, children should have achieved conservation skills. (See chapter 6 for more information on conservation.)

Conservation develops in conjunction with the ability to manipulate objects in one's mind—called *mental rotations*. Mental rotations address the fact that one can see an object in her mind and then think about what that object would look like if it were rotated in various directions. This skill is critical for many types of problem solving. Shape-o toys for toddlers are round plastic balls that have openings of various shapes arrayed across the surface—a square, circle, oval, triangle, cross, star, and so forth. There are plastic shapes that match the various openings. When a proper piece is fitted to the correct opening, the piece falls inside the Shape-o toy. Toddlers will try to force pieces into openings where they obviously do not fit. Their success at matching pieces with the appropriate opening is random. As a child learns mental rotations, he not only can recognize the shape that matches the opening, but he also can figure out which way he needs to turn the piece so that it will fit. This same skill applies to correctly locating and connecting pieces in jigsaw puzzles. Therefore, as children develop their abilities to rotate objects in their minds, they can solve more complex jigsaw puzzles with more pieces than they could at a previous stage of development.

Language

The ability to use language continues to improve as a child moves through the elementary school years. By age six, children have an average of 10,000 vocabulary words available to them and if they live in a bilingual environment, they can easily distinguish between words of their native tongue and words of the second language. In fact, the grade school years are ideal for children to begin learning a second language.

Not only can five-year-old children speak more clearly than they could earlier, but they also can begin to read printed words. By the end of kindergarten, assuming they have been trained to read sight words (words that one learns using flashcards or some other rote process), children should be able to read several small words, their names, and maybe even some larger words if they are repeatedly exposed to them (names of siblings, words in favorite books, etc.). By the end of the second grade, children can read between 500 and 1,000 words and by age eight, they can read several thousand words. Literacy is one of the most important cognitive skills in a Western culture. By the end of your child's school career, he will have taken many standardized tests. If your child is in public school, in the third grade he will most likely take his first intelligence test, he will take competency tests in each grade, and in high school he will take the Scholastic Achievement Test (SAT). Literacy, specifically vocabulary, is directly related to success on these instruments. Encouraging reading, limiting time in front of the television and computer, and reading to your child are ways you can help your child become a better reader and improve his or her vocabulary.

Intelligence

One of the most elusive issues in psychology is intelligence. For decades psychologists have tried to identify what intelligence is and to find a way to measure it. Today there are dozens of ways to talk about intelligence and hundreds of ways to measure it, but the validity of those definitions and measures remains the focus of extensive debate. Intelligence is sometimes referred to as IQ, taking its name from a mathematical quantity known as the intelligence quotient. IQ is calculated by dividing one's chronological age (the child's age at the time of testing) into one's mental age (as measured by a standardized test). This quotient is then multiplied by 100. Mathematically it is represented as $IQ = MA/CA \times 100$. (Interesting fact: The only reason we multiply by 100 is to make the number bigger and to get rid of decimals. Who wants an IQ of 1.2?) On many measures, an average IQ is 100 and the range of normal IQ is between approximately 70 and 130, although most people (about 68 percent) have an IQ score between 90 and 110. Yet this is only one way to evaluate intelligence. Some theorists argue that traditional intelligence tests measure only one or two areas of intelligence (vocabulary and math). To compensate, they have created measures of intelligence that address more than just language and math skills. Howard Gardner's multiple intelligence measures, for example, include eight different measures: linguistic, logicomathematical, musical, spatial, bodily-kinesthetic, naturalistic, interpersonal, and intrapersonal intelligence.

Regardless of how it is measured, intelligence is fluid until around age eight. Any measures prior to that age do not necessarily reflect intelligence measures in adolescence or adulthood. Therefore, I discourage parents from pursuing intelligence testing until third grade or later unless some evidence of exceptionality is obvious. After age eight, IQ stabilizes and remains about the same throughout the rest of one's life.

With standard IQ scores, giftedness begins around an IQ of 125 or 130, and an IQ of 70 or less is considered mental retardation. Even when one is considered mentally retarded, there are many variations of retardation. With mild retardation, a child can learn to function, eventually marry, hold a job, and even bear children with normal IQ. Yet, as mentioned above, most intelligence tests measure verbal ability, spatial ability, and mathematical skills. While IQ scores are often correlated with academic success, financial success, and happiness, there is clearly no direct cause-and-effect relationship. Low scores do not guarantee failure and exceptional IQ scores do not guarantee success. Therefore, if your child is measured below normal, don't suppose that his future is set. Many times I have worked with both children and adults who were thought to be mentally retarded but who overcame their deficits in many ways. I also have worked with children who have lived down to their parents' expectations because of test scores. During my career as a college professor, I have had several students of genius IQ (140+) who flunked out of college. Regardless of IQ measures, work with your children where they are, challenge them without defeating them, and when in doubt, seek professional assistance. You should never require more of your child than he or she is capable of delivering and neither should you accept less than he or she is capable of accomplishing.

Learning Disabilities

By the time children start school, they are regularly tested on a variety of measures—language, speech, and so forth. Likewise, based on teacher observations, extra testing is sometimes suggested if the teacher suspects a learning disability or other problem that may inhibit the child's success in school. For many children, if their difficulties are addressed early in their development and early in their educational careers, the problems are easier to address than if they are treated later and they also have a far better chance of succeeding in their academic and social lives. However, inappropriate testing and mistaken evaluations can incorrectly label a child, place him or her in a corrective program when it is unnecessary, and have a long-term detrimental effect on the child. To avoid these problems, ensure that any evaluation of your child is made by a qualified examiner. While pediatricians, teachers, and school administrators may have ample experience dealing with attention deficit disorder, behavior disorders, and learning disabilities, their experience alone does not qualify them to diagnose these disorders. Many behaviors can mimic symptoms of these disorders and misdiagnosis is not uncommon. When that happens, not only is the child treated for a problem he does not have, but the real problem is not addressed.

School counselors, child therapists, and clinical social workers are usually trained to make these diagnoses. Pediatricians and other professionals who deal with children also can receive training that qualifies them to make these diagnoses, but you should not assume that because a pediatrician understands your child's physiology and development, she is qualified to make psychological evaluations. You should not accept the diagnosis and/or intervention plan of any untrained person as definitive in regard to your child. If in doubt, seek a second opinion from a trained and experienced child therapist or a child psychologist to confirm that the diagnosis you have received is correct and that the treatment plan is appropriate.

Memory

A child's memory abilities improve dramatically between kindergarten and third grade. At age five, most children have minimal strategies for remembering. When asked to remember something, they recall most effectively if they can see or touch the thing they are supposed to remember. For example, one study showed that when children were asked to remember which cup in a series of three a rubber ball was placed under, they could remember best if they touched the cup that had the ball under it. Many kindergarten teachers help children remember to walk quietly in the hallways by having them place their finger to their lips. Like their younger counterparts, five-year-old children will not recall several directions given at once, but by age eight they should be able to do this effectively. Memory skills improve as one moves away from rote rehearsal (the memory strategy that involves simple repetition) and toward memory organization and elaboration. These latter skills involve giving meaning to things to be remembered and deliberately organizing those memories. This skill is present by age eight and will improve with practice. Many college students rely on rote memory when studying for exams because they have never been taught more effective ways to retain information. Children who are taught memory skills, even at age five, perform better on memory tasks than children who must find their own strategies, but even then, unless they are reminded to use the strategies they are taught, they will forget to use them. Be patient with your child and teach him how to remember things, at the same time remembering his memory limitations.

FEELING

Between the ages of five and eight your child will learn to read facial cues, thus helping her to interpret the feelings and thoughts of other people, and she will begin to attribute meaning to the behaviors that she sees in other people. Those attributions will often be incorrect, but as she learns to consider facial and behavioral cues in varied contexts, she will continue to improve her ability to make hypotheses about motives for the behavior of others. She will refine her abilities to take someone else's perspective and she will improve her coping skills, which in turn will help her refine her problem-solving strategies. Each year during this four-year span of time, you will notice a difference in these areas.

In the following sections I will address a child's need to feel productive, his fears and how to deal with them, and the effects of divorce on a child during this stage of development. I will also address television and video games, mental illness, normal and abnormal childhood problems, and moral development.

Productivity

Between the ages of three and five, children are concerned about thinking up ideas on their own—a concept known as *initiative*. Between ages five or six and continuing until puberty, children not only want to think up their own ideas, they also want to want to be good at what they do—a concept known as *industry*. Prior to the industry stage of development, when your child colors a picture for you or makes a Play Dough creation, she will be satisfied with brief praise. During the industry stage, however, children will make sure to point out several important characteristics of their drawing or creation. "Did you notice the people's faces in the airplane window?" a child might ask his mother as she looks at his drawing. "See how I drew Daddy's truck and put the dog in the back?" Details matter because these children not only have created something, they have endeavored to do it well. A child who cleans her room will make sure you notice that she swept under the bed and straightened her sock drawer.

Prior to this stage of life, children will color a picture with a single crayon, but between the ages of five and eight, they will work very hard to stay within the lines of a coloring book and will use many different colors as they perfect their drawings. Even when they are toddlers, it is always good to comment on something specific in what your child does. This lets your child know that you have seen what they have done. But during the industry stage, it is especially important to praise the details of what your child does. This encourages the child's focus on details and lets her know that details matter. Perhaps equally important is the fact that the same details that matter to her are also important to you. This builds esteem.

Fear

By age five, most children are afraid of the dark. They may also be afraid of being left alone, afraid of monsters, and afraid of being eaten by wild animals. These are all fears spawned by imagination and often are unrealistic. By age eight, your child's fears will become more realistic—fear of disease, nuclear war, or burglars. On September 11, 2001, terrorists attacked innocent men, women, and children in our country, using civilian airliners to do their cowardly dirty work. Around the country, all of us were forced to face our own fears in regard to this horrible event. Repeatedly, the news replayed the images of planes crashing into buildings, buildings in flames, and the World Trade Center towers collapsing in New York. Witnessing these events was traumatizing to adults and even more so to children, who had no context within which to place these events.

Whether it is an event of the magnitude of September 11 or more mundane daily news, preschool children should be shielded from events and images that feed their fears. They do not have the skills to cope effectively with the fears such images and stories produce. Through pubescence, children think that bad things happening somewhere in the world could easily befall them. For example, it was not uncommon after the September 11 attacks for children to believe that Osama bin Laden knew their names and was coming after them. When I was eight, Charles Manson and his minions were convicted of murdering several people in California. By the time I heard his name, Manson and several followers were already in jail and on trial. We lived in the Midwest, miles from California, but I clearly recall lying in bed fearing that this evil man would climb in my bedroom window and kill me.

Address Fears on the Basis of Age

Children younger than five or six should be shielded from television footage and should not be involved in discussions about terrorism, plane crashes, war, murder, and rape. They are too young to process the information or to understand cause-and-effect relationships. If they see images of planes crashing or buildings falling—if they hear parents or news anchors talking about a terrorist who wants to kill Americans—children at this age will assume planes will crash into "their" building and that terrorists are hunting for them personally. Just as you cannot convince a young child that there are no monsters in the closet, once a child begins fearing plane crashes and terrorists (or Charles Manson), it will be very hard to comfort him or her. Preventing exposure to those issues can save both child and parent a lot of anguish. For young children who have been exposed to these fears already and who are exhibiting fear responses, parents will need to spend extra hours with them—not only consoling and reassuring them, but also snuggling, reading together, and just being together. For children of this age, their primary sense of security is in the parent-child bond. The stronger that bond, the better a young child can cope with fear. Extra time together can strengthen that bond and ease their fears.

Some information may be necessary, especially for children who are in grades one through five. Even if you shelter your children from world events, they will hear rumors and gossip from their friends. What is worse, the gossip they hear will most likely be significantly distorted. Therefore, parents of children of this age should proactively discuss the events with their children, providing basic facts about what is happening. Address questions about these frightening issues with children of this age as you would address questions about sex—just the basic facts and just enough to satisfy their curiosity. Do not lie to them about events, but do not volunteer too much information, either. Children of this age need to be reassured that they are going to be OK and that you will protect them. When fear and anxiety arise, provide reassurance and information.

Children who are middle school age or older need to be well informed. Parents should talk to their middle and high school children openly about the violence and frightening things that are a part of our world. These children need to be comforted as best you can, but by this age they must begin to learn to deal with the realistic fears that are part of life. These events are an opportunity to address the facts with your child, as well as for parents to teach a life skill—coping with stress.

Family group discussions can be productive as long as very young children are not present. Family members can express thoughts, fears, and anxieties as well as share strategies for dealing with discomforts that arise from frightening experiences. Parents can act as moderators and leaders directing the discussion, but they also can participate. This demonstrates to children that we all have fears and worries. Your children will learn that life is not about the removal of all fear and anxiety, but effectively coping with fear and anxiety. Once again, however, it is important that young children not be exposed to a "frightened parent."

For families who are involved in religious practices, a discussion of how one's faith can help overcome one's fears or concerns can be very helpful. Reading from holy literature as it pertains to specific concerns can be very comforting to those within a given faith if the references are not too abstract. For example, in the holy writings of Protestants, Catholics, and Jews, Psalm 46 directly and concretely addresses why the believer should not fear wars, tragedies, and disasters such as the terrorist attacks on our country in September 2001.

Discussions within the family, whether as a group or in parent-child dyads, keep the lines of communication open and let children know that it is acceptable to talk about their concerns. Many parents are afraid to talk about a subject because they don't want to upset the child. However, the child interprets the awkwardness and silence as an indication that talking is not acceptable. You should provide opportunity for your child to talk about his or her thoughts.

Watch for Symptoms

Many children deal with traumatic events like the tragedy of September 11 and similar frightening events with minimal difficulty. There will be some, however, who will need professional intervention. It has been clearly documented that observers of a tragedy can easily suffer post-traumatic stress disorder (PTSD) symptoms just as if they had experienced it in person. Watch for the following symptoms: school problems, anger, sleep disturbances, bedwetting, difficulty eating, mood swings, numbness, avoidance of the topic that caused the fear response, diminished interest in normally pleasurable activities, difficultly concentrating, or a sense of foreshortened future. Many of these symptoms directly reflect the *DSM-IV-TR* diagnostic criteria for PTSD.

Watch for the appearance of the event in your child's drawings and play. Should the event show up in these media, use it as a catalyst for conversation and save the drawings. They could provide valuable diagnostic information to a therapist if you choose to take your child to a professional counselor.

Learning to cope with fear is one of life's necessary skills. Parents should talk openly with their children about the things that frighten their children and reassure them as much as is truthfully possible without providing too much detail. Most fears of children between the ages of five and eight are unlikely to befall them and it is easy for a parent to reassure children that they don't need to worry.

Fear vs. Terror

Sometimes a child's fears inhibit his ability to function normally. For example, by four or five years of age, children occasionally find it difficult to go to sleep because of their normal nighttime fears. Parents struggle with the frustrations getting their children to deal with the fears and their own irritation with a child who repeatedly gets up because he is afraid. Whether to force the child to stay in bed is, in part, based on the difference between fear and terror. All children have fears and they must learn to deal with them. They also need their sleep. Therefore, after doing your best to help ease her fears, it is necessary to force the child to stay in bed and deal with the fear. Over time, children will learn to cope with their irrational fears. Terror, on the other hand, is not normal and won't go away on its own. Terror is often the result of a traumatic experience. That experience can be a personal one (for example, being in a car accident or experiencing a burglary at home), or it can be the result of exposure to someone else's trauma. Television and movies are a likely source of the latter. I am amazed when I attend a scary movie and I look around the theater and see young children in the audience. I'm glad I don't have to be the one to help them get to sleep at night. Horror movies are never appropriate for young children for obvious reasons, but even movies that might seem entertaining to children can create terror. The mother of a six-year-old child brought him to me because he was terrified anytime there was a storm. In such a situation, especially if they were outside, he became hysterical and she found it nearly impossible to calm him. In the process of therapy, I discovered that he and his father had regularly watched a videotape of the movie *Twister*. In this movie, a tornado sucks a father out of a storm cellar and storms threaten the movie's characters from beginning to end. Storms terrified this child because he saw what they could do to him. Like most children his age, he reasoned that a tornado was after him, trying to kill him.

When a child is terrified, parental comfort and reassurance are necessary. Snuggles, patience, and working through the terror together are imperative. If your children are terrified in the night, for example, you might let them sleep with you for the night. Extreme and ongoing terror may require therapy or even medication. Most terror, however, can be prevented by shielding your child from terror-inducing stimuli in the environment (for example, the news, scary movies, television shows, and books).

Divorce

Divorce is hard on everyone. Even in the most amicable divorce, the pain of a lost relationship and anxieties associated with starting a new life are overwhelming. Children, especially, are adversely affected by divorce. Given their egocentric worldview, they assume not only that they must have done something to cause the divorce, but that if they are good enough or if they work hard enough, they can fix the relationship and get mom and dad back together. The research on children of divorce indicates that not only is it difficult for them to recover from the trauma of the divorce, but in some cases the symptoms get worse as the children get older.

There are cases where divorce or at least separation is advisable. In cases of abuse (spousal abuse, child sexual abuse, significant marital turmoil, or child physical abuse or neglect), divorce may be the lesser of two evils. Many divorces, however, are the result of disagreements and personality conflicts rather than serious issues that compromise the health, safety, and well-being of children in the family. If or when difficulties arise, a couple should weather the storm as long as possible for the sake of the children.

Television and Aggression

Children love to watch television and to play with personal game devices and computer games. None of these objects are bad in and of themselves. Problems arise with one's choice of programming or when children spend too much time with game devices or in front of the TV. Study after study has indicated that children, especially those who are already aggressive, become more aggressive when they are exposed to aggressive models (for example, television and video games). There are plenty of innocuous computer games and television programs to choose from without having to resort to violent and aggressive programming. Even better, there are many educational and productive television shows and every day new computer games are developed that help children with their reading, math, geography, and history skills. Since these forms of programming are available, there is no reason to resort to mindless and violent television programs, movies, and video games. They serve no purpose and the research is reasonably clear that such programming can easily lead to violent behavior.

Mental Illness in Childhood

It may seem odd to think about children as being mentally ill, but it happens. There are many mental disruptions that are not uncommon in children—obsessive-compulsive disorder (OCD), depression, oppositional defiance disorder (ODD), learning disabilities, behavior disorders, Asperger's syndrome, and attention deficit/hyperactivity disorder (ADHD), to name just a few. Diagnosing and treating mental disorders in childhood not only helps the child function better at home and at school but also can make one's job as a parent easier. A counselor, therapist, or psychologist can be an invaluable ally for the parent of a child with a mental illness.

Problems of Diagnosis

As I discussed in the section on learning disabilities, clinical diagnosis of disorders requires experience and training. Unfortunately, diagnoses often come from unqualified individuals. Non–mental health professionals (for example, teachers) who work with children may assume that since they have seen many cases of one disorder or another, or because they have had some experience with the process of diagnosing disorders, they are qualified to make such evaluations. This logic is as flawed as if I were to make a medical diagnosis just because I have repeatedly seen a particular medical condition. Even within the field of mental health, therapists who do not routinely work with children can fail to consider the many nuances that affect the diagnostic process. Development, chronological age, social environment, cultural context, family constellation, and the broad range of behaviors among children are only a few of the things that are involved in the diagnosis and treatment of childhood mental disorders. It is often difficult to apply the diagnostic criteria in the *DSM IV-TR* (*Diagnostic and Statistical Manual,* 4th edition–text revision), the manual most often used to diagnose mental illness, to children. As with any diagnosis, whether of a psychological or a physiological condition, it is wise to seek a second opinion, even when you have confidence in the professional making the assessment. Many times I have worked with children who have had four or five different diagnoses over a short period of time. Therapy had been unsuccessful because the respective therapists were treating the wrong problems. Proper diagnosis is possible when qualified clinicians carefully examine the child, and with proper diagnosis the establishment of an intervention plan can lead to problem management or recovery.

Normal Childhood Problems

There are a host of behaviors that are not uncommon in children. Fear of specific environments, especially the dark, and fear of strangers as well as large animals are not unusual. Especially shy children may be clingy and you may find it difficult to get such a child to try new things. Clinginess should wane as the child approaches age seven or eight and as he or she is exposed to more environments that require separation from the primary caregiver. School anxiety is not uncommon. Some children fear the unknown of new situations like starting school, and they are unsure of how they will be received by their peers and teachers. Children going into kindergarten who have not been exposed to structured environments or who have not been in preschool may be especially anxious. Even though most children eventually accommodate to school, some are so stressed by the setting that parents are forced either to homeschool the child or to hold the child out of school and wait for the following year to start kindergarten. Most parents do not want their child to be a year behind, but sometimes this is an option that is most beneficial to the child.

It is not unusual for children in their early years to walk, talk, and move around in their sleep. Crying out in the night is not unusual. It is not normal, however, for these sleep disturbances to lead to a lack of sleep. Even though they may seem to rest poorly, children rarely remember their bad dreams or other sleep disturbances.

Finally, it is not unusual for children to regress to earlier behaviors. Children of age five and six are more prone to do this than older children. The presence of a new sibling can easily trigger regressive behaviors as the older child recognizes that the sibling is receiving attention for those behaviors. Baby talk, thumb-sucking, and whining are some regressive behaviors that you might see.

Abnormal Childhood Problems

There are many problems that are abnormal in children, including autism, eating disorders, and speech problems. Not every child who exhibits these problems needs long-term therapy. Some types of problems can be corrected within just four or five visits. Parents must recognize, however, that early intervention is often the key to interrupting these disorders and helping the child productively cope with and compensate for the problems that created the symptoms in the first place. Waiting for intervention is usually not helpful and, in fact, may lead to other problems. For example, a child who has a physical problem that leads to loss of bladder control may then exhibit humiliation at the inability to maintain bladder control in front of friends. This humiliation can lead to other emotional problems that would never have been an issue if the physical problem had been addressed quickly.

There are very few behaviors that are nearly always considered abnormal with children. Three specific behaviors always give me pause when I evaluate a child: cruelty to animals, fire setting, and bladder control problems.

I discussed these issues, called the terrible triad, in the previous chapter. (For more information, see chapter 6.)

Moral Development

Around the time your child turns two, she begins developing a rudimentary sense of morality—right and wrong. Adults tend to think of morality in relationship to religious teachings; however, developmental morality is different from religious beliefs, although it can be related to one's religion. Prior to age nine or ten, children are incapable of understanding the abstract nature of religion. Their ideas about right and wrong are based on sets of rules. These rules change as the child matures. Rules are established by parents, sometimes based on religious background but also based on the parents' beliefs about what is acceptable and what is not. In early childhood, children cannot distinguish the difference between a religious taboo and something that "we just don't do" in the home. For example, in many homes, smoking may be prohibited and children may be taught the dangers of smoking. In these homes, young children interpret smoking in the same way they interpret behaviors like hitting or using profanity—it is "sinful" (although they would not use this term). Even though smoking is usually considered a social taboo rather than a religious taboo, children make no distinction between the two.

Starting at age two, children are able to understand that there are things they are expected to do and things they should not do. One of the first words they learn is "no." When a child uses the word "no" correctly, she is demonstrating intent. She knows what is expected and is intentionally defying that expectation. What is right or wrong at this early stage of development is based completely on whether or not one gets into trouble for doing the thing in question. If one does not get into trouble or get caught at the behavior, it is acceptable. (I find it fascinating that many adults operate on this same immature belief system.) At age five or six, children are concerned with how others perceive them. Being perceived as a good child is closely related to one's view of morality. Therefore, at this age, not only do some children still relate morality to getting into trouble, they also begin to believe that something is morally wrong if people will be mad at you if you do it. If you can do something and others will not be angry, or if they will be pleased with you for doing it, then the behavior is "morally" acceptable. For example, if a child's friends like him better because he steals candy and shares it with them, stealing in this context is not as bad as other forms of stealing.

By age eight, however, children move into yet another stage of moral decision making—morality that is based on a fixed set of rules. In other words, for children between eight and ten, something is wrong if it is against the rules—period. These children tend to be legalistic and they are incapable of understanding the many nuances that accompany judging a wrongdoer and deciding punishment. Nearly all children under age ten will be frustrated if they see someone getting away with something that they recognize as wrong. For this reason, tattling is common.

Fair?

The meaning of the word "fair" changes as we get older. Well into their elementary school years, children believe that fair means total equality; this is especially true at ages five and six. If you get ten jelly beans, it is only fair that I get ten jelly beans, too. Between the ages of six and seven, children shift their attention to what they earn. They believe that "fair" is related to merit and how hard they work. Therefore, they will get upset with you if they think they worked harder at something than a sibling, yet both they and their sibling receive the same reward.

Fairness as children understand it is difficult to apply and sometimes it is best if parents do not try to be "fair" in the sense of equality. Older children, for example, may argue that it is not fair that their younger siblings get away with something that they can't (for example, a small tantrum). Yet what the older child doesn't recognize is that because she is older, there is a different set of expectations. Younger children may argue that it is not fair that an older sibling gets to stay up later than they do. Again, there are different needs because of the children's ages. Fairness is not as important as meeting the child's needs. My elder daughter has always been very good at getting up in the morning. Therefore, as she got older, we allowed her to choose her own bedtime. My second child has never been good at getting up early and it took her forever to prepare for school when she was in early elementary school. Therefore, even though my eldest child was allowed to stay up until a certain hour when she was in third grade, my second child did not have that privilege until later because she had not earned it based on her behavior. As a parent, I tried to be fair by considering their developmental ages and their levels of responsibility, and by meeting their needs instead of making sure they always were treated exactly the same way.

DOING

During their grade school years, children grow between two and three inches per year and gain between three and six pounds each year. Their average weight at age six is 45 pounds and their average height is 3.5 feet.

Girls remain smaller than boys until age nine. Both their fine and gross motor skills refine as they approach preadolescence. By age six, most children can hop on one foot, throw and catch, ride a bike, and skip, and they can begin to use a table knife. Unlike three-year-olds, who grip a pencil or pen in their fist, grade school–age children can hold a pencil as an adult does.

Accidents are among the most common physical injuries to children in this age group. Children should always use seat belts while riding in a vehicle and they should always wear a helmet and knee pads while riding bicycles, rollerskating, and skateboarding. Head injuries due to falls from bicycles, roller skates, and so forth can cause permanent brain damage or even death, and are almost totally preventable by wearing a helmet.

In the United States, obesity is a major problem with children. The two most significant causes of obesity in children are poor diet and lack of exercise. The widespread acceptance of home video games, cable and satellite television, and personal computers has exacerbated the problem. Children spend time on a couch or sitting in their rooms instead of playing outside, running, or riding a bicycle. Electronic devices have their place, but when they substitute for exercise, they are destructive and they promote a lethargic and sedentary lifestyle. Parents should place daily time limits on a child's use of any of these devices and they should also carefully monitor their child's diet. Nutritional needs for a child are perhaps even more important than in adulthood because vitamin deficiencies and other dietary deficits can lead to stunted growth, cognitive deficits, attention problems, and behavioral problems. Some of these problems are irreversible. This doesn't mean that children should never eat sweets, but it does mean that snacking between meals, when it substitutes for healthy mealtime foods, is a problem. Vary healthy snacks with sweets and carefully watch how much your children eat at mealtime. Snacks should not substitute for meals. If your children are hungry during the day, apples, carrots, and other healthy vegetables and fruits can be available to them.

Teeth

Between the ages of five and eight, your child will lose several teeth as his or her permanent teeth prepare to break the surface of the gums. Pulling teeth is frightening to children because they do not know what to expect. Don't try to pull teeth too soon or it can be painful, thus making cooperation from your child less likely when other teeth are ready to pull. On the other hand, when the tooth is attached only by gum tissue, it will be extremely loose and the child risks swallowing it. Using dental floss or thread looped around the tooth in a square knot is often all it takes to pull the tooth. Bleeding is not unusual, but rinsing in cold water for a few minutes should stop the bleeding. After pulling a tooth, the child should avoid abrasive foods (potato chips, hard candy, etc.) for about 24 hours. Consult with your pediatrician and/or pediatric dentist for professional guidance about tooth loss, pulling teeth, and potential need for orthodontic treatment.

The Tooth Fairy

Many parents are concerned about perpetuating fantasies such as the belief in Santa Claus, the Easter Bunny, and the Tooth Fairy. There is no research that demonstrates any negative effects in most children due to the belief in these fantasy characters. If you don't want your child to believe in these characters, don't participate in the fantasy games involving them, but you don't have to worry that it will harm your child. Some parents are concerned that if they play along with the fantasy, their children will not trust them when they discover that the characters do not exist. This is an unrealistic fear. On the contrary, knowing that the Tooth Fairy will bring a surprise during the night helps gain a reluctant child's cooperation while pulling a tooth. Do not push your children into these fantasies, but if they choose to believe in them, play along until they either express concern or question the existence of the character. In our home, we saved the teeth from each of our children in a small plastic bag in my bedroom dresser. When my younger daughter was seven, she still believed in the Tooth Fairy, but she stumbled across this bag of teeth. She asked me where those teeth came from if the Tooth Fairy took them. Instead of making up a lie to perpetuate the fantasy, I simply told her the truth. (She continued to believe in Santa Claus for two more years.)

Lateralization and Hand Preference

Handedness is most likely determined by genetics. Infants will begin to show preference for one hand over the other, but preference will not be clear until a child reaches five or six years of age. Handedness will become most obvious when a child is using a spoon or fork, or while drawing with a pencil or crayon. Even though there are disadvantages to being left-handed, there is nothing abnormal about left-handedness. There is absolutely no reason to force a child into a hand preference that is unnatural for her. Let the child pursue whichever hand preference she wants and provide appropriate equipment (school desk, ball glove, etc.) when handedness is solidified. Left-handedness is slightly correlated with learning disabilities, but it is also slightly correlated with giftedness. The major disadvantage to being left-handed is that most things are produced for people who are right-handed. Through-out life, left-handed people are forced either to find special equipment (guitars, golf clubs, etc.) or to learn to accommodate to right-handed equip-ment. Otherwise, there is little disadvantage to being left-handed.

Drawing Skills

Your child will make tremendous strides in his ability to draw between ages five and eight. At four or five years of age, when you child is asked to draw himself, he may draw a circle with stick-shaped arms and legs protruding from it. He likely will omit fingers and toes, and he may omit details such as ears, a torso, hair, and clothing. He may use only a single color when decorating the picture and he will make little attempt to color within the lines of his drawing. However, by age eight, his drawings will look completely different. His pictures will contain minute detail—fingers, toes, torso, hair, ears, eyes, eyelashes, and clothing. He will work very hard to color within the lines, will use multiple colors, and very likely will begin to use shading in his drawings.

Playtime

Like preschool children, children in elementary school need lots of playtime to exercise their bodies, practice social interaction, and develop their imaginations. A child's play changes between ages five and eight. Like their younger siblings, five-year-old children engage in fantasy play, but their cooperation, while better than that of children age three or younger, is still limited by their possessiveness, their inability to take another person's per-spective, and their inability to set aside their immediate wishes. Fighting with playmates is to be expected. By age eight, children engage in elaborate dra-matic and make-believe play. They give each other instructions about what to say and how to engage in their own made-up games and fantasies. At age eight, children can play together for two or three hours without serious conflict.

Guns and Aggressive Play

Boys are more aggressive than girls. While some of this difference is due to social factors (parents tend to excuse aggressive behavior in boys while condemning the same behavior in girls), there is no question that body chem-istry also plays a major role in this difference. Boys are more likely to hit, wrestle, and "pretend" fight. Even in homes where parents try to teach boys not to be aggressive and where weapons are not present, most boys will still be fascinated with weapons and "pretend" fighting. Whether or not to provide toy guns and swords is a parental choice, but when these toys are unavailable, boys will make their own pretend weapons. A parent should not suppose that avoiding toy guns will squelch aggressive play. Television programs, movies, and video games with aggressive themes will compound the aggression that is already a part of your male child's psyche. If you don't want your son mimicking the aggressive behavior he sees on TV and in the movies, don't expose him to those models.

Controlling aggression is one of the most important roles that fathers play in the lives of their sons. By wrestling with their sons, playing hard, and providing positive masculine models, they teach their sons that aggressiveness is inappropriate only when it is channeled inappropriately. Men who are physically abusive to their children and/or spouses not only model abusive behavior that will very likely be a part of their children's future relationships, they also are providing a dysfunctional model for their sons as to how adults express their aggressive drives that could easily be generalized to school, church, or any other environment in which the child is placed.

Choosing a Bedtime

When children start school, especially if they have not been in day care or preschool, they will be exhausted by the end of the day. Children ages five to eight need a minimum of eight to ten hours of sleep each night. You can let your child's behavior determine whether she needs more or less sleep. If your child gets up easily and isn't grumpy or falling asleep all day, then you have found the right time. If your child lies in bed for an hour without sleeping and gets up earlier than he has to, he may be going to bed to early.

Many children run at full speed, but when they lie down and are forced to be still for a few minutes, they immediately fall asleep. Children do not know how to prepare their minds and bodies for sleeping. You can help your child unwind from the activity of the day and prepare for bed by reading stories and helping your child relax before time for sleeping. These routines can condition your child's body to slow down and relax. Expect your child to lie awake when she is excited, when her routine has been interrupted, or when you have visitors. Bedtime is a bad time for tickling and wresting because your child will have difficulty transitioning from very active play to preparing for sleep. Do not worry if your child lies in bed and plays quietly as long as she gets enough sleep during the night. Quiet playtime in the dim light of the bedroom can help her prepare for sleeping and also gives parents some quiet time in the evenings.

Allowance

It is a good idea to begin saving money for your child as soon as she is born. A bank account provides a convenient place to store gifts of money that your child receives when she is too young to know how to spend it. Saving a little each month also helps prepare for big expenses later in life (for example, college, marriage). Before children can understand money, there is no need to provide them with an allowance other than directly depositing it in their bank account. Even when they begin to understand money, sometime around the first grade, they are still too young to set their immediate wishes aside. Given the opportunity, they will spend their money on the first thing that catches their fancy. By age seven or eight, children can begin to postpone their desires and an allowance can help teach them how money works and also how to budget. Limit how much they can spend, because they will make many bad decisions for several more years.

The amount of an allowance is based on its purpose. For children ages five through eight, the purpose of an allowance is not for your children to buy their own toys, pay their own expenses, or manage money. The purpose is to begin to teach the value of money and stewardship. Therefore, a dollar a week or some other small amount is plenty. Not until your child is an adolescent does the purpose change. In adolescence, the child not only needs to learn stewardship and budgeting, but also will have many financial interests from which to select. A larger allowance helps the child learn to make these decisions and teaches the child self-control, how to set aside immediate needs for future rewards, and the value of the things that he purchases.

School Choices

As you prepare to send your child to school for the first time, you have several choices. Public schools require no tuition, they offer free transportation (paid for by your tax dollars), they are usually within a reasonable distance from your home, they offer many services (computers, breakfast, athletics, clubs, assistance with special learning needs), and they are carefully regulated by the government both in hiring practices and in outcomes. Public schools, however, because they are often large, have a higher student–teacher ratio than other options, they cannot make exceptions to their rules that might be possible in smaller private schools, and there can be no religious component to their curriculum. Private schools offer smaller student–teacher ratios and many of the same services found in public schools, and they often are supported by religious organizations. Therefore, some religious teaching is part of the curriculum. Teachers in religious schools are more likely to see their jobs as a calling than as a job. Hence, they may be more committed to your children than some teachers in public education. (This is a generalization, of course, and many teachers in public schools are deeply committed to their students and their profession.) Private school is often expensive, transportation is either inconvenient or unavailable, and the school may be much farther from your home than a public school. Because they are often smaller than public schools, private schools may offer fewer academic and extracurricular opportunities than public schools. They may or may not be regulated by accrediting associations. Therefore, oversight and outcomes evaluations may be minimal.

In recent years, many parents have chosen to educate their children at home. Homeschooling was once practiced almost exclusively by conservative religious families or by families whose children were housebound due to health problems. Today, homeschooling is very common in many parts of the country and is practiced by both religious and nonreligious families. It offers many advantages over public or private schools. It is cheaper than private school, although parents must purchase curriculum, books, and other materials. Many parents find that they can provide instruction at home of as high a quality as the child would receive in a public school simply because the child has one-to-one instruction. Children who are homeschooled are not bound to the public school calendar. Therefore, they are free to travel with the family at their leisure, and when they are ill, making up work is very simple. Also, because children are not forced to move in groups and conform to the daytime routine established by the school, parents can often complete the academic portion of their homeschool day in much less time than would be true in a structured school setting. Therefore, children have more free time than in public school.

With homeschool settings, parents have control over the curriculum, can choose what approach to education they like, and can add educational components (for example, religious instruction) if they choose. Finally, even though children in homeschool groups may have fewer opportunities for field trips, extracurricular activities, and social interaction than children in structured school environments, many areas have homeschool organizations where families join their resources to offer these services and opportunities. Likewise, some public schools will allow homeschool children to participate in some extracurricular activities (for example, band, athletics) even though the children are not in the academic program at the school. Homeschooling is very demanding on the parent's time and energy, however, and if one is not committed to the process, another school alternative should be pursued.

Parents worry that if they homeschool their children, colleges will not accept a child's high school diploma, but this is usually not a problem. Each state differs in its approach, but competency exams (tests that the student would take if he or she were in public school prior to passing on to the next grade) can easily validate the child's abilities and in some states they are required for homeschooled children. Scores such as on the Scholastic Achievement Test are standardized measures that hold great weight in an admissions officer's decision. Therefore, regardless of educational history, how one scores on these standardized measures is very important and can validate your child's competency regardless of his or her school history. After many years of teaching college, my general experience has been that homeschooled children are at least as likely, if not more so, to be academically prepared for college as children from either public or private educational backgrounds.

Getting Started in School

The first three years of school are very important. During this time, a child learns to like or dislike school, teachers, and administrators. The most important job for kindergarten and first-grade teachers is to teach children to love learning. If children believe that school is a fun and worthwhile place, they will want to learn. Therefore, it is especially critical that a parent of a younger child pay close attention to her child's needs during these impressionable years.

One way to help your child adjust to school and acquire a love for learning is to become involved in your child's school. Be a volunteer tutor, have lunch with your child, participate on parents' day, and show up for parties and special occasions. Get to know your child's teacher and go to open houses at your child's school. Even though I have a busy schedule, from the year my oldest child started school, I have had lunch with at least one of my children every week. I regularly read to my children's classes when they were younger and I often go on field trips. My wife, also very active in the school, does many of the same things. Our involvement teaches our children how important we perceive school to be and that we are all in the educational process together.

As the summer winds down and the beginning of school approaches, your children will need to adjust their sleeping schedules to accommodate their sleep needs. Some children need more sleep than others. Begin changing bedtimes of younger children a week before school starts. Get them up during this week at the same time they would need to be up during the school year. This will help their bodies adjust to going to bed earlier and to getting up earlier before they actually are in school. Four or five days of an adjusted schedule should make the transition to the classroom easier.

It is also easy to get into bad eating habits over the summer. A healthy diet is critical to learning. Children who eat too many fatty foods are less alert and too much sugar can make it difficult for them to pay attention. Sugar burns very quickly in the body, causing them to become tired quickly. Once that brief boost of energy is used up, the child becomes tired and lethargic. It may seem obvious, but fresh vegetables, fruit, and some protein every day make for a good diet.

School Problems

Teach your child to respect all teachers even though he will have both good and bad teachers throughout his school career. Never display your frustrations with teachers or administrators in front of your child. Problems will inevitably arise. Some of those problems will be the fault of the teacher and others will be your child's, either behavioral or academic. It is difficult for parents to admit their children misbehave and we may be quick to place blame on the teacher. If you find yourself disagreeing with your child's teacher or if your child is having problems, go directly to the teacher with your concerns. If the teacher is at fault, kind but direct conversation may be all it takes to fix the problem. If the teacher's intentions are good, he or she will be happy to clarify issues and let you know what is going on. Don't start with the principal. It only increases the tension between you and the teacher. More important, it increases tension between the teacher and your child. If your child is at fault, take advantage of your alliance with the teacher by working as a team. Children will quickly catch on if you aren't working together and they will use that to their advantage. Support the teacher and his or her system as much as possible, even if you don't like his or her decisions. Teachers are professionals and have reasons for the systems they have in place.

Perhaps the most unrealistic suggestion I could present in this book is this—*do your best to be objective.* Any teacher can tell you that teachers rarely get calls from parents whose child is at fault. When our children act up, it is a poor reflection on us and we don't like it. We like to think our kids are perfect. We can point out weaknesses in our children, but we don't want others to do so. Yet parents have to understand that discipline is a valuable part of development and if we make excuses for our children, we are cheating them of a skill they need to function as healthy adults. It is also possible that your child's behavior problems are the result of an undiagnosed medical condition (hyperactivity, diabetes, and even poor hearing or poor vision). Rationally discussing possibilities with the teacher may help identify a plan of action that will be helpful to the child in the long run.

If talking with the teacher doesn't relieve your frustrations, talk to the principal. I have known teachers who called their students "dummies," who picked on students they didn't like, and who did not need to be in the teaching profession. This kind of behavior is unacceptable. Teachers engaging in this sort of behavior need either to deal with their personal problems that are causing this kind of unprofessional behavior or to find a new career. It is not unreasonable to expect the principal to do something about poor conduct by a teacher and you should follow up to see that something has been done to correct such a situation. Keep in mind, however, that even if your child has a poor teacher, you can compensate for that deficit by involving yourself in your child's academic life.

Teach Your Child to Be a Student

Many parents fail to recognize the limitations children have as they start school. They do not know how to schedule their time, to study, or to take tests. They often have no idea why they are doing what they are assigned and they do not see the connection between one subject and another or between homework, studying, tests, and grades. It is the parents' job to support the child's academic program at home. Help your child learn to organize his or her assignments, subjects, homework, papers to be turned in, and forms to be completed. Daily, go over your children's assignments, checking for errors, and have them correct mistakes before they play. Homework doesn't have to be "done before supper," as many of us recall from our own childhood, but the routine in your home should allow plenty of time for the child to finish homework before bedtime.

Teach your child how to study by helping her prepare for tests. Creating flash cards, reviewing spelling words, defining terms, and practicing math tables are all ways to help your child learn how to study and to be a better student. By far the most significant deficit that I find in my freshman college students is that they do not know how to study efficiently. For some reason, they were never taught how to manage their time, study, or prepare for tests. If you begin working with your child in kindergarten and first grade, she should be prepared as an efficient student when she reaches high school and college.

Youth Activities

Even at four or five years of age, children are not too young to take lessons—piano, dance, and even karate. Children will be limited by their attention spans and they will also have physical limitations. Some sports, such as baseball (T-ball), involve too much standing around, and children with attention problems will easily disengage and become bored. Soccer, especially on a small field with three-on-three competitions, allows all the children to be involved and helps maintain their attention.

One of the difficult questions parents have to address is what to do if a child wants to quit an activity before its scheduled termination. Most of us recognize that it is important to teach children to follow through with activities once they begin, but we also do not want to frustrate them to the point that they hate the activity and dread the time they spend doing it. For example, a child who is playing on a basketball team may decide midseason that he does not want to play any longer. The dilemma for the parent is balancing the child's commitment to the team, the need to learn to follow through with a commitment even when one is not enjoying the activity, and the mental well-being of the child. There are several steps in making this decision regardless of whether the activity is a sport, music lessons, scouting, or some other recreational activity.

First, as always, consider the child's age. Very young children, especially preschool age, lose interest in activities very quickly. Children of this age should not be allowed to begin an activity unless they have asked about it many times. That provides evidence that their interest is not a whim. Yet one can expect that in the process of finding the right "fit," children may try several different activities during their childhood before they find what is right for them. Unless she is completely miserable, I suggest that the child continue with the activity until a recognized break (tuition due date, end of the season, or something of that nature). Then she will be free to disengage and perhaps try some other activity.

Second, determine why the child wants to disengage. Many times, a child will not give you the real reason. It may be that he simply does not enjoy the activity. On the other hand, the child may have been called down or embarrassed by a coach or director, or other participants may be teasing or threatening your child. It could also be that the child had a bad day at the event, feels incompetent, and is embarrassed to go back. Tragically, it is also possible that an adult or an older child is physically or sexually harming your child. Child molesters do what they can to get in positions of power over children. They can easily do this by volunteering to be a coach, youth worker, or scout leader. Never jump to the conclusion that this is why your child is unhappy, but it is important to consider this as one of many possible causes for your child's unhappiness.

Third, support your children in their activity choices, but do not push too hard. Your children may have lost interest because you do not seem to have any interest in what they are doing. On the other hand, do not make them pursue an activity just because you think they should like it or because you personally like it.

Fourth, determine the level of stress the activity is causing your child. All of us have times where even pleasurable activities require work. We may not feel like practicing, but we know that in the end we have more fun than displeasure. If it becomes evident over time that your child's displeasure is exceeding his or her pleasure, then the activity is not the right fit.

Fifth, do not overschedule your children. One or two activities are plenty. If your children are on the go every night of the week, they probably are overscheduled. Your children need plenty of free playtime along with their schoolwork and recreational activities.

Finally, make the decision to quit final for the present. When children quit an activity, they must know that they cannot pick up again on that activity anytime in the near future. A year or two later is OK, but allowing your children very quickly to get in, out, and in again will teach them that they can quit when the going gets tough and then reengage to enjoy the pleasurable part of the activity. When your child quits, he is done for the remainder of the season.

It is important to start looking for an area of interest and competence for your child in these early years. Through starting early, by the time your child reaches adolescence, he or she will have had several years' practice in some activity, sport, or skill. This competence is very important during adolescent years. Sports, theater, and music are important parts of the development of a child's esteem. The right fit between the activity and the child makes for a stronger, more secure child.

Little League Violence

Little League violence is a problem all over the country—not violence between little boys and little girls, but violence between the adults who attend these games. There are numerous recorded incidents of violence at Little League games around the country where coaches, parents, and others have spit on, hit, shot, and stabbed others over issues surrounding the game. Several times these episodes have ended in murder. Violence is always troubling, but it is exceptionally frustrating when it happens over something so trivial as an official's decision in a Little League game. Not only that, but these episodes happen in front of impressionable youngsters on the athletic field and in the stands. There are several reasons parents get so emotionally consumed with Little League games.

One reason is that these events involve our children and we are very protective of them. If we perceive that our children are frustrated, angry, or being mistreated by a coach, an official, another player, or even a spectator, we feel the need to defend them. Often, however, children perceive a parent's intervention not as a defense but as an embarrassing intrusion. More often than not, they would prefer we keep our mouths closed.

Second, parents take the game far too seriously. They get wrapped up in the excitement of the game and expect it to be error- and injury-free, but this is an unrealistic expectation. Part of athletics is learning to deal with the normal disappointments and errors of the game. Umpires make mistakes, fans say thoughtless things, and coaches make decisions you do not like. Little League athletics exist to teach sportsmanship and the rules of the game, to provide recreation and social interaction for children, and to help children as they seek an activity that they like and want to pursue. The purpose of Little League, contrary to the opinion of some parents, is *not* to provide a proving ground for future professional athletes. Life is full of disappointments, "unfair" decisions, and frustrations. Little League provides a place for children to learn how to cope with this normal part of life. Many times, though, parents and coaches miss the opportunity to teach a life skill, instead demonstrating poor coping skills through their anger, catcalls, and aggression.

Another reason for this aggression is that some adults have not learned to control their anger. Not only do they act out on the athletic field, they also drive aggressively, lose their tempers at work and at home, and generally have poor coping skills. The Little League field is just another forum for them to demonstrate their inability to control their behavior. For these individuals, anger management or personal counseling may help to bring back for all of us the joy of the game that has been lost.

Finally, our culture has sanctioned poor personal conduct. In 1996, Baltimore Oriole Roberto Alomar spit in an umpire's face. His behavior, while condemned in the media, brought him only a slap on the wrist and, perhaps worse, the fans cheered his return to the field when they should have protested the decision to allow him to play. Numerous examples of atrocious behavior in various sports could be listed, but the point is, we accept outrageous behavior from professionals who should know better. The days of athletic gentility—days when Bill Russell dominated the basketball court, Arthur Ashe led on the tennis court, and Walter Payton inspired us on the gridiron—are gone. Replacing these heroes and gentlemen are arrogant individualists. It is to these misfits that our children look for inspiration.

Research has demonstrated that parents' unreasonable behavior will directly contribute to the decision of over half of the millions of children who play Little League athletics to discontinue organized sports by age 13. As a parent, you can combat these problems by setting a good example for your child.

Responsibility

From your child's very first days, your goal is to prepare your child to live on his own. Therefore, one of your primary tasks is to teach the child to be responsible. How a child approaches responsibility at this stage will, in part, determine how he approaches responsibility in his teen years. By the time a child reaches age six or seven, he should be capable of taking on routine responsibilities. Caring for a pet, cleaning one's room, and attending to some weekly or daily household chore is reasonable. Requiring these responsibilities of a child at this age helps move the child out of a long-held belief that he should be allowed to play whenever he wants. Not only will distribution of household chores make your life easier, but at the same time you are teaching your child that life requires some responsibility and that a family works together. As children accept and fulfill their responsibilities, they should earn freedom. As children fail in their responsibilities, they should lose freedom. For example, as I discussed previously, my eldest child was very responsible about getting up and preparing herself for school when she was in the third or fourth grade. Because of her responsible behavior, we extended her bedtime. As she entered middle school, we eliminated a set bedtime altogether. Our rule was that as long as she wasn't bothering others who were sleeping and as long as she got up on time, wasn't grumpy, got ready for school on time, and wasn't falling asleep in class, she could set her own bedtime. She appreciated this freedom. It made her feel grown-up and good about herself, but more important, it taught her the relationship between the potential unpleasantness of working at being responsible and the pleasure of the freedom a responsible person earns.

I have been a part of a college environment for more than 25 years. During this time I have witnessed a broad response to the freedom of college life in young people. Some of them, even in their first year, study hard, get to class on time, and live up to their obligations. Others goof off and end up in serious grade trouble within the first semester. There are many things that cause irresponsible behavior, but it is clear to me that some of these young adults enter college never having had to make decisions on their own. Their parents made all of their decisions for them and did not allow them to make mistakes or take initiative in their lives. Many times, these parents were very well-intentioned and good parents. Their desire to protect their children and keep them free from pain and the effects of poor decision-making led them to fail to teach the child how to make decisions. While college may seem a long way off for your seven-year-old, you are building the foundation on which that future responsible or irresponsible person will act.

SUMMARY

When your child enters this stage of life, he is beginning kindergarten. His motor skills are still developing and limits in his physical abilities are still obvious. His attention span is short, as are his patience and ability to post-pone self-gratification. By the end of this stage he will be experienced with school and he will have learned to read, write, and study. He will have many friends outside your home, his attention span will have increased dramatically, and he will occasionally be able to postpone immediate gratification for some future reward. In just a few years your children will lose their baby-faced qualities and you will say goodbye to your little boy or girl as they enter adolescence. It will be easy to get discouraged during these years because of your busy schedule, shuttling children among soccer practice, piano lessons, school, and other activities. You will sit through many open-house lectures from school administrators, PTO meetings, and school orientations. Enjoy these years, because they will go by in a flash and you will wonder where they went.

CHAPTER 8

The Last Days of Childhood: Middle Childhood (Ages 8–12)

You don't have to be afraid of change. You don't have to worry about what's being taken away. Just look to see what's been added.

——Jackie Greer

How do geese know when to fly to the sun? Who tells them the seasons? How do we humans know when it is time to move on? As with the migrant birds, so surely with us, there is a voice within, if only we would listen to it, that tells us so certainly when to go forth into the unknown.

—Elisabeth Kübler-Ross

I have traveled many miles over the years and each time I have taken a trip, I have brought home gifts for my children. I loved the days when all my children were preschool and early grade school age because gift buying was easy. They would get excited over a pen from the Smithsonian Institution or a super ball that lit up when they bounced it. But by the time they reached puberty, gift buying was much harder. Not only were gifts more expensive, but finding just the right thing that wouldn't make them feel like "babies" or wouldn't embarrass them was very challenging. I had to try to keep up with what was "cool"—a rule system that seemed to change by the minute. Even with a Ph.D. and years of experience working with children, I couldn't keep up with it.

I loved the simplicity of those earlier days of childhood, but as the children's lives became more complex, they developed new skills and abilities that greatly changed the way we interacted and increased the number of things that we could do together. At eight years of age, children are not quite ready to be grown-ups, but by the time they are twelve, they perceive themselves as nearly adult. They will see any suggestion that they are not fully mature as an insult. In fact, with the onset of puberty they enter adolescence and they will seem more mature both in their appearance and in their actions. Physically, they will change dramatically. They will have most, if not all, of their permanent teeth; their round, baby faces will begin to stretch; and they will grow several inches, approaching their eventual adult height. Their interests, attitudes, and social needs will also change. Some days they will seem so mature and adultlike that you will wonder where their childhood went, yet other days they will argue with siblings and fight just as they did when they were small. They will seek new freedoms and responsibility as they prepare for adulthood and they often will live up to those responsibilities. Relationships between parents and their children will change as children approach puberty. Even though children will always need their parents, puberty brings a need to take care of oneself—to find an identity separate from parents. Many parents get discouraged when their sons and daughters no longer want to snuggle or kiss their parents goodbye. Don't be discouraged. This is a normal part of a child's need to be independent.

Middle childhood, the years between ages 8 and 12, represents the threshold of adolescence. This chapter addresses the many cognitive changes that occur during these years and how those changes affect a child's abilities and social interactions, and the educational implications of those changes. Also discussed is the onset of puberty and the physical changes that accompany pubescence.

THINKING

The cognitive changes that take place during these five years increase a child's abilities most noticeably in school tasks. During this stage, children improve their abilities to think abstractly, their memory skills improve, and they are more proficient at studying and preparing for tests. Improvements in monitoring their own behavior, as well as regulating their emotions and behaviors, provide new opportunities for teaching responsibility, discipline, and freedom. The combination of all of these new skills allows for subjects to be addressed that could not be taught in earlier years. Advanced math, issues concerning social injustice, and complex social systems are among the topics that may appear in their school curriculum (and that they would have been unable to comprehend just a year or two earlier).

At ages eight, nine, and ten, your child will prepare to leave elementary school and move into a new system of education in a middle school. Middle school systems take advantage of children's new abilities by allowing them more freedom of movement, changing classes, caring for their own lockers and possessions, and providing more elaborate field trips (for example, overnight trips to historic places like Washington, D.C.). Even while they are still in elementary school, however, the transition begins. Third grade is the time when many school systems begin assigning grades to a child's work rather than general statements regarding meeting or failing to meet expected criteria. Children in upper elementary school may change classes for some subjects, earn positions of responsibility such as serving as helpers in kindergarten or first-grade classrooms, or functioning as hall monitors or safety patrol officers. The child's increased ability to pay attention, her improved fine motor skills, and her growing responsibility allow her a first exposure to band, chorus, or orchestra. Even though children can play musical instruments long before age eight, their size, limited ability to concentrate, and limited fine-motor skills greatly limit how far they can go in perfecting their skills with an instrument. The developmental changes of middle childhood come at a time when the door to limitless possibilities springs open.

Memory and Organization

Prior to age eight, children's memory abilities are limited and their strategies are haphazard. When they are younger, they have little ability to monitor their memory skills, or even to think about their memory strategies—a skill called *metamemory*. For example, if you ask a first-grade child if he can remember a list of words, he will almost always say "yes." No matter how long the list, he almost always suggests that he can remember the items because he has no ability to think about his memory abilities and limitations. Even though children younger than eight years of age can remember some things astonishingly well, they have no formal strategies for remembering. Young children remember best when they are interested in the thing to be remembered. If the child has no interest in the thing to be remembered, it is easily forgotten. By third grade, however, your child will readily recognize her limitations. She may not know her limitations in detail, but she can quickly identify something that is beyond her capacity to remember. At this age, she will still need some training as to how to compensate for these limits, but the recognition of one's limitations is a huge developmental leap. During this stage of development, children can begin to use calendars, "things to do" lists, and other memory strategies that can help them improve their recall abilities and meet their obligations.

Despite their improved memory abilities, many children have come through my private practice because of difficulties in school related to memory problems. They fail to turn in assignments even when they have them completed, or they forget to bring home books they need for homework. Mothers and fathers are beside themselves with frustration when the child's report cards are less than stellar. Even after systematically following up on their child's assignments, they find completed assignments in the child's bedroom or tucked away in a book bag after it was due. These parents do not understand why the child does not simply turn in the completed work at the assigned time and they fear that the child's academic future is threatened.

Developmental delays, cognitive disorders, and psychological problems can cause this behavior, but it is equally possible that the child is simply not motivated to perform. One of the challenges for developmental psychologists is to recognize ability when it is present but not displayed. For example, many of these children have the ability to study, recall responsibilities, and organize their assignments, but for one reason or another, they don't care enough about it to perform the behaviors. When this is the case, a parent's harping, complaining, and punishing will have little effect on the child's behavior. The solution lies in finding a way to motivate the child. In earlier years, parents could motivate children by threatening to take away TV time or confiscating toys, but by late elementary school and middle school years, finding rewards and punishments that are motivational is much harder. When a child in this stage refuses to comply, forgets to turn in assignments, repeatedly forgets books and materials at school, and engages in other irresponsible behaviors, he can easily find himself repeating a grade.

The first step in correcting the behavior is to assume that the child may simply be disorganized. Many adults have difficulty keeping track of important papers, due dates, and assignments at work. Organization is a skill that can be learned and it is inappropriate to punish a child for the lack of a skill he has not been taught. Often, schools provide children with a calendar that is designed to help them keep track of their due dates and daily assignments and also allows parents to see what the child is supposed to be doing for homework on a given day. If such a calendar is part of your child's routine at school, teach him how to use it, reward him for succeeding, and work with his teachers to ensure he is correctly noting his assignments. Check your child's folders, notebooks, and calendars each day with him so that he can see where he is succeeding and where he needs improvement in his organizational skills. Small Post-it notes on his folder, books, or calendar can add emphasis to things that your child may forget (for example, to submit completed work at the beginning of the day). For children who are simply disorganized, learning how to organize themselves is esteem-boosting and it teaches them that they are not stupid and that with effort, they can perform.

A parent can also find motivators at home that encourage the child to focus on necessary memory tasks. Even though he is less likely to be motivated by punitive responses than younger peers, this doesn't mean that punishment and, even better, rewards for appropriate behaviors cannot work. Limiting privileges with computers, television, and other activities that a child values can serve as punitive responses. Likewise, allowing the child to earn extra privileges (for example, a trip to the movies after a week of improved behavior) can be a powerful motivator. In 20 years of working with children I have never failed to find a motivator that works with a child if I have had enough time and cooperation from parents. Rewards are always preferable to punishments if appropriate rewards can be found.

When necessary, utilize help from the school. Administrators, teachers, and school counselors have experience working with children who lack motivation or organizational skills. Use their experience and expertise as you intervene with your child. A team approach not only takes advantage of the expertise of several experts in solving the problem, but it also affects the child across environments. Some parents complain to their children about behaviors, but once the child steps on the school bus, he is free of intervention until he returns home. When the parent and school personnel work together, the child cannot escape or ignore his responsibilities as easily.

When these options fail, it may be necessary to seek professional help. Child therapists are trained to identify psychological disorders. Children in my practice who have had these types of school-related problems sometimes have needed to be referred to a physician for medication, or they may simply have needed encouragement from an objective third party. A few weeks of therapy, as well as teamwork between the parents, therapist, and teacher, usually works to correct these problems. Other times, school problems like those mentioned above are the result of a more serious problem—sexual or physical abuse, response to divorce or marital disruption, or other trauma. When this is the case, the problem most likely will not go away on its own and early intervention with a therapist can address both the immediate school-related problems and the underlying, and perhaps more serious, problem.

When all else fails, natural consequences may be necessary. Allowing a child to make his own choice to repeat a grade is not what you want for your child, but it may be what it takes to correct his bad choices at a time when those choices have minimal long-term effects. This sounds odd, because repeating a grade has long-term effects. The child will lose his friends as they move on without him. He will graduate a year later, and he may experience other academic and social frustrations because of his choice. However, repeating a grade and recognizing that his behaviors have serious consequences may be the very thing that prevents him from making much more serious mistakes when he is older that could lead to legal problems or may even be life-threatening to himself or others.

Focus and Attention

By age eight, children are capable of concentrating for long periods of time, even at school, but they are still more likely to be physical learners. In other words, they will learn better and find it easier to concentrate if they are physically active in the learning process. Experiments and instruction that involve the child will be more effective than lectures.

Centration, which was discussed in previous chapters as the process of focusing on a single attribute to the exclusion of other attributes, begins to wane during this stage of life. A joke once circulated about a five-year-old child who told a neighbor that she lost her dog. When asked what the dog looked like, she said that it had black feet, a black head, a black body, and a black tail. This child's description of her dog demonstrates centration. By age eight or nine, the same child would easily describe the animal simply as "a black dog."

Egocentrism will continue to be a limitation for children through their teen years. They will continue to see things from their own perspective for several more years. Parents get frustrated with their children because they make noise while others are sleeping or they talk on the telephone when someone else is waiting for a phone call. The child's egocentric worldview makes it difficult for him to think about another person's needs or interests while also considering his own needs and interests. In a similar way, during middle childhood, children cannot easily separate themselves from events. When something happens that affects them adversely, they have a difficult time seeing the event in the broader context of life. Much like their younger counterparts, they can easily be emotionally devastated by bad grades, a failed romance, or a broken friendship. These painful events seem overwhelming because children have difficulty thinking about a time when the present emotional pain will abate. In the reverse, when an event happens that does not affect them directly, they can easily dismiss its importance, regardless of the meaning of the event in a world or historical context. Children in this age group do not ordinarily have any interest in politics, world geography, or social issues to which they cannot readily relate. Given some instruction, children in this age group can empathize with, for example, starving children in Ethiopia, but they will not spontaneously pursue information on the subject because the issue does not affect them directly.

Abstract Thinking

Developmental theorist Jean Piaget taught that sometime around the onset of puberty, children develop the ability to think in abstract terms. Prior to acquiring this skill, they can think about some abstract issues, but only when they are represented in a concrete form. For example, several years ago one of my graduate students was convinced her five-year-old daughter could understand a map of the United States. Her daughter, she told me, could easily put together a puzzle that was a map of the United States. She said her daughter could point to the state where she lived and to the state where her grandmother lived. What my student failed to understand was that maps are indeed abstractions, but her daughter's understanding of "map" was directly linked to the physical puzzle map in front of her. This child could be taught to recognize states or other locations, but she could not understand that a map could be any size, any color, or potentially any shape. The "meaning" of the map was abstract while the map in front of her was concrete. I am certain that if I drew a picture of the United States on a piece of paper and asked this woman's daughter if it represented the same thing as her puzzle map, she would have said "no."

All of this changes around puberty, when children can begin to understand concepts like justice, hate, love, hope, and other ideas that can fully be understood only at an abstract level. They can hypothesize about events that have not happened and they can easily imagine situations that they have not experienced. This allows them to take the perspective of another person much more effectively than they did prior to acquiring the ability to think abstractly.

Self-Monitoring, Social Skills, and Problem Solving

By late elementary school years, your child will have developed study habits that may or may not be effective. If ineffective strategies are not replaced with effective ones, your child could easily continue using ineffective habits to prepare for tests well into his high school and even college years. It is important to study with your child in order to teach him effective study strategies. Even very young children will use effective memory and study strategies if they are trained and reminded to use them.

Self-monitoring is another advantage that children in this age group have over younger children. These children can think about their states of consciousness, think about controlling their thoughts, and think about ways to control their behaviors. By age 12, even though many children are still impulsive, they have the ability to anticipate events, how those events will make them feel, and various ways they can respond to the events and their feelings. Improved abilities to take the perspective of another are evident in their writings and in their drawings. This is a tremendous asset for teachers, parents, and therapists. The ability to think about the future and monitor one's behavior allows for practice of hypothetical events that children may encounter. This assists them in monitoring their behavior and displaying socially appropriate behaviors because they can prepare themselves well in advance for the situations they will encounter. Finally, as children approach their teen years, their problem-solving abilities improve. All of these events together make it possible for a child to think about an event that she has never experienced, consider possible responses to her feelings about it, and decide in advance how she might respond to it, as well as how her response might be perceived by others. This is a very complicated skill involving many simultaneous issues that, prior to puberty, most children cannot perform.

Preparing for Middle School

Around age 10 or 11, your child will transition from elementary school to middle school. This transition brings with it many changes in procedure as well as new and more demanding expectations. While your child is in elementary school, teachers and administrators assume the parent and child will interact daily in regard to assignments, coursework, and school activities. This assumption is not made as often at the middle school level. Also, in middle school, your child will maintain a locker, bus and class schedule, and travel from one activity to another without direct supervision by a teacher or an administrator. Therefore, children must be more responsible for their assignments and schedules than they were in elementary school. Even so, parents should continue to be involved with their children during these years. Many children still need help organizing their time and studying, and they may need to be reminded about due dates and other important events in their lives at school. Parents should attend parent–teacher orientation and visitation nights even if they have done so many times before. This not only potentially provides new information and awareness of the child's specific program and needs, but it also communicates to your child the importance of school and your dedication to the child's progress and education.

The level of difficulty in coursework increases during middle school years. Many parents find that they are unable to help their children with some of the subjects they are learning. Math, science, and other subjects may require an understanding of specific procedure as it is taught at school. I teach college-level statistics, but many times, have been frustrated because I was unable to help my children with their math homework. Even though I could solve the problems, I could not do it using the procedures they had been taught in their classes. Occasionally, a child's homework may involve an understanding of the subject that goes beyond the parent's level of knowledge. Therefore, parent and child may have to plan further in advance for test preparation and homework in order to get the help required for a given project. Use of a tutor may be necessary, and many schools offer tutoring before and after school as well as during study halls.

The transition to middle school is anxiety-producing for many children. They recognize that they will leave an environment where they are the oldest and where they are familiar with their surroundings for a new environment where they will be the youngest and where they will be totally unfamiliar with their surroundings. Some schools offer a mentoring program or a "shadowing" day where children can spend the day with a middle school pupil the year before they begin middle school. This exposure can ease anxieties about the transition and also answer many of the child's questions about the differences between elementary school and middle school.

Parents who are concerned about their child's academic or emotional preparedness for middle school should discuss their concerns with the child's teacher and/or school counselor. These individuals know your child and they also know what is expected in middle school and can provide the parent with an objective opinion as well as suggestions for preparing the child for a new academic year.

FEELING

Emotionally, children in this age group are blossoming. Between ages 8 and 12, children grow in their ability to recognize their own emotions, label those emotions properly, and control the display of their emotions. They are still children, but during this stage of life, they ebb and flow between exceptionally mature behavior and childish emotional outbursts. Patience is imperative; parents must understand that these two poles are normal.

Peers

Peers have an effect on children's thoughts and behaviors from age three on. What changes as the child gets older is the level of influence peers have on a child's behavior. Beginning around age seven or eight, children become very interested in what their peers think about them, what is important to them, the clothes they wear, the games they play, and the places they go. These behaviors have a growing influence on your child as he or she becomes concerned about fitting in with his or her peer group. Peer influence reaches its pinnacle of power during the teen years, but it begins to show itself during the late elementary school and middle school years.

During middle childhood, children engage their peer group in three ways. They may be *popular* because of prosocial behaviors (for example, good grades, athleticism) or they can seek popularity through antisocial behaviors (rebel attitudes). Those who do not achieve popularity feel *rejected* by their peers. These children may either withdraw or they may lash out aggressively. Finally, children who are not rejected by their peers but who do not fit in with their peer group are considered *neglected*. This type of behavior disturbs many parents, but surprisingly, research demonstrates that neglected children are usually well-adjusted; they simply do not socialize the same way as most children their age.

Competence

As children approach adolescence and their peers take more priority in their thoughts, children begin to strive for competence among their peers. They may choose to seek competence because of their appearance, their academic strength, their musical talent, or their athletic abilities. If they find that they are not competent in any of these areas, they may seek to be competent as "socialites." These are children whose gift is making friends, making people laugh, or getting along with others. It is important that children find a place to fit in with their peer group. Competence helps develop a strong esteem and gives the child the emotional strength to endure the inevitable disappointments and hurts that accompany preadolescence, adolescence, and eventually adulthood. This stage is what Erikson called "industry vs. inferiority." As children approach age 12, they continue to seek some area of expertise—something they perceive demonstrates their industriousness. Failure to achieve industry leaves children feeling inferior to peers and eventually leads to other social difficulties. It is at this stage that earlier exploration of activities (for example, sports, dance, karate) will have allowed them to find an activity they enjoy and one in which they can excel. (See chapter 7 for more information on this issue.)

Bullies

Bullying is a worldwide problem, especially in schools. Bullies have been around for years, but it has only been in recent years that psychologists and educators have focused on the problem of bullies. Schools are prime locations for bullying because in nearly all other environments where a child exists, the child can voluntarily separate himself from that location. For example, if a child is bullied on the soccer field, he can choose to withdraw from the sport. However, a child has no choice but to attend school.

In my book *Wounded Innocents and Fallen Angels*, I addressed the extent of the problem of bullying. In short, research on the problem of bullying is consistent. Studies show that a minimum of 10–16 percent of schoolchildren in the United States are bullied each year, and several research studies show numbers that are even higher. One study of over 800 children demonstrated that three-quarters of children between the ages of 8 and 11 ranked bullying as a bigger problem than racism, AIDS, or the pressure to try sex, alcohol, or drugs.[1] Bullying occurs equally in rural, suburban, and urban school systems and is not bound to any single race, gender, socioeconomic group, or area of the country. Even though bullying occurs among very young children as well as adults, bullying is most prevalent among children between the second and eighth grades.

Bullying includes several types of behavior—sexual, physical, verbal, and psychological. Some bullying involves sexual intimidation or harassment. Females are more likely to be victims of this form of bullying than males. With physical bullying, bullies may intimidate or injure their victims or they may extort money from them by threatening physical force. This type of bully may hit, spit on, kick, push, or pinch his victims. In the most extreme cases, bullies may even kill their victims. With verbal bullying, bullies intimidate or call their victims unkind names. Their words are deeply damaging and have long-term consequences. The emotional pain a bullied child feels is real and intense.

Psychological bullying is often overlooked. These bullies snub, ignore, or exclude a child. Psychological bullying also involves lying, blackmail, humiliation, and malicious gossip. This type of bullying is perpetrated more often by girls than boys and, because it is often overlooked, may explain why some people believe boys are more likely to bully than girls.

Name-calling or physical altercations alone do not qualify as bullying. The behavior must be repeated and regular, and the victim must also perceive himself or herself to be weaker than the bully. Even though bullies are often bigger than their victims, they do not have to be. The victim must merely perceive himself or herself to be weaker than the aggressor.

Some bullies are mean to their victims out of ignorance. They do not realize how much emotional pain they are causing, and when they eventually realize what they have done, they stop their bullying behavior. Other bullies are driven by weak egos, and pushing other people around makes them feel powerful.

Victims may be selected because they do not have the "in" clothes, because of their appearance (for example, glasses, braces, hairstyle, or a birth defect), or because of where they live, their race, or their religion. Victims are most often new children in a school, weak children, or children who do not fit in with a social group. When these children begin to affiliate with a social group, they are less likely to become victims of bullying. Therefore, addressing victim behavior involves helping the child attach to a social peer group.

The results of bullying can be devastating. Adults who were bullied in elementary school may harbor painful memories long into their adult years, and victims of repeated bullying suffer esteem problems, loneliness, and fear. Victims of bullies also experience humiliation and anxiety. In some cases they endure beatings, bloody noses, and even broken bones. At the extreme, victims of bullies have killed themselves because they believed their problem had no other reasonable solution and they could not stop the pain in any other way.

One of the most common responses from adults when children tell them that they are bullied is that the child should ignore the bully. Telling children to ignore bullies does not work. It takes 30 consecutive days to change behavior; therefore, the child has to maintain "ignoring" for 30 schooldays. This is unreasonable in some cases of bullying and the adult's suggestion to ignore the continuous bullying behavior only demonstrates to the child that adults cannot, or will not, help or intervene. It is interesting that in one study, only 25 percent of the children studied said that teachers had been helpful by intervening in bullying situations, while 70 percent of the teachers in this same population reported that they intervened effectively 100 percent of the time. Children need to learn to handle life's problems, but bullying is not a normal problem. No child should be forced to coexist in an environment where he or she is regularly afraid, embarrassed, humiliated, or shamed, and adults are their primary resource for structuring a safe environment. It is important for parents to take their children seriously if they indicate they are being bullied.

Symptoms that your child might be a victim of bullying include physical injury that is unexplained or where explanations do not match the injury, a sudden or unexplained fear of school, or anxiety in relation to attending school. As many as 10 percent of schoolchildren miss one day of class per month because of bullying. Many children will pretend to be sick in order to avoid school and their bullies. Sudden changes in your child's grades or self-esteem, self-destructive behavior, depression, frequent crying, behavioral problems or changes, avoidance of certain people or places, and nervousness are also symptoms of bullying.

Both bullies and victims can benefit from professional intervention. If bullies are not helped, they face a grim future. By their adult years, they are more likely to experience alcoholism, to engage in criminal behavior, to be diagnosed with a mental illness, and to require social support services. Victims fare better, but the short-term emotional scars of bullying can be difficult to deal with. Even more important is the daily ritual of trying to avoid a bully or cope with the harassment, embarrassment, humiliation, pain, or extortion of bullies.

It is always important to encourage your child to talk to you about all of his or her problems, but open communication is especially important with bullying. Talk to your child about what bullying is and what to do if repeatedly confronted by a bully. Children should feel free to talk to teachers, administrators, and especially to parents, if they are victims of bullying. Even though many parents are certain that their children will talk to them about issues like bullying, take the initiative and reassure them that you can and will help. Certainly, you should never minimize the effects of bullying on your child. The pain, fear, and anxiety that they feel are very powerful.

Teach your child problem-solving strategies that apply to the situation where he or she is being bullied and role-play those situations so that your child can practice using the skills you teach. Your child will be confronted with unkind people throughout life. Therefore, learning to cope with unpleasant people is a life skill. Help your child distinguish between bullying and normal teasing and unpleasant life situations. Teach your child ways to cope with hurt, embarrassment, and anger. As with problem-solving strategies, practice these coping skills at home so that your child will know how to employ them when confronted by a bully or other unkind individual.

Of course, you should model productive problem solving, coping skills, and anger management at home. Your child will learn by watching you. When necessary, do not hesitate to communicate directly with teachers or school administrators. Bullying not only can cause your child physical and emotional distress, it may also cause him or her to learn to dislike or avoid school, creating problems with grades that could adversely affect his or her long-range academic career.

Helping Behavior and Justice

Prior to age eight or so, children like to help mom and dad with chores and activities, but their desire to help is an egocentric one. They want to help so they can demonstrate their competence, abilities, and independence. By eight or nine years of age, children develop a sense of selfless benevolence. They have the ability to take the perspective of another person and they can think about what another person is experiencing. Using this skill, they can then imagine how their assistance can affect that individual. During this age, children will do the dishes, clean the kitchen, clean their room, or perform some other activity to help around the house because they know that their help will make life easier for their parents. They will engage in the same activities at church, school, or social clubs. At this age, children tend to believe that those who have less than they have deserve more of what they do not have. Therefore, children can be exceptionally generous during this stage of life.

At age eight, a child's concept of justice involves equality. In her mind, rewards and punishments are justly administered if everyone receives the same response. For example, if one child was punished for a given behavior and another child engages in that same behavior, the second child deserves exactly the same punishment. By age 12, children begin to broaden their idea of justice and recognize the nuances that may require "inequitable" distribution of rewards and punishments. Using the previous example, a pubescent child can recognize that even though both children engaged in the same behavior, their circumstances could be different; therefore, the punishments they receive could be different as well. (See also "Fair?" in chapter 7.)

Same-Gender Classrooms

For years, researchers have argued over the benefits and disadvantages of same-gender classrooms. Although most public schools do not segregate children by gender, many private schools do, as do other organizations—churches, summer camps, and clubs. There is no definitive answer to the question, but the research in this area indicates that there are some distinct advantages, especially for girls, in same-gender classrooms. Girls tend to talk less and interact less with the teacher in mixed-gender classrooms, especially in subjects like math and science. There are also advantages to teachers. Given a same-gender classroom, some presentations can be fine-tuned to address the gender of the class, as would be true with any homogeneous group. Likewise, the embarrassment and awkwardness that accompany children at this age are lessened when they do not have to worry about looking silly in front of children of the opposite sex—one or more of whom may be the object of their romantic attentions. Given a choice between same-gender classrooms and mixed-gender classrooms, I recommend same-gender classes.

Humor

Adults take humor for granted because it is so much a part of our daily lives. We hear a joke and we laugh. There are many kinds of humor—puns, sarcasm, slapstick, dry humor, and many others. Prior to age seven or eight, children have little understanding of jokes and humor. They will laugh at slapstick comedy, but they cannot easily interpret oral jokes. The presentation of a joke (for example, facial expression) or funny-sounding words makes them laugh—not the punch line. When my son was five, he wanted to tell me jokes. "Why did the chicken cross the road?" he asked me, trying to mimic a joke he had heard at school. When I said I did not know, he said, "To find a tree." At that, he laughed hysterically. Of course, this is not a joke. In his mind, the thing that was funny was talking about a chicken. He did not understand the components of humor—delivery, expectation, and punch line. This also explains why children will tell the same joke several times in a row. They fail to understand that most humor relies on one's expectation of a different outcome. Once the punch line has been delivered, there can be no surprise. They enjoy telling "jokes" because they like making people laugh. They suppose if the story was funny once, it will always be funny.

Prior to age seven or eight, children cannot understand sarcasm. This is because they have a limited understanding of the world and a limited vocabulary, but even more because they take words literally. A five-year-old asks his mother when they are going to have supper. She sarcastically replies, "Tomorrow." This troubles the child because he takes her words literally and supposes that she really means that they will not eat until the next day. By age eight, however, children have increased their vocabularies, they have a broader understanding of the world, and they should begin to understand the various nuances of words, tone of voice, and context that will allow them to understand sarcasm and other forms of humor.

DOING

Between ages 8 and 12, children change in physical appearance and ability. They outgrow their shoes, pants, and shirts almost as fast as you buy them. Children who play musical instruments improve in their physical agility with their instrument during these years as their control of the muscles of the fingers refines and they also improve in their ability to conceptualize musical theory, thus improving their skill with their instrument. Likewise, children make advances in athletic ability. For example, by age 12, children can easily jump more than 12 inches vertically and 5 feet horizontally. Males can throw a baseball at nearly 80 feet per second by age 12 and girls can throw a ball at nearly 60 feet per second by their 12th year. Nearly all of these changes are due to what is perhaps the biggest event during these years—the onset of puberty.

Puberty

In Western cultures, girls reach puberty as early as age eight and boys as early as age nine. Even though some children do not reach puberty until age 14 or later, most girls are pubescent by age 13 and most boys by age 14. The average age for the onset of puberty is about ten years for girls, and for boys the average is about a year later. Puberty is considered delayed if it has not occurred prior to age 13, although it is not inconceivable for children to reach puberty as late as their mid-teens. Puberty, by definition, is sexual maturation. With the onset of puberty comes the ability to reproduce. There are many changes that accompany pubescence. Various body parts grow at different rates. The arms and legs grow faster than the rest of the body, giving children a lanky and asymmetrical appearance. As their bodies change, they must learn to accommodate these physical changes, much as one learns to walk in a new pair of shoes. Wearing a "new body" on a regular basis accounts for some physical awkwardness that pubescent children experience. With hormonal production in pubescent children come acne, body hair, pubic hair, muscle tone, moodiness, and rapid physical growth. Even though there are many similarities, boys and girls experience different effects of puberty.

Girls

The onset of puberty is clear for girls. Puberty is marked by the first menstrual period, called *menarche*. First menstruation can be both exciting and frightening to young girls. In general, girls see menarche as a step toward adulthood, and despite their anxieties, its appearance indicates that they are no longer children. They may fear the pain, discomfort, and moodiness that sometimes accompany one's period that they have heard about during sex education discussions. They also may experience anxiety about dealing with "dirty" menstrual discharge, used napkins or tampons, and panty liners. However, many of these anxieties can be eased if the child is properly prepared for menarche. (See next section.)

Girls see other evidence of their maturation besides menarche. They begin to develop pubic hair, and the hair on their legs will grow faster and darker. Parents may allow their girls to begin shaving their legs and underarms around the onset of puberty, although when one shaves should depend upon the child's level of responsibility rather than age. Girls also notice a swelling in their nipple region that marks the beginning of breast development. When girls develop breast buds, they should begin to wear a camisole or training bra. This is yet another activity that gives pubescent girls a feeling of womanliness. As she continues to develop, the girl's body shape changes. Her face loses the round, little-girl quality as her cheekbones become more defined, her lips increase in size, and her body shape begins to develop more of a womanly curve, with her hips and buttocks wider than her waist.

Preparing Your Daughter for Menarche

It is not unusual for girls to be anxious when discussing menarche or their menstrual cycle. Sexual conversations are often awkward for both parents and children, but a parent can relieve a child's anxiety by discussing these events in a modest but matter-of-fact manner, remaining open to any question the child has. Conversations about menarche should begin long before puberty. Mothers should begin the dialogue about menstruation when their daughters are in early elementary school. These conversations can be short, even just a few seconds long, but they open the door for later, more in-depth conversations. Children are naturally curious when they find tampons or panty liners in the bathroom cabinet. Use their questions as an open door to briefly discuss the fact that women use them a few days a month for special needs. As they get older, their questions will get more specific and you can be more specific with your answers. By the time your daughter is seven or eight, you should have had several brief conversations about menstruation, and maybe one or two more extensive conversations. Prior to menarche, explain to your daughter that every woman is different in her experience and that menstruation is a normal part of a woman's life. Ease anxieties about the messiness of one's monthly period by reminding her that she urinates or has a bowel movement every day, and these are normal body functions that she easily takes care of. Ensure that your daughter understands that the length of one's period, the intensity, the starting point, and the ending point vary from woman to woman.

Never laugh at any sexual question your child has—even if it is funny to you. The child will not understand that you are laughing at the thought, but instead will feel that you are laughing at her. You can be sure she will not trust you with any other questions if you laugh at her or make her feel silly, stupid, or ill-informed. Expect your child to have misconceptions and strange ideas that she may have picked up from ill-informed friends. Honestly and openly correct her misconceptions without making her feel as if she is the only person who doesn't know the truth—a process I call *normalizing* thoughts or behaviors. When people have embarrassing or incorrect thoughts or behaviors, they fear they are the only ones who have ever experienced what they are going through. Normalizing involves letting the person know that many people have had similar misconceptions and that such misconceptions, while they need to be corrected, are not abnormal. When her first period arrives, she will see that most of her fears were ill-founded and she should quickly incorporate this new experience into her routine.

Boys

There is no event equivalent to menarche for boys, but even though they do not experience a single event that marks the onset of puberty, boys do experience many physical changes that make it clear they have begun to develop sexually. Puberty brings with it an increase in the size of a boy's testicles and penis. He develops pubic hair and begins to develop facial hair and chest hair; the hair on his arms and legs darkens and grows faster than in the past. As his larynx widens and extends, his voice occasionally cracks and then deepens. He gains weight much more quickly than before and his muscles take on clear definition, especially if he is physically active. Prior to puberty, boys can gain very little muscle mass, no matter how much they exercise or lift weights. By the onset of puberty, however, they have the potential to gain muscle mass in almost any area of their bodies—the neck, shoulders, arms, back, abdomen, and legs.

Even in infancy, males can experience erection, but until puberty, sexual arousal is almost always either an autonomic response (many males have erections when they sleep, or even during the day, for seemingly no reason at all) or because of direct physical stimulation of the penis or testicles. During puberty, however, boys may experience erections by viewing sensual materials, by discussing erotic issues, or simply by being in the presence of a female. Therefore, frequency of erection increases during puberty.

The majority of seminal fluid emitted during ejaculation by an adult male is made up of fluid from the prostate gland. Prior to puberty, when boys experience orgasm, there is no penile emission. At puberty, a boy's prostate gland begins to develop fluid that is the vehicle by which sperm travel during ejaculation. Therefore, at puberty, when a boy has an orgasm, he will experience ejaculation for the first time. He may also experience *wet dreams*. Wet dreams are nighttime penile emissions, often associated with erotic dreams. Wet dreams are completely beyond a child's control and one should never punish a boy for experiencing a wet dream.

Masturbation

In the 1940s and 1950s, two of the most extensive studies of sexual behavior ever conducted at that time were released in what became known as the Kinsey Reports. These reports concluded that by adulthood, about 92 percent of males and about 62 percent of females masturbated at one time or another.[2] Even though there have been many claims that these numbers are incorrect due to methodological problems, most research in the years since the publication of these reports has validated relatively high numbers in regard to the incidence of masturbation among both males and females. It is generally concluded that by adulthood, most (if not all) males have masturbated at least once and the majority of females (60–80 percent) have masturbated at least once. Masturbation is evident in children even in infancy, and many children as young as three or four years of age masturbate on a regular basis. By age 12, over half of all males and about 25 percent of all females have masturbated at least once. Prepubescent females rarely experience orgasm during masturbation, but they experience a swelling of the clitoris and labia minora that accompanies sexual arousal. Prepubescent males can experience orgasm, but they do not ejaculate. By puberty, both males and females can experience orgasm during masturbation, and males experience ejaculation for the first time.

Myths and false ideas about the effects of masturbation have circulated for centuries. Sometimes well-intentioned religious individuals perpetuated these myths in an attempt to use fear to stop autoerotic behaviors in children. This book is not a religious work and I understand that there are many religious issues that parents will want to consider as they decide how best to approach the issue of masturbation. However, physically and psychologically, there are few real dangers posed by masturbation. The most likely danger involved with masturbation is infection due to uncleanliness. Germs can be introduced into the vagina or penis by dirty hands or objects. Excessive masturbation can lead to infections, abrasions, inflammation, and soreness. Excessive masturbation is also one of many symptoms of sexual abuse in both males and females. (There is no standard for what constitutes excessive masturbation, but it is not unusual for individuals to masturbate daily. Masturbation three or four times a day or more would be considered excessive by most clinicians.) The use of autoerotic toys can cause abrasions or can become lodged in body cavities. In some cases, females have had to have objects removed from their vaginas after inserting them during masturbation. Adolescents and adults who experience sexual dysfunction, especially violent fantasies, feed their violent fantasies with pornography, imagery, and masturbation. This is obviously unproductive. However, with these exceptions, there is little evidence that masturbation is psychologically or physiologically damaging. The most likely psychological danger of masturbation involves guilt related to the behavior rather than the behavior itself.

Children must learn that autoerotic behavior is a private behavior and if parents are not concerned about the child's frequency, it should be practiced at home in the privacy of one's room—not in the car, a parking lot, the living room, or at school. Many parents have religious beliefs that condemn autoerotic behavior, especially in adolescence, since this behavior nearly always is accompanied by visual imagery and/or sexual fantasy. Teaching children one's religious beliefs can be done without chastising the child or humiliating him or her. Emphasizing the private nature of this sexual behavior and its place in one's religious framework may be all that is needed to curb the behavior. However, it is not unlikely that children will continue to engage in the behavior, but in secret. Excessive guilt due to uncontrollable sexual urges can have both physical and psychological ramifications. The intensity of sexual feelings during adolescence is difficult enough without parents compounding it with guilt. Consultation with a child psychologist who also is a practicing member of one's faith can help parents find ways to deal most effectively with masturbation without creating psychological problems and also without abandoning their faith.

Early and Late Maturation

Girls and boys respond differently to early maturation. Generally, research has demonstrated that early maturation is beneficial for boys but difficult for girls. These differences are most likely due to cultural issues and social relationships. Nearly all cultures worldwide value physical agility, strength, speed, and athleticism in males. When boys mature early, they are almost always physically stronger than their peers, making them better than their peers at most athletic activities. For example, when I was in the seventh grade, a boy in my class was already pubescent while most of the rest of us had just begun our sexual maturation. His added muscle tone, speed, and strength gave him a distinct advantage in nearly every sport he played. He held records in basketball, track and field, and football. Even though he was probably a gifted athlete anyway, his early maturation created a situation where in essence he was physically a year or two beyond the rest of us. Such a situation is similar to ninth graders competing with seventh graders. My friend's athletic prowess brought accolades from parents, teachers, peers, and the community. (This young man went on to play college football, and he later became a physician.) This social attention based on issues of cultural importance benefits the boy's self-esteem and ego.

Girls, on the other hand, respond very differently to early maturation. Instead of being proud of their early development, girls who mature before their peers are more likely to be self-conscious, nervous, and anxious. They are less likely to see menarche as a positive event and they experience more awkwardness with puberty than girls who mature at a normal age or those who mature late. Sadly, adults may interact with young girls based on their appearance rather than their chronological ages. A young girl who looks older than she is is far more likely to experience sexual advances from both teens and even adult males than are girls who mature later. Even though their bodies may be advanced by several years, their cognitive age is most likely equivalent to their chronological years and they are woefully unprepared for sexual relationships. The development of such relationships complicates the child's cognitive and social development and presents a skewed view of her self-worth—one that is tied to her physical appearance rather than more important issues. For these reasons, girls who mature early are more likely to have social and self-esteem problems than girls who mature at a normal age or those who develop late.

Boys who mature late are weaker, smaller, and slower than their peers. Even though there is absolutely no correlation between penis size and sexual prowess, many males, especially during puberty, make such judgments. Therefore, boys who develop late may easily be the victims of ridicule. They are more likely to feel shame and anxiousness around their peers than boys who mature at a normal age or those who mature early. On the other hand, girls who mature late are not burdened with the social problems, especially from males, which burden girls who mature early or on time. They are also less likely to suffer from esteem problems than girls who mature early.

The onset of puberty is biologically timed and there is nothing that a parent can do to delay or speed up sexual development. Awareness of the issues that accompany puberty for boys and girls, as well as the issues involved with early or late maturation, can prepare parents to guide children through these developmental experiences.

Sexual Latency

Freud called the ages between six and puberty the *latency* stage. He believed that during these years children are uninterested in their sexuality.

Freud noticed that during these years children tend to form friendships primarily with children of their own gender. Even though children sit with, play with, and want to spend time with children of their own gender, I believe Freud was mistaken in his interpretation of these behaviors. Prior to puberty, children are less interested in the opposite sex than they will be during puberty, but they certainly are interested in members of the opposite sex. They have girlfriends and boyfriends, they talk about who "loves" whom, and they develop infatuations, possibly with many people, prior to puberty. Children develop these emotional relationships with children, teens, and even adults. In fact, for many children, their first love interest is a teacher, baby-sitter, or other older person when the child is in early elementary school.

Freud's observation that children tend to stay within their own gender group is due to the fact that they lack the social skills to pursue relationships. They do not know how to express their feelings in general, but it is especially difficult when they are infatuated with someone. Instead, they pursue their romantic relationships from a distance. They may talk about their love interests, but they will not risk teasing and embarrassment from their same-sex peers and they will not risk rejection by their love interest. Part of a parent's job during these years is to recognize these relationships, help the child identify feelings that are associated with their interests, and find appropriate ways to express those feelings. Of course, I am not suggesting that seven- and eight-year-old children should pursue relationships with each other. Rather, I am suggesting that part of learning how to deal with the powerful emotions associated with infatuation (and eventually, true love) is the ability to recognize those feelings and learn how to express them. This expression can take the form of poetry, a diary, or discussions with parents or other adults.

Teeth

Between the ages of 8 and 12, children lose all of their baby teeth, which are replaced by their permanent teeth. By age 12, only the third molars are still beneath the gums, where they will remain until the late teens or early adulthood. Even though baby teeth will be replaced, dental experts advise that proper care of baby teeth is imperative because poor care of baby teeth can lead to their premature loss and future dental problems.

Although the teeth move easily within a child's mouth throughout adolescence, some orthodontists prefer to prescribe orthodontic appliances while the child is young, his mouth is growing, and the teeth can be easily adjusted. Adjusting the bite and positioning of a child's teeth in these early years can prevent the child from having to wear braces for longer periods of time later in childhood or adulthood. Orthodontic care is expensive and although there are many reputable dentists and orthodontists, one should seek a second opinion before subjecting a child to two or three years of the awkwardness, inconvenience, and discomfort of braces.

Injury and Health

The biggest health risk for children during this stage of life is physical injury. These injuries are often related to sports or accidents around the home. Accidents that are frequent among this age group are drownings, burns, and accidents related to bicycles, ATVs, motorcycles, skates, and skateboards. Death or injury due to automobile accidents is also common, as are injuries suffered from mishandled firearms. Nearly all of these injuries and deaths are preventable with proper supervision, proper storage of firearms and ammunition, wearing a safety belt while in an automobile, and wearing safety equipment while operating ATVs, motorcycles, bicycles, and skateboards.

Obesity is not an uncommon problem in the United States because of poor dietary habits and sedentary lifestyles. Encourage your child to play and do not allow him or her to substitute television or video games for activity. Adult eating and exercise habits have their roots in childhood habits. Teaching your child good exercise and dietary habits decreases the likelihood of a sedentary lifestyle in adulthood, where the ramifications of such a lifestyle are potentially fatal.

Divorce and Custody

Not too many years ago divorce was a relatively rare phenomenon. When I was in grade school, I knew of only one child in my entire grade school whose parents had divorced. We all knew who this girl was because of the rarity of her situation and because of our own fears that our parents might divorce. However, in recent years divorce has become common. In any elementary school or middle school around the country, it is a safe bet that nearly half of the children are from homes where at least one divorce has occurred. The percentage of two-parent families dropped from about 87 percent in 1970 to less than 70 percent in 1995, and many of the two-parent families in the 1995 survey included at least one adult who had divorced and then remarried. Regardless of one's religious or social opinion of these data, the fact is that divorce is a very real part of our culture, and it does not appear that this trend will change anytime soon.

The effects of divorce on children are long-term. It used to be thought that children suffered emotional distress initially following a divorce, but then, as time passed, the effects of divorce waned. The most recent research has called that assumption into question. Data have shown that children continue to experience negative effects of divorce into their late teens and early adulthood. Adults do not fare much better. In a 2002 study of more than 5,000 married people who were tracked over five years, researchers found that two-thirds of those couples who were unhappy yet stayed married reported that they were happier than they were five years earlier. Likewise, those who were unhappy and divorced were found not to be any happier five years later.[3] At the very least, divorce creates emotional turmoil in both adults and children and those emotional effects are long-lasting.

Generally, divorce has more immediate negative effects on boys than girls. They are prone to more acting out and school problems than their peers from intact families. This may be due to lack of a male role model at home, since women are more likely to have custody of children, both boys and girls, than their ex-husbands. Even so, the effects of divorce are also measurable in females. Girls are more likely to have long-term relationship difficulties, both with their mothers and with males. These difficulties also are very likely related to lack of a father figure at home.

Children who live in single-parent homes are more likely to be left alone in the afternoons after school than in two-parent homes. These children, called latchkey children, are more likely to experience a host of problems associated with lack of supervision, such as accidents or misbehavior with siblings or peers. They also have no access to help with homework and no parent at home to discuss the events of the day or issues that may be troubling them. Parents who keep in contact with their children, even if only by telephone, and who know where they are and what they are doing increase the likelihood of adjustment and reduce the likelihood of accidents or injury.

There are many reasons why couples divorce. In cases where children are at risk of physical abuse, sexual abuse, or neglect, the negative effects of the dissolution of the marriage are offset by the advantages of the children's safety. In homes where extreme and regular turmoil exists, divorce also may be beneficial. Spouses who verbally or physically abuse one another on a regular basis expose their children to dysfunctional models that increase the likelihood they will engage in the same behaviors in their own future relationships. All this being said, many relationships end simply because adults are unwilling to invest the energy and work it takes to repair their damaged relationships. *No problem is so big that a couple cannot overcome it if both parties are willing to work at it, and no problem is too small to destroy a marriage if one or both people in the relationship are unwilling to work to overcome it.* For the sake of the children, the adults should make every effort to maintain their marriage unless the health and safety of the children are at risk.

Dating Again and Blended Families

The term "blended families" describes the union of couples with children after divorce or death of their respective spouses. When a parent elects to marry another parent, the newly created dynamic can be complicated. The children of each adult may still harbor a host of emotions regarding the divorce of their biological parents—resentment, anger, relief, hatred, and anguish. At the time of the divorce they had little or no control over the decisions their parents made. Lack of control over one's life is a very hopeless feeling. Then, when remarriage is in the offing, decisions again are made beyond their control. Even if the parents ask the children's opinion, the children are forced to choose between what they may really want and the fact that their decision may mean mom or dad cannot pursue a happy relationship with the person he or she is thinking of marrying. It is an unfair position in which to be placed. Unless the children really want their parent to remarry, they lose no matter what answer they give.

With the new union comes the logistics of either moving into a home with new brothers and/or sisters or having new people move into one's own home. Imagine being forced to move into a home belonging to a workmate or having that workmate move into your home, share your bathroom and perhaps even your bedroom. Even if we liked our workmate, few of us would enjoy being forced into a situation like this, and yet it is this very scenario that children of blended families are forced to endure. This doesn't mean that the difficulties are insurmountable and it doesn't mean that children cannot accommodate to the new living arrangements. Rather, it is important to consider the dramatic emotional and logistical effects of blending families on the children involved. Many times in therapy I have worked with blended families whose children were experiencing rebellion, school difficulties, or incorrigibility. The behaviors were clearly the children's response, at least in large part, to divorce and remarriage, yet the adults failed to consider how their decisions would affect their children. Even if they do consider those effects, many times the adults just assume the children will easily overcome those problems and they marry anyway. Parents should consider how potentially traumatizing blending a family can be even prior to engaging in a romantic relationship. Some experts suggest that parents should not even date while they have young children. This suggestion often is not very realistic, but it does emphasize the seriousness of dating and the many complicating issues involved in divorce, new romance, and remarriage.

Parents should seriously consider maintaining only casual relationships while their children are small. It is very easy for children to experience hope (or fear) that each new man or woman the parent dates could be the next new dad or mom. In their attempt to fit in, these potential mates bring presents and treat these children kindly, thereby only compounding the child's hurt and confusion when the relationship dissolves. I have seen many children in my clinical practice who have divorced mothers or fathers who date. The child reexperiences the pain of divorce each time a new man or woman comes into the parent's life and then disappears. For this reason, if you plan to pursue romance, it is best to keep your relationship separate from your children and your family life. Only when marriage is likely should the potential spouse be introduced to and become a part of your children's lives.

When blending a family, parents should make their best effort not only to respect their children's physical space—their bedrooms, bathrooms, and possessions—but they also should be prepared for an emotional reaction from their children. While some children may resent the parent's new relationship, others are happy that the parent has found love again. Even so, they will be torn between many conflicting emotions. Providing ample time for discussion of feelings, hopes, and dreams can help ease this transition. As your child expresses his or her thoughts about the relationship and the potential family blending, listen carefully for clues to what your child really wants. Respecting your child's wishes as best you can will empower your child and make him or her less resentful when blending occurs. When necessary, professional therapeutic intervention can help.

Freedom and Responsibility

Beginning at age two, children seek their own independence. They want to do things for themselves and they want to demonstrate their competence to themselves and their parents. As children approach the end of their elementary school years and enter middle school, their struggle for independence picks up speed. At puberty, and certainly by their teen years, independence is of primary importance. Children will walk ten yards in front of their parents when they are out together, they will find every possible flaw in their parents' decision making, and the words "I know" will appear daily—even if the child doesn't know.

Prepubescent children want to do more things on their own and with their friends. As they approach their teenage years, they begin to resent parents' involvement and they feel as though people see them as children when they are supervised. Unfortunately, at this age, children want all of the benefits of freedom without accepting its responsibilities. For example, children expect their parents to provide things for them (food, clothing, shelter, etc.), but never consider the fact that those provisions cost money and time and, in fact, demonstrate the parent's concern and love for the child. Instead, egocentric children at this age expect clothes that fit their social group's dictate of style, they want to take trips or outings that cost money without considering the cost to parents, and they want to go and do whatever they want, regardless of the cost (financial, time, energy, schedule, etc.) to the rest of their family. These children dream about living on their own and doing whatever they want, but they cannot, at this age, fully understand the practical responsibilities of adulthood. In short, they do not recognize the connection between freedom and responsibility. With every freedom, one must accept its responsibility.

As children demonstrate their ability to be responsible, parents should give them more responsibility. As the parent, you not only should expect obedience from your children, you should also look for ways to allow them to make decisions for themselves—even when you know they will make mistakes. Of course, you don't want to set them up for failure, but you should not be surprised when they make poor decisions. These are the years for practicing decision making and for learning the consequences of actions. By allowing freedom, but also closely wedding freedom to responsibility, parents not only give children what they want (freedom), but also teach them that freedom and responsibility are inseparable.

Continue to allow freedoms for your child as he or she earns them and demonstrates an ability to behave responsibly. Make sure you encourage your child when you notice him behaving responsibly, so that he can begin to see the connection between responsibility and freedom. For example, as you notice your child responsibly turning in homework assignments, performing household chores, and behaving responsibly with keys and money, laud him for his behavior and reward him with new freedoms, such as a later bedtime or more freedom on the computer or TV and movie choices. Do not give your child freedom simply because he reaches a certain age, especially if he is irresponsible. If you do, you can be certain he will not see the connection between responsibility and freedom and when he is older he will likely make irresponsible decisions when the consequences are very high (for example, driving irresponsibly, which may lead to his own death or the death of others).

Pets

By age eight, children are old enough to care for a pet. They are still at risk for injury, especially from large dogs, but they are old enough to be responsible enough to care for a pet regularly. Caring for a pet is a major responsibility and parents should carefully consider the child's maturity and level of responsibility before acquiring any pet. The life expectancy of dogs and cats is well beyond a decade, so parents must recognize that giving a home to a cat or dog is a long-term commitment. Do not be deceived by the cuteness factor. Many abandoned animals were acquired as puppies or kittens when they were small and cute. However, when owners realized the amount of work and the financial commitment, they abandoned them.

There are many books available to help parents select a pet. Many experts argue that mixed-breed dogs make better pets than full-blooded dogs. Mixed-breed animals often have the positive qualities of the various breeds in their genetic makeup and they are also less expensive—sometimes free (usually from people whose pet has had a litter they cannot keep). Humane societies and animal shelters offer animals at low cost that includes shots and neutering. Regardless of the type of pet you acquire, it will require care, regular shots and checkups, and human interaction. Before choosing a pet, consider your financial resources, the time you have available to care for the pet, and the space available for the pet. Also understand that even during adolescence, children will need to be reminded to care for their pets.

One final issue regarding pets comes from insurance companies. Owning a pet, especially a dog, increases one's personal liability. The likelihood of being sued increases dramatically when one owns a dog. Liability doesn't result just from dog bites. Pet owners have been sued when their non-neutered pet has impregnated another person's pet. Insurance companies suggest that homeowners not only ensure that their pets are properly restrained (for example, in a fenced yard or on a leash), but also that they are neutered and are properly cared for. Neglected and abused pets are much more likely to bite. Finally, have your insurance agent review your homeowner's policy to ensure that you are adequately covered in case of a lawsuit regarding your pet.

SUMMARY

The years between 8 and 12 are exciting, but they can also be a sad time. You will say goodbye to your baby during these years. But as you see the baby appearance and behaviors fading into the past, you also see the emergence of your adolescent child. By age 12, even though our culture does not consider children of this age "adult," they take on adult characteristics in their relationships, their thinking, and their behavior. Puberty may be the biggest and most obvious experience you will go through with your child during these years. Puberty has a profound effect on the developing child. Physical appearance and behavior are affected, in part, by hormonal changes associated with pubescence. Yet there are many other changes during these years as well. Cognitive changes, most noticeably the broadened ability to think abstractly, solve problems, and empathize, greatly increase your child's ability to think, analyze, and study. Your child also changes in his or her approach to social relationships. Friendships are increasingly important. Even though your child will always need you, your role as a parent changes during these years and it will continue to change throughout your child's teenage years.

Throughout your child's life, you should be moving toward providing less direction and giving more responsibility. From birth, we are preparing our children to leave us. In the next chapter, you will see a noticeable transition in the parent's role. Young adults need to be free to make decisions, both good and bad, and to experience freedom. The quest to be free begins at puberty.

PART IV

Adolescence

CHAPTER 9

Emerging Adults: Adolescence (Ages 13–18)

When children turn thirteen, you should put them in a barrel and feed them through a hole. When they turn sixteen, plug up the hole.

—Mark Twain

One does not discover new lands without losing sight of the shore for a very long time.

—Andre Gide

Even though Mark Twain was joking, many parents have felt this level of frustration with their teenage children, but it doesn't have to be this way. Teenagers are developing human beings experiencing one of the most exciting times of their lives, but a time that is also perhaps one of the most difficult. They change by the week in their physical appearance, their hormonal levels, and their cognitive abilities. They are pressured to think like adults when we ask them what they want to do for a living, where they want to go to college, and when we tease them about romances. We expect them to be mature and when they aren't, we say, "You are old enough to know better." On the other hand, we still have to supervise them, make some decisions for them, and discipline them. Therefore, they see themselves as young adults and others see them as adults as well, yet in many ways they are treated like children. Surely it is a confusing time.

Beginning in their earliest childhood playtime, children pretend to be adults. When they play house and dress-up games, their desire to mimic what they see in the adult world is obvious. Early adolescence is the final practice game before the real event. Adolescents long to be adults and at times they are very mature, but in other ways and at other times they are still children. Just as with two-year-olds, much of what frustrates parents about this stage of development is actually desirable. Teenagers *should* begin to question their parents. They *should* begin to stretch and seek more freedom, and they *should* begin to develop concern for their appearance and interest in the opinions of their peers. They *should* want more responsibility, and they *should* begin to develop their own way of thinking. The parent's job is not to stifle these normal and desirable behaviors and thought processes, but rather to help the emerging adult to harness, channel, and polish them. Preparing teens for the adult world requires providing them with responsibilities, allowing them to make their own decisions, and even letting them fail—all while under the parent's supervision. When your child was just learning to walk, you walked along behind her with your hands just inches from her sides in case she fell. You recognized that in order for her to learn to walk on her own, you had to risk falls, banged knees, and scraped elbows. In adolescence, metaphorically, parents do the same thing. They allow their teens to walk on their own, but are never too far away to catch them if they start to fall or to help redirect them if they unknowingly approach hazards in their way. Yet they must walk on their own if they are ever to master self-sufficiency. In a sense, adolescence is an apprenticeship for adulthood and the parent is the mentor. This chapter addresses the issues that parents must be aware of as they prepare their children for adulthood.

THINKING

The years between preadolescence and adulthood mark one of the most dramatic changes in the way children think. Most significant is the ability to think in abstract terms, but adolescents also improve in their ability to solve problems and use deductive logic. As they expand their worldviews, they begin to doubt some of the truths that they once believed. This section addresses these issues as well as learning disabilities and how a parent can help the child overcome limitations.

Abstract Thinking

During early adolescence, children enter a new phase of their cognitive development. From around age eight or nine until puberty, a child's mind is preparing for a form of thinking that he was incapable of prior to that time. Abstract thinking is the ability to think about concepts that cannot be seen.

The word *abstract* means to express a quality apart from the object. Prior to the ability to think abstractly, children cannot understand metaphors, puns, clichés, sarcasm, or similes. For example, if you say, "People who live in glass houses should not throw stones," a child who cannot think abstractly will only understand the concrete example that throwing stones can break glass. He will miss the real point, which is that a person should have his own life in order before making accusations about others. Even more difficult is understanding words that, in order to be fully understood, cannot be thought of in concrete form. For example, very young children understand the word "fair," but their understanding of the word is limited to a concrete demonstration of what fair is. For young children, fairness means equality. If one lets another play with his toy, it is fair if the other child lets the first child play with his toy. In this example, a child can do something fair, but this is only a concrete example of one meaning of the word. In other words, fair is what you do. At a much deeper level, fairness involves much more than equality. The abstract meaning of fairness cannot be fully seen. Fairness is about getting along with one another, respect for others, and treating other people in a way that you want to be treated. None of these concepts can be seen in any concrete way. They can only be pondered in one's mind. Therefore, they are abstractions. It is only when a child reaches puberty and beyond that he or she is capable of fully understanding abstract concepts, and the ability to think abstractly will change the way a child views social justice, honor, religion, parents' rules, and other complex issues.

One of the advantages of this new cognitive ability is that parents can talk with their children in ways they never could before. For example, when my elder daughter was 13, she and I had a disagreement. She was very angry with me because I had punished her for some misbehavior. After an hour or so, I asked her to go for a walk with me. During our 30-minute walk, I explained my reasons for what I had done and why she had been punished. I was able to talk to her about my hopes and fears as a parent and how much I wanted her to have a good childhood. I also told her that I was willing to risk her being angry with me in order to teach her respect, manners, and proper behavior. I shared some experiences from my own childhood and how I wanted some things to be different for her. In the end she understood me and we hugged. It was a very productive conversation and her behavior improved. More important, our relationship was stronger. I could not have had a conversation like this with her even a year earlier. At an earlier age, her inability to think about issues beyond the present situation (e.g., my hopes and dreams) would have prevented her from fully understanding me. Likewise, not long after the terrorist attacks of September 2001, I had many conversations with teenagers about the attacks and their meaning. Because they were capable of thinking abstractly, they were able to understand issues related to religion, history, hate, love, hope, and tragedy. We could talk at length about coping with loss, growing up, our hopes and our fears, and how to deal with them. I could not have conversations like these with younger children.

Deductive Reasoning and Problem Solving

Adolescence marks the beginning of the ability to think deductively. Young children, when presented with a problem, depend on adults to solve it for them. By late elementary school, children should be able to develop a plan for solving problems both in their schoolwork and in life, but their abilities are still limited. It is not until adolescence that they can fully develop a logical plan for testing their hypotheses about problems they face—a skill called *hypothetical-deductive reasoning*. Once a plan is created, they can then execute it by using *hypothesis testing* and *logical combinations*. For example, a word jumble is a puzzle in which the letters of a word are mixed up and the goal is to rearrange them to form the correct word. Children haphazardly try letters in various positions until they find a combination that works. However, as an adolescent develops a plan for trying combinations of letters until she solves the puzzle, she will quickly eliminate, for example, letter combinations that never form words (for example, "b" and "v"). A trial-and-error approach may eventually result in the correct solution, but using logical combinations will, on the average, help a person solve a problem more quickly and more often. Problem solving is a life skill that must be mastered if one is to overcome the difficulties in finances, relationships, jobs, and logistics that are an everyday part of living.

Doubt

One of the many frustrating things about the teen years for parents is the fact that their adolescent children do not automatically believe them just because they say something is so. But doubt is a normal part of cognitive development. Learning to think for oneself, like problem solving, is a life skill that must be acquired if one is ever to achieve full cognitive independence.

During middle and late adolescence, teens think they have most of the answers to life's questions. As a college professor, I occasionally come across a student who knows so little about a subject I teach that he doesn't even know what he doesn't know. He may know a few terms or perhaps he may have been exposed on a very surface level to the subject, but his understanding is extremely shallow. In other words, in his ignorance he believes that he understands the material when just the opposite is true. He is so confident in his knowledge that he cannot see how much he does not know. (The term for this misperception is the *illusion of knowing.*) Therefore, it is very difficult to demonstrate to the student the flaws in his thinking. His misplaced confidence inhibits his ability to hear my comments objectively. During adolescence, teens are exposed to some of life's issues—sexuality, love, religion, social interaction, money management, driving—yet their understanding of these issues is so shallow that they often do not have the slightest notion about how much they still do not know. They doubt their parents' ideas and are certain they have a better answer, but just like my students, their confidence is based on ignorance and inexperience. This frustrates parents because they recognize the lack of understanding in their children and they think, "If only they would listen to me . . ." The more a parent tries to force the teen to accept his or her point of view, the more the teen digs in his heels and refuses to listen.

Even though you can expect your child to doubt your word, your religious beliefs, and your teachings, don't lose heart. Doubt is a necessary part of growth. It is the thing that helps one move from externalized beliefs to the far superior and more powerful internalized beliefs. When children move beyond this stage in their lives, they will recognize the stability of your beliefs and the value that they hold. As they learn more about the world, they very likely will return to many of the core beliefs they were taught in their early years.

Learning Disabilities

There are many identified learning disabilities. Some affect a person's ability to read or study, while others affect only certain academic areas (for example, math). Disabilities may have a physical cause, such as hearing, vision, or motor skills problems, while others may be due to developmental delays, mental retardation, or other conditions (for example, ADHD). These disabilities interrupt the normal learning process and contribute to lower academic grades, poorer social interaction, and a variety of difficulties related to school and social functioning.

While I do not doubt the existence of learning disabilities, experience has shown me that the most effective response to disabilities has come from students who not only recognize their disabilities, but also take responsibility for overcoming their limitations. Rarely do I have a student who has learning disabilities who doesn't succeed when he or she refuses to make excuses based on the learning disability. These students succeed because they focus on what they can do rather than on what they cannot do. On the other hand, even though I am willing to accommodate students with learning disabilities, students who approach me at the beginning of a semester and tell me what they cannot do will more often have significant trouble during the semester. Expecting the system to change to accommodate one's disability without investigating ways to overcome one's limitations addresses only half of the problem. A bigger problem than a learning disability is an attitude of "I can't."

I once served on a college admissions committee. An applicant indicated that he had many learning disabilities. Among them were disabilities that affected his ability to read, study, take notes, take tests, organize his time, and maintain his personal schedule. Almost none of these disorders exist in the *Diagnostic and Statistical Manual of Mental Disorders* (*DSM*),[1] but even so, he said he would need individual assistance in all of these areas. I wondered aloud to whom we would give a diploma if this person ever graduated. Even supposing that he had correctly been diagnosed with disabilities in all of these areas, it was evident that his approach to his disabilities was to seek change in the system rather than to find ways to overcome his limitations. If your child is diagnosed with a learning disability, it is certainly reasonable to look for ways to work within the system to accommodate those disabilities, but you should also investigate ways to help your child overcome his or her limitations. This is yet another life skill that will help long after a child has finished her formal education.

FEELING

As teens enter puberty, their bodies begin producing hormones at a fantastic rate. As these hormones course through their bodies, they affect moods and behavior. In a sense, it is as if they are on drugs—drugs that are naturally produced in their own bodies. The fluctuation of these hormones causes acne, growth variations, and mood swings. Because of their emerging ability to think abstractly, children in their early teens begin to experience a new phase in friendships and romance and their emotions are more intense. Their developing sexual interests compound their emotional connection to members of the opposite sex. Yet relationships with the opposite sex are not the only relationships that are affected by their emerging emotional selves. This section addresses a teen's view of morality, deity, and religion, as well as mental illness in adolescence and the importance of intervention during the adolescent years.

Love

Love is an emotion interwoven with a web of confounding components that is very difficult to unravel. Infatuation is shallow love that is based on appearance, sexual arousal, or selfish desire. True love is based on commitment, empathy, and compassion—components that give rise to physical arousal rather than follow it. Prior to adolescence, a child is capable of loving another person, but that love is based on the need for comfort and attention. A child can fall in "love" with a teacher, classmate, or neighbor, but his love is based on the person's appearance (she is pretty or he is handsome), an undefined raw emotion within, and the attention the child gets from the person. Children think about marriage, but their ideas of marriage are shallow and egocentric. Even though they are capable of doing nice things for the object of their devotion, their love is largely based on what they receive. (See also "Expression of Emotion" in chapter 6.)

Adolescent love is the beginning of real hopes for marriage, sex, and commitment. Theorist Robert Sternberg proposes that healthy adult relationships have three components—*commitment*, *intimacy*, and *passion*. Adolescents are capable of commitment, which is the drive to stay together, but their commitment is limited. Few high school romances lead to marriage. Adolescents are capable of intimacy as well. Intimacy is the ability to share one's emotions, thoughts, and dreams. Teens can form powerful bonds with friends in whom they confide their secrets, hopes, fears, and dreams. Likewise, teens are capable of passion, which is the erotic or sexual component of a relationship. They experience erotic arousal even if they do not act on it.

Even though teens are capable of experiencing all three of these components, they cannot balance them over a long period of time. For example, two adults can coexist quite happily in a marriage without sex if one of them is incapable of performing sexually (for example, because of a spinal injury). They can do this because their passion is based on more than sexual desire. It is balanced by their intimacy and commitment to stay together. Few teens can balance these three components, but adolescent romance allows time to learn these components and what place they hold in one's relationships. During these years, teens learn the importance of each component and how to express it most appropriately. Learning to express love and the place love holds in one's life is one of the difficult tasks in learning about love and romance.

As they struggle for a place in the world, especially in the world of relationships, broken romances are very painful for teens. Not only do they have difficulty identifying and coping with their feelings, but their egocentric worldview makes them feel as though their hurt will never go away, no one will ever love them again, and they will be alone the rest of their lives. Even though adults experience these same feelings when their romances dissolve, they usually have the ability to cope much better than most adolescents because they have experienced broken relationships and they are aware that time heals these wounds. For teens, their limited experiences inhibit this confidence. Therefore, broken relationships are extremely hurtful. In fact, one of the risk factors for suicide during adolescence is a broken romance. Take seriously the pain that your teen feels when rejected by a girlfriend or boyfriend.

Emotions are confusing. We learn to identify them by context and experience. Something in the environment arouses our affect, we search our experience for context and prior similar situations, and then we label the emotion. As we get older, we recognize that we rarely feel a single emotion. More often, we have many emotions operating at any one time—happiness, nervousness, apprehension, excitement, and so on. Sorting out these emotions and learning how to handle them takes years to refine, and some adults never fully master it. You can help your child through love's ups and downs by helping him or her label emotions and find ways to cope with all of the complex feelings that make us human.

Sexual Interaction and Romance

By adolescence, the depth of infatuation changes. Teens are capable of thinking about the future, marriage, and children, and their love for another person can be very deep. It is very difficult for teens and adults alike to distinguish between erotic infatuation and mature love. Therefore, when teens are sexually involved with another person, the emotional bond to that person can be very powerful. They mistake the emotionally powerful passionate love for true love. Yet, the newness of sexual play ebbs in all relationships and if the relationship is not built on something more substantial, over time passionate love will always wane. This doesn't mean that adults who are married for many years do not enjoy sexual relations with one another. Of course they do, but their sexual attraction is not based on appearance. It is based on the deep commitment and intimacy they have with one another. In the most stable relationships, sex follows commitment—it doesn't precede it.

Adolescents may be possessed with sexual thoughts and even young people who are committed to abstinence will be tempted to engage in sexual play, fondling, and intercourse. Preventing unwanted sexual exchange requires planning. Encourage your teens to plan their dates. Knowing where they are going, how long they will be there, and when they will be home reduces the likelihood of engaging in any behavior that should be avoided. Teens get into trouble in many ways when they find blocks of time with nothing to do. Also encourage them to avoid situations that would allow their passions to overtake them. For example, lying on a couch in a house where no adult is present is certainly a setup for sexual play.

There are many reasons to encourage abstinence in teens, including sexually transmitted diseases, pregnancy, and religious teachings. If you want your child to maintain his or her virginity during adolescence, help your child plan for it. For example, when my girls became teens, I bought each of them a ring of her choosing. It was the nicest piece of jewelry either of them had ever owned. I discussed with them the meaning of the ring. It represented their promise to maintain their purity until marriage and it was a reminder to them that I loved them deeply and that my behavior with them was characteristic of real love—not passion or selfishness.

Stalking

The power of love makes it difficult to manage the emotional turmoil of relationships, especially when love is unrequited. Stalking is a serious problem among both young people and adults. It includes repeated and unwanted advances, telephone calls, harassment, and gift giving, and it is a crime in every state. Especially at risk are people who have few social skills, who have few or no friends, and who are immature. Helping an adolescent pursue a relationship or cope with a broken relationship involves learning social skills, reading social cues, and developing a social network. People with even a few close friends are less likely to stalk or harass an individual than are those who are socially isolated. Watch your child for signs of stalking behavior and take it seriously if your child is a victim of a stalker. While most stalkers are not dangerous, many school shootings have been the finale of a long history of stalking by a scorned boyfriend.

Moral Development, Religion, and Conversion

Adolescence is a time of tremendous cognitive and emotional growth. The ability to think abstractly, combined with the fact that children begin to form their own opinions about life, leaves them searching for answers. Adolescence, therefore, is a time of soul-searching and increased likelihood of religious awareness and conversion. It is during this stage of life that people are most likely to seek a higher power and involve themselves in religious activity. Even if your child has been involved in religious activities since early childhood, his newly developed abstract thinking skills will cause him to realize the limited knowledge of his religious life prior to adolescence, thus precipitating conversion experiences.

Unfortunately, most of the research in morality, religious involvement, and measures of character show little correlation. In other words, the level of religious involvement is not necessarily directly related to how people behave. For example, even though it seems that it should be otherwise, according to a 2002 study published in the *Journal of Adolescent Health*, the level of a parent's religiousness has little effect on girls' sexual behavior.[2] These results are common in studies that examine religious involvement and sexual behavior in adolescence. Many other studies have noted that religious affiliation has little affect on honesty, as well. Young people who are active in their religious communities are no less likely to cheat on tests, for example, than those who are not actively involved.

But these data do not always present an important distinction regarding religious and moral teaching and behavior. Some studies, for example, have shown that active religious involvement is positively related to lower rates of sexual involvement. A study of more than 2,000 15–17-year-olds in 1988 showed that a teen's belief that sexual behavior was wrong was a statistically significant factor related to maintaining virginity.[3] What appears to be consistent in regard to behavior is that *internal* moral codes are more powerful in affecting behaviors than *externalized* codes. Therefore, mere attendance at church, synagogue, or mosque does not increase honesty or decrease sexual behaviors, but internalized beliefs, while they may also lead to regular attendance at religious rituals and meetings, are really the cause of moral behaviors. In summary, the difference seems to lie not in the practice of religion but in the internalization of moral codes. If beliefs are externally controlled by parents, religious leaders, or ritual to the exclusion of an internal drive to perform those behaviors, religion appears to have little affect on behavior in adolescence. On the other hand, when a moral code is internalized, behavior reflects that code even in the absence of external reinforcement. (See also the earlier section in this chapter, "Doubt.")

Mental Illness

Many adults mistakenly believe that mental illness affects only adults, but children suffer from depression, neurosis, obsessive-compulsive disorder, a disorder where the child pulls out his own hair (called *trichotillomania*), attention deficit disorder, and even psychosis. Eating disorders and self-mutilation are especially common among adolescents. Any disorder, especially those named above, is a serious issue that needs to be addressed by a trained professional. Situational issues are sometimes the cause of disorders and symptoms may abate over time, but this is not always the case. Assuming that symptoms will go away can be very dangerous. Eating disorders, depression, and self-mutilation, for example, are often present in cases where young people have later attempted or committed suicide. Some of these disorders have lifelong health risks associated with them as well.

If your child exhibits symptoms of psychological disturbance, an appointment with a trained therapist, psychologist, or psychiatrist will aid in diagnosing the cause of the symptoms and provide a plan for treating the symptoms and the underlying causes. Medication is sometimes a short-term solution, although not always. Many parents are apprehensive about medication, but mental illness can be debilitating. Medication can aid in stabilizing a person's affect, thus allowing him or her to function more effectively and to learn more effective ways to cope with circumstances. Once this is accomplished, the child may no longer need medication. Other times, medication makes up for physiological deficits, much as insulin accommodates for the physical deficits of diabetes. There is no shame in taking medication and it can improve not only your child's functioning but also his or her quality of life. Medication should always be monitored by a physician and used in conjunction with therapy, which will help the patient learn new ways to deal with his or her situation.

DOING

Without a doubt, one of the most common questions I receive from parents concerning their adolescents regards sexual behavior, sexual maturity, dating, and relationships. This section addresses those issues as well as other important considerations as young adults approach their final days at home with parents. Important issues regarding driving, planning for college, health, discipline, and finances must be addressed by parents as they prepare to launch their children into the adult world.

Physical Growth

One can expect early adolescents to experience a growth spurt. Parents are sometimes frustrated at how quickly children grow out of their clothes and shoes. They eat more than ever, seeming never to be full. Some experts estimate that a female's caloric intake increases by as much as 60 percent during adolescence, and a male's by as much as 90 percent.

Children in this age group may look and act awkward for several reasons. One reason is related to their developing social awareness. The awkwardness adults feel when they speak in public is somewhat similar to what emerging adolescents feel anytime they are in public. They feel all eyes upon them and their self-consciousness and the accompanying nervousness make them appear awkward. A second reason for their awkwardness is their ever-changing bodies. When an adult buys a new pair of high-heeled shoes, she may find it difficult to balance for at least the first few minutes, if not the first few times, she wears those shoes. Children's bodies are changing in early adolescence and almost weekly they have new legs, new feet, and new arms. They have to get used to these developing body parts just as adults have to accommodate to new shoes. A final reason for their awkwardness is *asynchronous* growth, which means that body parts do not all grow at the same rate. Therefore, arms and legs may not grow in proportion to their bodies. Eventually, all body parts will align, but asynchrony makes teens look and feel awkward.

Sex Education

Many parents perceive the discussion of the facts of life as a single conversation that occurs at puberty. On the contrary, a parent should look for appropriate opportunities to have short discussions on the topic throughout childhood. For example, when my elder daughter was 11, she and I were driving home together after watching a Christmas program. We began talking about the "miracle of the virgin birth" that we had heard about. I asked her if she understood what a virgin was. That question was an open door for a conversation about the facts of life. Likewise, when my sixth grader asked me what AIDS was, that gave me an opportunity to talk about sexually transmitted diseases. My wife also talked with both of my daughters several times about a woman's menstrual cycle when they were young. Discussions about sexuality and the facts of life can be addressed at almost every age. The difference in the conversations from one age to another is the level of detail.

In a child's early years, sex education may involve only a discussion of body parts. As children get a little older, they are ready for more information. When my wife was pregnant with our son, my younger daughter was only three. Discussions about the pregnancy with her were very limited, but she knew the baby was in her mommy's tummy. My eight-year-old daughter, however, was old enough to know more details. We looked at a computer program that showed three-dimensional images of the body, the skeleton, and internal organs. Among the many things we talked about was the uterus. I was able to show my older daughter where the baby was and how she, as a female, was different from me as a male.

When you have many conversations like these with your children, the detailed discussion about intercourse is just one more step in a very long line of discussions. This process makes these conversations less threatening to both parent and child. It also reduces the likelihood of confusion. If a child doesn't understand in a single conversation, he or she may be too embarrassed to ask questions. If the dialogue continues over several years, he or she will be more likely to ask questions, will be less threatened, and will be more likely to develop responsible habits.

Even if you think your children know the facts of life, they may not. One of the reasons for pregnancy in the teenage years is misinformation about sex. Even in elementary school, children are aware of sexual issues. They are informed (and often misinformed) about sexual issues because nearly every aspect of sexuality is portrayed in the cultural media that surround them. Much of their information comes from their friends who don't know any more about sex than they do. Unless parents make a concerted effort to teach their children, we can expect misinformation and ignorance to direct them.

Sex education in the school should not threaten you. It is your job as a parent to teach your children the biology of their sexuality as well as your religious view of it. If you have many conversations about sex and your family's views of sex during your children's childhood, one or two lessons about sexuality at school will have little impact. Some sociologists and psychologists portray teenagers as mindless automata who are entirely at the mercy of their primitive drives. These researchers and activists believe the only way to stem the tide of premarital pregnancies and the spread of disease is to teach "safe sex" and to distribute condoms and other contraceptives. I give our youth more credit than that. Many youth today do engage in various degrees of sexual contact and I am not opposed to teaching safe sex, especially among high-risk groups. However, many young people have chosen to abstain from sex until marriage. Teaching a message that abstinence is acceptable and providing young people with ways to maintain their sexual purity until marriage is a very effective form of contraception and strategy for the prevention of disease. A child can't get pregnant or contract a sexually transmitted disease if he or she is not sexually active. It is a parent's job to communicate this information, not the school's. If a parent does his or her job properly, the ongoing discussions of sexuality will be far more effective than any school-based sex education program.

Look for appropriate opportunities for short conversations about many important topics. Sex is just one of them. The responsible approach to teaching sexuality to your children involves being active with your child as well as thinking and planning for the pressures your child will encounter. Don't

leave to chance something so important as learning responsible sexual behavior. Rather, proactively engage in processes at home that consistently
communicate a healthy approach to sexuality that is consistent with the religious and moral beliefs of your family.

Sexual Behaviors and Experimentation

With the onset of sexual maturation, early adolescent children experience
an awakening of sexual interest, although the level of interest varies greatly
from one child to another. Sexual energies are undifferentiated during this
stage of life, which means that a child's sexual energies could easily be directed into any of a number of areas—incestuous sexual play, homosexual
behavior, and pornography, as well as cross-gender sexual behavior. Sexual
interest can be intense throughout adolescence. Parents express concern
about finding pornography in their child's room. Even though the use of
pornographic material by minors is illegal and undesirable, it is not unusual.
If one's religion prohibits the use of pornography, the parent must be cautious in how he or she addresses it with the child. A child's sexual curiosity
and energy must be understood and properly channeled, not squelched.

Likewise, sexual foreplay between adolescents is not uncommon. Again,
it is not desirable, but it is not unusual. The wise parent will control his or
her temper, address the behavior, and use the situation to teach proper conduct. A response from a parent that is too punitive will only ensure that the
child will *not* come to the parent to discuss the sexual urges that are an inevitable part of growing up. During adolescence, parents give their children
more freedom. As always, however, reasonable supervision and guidance will
reduce the likelihood that your teen will engage in inappropriate sexual behaviors.

Even though sexual play between siblings is not uncommon, it may be
illegal—especially if one child is several years older than the other. This type
of sex play can easily become forced and may indicate disturbance in the older
child. All incestuous sexual play should be addressed with the children involved and parents should consider the possible need for professional intervention with a child therapist. Addressing sexual dysfunction in adolescence
greatly reduces the likelihood of sexually inappropriate behavior in adulthood
(for example, rape or molestation).

A study done in 2002 demonstrated that a young man's sexual behavior
is affected more by conversations about sex with his father than by conversations with his mother.[4] This same study of over 2,000 subjects (parent-
child pairs) showed a correlation between higher education of parents and

females delaying sexual behavior. Also correlated with delayed sexual debut in females were good relationships between mother and daughter, good communication between mother and daughter about the child's friends, and strong disapproval by the mother of the daughter having sex. It was interesting that this study disclosed that many parents of sexually active teens were unaware of the child's sexual behavior. In summary, a good relationship between parent and child and open channels of communication enhance the probability that your children will maintain behaviors consistent with your family's moral position.

Dating

There is no magic age at which a child is suddenly ready for the responsibility of dating. Several considerations are important. First, learning the dating process begins in the early elementary school years. A parent should take his or her child out on simulated "dates" in order to teach the child how it works. When they were young, I took my daughters on dates to dinner, the movies, and other events. I wanted them to see how they should be treated on a date. As they reached the ages when they went on dates without me, they knew what to expect and what behaviors were unacceptable.

As a general rule, age 16 is a good starting place, but the child's development should be considered when deciding when he or she is ready to date. Some children are socially and emotionally underdeveloped at a traditional age for dating (16 years, for example) and, therefore, they might be unprepared to handle the responsibilities of dating. Other children may be ready around age 16. The way you know is by examining the way your children handle responsibilities like schoolwork, homework, and household chores. If the child is deceptive, dishonest, or irresponsible in these areas, it is likely the same characteristics will present themselves on a date.

Plan to meet your son or daughter's date. If your child is ashamed or afraid to introduce the date to you, or if the date is unwilling, your child should not be going out with this person. Also, make sure your child has a clear plan for the date. Where will they go? What will they do? Who will be there? When will they return? Simply providing a curfew may leave too many things to chance. Young people who "hang out" with nothing to do are much more likely to get into trouble than those who plan their dates.

Dating is an important part of learning social skills, social responsibility, and compatibility. It is also a risky behavior that irresponsible young people can use to engage in risky and irresponsible sexual behavior as well as other potentially damaging or dangerous behaviors. Teaching children to be responsible during the years leading up to dating and providing a home that encourages responsible behavior is the beginning point for preparing them for the responsibility of dating.

Pregnancy and Contraception

There are many things we fear in regard to our children. While they are still in the womb, we hope for a healthy child, all body parts in the right place. We want them to be free from injury and disease. As they become teenagers, we want them to make good choices, to stay away from "the wrong crowd," to avoid trouble with the law, and to avoid habits that would compromise their health and safety. But we know our children will get sick on occasion and sometimes they will make bad choices. Some choices have short-term consequences while others may have wide-reaching impact. Teen pregnancy is a problem that has lifelong consequences.

When a teenager gets pregnant, parents can't help but feel hurt, anger, and fear. They may experience social embarrassment and feel they have failed as parents. They know the difficulties that lie ahead and they wish their children had made wiser decisions. Dealing with these emotions takes time, but parents must temporarily set them aside for the best interest of the girl and the baby that she carries. The pregnant teen needs emotional, physical, and financial support. Deciding what to do will be one of the most important decisions of her life. Among her options are abortion, raising the baby alone, marrying the father and raising the child in a family setting, and giving the baby up for adoption.

It is my opinion that abortion is an inappropriate choice. Advocates for abortion rights argue that a woman has the right to choose what to do with her body. As I stated in chapter 2, a woman has the right to choose not to get pregnant, but once she has made a decision to engage in behaviors that have led to pregnancy, her personal rights should not override the rights of the child inside her body. (See "Abortion" in chapter 2.) Even though my personal belief is that abortion is an inappropriate choice, it is a legal option in the United States and many other countries. Women are free to take advantage of this option if they choose. Discussion of this topic is difficult, and regardless of which side of the debate one takes, emotions can easily obscure objectivity. Instead of debating the pros and cons of abortion, this discussion might be most productive if one concedes that there are other options for dealing with pregnancy that do not require one to make a life-or-death decision in regard to the fetus.

The teenager could choose to raise the child by herself. A teenage mother faces many problems when raising a baby alone. First of all, no adolescent is physically or emotionally mature enough to be a mother. Research shows that teenagers raising babies are more likely to neglect or abuse their children. These babies also have poorer test scores when they reach their school years, they are more likely to have mental health issues (for example, ADHD, learning disabilities, behavioral disorders), and they are more likely to have relationship difficulties in their adolescent years. Young mothers must work to provide for their children, making it difficult to continue their education. Marrying the father and raising the child together is possible, but marriages under these conditions are very unstable and are much more likely to end in divorce than marriages between adults.

Yet another option is to deliver the baby but give it up for adoption. Most of the criticisms about adoption refer to disadvantages and the wants and needs of the mother and/or father. Yet all things considered, adoption holds the most advantages for the child. There are many loving couples who desperately want to have a child. Through adoption, the child can grow up in a financially stable home with two parents who are psychologically and emotionally prepared for the daunting task of parenthood. When the teenage mother places her child up for adoption, she can have her prenatal care financed by the adoptive parents. After the delivery, the mother can continue life without the many complications of motherhood and perhaps have children at some future time when she is more adequately prepared for the task.

Many argue that the adopted child will feel unloved or have adjustment problems when he or she has to deal with the reality of being adopted. Even though many adopted children long to meet and know their birth parents, I have never met any adopted child or adult who was raised in a loving home with two parents who had significant adjustment problems because of adoption, and I am aware of no research that demonstrates any significant problems for adopted children in these circumstances. Likewise, the potential disadvantages of adoption are no greater than the potential disadvantages of being raised by unprepared adolescents. When a mistake is made, the responsible person seeks to respond in a way that is best for all considered. For this reason, when a teenager is pregnant, even though giving a child up for adoption would be difficult for the parents, grandparents, and others, it is very possibly the most loving thing to do for the baby.

Contraception

Many times I have been asked if I thought adolescent girls who were sexually active should use birth control. The answer to this question is simple—of course they should, unless you want to run the risk of pregnancy. The more important question involves whether or not the parent is aware of the teen's sexual behavior and her receipt of a prescription for the pill or other birth control method, and whether or not the parent is in control of the child. For example, during a question-and-answer session at a parenting seminar, a woman told me her daughter was sexually active and she could not seem to contain her daughter's wild behavior. Should she get a prescription for the pill for her daughter? This woman had several problems. Her first and most immediate problem was that her daughter risked pregnancy. Giving her the pill could be construed as permission to continue that behavior, but the woman said the girl was already sexually active. There would be little lost in this situation and the consequences of not protecting her from pregnancy were very real, imminent, and dramatic. The last thing this family needed was an unwanted pregnancy. Her second problem was that her daughter was out of control. The child would not obey or respect her mother. Even though this was not the most pressing problem, it was in fact the bigger problem. Finally, because of the girl's behavior, she risked acquiring a communicable disease—a consequence that could be fatal. No form of birth control, other than abstinence, would fully protect her from AIDS, syphilis, herpes, or a number of other diseases.

A highly publicized study published in the *Journal of the American Medical Association* in 2002 showed that requirements that parents be notified when their children attempt to acquire contraceptives or STD testing greatly reduced the likelihood that girls 14–17 would use these services.[5] This study was the result of a poll of 950 sexually active girls in Wisconsin who were treated at Planned Parenthood clinics in 1999. While African-American girls and girls 17 and older were less likely to stop using sexual health care services than younger girls, even then 56 percent of 17-year-olds and 49 percent of African-American girls said they would terminate services if parents were informed.[6] This controversial issue is not only about the rights of parents to be informed when their daughters receive medical intervention. The AMA staunchly defended patient-physician confidentiality in order to provide services to young females that can greatly reduce the number of unwanted pregnancies and the transmission of STDs. Opponents argue that the same child who wishes to receive contraception and/or testing for STDs could not get an antacid from a school clinic without parental notification. Issues like these are highly politicized. Whether birth control is provided, with or without parental permission and knowledge, is an important but separate issue from the use of birth control and the issues addressed above. In normal circumstances, you should not acquire birth control pills for your child unless you want to place your stamp of approval on sexual behavior. On the other hand, in extreme circumstances like the ones mentioned above, it is the lesser of two evils.

The pill, one of several forms of birth control, is not only a form of birth control. It is also a common prescription for adolescent females who are not sexually active but have difficult menstrual periods. An adolescent who is having difficult and/or irregular menstruation might easily benefit from taking the pill. (See chapter 2 for more information on birth control.)

Homosexuality

As children reach pubescence, they experience a host of emotions. Just as it is not uncommon for pubescent children to experiment with pornography, masturbation, or sexual contact, it is not atypical for children to have homosexual thoughts or even brief homosexual encounters. The fact that it is not atypical means that parents should not necessarily be alarmed, but it doesn't mean that homosexual behavior is desirable any more than it is desirable for an early adolescent to engage in heterosexual behavior. The cause of homosexuality and, more important, the culture's opinion of homosexuality, are hotly debated topics. Just as I may have alienated some readers with my position on abortion, I recognize that no matter which position I take on this issue, there will be those who adamantly hold the opposite view. Nevertheless, it is a pertinent issue in adolescence and it must be addressed. I have included arguments from both sides of the issue.

Many homosexuals argue that they first realized their homosexual interests in early childhood or early adolescence and, indeed, there is a body of research evidence that indicates homosexuality is a part of one's personality. Personality is largely based on one's genetic makeup and is very difficult to change. Homosexual advocates use research that supports this claim as reason not to dissuade one from pursuing same-sex relationships, even in adolescence. They argue that a homosexual is genetically made that way and can no more change his or her sexual orientation than a heterosexual can. Indeed, many homosexuals have deeply desired to change to a heterosexual lifestyle, but have found it nearly impossible. Opponents to this argument propose that similar genetic arguments can be made for drug addiction, compulsive behavior, gambling, pedophilia, and even serial killers. All of these behaviors have some evidence of genetic links and people who struggle with these issues find that they are driven to pursue their goals even when they want to change. Many people who have these drives first realized their interest in these issues during childhood or adolescence. Yet few people in the mental health community would argue that because pedophiles, for example, may be genetically predisposed to pursue sex with children, the community should accept the behavior as normal and/or desirable. (Hard as it is to believe, there actually are a few mental health practitioners who *do* make this argument.)

Gay and lesbian advocates state that as children reach pubescence, their sexual awakenings should not be stifled, arguing that teens should be free to pursue their sexual orientation as it develops. They say that the cultural oppression of such drives only makes these children feel bad about who they are and creates internal confusion. While some of what they say is true, opponents argue that children have many sexual urges in adolescence. Pursuing these urges just because they exist, especially during a time in emotional and cognitive development when one is incapable of making mature decisions, is irresponsible. Teenagers have powerful *heterosexual* drives, yet most counselors do not advocate heterosexual promiscuity.

Homosexual advocates argue that the taboo against homosexual relationships has its roots in the Judeo-Christian ethic. This ethic, they claim, is a man-created view that has been accepted for centuries. They point to similar times in history when religious bodies oppressed entire groups of people. For example, the mentally ill once were thought to be demon-possessed, but the religious world does not routinely hold that position today. Mental illness is recognized for what it is, though it was not until it was pointed out how the church had demonized people just because they were different that any progress was made. Likewise, divorced people, especially divorced women, were once shunned by the Protestant churches, but in recent decades churches have begun to accept divorce even among the clergy. On the other hand, opponents to this argument say that even though a long religious history doesn't automatically make something (e.g., the Judeo-Christian ethic) correct, neither does having a long religious history automatically make something wrong. Religious writings in Judaism and Christianity directly forbid homosexuality.

So who is right and what role does homosexuality play for developing adolescents? The United States is a free country and adults are free to practice this behavior if they choose. A person's sexual orientation makes him or her no less worthy of equal treatment under the law than any other citizen. However, adolescents are too young to make decisions about their sexuality, whom they will sleep with, and whom they will marry. It seems irresponsible that educators, doctors, or mental health professionals would isolate something so important as sexual orientation and suppose children are capable of making decisions at 13 or 14, and yet not also allow them to make decisions about marriage, sleeping with classmates, or engaging in sexual behavior with adults.

The powerful emotions that drive arguments on each side of the issue inhibit one's ability to see that a person exists beyond the behavior. Any parent who has a child struggling with the issue of homosexuality can confirm that it is much harder to take an antihomosexual stance when it affects one's own child. Only through objective discourse can one arrive at a reasonable conclusion about homosexuality, its cause, its meaning, and one's response to it. It is your responsibility as a parent to decide what to do with this information, and to make up your own mind.

Sexual Abuse

Pedophiles prey on children of all ages. Young children are at risk from predators because they have limited means to protect themselves or to communicate what has happened to them after the fact. As children move into their early teens, parents want to give them more freedom and responsibility, but no matter how responsible these children may be, an adult can easily overpower them. Therefore, they are still at risk of becoming victims of sexual abuse. Teens like to think they are in control and that nothing bad can happen to them, but they are more vulnerable than they believe. A sly pedophile can easily overpower a teen or lure her into an area where she cannot call for help. Even though you need to give your child more freedom, she still needs some supervision.

Open communication is important in the tragic case that your child is sexually abused. Dealing with abuse from a parent, relative, neighbor, teacher, or stranger requires that the parent and child have the opportunity to discuss it. The child must trust the parent and feel free to discuss the situation if the parent is to be of any help. This requires a relationship that is fostered over time. Parents should also be aware of the symptoms of sexual abuse (for example, vaginal discharge, shame or fear of one's body or sexual issues, change in school performance, risk-taking, or suicidal behavior), so that if the child does not open a dialogue with the parent, the parent can be the one to initiate the conversation.

School Safety

A big part of my professional work involves homicide investigation and prevention. I've spent much time studying homicide, lecturing on the subject at the FBI Academy in Quantico, Virginia, and addressing schools, law enforcement groups, therapists, and businesses on homicide prevention and risk assessment. Every day, somewhere in the country, school shootings, rapes, bullying, and other violent acts take place. School violence is especially troubling because it occurs in a place that we assume is safe. Most of the school shootings I have studied (those that did not involve drugs or other crimes) have happened in quiet suburban communities where people believed they were safe from violence.

There are several things parents can do to help keep their children safe. First, make sure your children know that any threat made by another student, no matter how unlikely it may seem, should be taken seriously. Many times in recent years, plots have been uncovered when a student told an adult of the plan. The conspirators may not have followed through with their plans, but the risks are too great to take chances. Threats to shoot, stab, blow up, or otherwise harm self or others are always worthy of attention. This may seem self-evident, but in many cases where school shootings have occurred, others knew of the plan but didn't believe it would happen.

Certainly parents should supervise their children. The boys in Littleton, Colorado, not only left evidence of their plans in plain view in their own bedrooms, they spent hours preparing the pipe bombs they later carried to the school, not to mention the vile videos and web pages they created. One might ask how these boys could have made such extensive preparations without their parents becoming suspicious. The rooms that your children occupy in your home are not their rooms. They belong to you and you allow the children to use them. Parents can go overboard respecting the privacy of their children to the point that they don't supervise them appropriately. Parents must walk a fine line between disrespect for a child's space and poor supervision.

Certainly a parent must recognize warning signs of violence. Suicide attempts or ideation, fascination with death, weapons, and violence, as well as cruelty to animals or people, are troubling signs. These behaviors are not normal and are always worthy of attention. Don't believe it when you hear people saying, about someone who has killed another person, that there was no indication that the person would commit a violent act. There are always warning signs.

Finally, stay involved with your children. Desperate people commit desperate acts. When children see a future, have hope, and know they do not stand alone in this sometimes frightening world, they are less likely to pursue acts of desperation and more likely to believe they can endure current struggles. Family unity and involvement foster a realistic perspective on life and can help one endure life's difficulties.

Driving

Once children have a driver's license, they want to drive everywhere they go. Before you relinquish the car keys, consider some reasons not to give your child unlimited access to a car. Driving a car is probably the most dangerous thing your children will ever do. The roads are crowded with other drivers, and road debris, potholes, and other obstructions create a challenge even for proficient drivers. Extra surprises like deer and stray animals, as well as careless or aggressive drivers, make safe driving a complicated task requiring great skill and maturity.

Teenagers are among the poorest and least skilled drivers. Even very responsible and mature teens are limited in their ability to handle an automobile efficiently. That does not mean they are all bad drivers per se, but they have more accidents than the rest of us for a reason. They lack experience; it will take time for them to polish their driving skills; and they are easily distracted, especially if there are other teens in the car with them. Even experienced drivers are at greater risk on the road when they are talking on cell phones or tuning the radio. Another reason teens are poor drivers is that they do not understand the laws of physics. Again, even some experienced adult drivers fail to adjust for changes in road conditions, speed, condition of the automobile, and weather, but novice drivers are most at risk for such errors. Finally, teens perceive themselves as invincible and they tend to believe that accidents happen only to other drivers. Because of their inexperience and immaturity, dents and scratches should be expected eventually on any car they are allowed to drive.

More teenagers die in automobile-related deaths than by any other means. We all want our children to live to adulthood and yet our decisions sometimes do not demonstrate that. Just because a child reaches age 16 does not mean he or she is prepared to drive a vehicle. This does not mean that teens should never drive, but parents should carefully evaluate their children's level of maturity and responsibility as well as their skill behind the wheel before letting them drive the family car. Consider where they want to drive and with whom. Also consider whether they will be driving in daylight, at night, during inclement weather, or on poorly maintained roads or roads that have a high frequency of accidents. As children improve in their skills and grow in maturity, they can earn the privilege of driving more places, more often, and with a wider variety of passengers.

Several states have proposed bills increasing the minimum driving age, only to have them defeated by vocal objections from citizens. I can think of only two reasons that would lead parents to oppose raising the driving age—the inconvenience of having to drive their children everywhere and a desire to appease their children. Unpopular as my suggestions may be, more children will live to see their twenties if parents and teens set aside their personal interests and follow these precautions.

Planning for College

Planning for college includes planning for finances, selecting a college, visiting and applying to a college, and planning for a career. There are few decisions that occupy as much time and money for young adults as where to attend school following high school graduation.

Finances

Financial planning for college begins many years before your child graduates from high school. College tuitions and fees have risen disproportionately to the cost of living over the past several years. Currently, private education routinely runs between $10,000 and $20,000 or more per year. Public education is less expensive, but still potentially cost-prohibitive without financial aid, loans, long-term savings, or a combination of the three. There are many sources for financial aid and very few college students actually pay full tuition and fees. Grants and scholarships are available from federal, state, institutional, and private sources. Some of these sources not only pay tuition and fees but may also cover housing, books, and even stipends for personal living expenses. Student loans through the government or your bank are also low-interest ways to finance college expenses.

Academic scholarships are one source of financial aid. Universities want to attract quality students as much as they want to attract musicians, artists, and athletes. Therefore, a high grade-point average and high scores on standardized instruments like the Scholastic Achievement Test (SAT) can lead to college funding. Your child can prepare financially for college by getting a job during the high school years, but those dollars are quickly spent. I have instructed all of my children that their job during high school is working on their grades. They can potentially earn far more college tuition dollars through scholarships because of good grades and high SAT scores than they would ever earn working at a fast-food restaurant or a shoe store.

There are numerous companies that sell information about grants and scholarships. Most experts in college financial aid discourage paying for this information. Most of the information these services provide is available for free. You are paying them to put it together for you. Likewise, many of these compilations of financial resources are from sources for which your child will not qualify. Invest your energies seeking funding from government sources, financial aid through the college or university your child plans to attend, and through organizations you are a part of—work, church, or civic groups.

Campus jobs are another source of income. Students can work in a campus job, and even though the pay is less than they might make off campus, the job flexes around their class schedule, and since it is on campus, they do not need an automobile—further saving money. Many colleges and universities use student workers in campus offices, housekeeping, and buildings and grounds departments, as assistants to professors, and in the dining and residence halls.

Financial aid is based on the previous year's income tax return—documentation you will need to complete most federal financial aid forms. Apply early for all forms of financial aid. Even though a college may have an application deadline for financial aid of May 1, once its aid dollars are expended, there may be none left even for qualified students.

Financial aid regulations change frequently. Get to know the financial aid officer at your child's prospective institution and make sure you do not make any assumptions from year to year regarding the aid for which your child qualifies. Most financial aid forms have to be resubmitted each academic year.

Selecting a College

Which college your child attends depends on what he or she wants to do when finished. A college's reputation, location, faculty, and convenience are all important considerations, but if your child cannot pursue his or her career path upon graduation, then it is the wrong choice. Take into account the amount of financial aid your child will receive from federal and private sources as well as from the institution. A college or university that may have at first seemed too expensive may actually be comparable in cost to less expensive schools once you have computed financial aid. Job placement and assistance in pursuing graduate school admission are also important considerations. Does the college or university have an office or an individual in your child's department who is responsible for helping your child find a job or graduate school upon graduation? You also should consider the institution's graduation rate, job placement rate, and success rate for admission to graduate programs.

Most colleges and universities have Internet sites that provide much of this information, including virtual tours, telephone numbers and e-mail addresses of people you will need to contact, and other important information. Financial information is often omitted from web sites because it changes frequently and varies from person to person, depending upon the applicant's grades, standardized test scores, residency, and financial aid. Consultation with the financial aid officer will answer all of your finance questions.

Visitation and Application

When your child has narrowed his or her list of potential colleges to three or four, plan a visit to each institution. Many colleges offer prospective student visitation days, but I encourage students to visit the campus during normal operations. That way they can see the college as they would experience it.

Whenever possible, let your child spend the night in the dormitory with a student, attend a few classes, take a campus tour, and meet with admissions and financial aid counselors.

Application fees are waived at many colleges and universities if the applicant applies through the school's web site. Keep copies of your application materials so you will know to which colleges you have applied and will have pertinent information handy for reference when filling out other applications you may need to complete.

Residency

If you can afford it, let your child live on campus. College life is very demanding. Living on campus saves your child time commuting and makes it easier for him or her to use the library, laboratories, and other facilities. On-campus jobs further accommodate the busy life of a college student, making an automobile unnecessary. Social activities are one of the most enjoyable things about one's college years and commuters miss out on many of these activities. Nightlife, dorm life, and socializing will be parts of your child's college experience that will never be forgotten. Living on campus also provides a time of transition for learning the responsibility of living on one's own.

Health

One of the most obvious health issues during adolescence is acne. There are many causes of acne, but during adolescence, the production of hormones and the presence of excessive facial oil cause acne. Acne is unavoidable, but it can be controlled by regular cleansing and sometimes through medication.

The most likely threats to your child's health during adolescence are accidents and drugs. Accidents include falls from bicycles, skateboards, motorcycles, ATVs, or horses. Anyone riding any of these should wear protective gear (for example, a helmet). Many children are injured each year in sports-related activities as well. Without question, most deaths during adolescence result from auto accidents. Wearing a seat belt and having limited access to an automobile can help save your child from injury and even death. (See section on driving in this chapter.)

Drugs

The use of illegal drugs and the misuse of prescribed drugs have been problems for years. In recent decades, the problem invaded the youth culture, in large part because of availability. Despite laws that prohibit selling alcohol and tobacco to teenagers, these are readily accessible to most teens. Even cocaine, crack, crank, LSD, marijuana, Ecstasy, heroin, and meth-amphetamines are not hard to find, regardless of where one lives. In short, if your child is motivated to use drugs, he or she will find them. Drugs offer users a chance to escape problems, to fit in with their peers, and to rebel.

Drugs have many physical, behavioral, and psychological effects. Knowing the symptoms of drug abuse is necessary in addressing the problem with your child. Lying, stealing, weight loss, loss of appetite, mood swings, flat affect, agitation, school problems, legal problems, unexplained absences, and certainly the presence of drug paraphernalia (for example, bongs, roach clips, cigarette paper, pipes) are all symptoms of drug use. Drug addiction is very difficult to overcome and some drugs are addictive after just one or two uses. Professional treatment is imperative and the sooner the problem is addressed, the higher the likelihood of success. Drug treatment programs address environmental changes, they create accountability, and they address the issues that led to the use of drugs in the first place.

Drugs like GHB (gamma hydroxybutyrate) and rohypnol are a current problem, especially on college campuses. These drugs are odorless, tasteless, and colorless. Some people use these drugs for personal pleasure, but they are called "date rape" drugs because they have been used to incapacitate another person in order to take sexual advantage. These drugs cause the victim to become totally lethargic or to lose consciousness. In either case, the perpetrator is then able to take advantage of the victim without resistance. In some cases, victims have no memory of the event even if they did not lose consciousness. These drugs are often used in conjunction with alcohol. Therefore, many victims pass out and, upon awakening, think their loss of consciousness was due to having had too much to drink when in fact they were intentionally drugged. Some victims have died after being given these drugs. Make sure your child is aware of these drugs and how they can be used.

Sexually Transmitted Diseases (STDs)

Just a few decades ago, sexual experimentation led, at the worst, to pregnancy or a sexually transmitted disease that could easily be treated. Today, while pregnancy is still a possible outcome, several sexually transmitted diseases are incurable and a few are fatal. In other words, sexual experimentation is potentially fatal. Sexually transmitted diseases are conveyed from one person to another in part through lack of understanding of the diseases and how they are spread. The people at highest risk for contracting most sexually transmitted diseases are sexually promiscuous individuals and those who share needles with others. However, anyone who has sexual contact, even once, with an infected person can contract one or more of these diseases. While some STDs have been transmitted through blood transfusions, sexual contact is by far the greatest risk. Many STDs are transmitted when body fluids (semen and blood) come into contact with soft, mucus-lined tissues of the body (mouth, vagina, anus, urethra) or open cuts, sores, or blisters. Teens, and even some adults, mistakenly think that abstaining from intercourse, but engaging in oral sex or casual sexual contact (not intercourse), will protect them from sexually transmitted diseases. Likewise, some well-intentioned organizations have falsely communicated that use of a condom will prevent the spread of STDs. While condoms help, they do not guarantee that one will not contract an STD.

Depending on the type of STD one contracts, the disease can cause pain, fever, inflammation, lesions, itching, and growths of various kinds. Left untreated, they can complicate pregnancy and delivery, they can be transmitted to a fetus during birth, and they may eventually lead to senility and even death. Among the many diseases associated with sexual contact or sexual intercourse, perhaps the most frightening is HIV/AIDS.

HIV/AIDS

At the end of 2003, it is believed that AIDS (acquired immunodeficiency syndrome) had killed over 21 million people worldwide and that over 5 million new cases of HIV (human immunodeficiency virus) occur each year. Homosexual males are at very high risk for the transmission of HIV. There are no consistent and reliable data concerning sexual promiscuity among homosexuals, but what few data exist demonstrate that promiscuity is a common behavior among homosexual males. Any sexual promiscuity, whether homosexual or heterosexual, increases the likelihood of contracting and spreading sexually transmitted disease, but male homosexuals are especially at risk for contracting AIDS because of the practice of anal intercourse. Anal sex increases the likelihood of contracting HIV because the anus is not large enough to accommodate an erect penis and, therefore, tearing of the anal tissue is not uncommon during intercourse. These openings provide a point of entry for the transmission of the HIV virus. Drug users also are a high-risk group because of the practice of sharing needles. While it is rare, mothers can transmit AIDS to their babies via breast milk and it is possible, although unlikely in the United States, for AIDS to be transmitted through blood transfusions. Anyone who engages in sexual contact with an infected person is at risk for contracting HIV.

Once a person contracts the HIV virus, he or she is positive for HIV. The virus remains in a person's body throughout life. Eventually, the HIV virus gives rise to AIDS. Once this happens, AIDS is almost always fatal. However, in some cases, people carry the HIV virus and never develop AIDS. Physicians and researchers are frantically seeking answers to the question of why some people carry HIV but do not develop AIDS. A clear answer has eluded them. When AIDS develops, there are drugs available to control the symptoms, but eventually the body's defenses deteriorate and the person dies of opportunistic infections or illnesses.

When an invader moves into the body, cells called *T-* and *B-cells* that are produced in the bone marrow surround the invading cells and latch onto them. Once captured by T- or B-cells, the invader is rendered harmless and is eventually disposed of by the body. The HIV virus invades the body and as special T-cells called *CD4 T-cells* attempt to capture the virus, instead of being captured, the virus invades the walls of the CD4 T-cells. Once inside the cells, the virus converts the CD4 T-cells' RNA into DNA and tricks the cells into copying the HIV virus. Infected CD4 T-cells then move into the lymph nodes and organs of the body where many other T-cells gather, and form strands of CD4 called *follicular dendritic cells* or *FDCs*. There, the virus begins to reproduce itself, invading uninfected CD4 cells in the FDCs, rendering them useless for fighting other invaders. Over time, the number of infected T-cells increases and the body cannot produce enough new T-cells to fight infections. When this happens, what would ordinarily have been relatively minor infections overwhelm the body. At this point, the person is said to have AIDS. Therefore, no one dies of AIDS. Instead, they die of illnesses that most likely would have been repelled if the person did not have the HIV virus—pneumonia, infections of the lungs, intestines, and brain. AIDS victims may suffer blindness due to infections in the eyes, weight loss, cancer, and also many side affects from the drugs used to treat AIDS.

HIV is called a *lentivirus* or "slow" virus, which means that even though it reproduces quickly, there is long time between infection and the presentation of symptoms. Therefore, a person can be HIV-positive for many years before developing AIDS. In fact, a little more than ten years is the average period from HIV infection until the onset of AIDS. When the virus first became widely known in the early 1980s, many of those who were developing AIDS at the time had been infected with the HIV virus a decade or more earlier. This is especially frightening when one considers that an adolescent engaging in sexual experimentation could contract the HIV virus at age 16 or 17 and yet not exhibit AIDS symptoms until his or her thirties—a time when the person may be married and have children. If the AIDS victim in this scenario is female, she may have transmitted the disease to her children during childbirth, all while being unaware that she was HIV positive. One's life, and perhaps the health of one's spouse and children, would be compromised because of one's behavior during adolescence.

Other STDs

Even though AIDS is a frightening disease and attracts a lot of public attention, there are many other STDs, and some of them affect far greater numbers of people than AIDS. *Pubic lice*, also called crabs, can be spread through sexual contact or by shared clothing or bedding. This disorder is treatable, but lice are tenacious parasites. Even when active lice are killed, their eggs can hatch, providing a new batch of lice that quickly reproduce. *Gonorrhea* and *syphilis* are diseases that can be spread through sexual contact (anal sex, oral sex, sexual intercourse) or by contact of contaminated fluid with an open cut or sore. Effects of these two STDs can be dramatic, but they are easily treated with penicillin. *Hepatitis* (A and B) and *genital herpes*, while usually not fatal, are incurable diseases. *Genital warts* are extremely contagious. Left untreated, they develop into large, cauliflower-shaped warts in the genital region. Individuals infected by genital warts can transmit the disease even when they have no visible symptoms. Genital warts can be cured using topical acidic solutions administered by a physician. Even though it can be treated, *chlamydia* is an STD that many people are unaware of. It is the fastest-spreading sexually transmitted disease in the United States and it is easily transmitted by sexual contact.

The safest way to protect oneself from STDs is either by abstaining from sexual contact or by having a single sexual partner. The more sexual contact one has, the more likely one is to contract an STD.

Peer Trademarks

Peer trademarks are styles of dress, hairstyles, jewelry or other items that members of a peer group use to identify each other. In the 1960s and early 1970s, long hair was a peer trademark. My father allowed me to decide how long to let my hair grow during my high school years. Even though I'm positive he didn't like my choice, he recognized that he needed to allow some things he didn't like so that I could feel like I fit in with my peer group. He realized that parents eventually have to let go and allow their children to make some choices on their own.

Tattoos, a current peer trademark, are inappropriate for teens. Diseases such as hepatitis can easily be transmitted during the application of tattoos and even though tattoos can be removed with laser surgery, it is expensive and usually leaves a scar. Teens are not old enough to know what they will want ten years in the future and they generally are too easily swayed by fads. Body piercing is also a current peer trademark. A parent has to make the decision whether the area of the body that their teen wants to pierce can be pierced without permanent damage or contracting a disease or infection. Belly buttons and earrings are fairly safe sites, but generally I would discourage piercing tongues, lips, eyebrows, the nose, or other areas of the face. If your child really wants to express herself this way, she can do so when she is an adult.

Makeup

Adolescence brings an increased focus on self, self-worth, and appearance. Females will want to use makeup long before they reach adolescence, but it will become a pressing issue for parents of adolescent girls. Using makeup symbolizes the transition toward adulthood for young women. Girls should be allowed to use different types of makeup in stages as their behavior demonstrates responsibility. We allowed our daughters to begin to wear clear lip gloss when they started middle school. By this age, many of their friends were wearing all types of makeup. We believed it was important to allow them at least some things that helped them fit in (peer trademarks). The following year, after they had demonstrated their willingness to comply with our limits, we allowed some colored lipstick and base makeup. By the time a girl reaches age 13 or 14, her complexion can be affected by acne. Base makeup allows some of that to be covered (although facial makeup can actually increase problems with acne). During the high school years we had some limits on what our daughters could wear, but each year we allowed a little more freedom of choice. This gradual process demonstrates your willingness to compromise, but you still retain some control over what your child does and the message she communicates about herself by the way she looks.

Of most concern is what makeup communicates to the child. Teens do not need makeup. They usually have natural skin tone that is lovely by itself. More important, makeup at this very early age communicates to the child that she is not acceptable the way she is. Even if they wear makeup, developing teens should also be taught to appreciate themselves for who they are rather than who they can be with the "right" clothes or makeup. Ultimately, choice of what makeup to allow is the parents', but at the very least, I encourage you to carefully consider *why* the child wants to wear makeup. It is not a rite of passage and there is nothing about wearing makeup that makes one an adult. Teaching your child self-worth is as important as teaching the appropriate use of makeup.

Discipline and Supervision

My father used to say that my sisters and I would never be too big to spank. Even though he never spanked us during our teen years and I doubt he ever intended to, one should never spank adolescents. Even though I do not propose that children should never be spanked, it is something that should never be done without great forethought. Receiving a spanking is embarrassing to a child, but it is especially humiliating to an adolescent. This does not mean that teens do not need to be disciplined. None of us is ever too big to be disciplined. Discipline helps us identify ways that we have erred; it provides the motivation to correct our behaviors; and, perhaps most important, self-discipline gives us impetus and courage to do what needs to be done even when we don't want to do it. Instead of hitting your teen, find other ways to punish misbehaviors (for example, withdrawal of privileges, extra chores) or, even better, find ways to reward the positive behaviors that you want to see repeated. (See "Discipline" in chapters 5 and 6.)

Finances and Allowance

Until children understand money, they see it as just another toy. Depositing a younger child's allowance into a savings account will help build up a fund for her when she is older and better able to appreciate the value of the money she has. For older children, an allowance enables them to have spending money for things that you consider elective expenses. One's own money can be used for movies, eating out, music, or other forms of entertainment. Your children also can use their own money if they are not happy with the clothes or shoes you offer to buy them or when they want something more expensive. You can pay the amount that you would have paid and your child can make up the difference. An allowance also teaches your child the value of money, how to manage money, and to save for important items. Offer to match your child's savings dollar for dollar. This will encourage saving and help him appreciate the work he invests in waiting for a desired item.

Don't pay your children for doing their share of household chores and do not use money as a reward for grades or good behavior. Instead, you can pay your adolescent for extra work around the house—washing the vehicle, painting the house, or other jobs that are not part of routine chores. This way she can earn money she wants rather than expecting it to be given to her, and you will benefit as well. Teach your child how to save, plan, and spend money wisely. Wise use of money is by far one of the most difficult skills to acquire in adulthood.

SUMMARY

A colleague stopped me one day and asked me about his teenage daughter. She had started to question his authority and to rebel against his wife and he was frustrated with her ever-changing moods. One day she would seem to be an adult and the next day she would be rebellious and difficult to communicate with. As difficult as it is to accept, some of this behavior is to be expected from adolescent children.

From the very earliest years, children begin to question the authority of their parents. One of the first words children learn is "no." Two-year-olds test nearly every boundary as they become mobile and understand limits. However, the most significant challenge to the authority of one's parents comes in adolescence. Children shift their focus from parents to peers. No longer will they accept the parent's word as a rule. Children are much more concerned and aware that other parents do things differently. Even more difficult for them to understand is how some parents can do things or allow their children to do things that are in opposition to what they have always been taught.

In early adolescence children transition away from dependent thinking and toward more independent thinking. Unless a person begins to question what she has been taught, she will never learn to think independently. Arguments from children at this age are often the result of the child trying to understand where he fits in the adult world of which he is just becoming a part. It is necessary and desirable. The challenge for parents is to see adolescence as a time to teach their children to think for themselves. Parents can help their children through this stage with patience, loosening their control, and discipline with consistency. As children become adults, they should be given more responsibility, but with responsibility comes accountability. Consistency is important because children need to know that their parents are reliable. Stability is comforting to them. Parents should expect that their adolescents will begin to question "expected" behaviors. As their children experiment with what they perceive to be adult behaviors, parents should balance control and oversight with freedom so that by the end of adolescence, a young person is prepared to take on the responsibility of living on his own.

In many cultures adolescence does not even exist. Children transition from childhood directly into adulthood. In Western cultures, children are allowed the luxury of several years of transition between childhood and adulthood. We call this period of time adolescence. Your child's sexual awakening moves to the forefront of the developmental issues addressed in this chapter, but there are many other changes as well. These years bring many notable physical, social, emotional, and cognitive changes. These few years are also the last years most parents will have their children at home. By the end of adolescence, your child will be grown, in college, and possibly even married. As frustrating as these years can be, the frustrations are not insurmountable. Enjoy this stage as you have enjoyed every previous stage of your child's development.

PART V

Conclusion

CHAPTER 10

Summary

Remember, your basic assignment as a parent is to work yourself out of a job.

—Paul Lewis

Where does the time go? Yesterday you were holding a tiny baby in your arms, a parent for the first time. Today you watch in the rearview mirror as you drive away from a college campus, leaving your *youngest* child on campus as a freshman. It seems like yesterday that you rode your toddler on the back of a bicycle and only days ago that he was starting school, performing in his first play, and singing his first solo. With my own children, I look back on the many mistakes I made and wish I could undo them. I remember the many times I was too busy to play on the floor with my children. I have time to play now, but they do not. Yet I also have many good memories, like our walks in the woods, vacations, and reading stories in the big chair in the living room. The journey from having children to launching them as adults is paradoxical—long but short, disappointing but joyous, stressful but delightful. It is an exciting journey, but one that doesn't end when they leave home. Your job as a parent is never finished. It only changes. Still to come are college days, marriage, and grandchildren, as well as new careers, disappointments, buying houses, and many of the things you went through in early adulthood. Your role as parent shifts, but if you have fostered a deep relationship with your children, your lives together will continue to grow deeper as they enter the adult world.

The more they learn about the world through their own experiences, the more they will appreciate your challenges, sacrifices, and discipline when they were children. They will call you and say, "I heard words come out of my mouth that you used to say and that I thought I would never say. Now I know why you said it." It will be satisfying when they tell you they used to resent something that you had done, but now, as adults, they understand why it was important, and they are glad you did.

LEAVING HOME

By their late teens, your children will most likely leave home. They may marry, join the military, enter college, or leave for a life on their own. In any case, when they leave, your home will never be the same again. It is the time for which you have prepared them their entire lives. As your role as a parent changes, you will become more of an adviser than director—a mentor rather than a day-to-day guide. Other things will change as well. You will be only one of the people that your children will want to see during holidays. Their jobs, marriages, and personal lives will sometimes keep them from calling or visiting. They may live in another city, another state, or even another country, making it difficult to visit or even call. It is at this time in your life that my words from the earlier chapters, "Enjoy your children while you can," will be most real to you.

Launching your children is not only a sad time, it is also exciting. When a child leaves the nest, you will have more time for your other children still at home and you and your spouse will have more personal time together. When your last child leaves the nest, you can come and go as you choose. Your life will no longer be dictated by school schedules, recitals, soccer games, or other activities involving your children. Life will be cheaper. Your budget will no longer require buying clothes and shoes for more than you and your spouse. No more school expenses or fees for athletics, activities, or music lessons. Dinner in a restaurant will be for two and flying for vacations will no longer require three, four, or five tickets—only two. Life changes, but it isn't without advantage.

When your children leave home, you will have to prepare yourself to be an in-law, a grandparent; and at the very least you will have to prepare yourself for a new relationship with adult children. For nearly two decades you have mentored, disciplined, corrected, guided, taught, and encouraged your children. Now, as they enter the adult world, you will still see them evolve as they continue through life's developmental stages, just as you yourself are doing; you will see them realize some of their dreams, fail to realize others, and pursue their life's goals. You have been letting go, little by little, since they were children. Now is the time to release them and let them experience life on their own. They will make choices regarding career, education, leisure, religion, and spouse that you may like, as well as some you may not, but you must let them be free to choose. Adulthood is where you help your children live their dreams rather than trying to force them to live yours.

MARRIAGE

Historically and across cultures, most females marry while still in their teen years. In recent years in the United States, the average age when both males and females marry is increasing. In this country, most young people marry in their twenties, but some marry as early as 16 or 17 years of age. At this age, neither males nor females are mature enough to make the decision about whom they want to spend the rest of their lives with and they are not mature enough to handle the responsibility of marriage. This hasn't always been true, but American culture does not require young people to mature as fast or accept responsibility as it did many decades ago. By age 18, your child is old enough to legally make decisions about marriage, but generally, the longer people wait to marry, the longer their marriages last. Adolescents change tremendously between the ages of 17 and 21. Their interests change, their plans for the future change, and their worldviews change. All of these changes make marriage in the teen years extremely risky.

LIVING WITH REGRET

If you are reading this chapter after your children are already grown, you can't change the past. You may look back on the years that have flown by and find yourself experiencing deep regret. You know that you did not take time with your children or put their interests first. Perhaps you were a thoughtless or irresponsible parent, a cruel parent, or just a misinformed parent. In any case, it isn't too late to work on repairing the damage that has been done. It is never too late to change your way of living and over time, your children will see your intent to do what is right. You can improve your relationships from this point onward—change that will have generational effects because you then will have better relationships with your grandchildren and perhaps even great-grandchildren. Two of the most powerful words in the English language are "I'm sorry." Making amends as best you can is a refreshing and liberating experience. Even if your children refuse to accept your apology, at least you will know you have done what you could. If they do accept your apologies, you still have decades with them, not to mention years with your grandchildren and even great-grandchildren.

IN CONCLUSION

As I stated in the opening pages of this book, one of my biggest fears is that I will appear to set the bar for parenting so high that parents simply give up—a standard that instead of encouraging people and giving them something to strive for, defeats them when they believe they cannot live up to the many suggestions contained within these pages. If you feel discouraged and think you are failing as a parent, you are in good company. A study of over 1,600 parents of children ages 5 to 17, released by Public Agenda and funded by State Farm Insurance Companies in 2002, showed that most parents doubted their abilities to do the job. More than 65 percent of the parents in the survey indicated that they believed they were failing in their ability to teach self-control and discipline to their children and only 55 percent said they were succeeding at teaching their children to be honest.[1] Even more discouraging was the fact that about half of all respondents said that parents today were doing a worse job at raising their children than their own parents had done.[2] Parenting is hard work, but it is not insurmountable. We all will make many mistakes and no one, including me, has all of the answers. A major difference between good parents and irresponsible ones is that good parents work at being a parent first and foremost. Irresponsible parents seek their own pleasures, even at the expense of their children. The 2002 Public Agenda study was encouraging in that many parents believed they were working hard, they took their role as parents seriously, and they had given a lot of thought to the place television, dating, computers, movies, the media, and other important issues held in their families as they raised their children. By far the most encouraging thing I see in parents of the children in my clinical practice is the desire to do better. We mustn't forget that we cannot be perfect and if we worry too much about our parenting skills, we will forget to have fun and enjoy the process. All anyone can ask of you is that you do your best.

Even as hard as I work at being a good parent, I can't help but think about what my children will see in me when they are grown. So many children have come and gone through my office over these many years. In one way or another, most of them loved their parents, even when the latter were seriously abusive or neglectful. What frightens me most are the hundreds of adults I have seen over the years who harbor deep resentment about their upbringing decades after they left home. I wonder if my children will feel that way about me. If you are like me, you find that you work hard to be a good parent and yet many days you feel like you're moving backward. No matter how much you give of your time and effort, it never seems to be enough. Frequently you hear "I want . . . ," and yet how rare are the words "thank you" from your children. I know I'm not alone in this experience.

I wonder if my children will remember the good things I did for them—the many hours we spent playing together, our trips, vacations, lunches at school, bicycle rides, and bedtime stories. Will they remember the many times we all snuggled together in one big bed on a Saturday morning, or the times we tickled each other in front of the fireplace on cold winter evenings, laughing until we cried? Or will they just remember my mistakes—times when I lost my temper, failed to listen to their stories carefully, or when I seemed too busy, uncaring, or distant? Perhaps they will remember only the time that I was away from home rather than the time that I was there. It grieves me to think it might be this way.

In a blink of an eye, my house will be quiet. My children will be grown and gone. The time between visits will seem like forever and I know I won't hear from them as much as I want. Sooner than I know, the little feet running in the hall on the second floor of my house will not belong to my children, but to my grandchildren. I hope that my children will look to me as a model for parenting rather than what they do not want to be.

When those days come, the frustrations I feel today will be long forgotten. I will not remember the many times homework was forgotten in a locker at school, the petty arguments about who sits where in the van, who gets what glass at the dinner table, and who left dirty socks on the floor. Also forgotten will be the frustration of entire weekends spent driving to and from soccer games and dance recitals, sitting through 90-minute programs waiting for the minutes when my child recited her one memorized line. Completely in the past will be any memory of the constant nickel-and-dime expense of school supplies, cheerleader uniforms, dues for scouts, and "voluntary" contributions for costumes and productions at school and church. I am positive that things like these, which make my day-to-day job as a dad frustrating, will be hard to recall when my kids are grown.

All in all, I know that every day I think about being a parent and I take that responsibility very seriously. My children won't remember all the times when I was the only dad on a field trip or the prestigious professional opportunities that I let pass because they required me to be away from home too much—but I will know.

I know, despite what they might think of me when they are grown and gone, regardless of what they will remember, I have done a good job. They *will* remember me as the one who always had time for them and the one who loved them even when they were unkind to me. They will call me when they need help because they know I have always been there for them, even when they have ignored me. They will remember me as the one who celebrated their successes even when they were too "cool" to acknowledge that they were glad I was proud of them. They will see, I hope, that being a parent was a joy for me and they were never a burden—that when I look at them, I cannot believe such incredibly beautiful, brilliant, talented, and wonderful people came from me. The future frightens me, but I know, even when I make mistakes, that I've always done my best to show my children that I'm so very glad I'm their dad. That, I suppose, is the best that any of us can do.

CHAPTER 11

Miscellaneous Topics

Life is change. Growth is optional. Choose wisely.

—Karen Kaiser Clark

Throughout the book I have discussed dozens of topics, but as I conclude, there are a few odds and ends that may be of interest to you as you raise your children. These topics did not fit neatly into any single chapter, so here they are, together in one chapter.

TRAVELING WITH YOUR CHILDREN

The summer brings travel for many families. Even short trips begin with the hope that you will have minimal arguing, screaming, or asking "How much longer?" Your children will be most annoying when they are bored. Anticipate their boredom and plan for it before you leave the house. This will save you many minutes of frustration in your vehicle. Whether long trips or short, there are many ways to keep your children occupied while you travel.

Videotapes or DVDs are both fun and great time fillers. Many vehicles, especially minivans and SUVs, come with a built-in TV/VCR as an option, and some have DVD players. This is an expensive option, but you don't have to buy one with your vehicle. You can find nine-inch TV/VCR combinations for around $300 at department stores and discount electronics stores. With adapters, you can also connect play stations to a TV in your vehicle.

Audiotapes will also entertain your children as you travel. Bookstores and discount stores have many audiotapes for children. You may tire of some of the audiotapes, but your children, especially young children, will enjoy them over and over, and they help them pass the time. You can also purchase books on tape or check them out at a local library.

Save yourself some frustration by planning reasonable travel days. Some parents never stop until they reach their destination. They don't enjoy the trip, but instead see the distance between home and the destination as an inconvenience to be overcome. Try planning your vacation travel so you stop more frequently. Spending a night in a city with an aquarium, a museum, or a historical site breaks up long drives and gives children something to look forward to along the way. Teach your children to enjoy the journey as much as the destination.

Take low-calorie snacks. Sugary snacks may taste good, but when a child eats a candy bar, the sugar is very quickly metabolized into the system, making him fidgety and anxious. Take carrot sticks, apples, oranges, or bananas. Even if your children complain, they will eat these snacks if they are hungry.

Learn road games. At a bookstore or the library you can find books of games that you can play in the car. Many games don't require reading, paper, or game boards or pieces, making them convenient for young children. Some games require the players to be observant of their surroundings and others may help practice reading.

If your children are age seven or older, teach them to read a map. Children younger than six or seven will have trouble understanding the concept of a map. You can find maps for children in a library or at a bookstore. Let your children keep track of where you are on their own maps. They will learn a necessary skill and have fun at the same time.

Set aside 30 minutes or an hour of a long trip as quiet time. After a meal and a bathroom break is a good time. Let your children read quietly, sleep, or do some other quiet activity. This will give the driver, children, and other passengers a nice break.

SUMMER PLANNING

When summer arrives and children are out of school, many parents find themselves wondering how to entertain their children all summer long. Routines are important, especially for young children, so that your child will know what is expected each day. Do not wait until the first week the child is home to try to think up things for him or her to do. At the very least, sketch out a rough weekly calendar for your child. Include chores, activities, playtime, rest time, and educational time. Planning your child's summer in advance will make your job as a parent much easier.

Avoid the temptation to let your child sit in front of the television all day. A limited amount of television viewing is not a problem, but confine television viewing to an hour or two each day. Give your child a list of programs or videotapes from which to choose. Local libraries have a selection of educational and entertaining videotapes you can check out, or you can rent from a video store. Plan TV time and stick to the routine. If TV viewing is on a routine schedule (for example, every afternoon from 3 to 5), then it will be easier to say "no" if the child wants to watch at some other time.

Have a 30-minute to 1-hour quiet time every day. Quiet time may be most productive in the early afternoon, when it may be too hot to play outside. During this quiet time, the child can read, sleep, or play quietly with a puzzle or toy. This will give both you and your child a break.

Plan a structured outdoor activity every few days. This could be anything from finding all the types of plants that grow in your yard to finding bugs, looking at clouds or birds, or going for a walk. Local libraries have numerous field guides on clouds, trees, plants, bugs, birds, rocks, and so on. You and your child can learn together. County extension offices are also a good resource for free information about the environment around your home. You also can have your child participate in indoor projects once or twice a week. For example, most children will enjoy the opportunity to do a craft or to help in the kitchen, making lunch or baking cookies.

Have routine playtime outside if the weather permits. American children are the most privileged in the world and yet they are in very poor condition relative to children in other countries. One reason is that they don't exercise enough. If the weather is extremely hot, make sure the child wears sunscreen and drinks plenty of water (avoid carbonated beverages). If it is raining, and there is no risk of lightning, let your child play in the rain. I guarantee your children will never forget a few minutes of playtime in the rain, especially if you join them—fully clothed. A child who exercises will maintain better health, will eat better, will be less moody, and will sleep better.

A weekly trip together can break up the week. These trips can be expensive, such as trips to water parks, amusement parks, or museums, but they do not have to be. Historic sites, your state capitol, or other public parks or buildings are great places to learn, and they are usually free or have very reasonable admission. Airports, fire stations, police stations, courthouses, and other public facilities may be willing to give your family a tour if you call and ask. Activities like this may be even better if you get friends to go with you. The fire station, for example, may be more interested in a group of ten than a group of two or three. Planning one or two major activities, such as a trip to an amusement park or the beach, if your time and budget allow, will break up the summer and give your children something to look forward to. You can also use the trip as a reward for good behavior.

Many local libraries have summer reading programs that can broaden your child's understanding of the world. Many of these programs have incentives, such as free food or refreshments at area restaurants. Reading is a very important skill, and learning to love reading begins during the toddler years. Plan a trip to the library once a week.

Your child's summer routine should include regular participation in household chores. Children of almost every age can contribute to the home by taking responsibility for chores every day. Young children (ages two–four) are capable of cleaning their rooms and making their beds, although they will need help. Older children should be given reasonable chores to perform every day or two in addition to reasonable care for their bedrooms. For example, an older child can be responsible for cleaning a bathroom or helping with the dishes. When possible, have your child complete chores after breakfast each day so that they are out of the way.

Let your child keep a daily or weekly log of summer activities. This will help her remember what she has done and reinforce the learning that has taken place. A notebook purchased for this purpose can contain notes about all the plants, insects, animals, animal tracks, clouds, birds, and so forth that you find together during the summer.

Plan your summer. It would be discouraging for you and your child to reach the end of the summer and have only a string of television programs or video games as the content of a "What I Did Last Summer" essay. By utilizing some of these suggestions, you can use the summer to build productive habits as well as to teach your child a little about the world.

CHILD MALTREATMENT

Among my adult clients, especially women, the majority were sexually or physically abused as children. Among my child clients, many of them are, or have been, sexually or physically abused. Some of these children are physically abused or neglected by well-meaning parents or guardians who have used inappropriate forms of discipline. Most, however, are victims of brutal adults who elect to take out their wrath on those who are helpless to defend themselves or those who selfishly pursue their own physical urges regardless of the cost to their children.

Three terms are important to this discussion concerning child maltreatment: neglect, sexual abuse, and physical abuse. Neglect is failure to meet a child's basic needs (food, shelter, emotional needs, etc.). Sexual abuse is exploitation of a child, which includes fondling a child, forcing a child to watch sexual acts, intercourse with a child, and a variety of other forms of sexual contact or exposure. Physical abuse includes burning, scalding, pinching, bruising, cutting, breaking of bones, and other physical acts that injure the child either temporarily or permanently.

Abuse, both sexual and physical, happens in homes of wealthy families as well as in homes of the underprivileged. It occurs in both minority families and Caucasian families, and it is equally frequent in both religious and nonreligious homes. Abuse nearly always continues until there is some intervention—legal, religious, or therapeutic. Abusers sometimes want to stop but find they cannot. Abusers may sincerely apologize to children and to spouses for their behavior, and promises are often made that "nothing like this will ever happen again." These promises will be broken. Some abusers believe they have a right to engage in the acts they commit.

Spouses who are aware of the abuse wish it would go away, and ignoring or denying it often is the easiest way to deal with it. The reality of abuse is sometimes so painful to a spouse that he or she may simply refuse to believe what is obvious. Spouses also cannot bring themselves to deal with sexual or physical abuse that is being committed on a child by the partner because legal or therapeutic intervention means betrayal of the loved one. A bad situation, then, just seems to get worse. Abuse is far more likely in homes where alcohol or substance abuse is present, and it is also far more likely in homes where a stepfather, live-in male, or other adult is present.

Children who survive abuse grow bitter and apathetic, and are more likely to have relationship struggles as adults. They are more likely to become pregnant as teenagers and to engage in dysfunctional and abusive relationships. Abused children are also more likely to abuse their own children when they become parents.

I have seen children who have been burned with cigarettes for crying, and I have seen others who have watched as a sibling was beaten to death. Other children have been shot, had skull fractures, brain damage, broken bones, teeth knocked out, and noses broken—all by the very people who were responsible for their care. Some of the children and adults who have come through my practice were sexually abused from as early as age two and for as long as ten or more years.

The only hope for intervention is for the abuser to seek help or for the spouse to decide that enough is enough, and to help those who cannot help themselves. I am speaking for the helpless and I may be speaking for your child. Unless you act, the abuse will go on. For help, contact a member of your religious community, a therapist, or your county's Department of Family and Children's Services.

PSYCHOLOGICAL DISORDERS AND FINDING HELP

Attention Deficit/Hyperactivity Disorder (ADHD)

ADHD, commonly known as hyperactivity, is a condition in which an individual has difficulty maintaining attention on a task, is often loud and aggressive, and often has both social and academic problems at school. ADHD is most commonly treated through behavioral modification, contextual modification, and medication, or some combination of the three.

In recent years, the media have made it appear that physicians quickly prescribe drugs as an easy fix for ADHD symptoms, but ignore other problems. Some critics have implied that the condition does not even exist. While it is true that many times the disorder is inappropriately diagnosed and some physicians have been too quick to prescribe medication, these generalizations ignore the fact that medication can produce some amazing changes both in adults and children with ADHD. Often, even if medication is not the best long-term solution, it helps a child or adult focus long enough to get other problems in order. Hyperactive children are a challenge for parents. Once the child is on medication and his behavior stabilizes, more effective and long-term interventions are more easily implemented.

On the other hand, some criticisms of the diagnosis and treatment are valid. ADHD is over-diagnosed and medication is sometimes prescribed unnecessarily. Because medication adjusts behavior, it is very easy to terminate other clinical treatments upon receipt of a prescription. It is also easy to misdiagnose other disorders (such as oppositional defiance disorder or even attachment disorders) as ADHD. Because the medication often causes a change in behavior regardless of the diagnosis, the real problems are never adequately addressed. Therefore, children are treated for a disorder they do not have and the one that really exists is ignored. Competent and thorough evaluation by a qualified therapist, psychologist, or psychiatrist can help prevent such errors.

Behavioral modification can be a helpful alternative treatment to medication. Even for children who have been prescribed medication, once they learn to self-monitor and learn effective ways to control their behavior, they may no longer need the same level of medication (if any at all). With behavioral intervention, many of these children have maintained or even improved their behavior after withdrawal of medication. However, parents should always discuss withdrawing medication with the prescribing physician.

There are three reasons one would want to eliminate medication if possible. First, if it is an inappropriate prescription, the child certainly should not be taking the medication. Second, if the individual comes to believe that he or she cannot function without it, that belief can lead to unnecessary dependence on the medication for maintenance of behavior. Finally, medication often develops within a person a victim mentality—the idea that one does not have any control. This is never true. Even children who need medication for ADHD have some control over their behavior. Supposing that the medicine should do all the work is irresponsible.

ADHD is a real disorder that, when left untreated, can leave a child failing in school and frustrated at home. However, the dramatic rise in the diagnosis of ADHD gives one cause to reflect on the accuracy of such diagnoses. If you are the parent of a child whom you suspect has ADHD, have your child tested by a clinician who specializes in cognitive testing. If your child is currently diagnosed with ADHD and this diagnosis did not come from a qualified clinician, have your child reexamined by a qualified therapist to ensure that the diagnosis was appropriate.

Violent Children

It was not too many years ago that parents' major concern was their children skipping school, smoking in the bathroom at school, or using profanity. These days, parents' concerns include fear of weapons in school, sexual harassment, assault, rape, and even murder. Sexual harassment and intimidation have been found even among children in the second grade, and kindergartners have murdered their classmates. Without question, violent crime among minors has increased since the late 1980s.

It would be foolish to try to isolate one variable as a cause of any social problem. However, there are several variables that undoubtedly contribute to aggression in children. American culture is increasingly focused on individualism. Citizens are very quick to look to any issue to see how their personal rights are being affected. Lawsuits abound and the citizenry has lost any sense of personal responsibility. A fall on a wet floor in a store is not one's own fault for not being careful; rather, it is the store's fault for having a wet floor. Lawsuits frequently claim that one must be compensated regardless of one's own carelessness. As a result, children are raised in communities where the system teaches them to get what they can. For example, while traveling on a plane in 2002, I fell and broke my leg. It was my own fault and the airline in no way contributed to my injury, but repeatedly acquaintances asked me if I was going to sue. In such a culture, it should not be surprising that children resort to any means necessary to achieve personal goals, including violence.

The media contribute to the problem. Research has demonstrated that exposure to violent models makes violent behavior more likely. Shootings, stabbings, rape, and sexual aggression are commonplace on a wide range of shows, from afternoon tabloid TV and prime-time television series to the big screen. I am often startled at what movie critics describe as a "family movie." A well-known family psychologist has often said that the footsteps a child follows are most likely to be the ones his parents thought they covered up. Just as I have suggested that it would be naïve to isolate a single variable as the cause of any social phenomenon, it is equally naïve to suggest that the way of life to which we have become so accustomed (violent programming) has no effect on our children.

Absence of an empathetic and stable family is also a contributing factor. Over half of all children in elementary school have experienced divorce or separation of their parents and as many as 60 percent of young people have experienced physical or sexual abuse at home. The home should provide a place of safety, oneness, community, empathy, direction, and support. If these needs are not being met, children will try to compensate for the deficit. One way to compensate for instability is to strike out at others. In fact, many bullies are victims themselves and their violent behavior, in part, is an attempt to prove to themselves that they are OK, because they do not receive affirmation at home.

Even though children from lower-class homes are statistically more likely to engage in violent behavior than children from middle- and upper-class homes, and children from broken homes are more likely to engage in violent behavior than children from two-parent homes, family values are not determined by family income, nor are they determined by the marital status of the caregiver(s). A parent who is determined to teach responsibility to the child is what makes the difference. Parenting takes work. It is not the school system's job, nor is it any social organization's job to teach children responsibility and respect for others. It is the parents' job.

Movies, video games, or television shows do not make our children violent. Neither does our egocentric culture. Children have the freedom to behave appropriately or inappropriately, regardless of the good intentions and efforts of the parent. However, these factors, in concert with a home where no respect for others is taught, will be more likely to produce a child who has no respect for anyone else and, consequently, will be at higher risk for violent behavior.

When to Seek Help

Sometimes childhood and adolescent problems need more than parental guidance. When parents observe behavior in their children that they are worried about, or they do not see behaviors in their children that they think most children exhibit, it may be necessary to seek professional help. It is important to find qualified help for your child and your family. Interruption of dysfunction during childhood, close to the source of the problem, can prevent a lifetime of difficulties in social relationships. But it can be difficult to know when a professional is needed and when one is not.

The first step in answering the question is, as with any disturbance, to determine how much the problem is interrupting the child's life. If, for example, the child is extremely shy and doesn't seem to make friends easily, the more important question is how much the shyness is interrupting the child's ability to do the things that he or she enjoys. If the shyness doesn't interrupt the child's life and if the parents are able to do the things they need to do despite the shyness in the child, then professional intervention may not be necessary. Even if the child has a diagnosable disorder, it makes little difference as long as he or she is functioning well.

On the other hand, suppose a child has difficulty getting along with teachers and peers at school. The child has been disciplined numerous times at school and the parents have chosen to take the child out of more than one school because of behavior problems. This is almost certainly a problem, because the child is not functioning effectively in more than one environment and the behavior is causing problems for the parents. In a situation like this, there is a problem that needs to be identified and addressed.

Some problems are almost always serious. Children who are deliberately cruel to animals or human beings potentially are deeply troubled individuals. Even though many children occasionally harm animals by accident, it is highly abnormal to deliberately be cruel to living creatures on a regular basis. Depending on the behavior and the child's age, sexual acting out is also a sign of potential disturbance or trauma. Likewise, children who set fires deliberately and repeatedly are of concern. This specific type of vandalism has been directly correlated with serious mental disturbance. (See chapter 6 for more information on these behaviors.)

Sometimes problems exhibited by children are actually the result of problems with the parent or parents and not with the child. When parents are experiencing the stress of financial burdens, marital problems, abuse, or other significant life stressors, it almost always affects the children in the home. Children in these homes may act out aggressively, they may vandalize property, or they may withdraw. Older children may experiment with cigarettes, drugs, and alcohol. Even though the child is the one with the presenting problem, it is not uncommon for treatment to involve the whole family. Resolution of these problems requires treating the cause—the distress in the parents' lives. Help for the parents is a way to help the child, and parents must be willing to participate.

If the parent is unsure whether or not to seek professional help, it is better to seek help when it is not needed than it is to fail to get help for children who do need help. The earlier problems are addressed, the easier they are to correct.

Finding a Therapist

Even though there are many competent and exceptional psychologists in the field, there are also some who are not. Finding competent professional help can be a challenge. For many people, finding a therapist is as frustrating as buying a new car. There are options all around them, but they don't know where to look and when they do decide upon a therapist, they question whether or not they made the right decision.

Even though you could flip through the Yellow Pages to find a therapist, it is better to get referrals from people you trust—a minister, pediatrician, friend or relative who has had a child in therapy, or people you know in the profession. Make sure you pursue referrals who regularly work with children in an age range that includes your child. Therapy is very different at different ages and a counselor who is very good with adolescents may not have the necessary skills to work with young children.

Licensure is another important issue. In many states there are several levels of licensure. Licensed professional counselors, clinical social workers, marriage and family therapists, psychologists, and psychiatrists are a few types of practitioners who are overseen by state licensure boards. At a minimum, to receive a license, mental health professionals must have earned at least a master's degree, completed hundreds of hours of supervised clinical work, and they must have passed the state licensure exam. With licensure, counselors can (if they choose) accept insurance payments, they are overseen by the state licensure board, and they must engage in regular continuing education. Licensure does not guarantee that a counselor is a good one, nor does the lack of licensure mean one is unqualified. However, in some states with the exception of clergy, only those who are licensed can legally practice therapy.

There are differences between the licenses. Professional counselors generally have fewer license requirements than psychologists. Psychiatrists are also medical doctors and usually are the only people in the mental health profession who can write prescriptions. Competence, however, is not determined by the type of license one holds. Yet again, this is the value of getting a referral from someone you trust.

Once you have chosen a therapist, he or she should work with you to evaluate the problem(s), set goals for therapy, and establish criteria so you will know when those goals are met. Setting goals and criteria is crucial to therapy. For example, a goal might be to reduce aggressive behavior in a child. A criterion might be "five or fewer incidents at school in a month." Goals and criteria are individually tailored to the child, they may change as therapy progresses, and new goals may be added. If you and your therapist cannot at any point in time identify your goals and how you will know when you get there, you may want to reconsider your choice of a therapist. Long-range goals may take several sessions to establish, but even early in therapy, as the therapist evaluates the child, the goal may simply be "evaluation and rapport building." Your therapist should regularly remind you of your goals and provide a verbal or written progress report. I make it a point every week or two to discuss the goal(s) with the parents of my clients and let them know where I think we are. If my client's parents feel we are making no progress after several weeks, I will consider referring the client to another therapist. If your therapist has not reviewed your child's progress, ask. If he or she can't answer your questions regarding progress and goals, you may want to find another therapist.

Don't expect a therapist to give you an exact number of projected sessions. How long therapy takes depends on the skill of the therapist, the responsiveness of the client, and the level of involvement of the parent. One should not expect problems that have existed for five or ten years to be resolved in one or two visits. Therapy can be time-consuming and expensive, but the earlier problems are dealt with, the easier they are to correct. Remember that in correcting problems early, you are investing in your child's future.

THE MEDIA

"Then shall we simply allow our children to listen to any stories that anyone happens to make up, and so receive into their minds ideas often the very opposite of those we shall think they ought to have when they grow up?" This question was not asked by some modern conservative religious leader about television and movies. It was a question posed by Socrates to his

student Plato in Plato's *Republic*. It concerns me deeply what the media consider appropriate material for children and even more what parents allow their
children to watch. In her book *Viewing Violence*, psychologist Madeline
Levine decrees: "The debate is over. Violence on television and in the movies
is damaging to children. Forty years of research conclude that repeated exposure to high levels of media violence teaches some children and adolescents to settle interpersonal differences with violence, while teaching many
more to be indifferent to this solution."[1]

The average child watches four hours of television a day and it seems
absurd that anyone would suggest that what we watch on TV and in the
movies has no significant effect on us. If that were right, advertisers would
not spend thousands of dollars to get their products spotlighted in movies
and millions of dollars for commercials. It would be too simplistic to reduce
the cause-effect relationship between the media and any given behavior to
a one-to-one relationship or to assert that media exposure has the same effect on everyone. People are much too complicated for such assertions to
be made. Likewise, no specific program, movie, producer, actress, or actor
is responsible for all the ills associated with the media, but what we watch
clearly has an effect on us. The effects of media influence on our children,
whether it is violence, sexual behavior, or other standards of conduct, are
not trivial. The cumulative effect of the daily doses of violence, promiscuity,
thoughtlessness, prejudice, and stereotyping create callous and desensitized
individuals who are apt to copy the behaviors being modeled for them. As
Levine states, there is nothing to argue about. The effects are clear.

Levine also notes that the media, especially commercial television, have
as their primary agenda to round up the largest and most affluent audience
they can and deliver that audience to an advertiser. They are not concerned
with the welfare of families nor are they concerned about the welfare of children. Careless use of the media is psychological suicide. Children who are
heavy viewers of television score more poorly on nearly every cognitive task
than those who are light viewers of television, not to mention the fact that
they are more likely to be overweight and in poorer physical condition than
children who watch little television. To carelessly invite popular media ideas,
values, and attitudes into your home is to ignore the responsibility you have
as parents to socialize your children in that which is healthy, noble, and in
their best interest.

Television

Television is not all bad. There are many outstanding programs on television, but parents should consider television, movies, and other media as

useful but potentially dangerous tools. Cable channels that specialize in educational programming can be exceptional. Stations that specialize in time-tested programs (for example, *The Andy Griffith Show*) also provide whole-some family entertainment that a parent can watch even with young children without fear of having to explain some word or situation. Unfortunately, the major networks, because of their dependence on advertising dollars, seem bent on producing an endless stream of mind-numbing sitcoms and dramas, relying on sleaze and violence that in no way encourage the betterment of our minds, our culture, and our nation. These comments may seem too harsh, but a parent must recognize that the television is not an innocuous tool. It can be dangerous if it is not used properly.

Avoid using the TV as a baby-sitter; instead, limit your child's exposure to media. Ice cream is great, but we should not eat it at every meal. Some TV programming is fine if it is carefully chosen, even if it has no purpose but to entertain. Two or three hours a day of television viewing is plenty for any family.

Select programs purposefully. What does the show teach? What morals (or lack of) are conveyed by the program? Are these the morals you wish your family to embrace? Resist the temptation to turn the TV on and *then* decide what to watch by scanning channels. This is like starting your car, pulling out of the driveway, and then deciding where you want to go. Use a television guide to make deliberate and purposeful choices before the television is ever turned on. Sit down at the beginning of the week and select the television shows that you would like to watch or that you want your children to watch. Ask yourself what the program provides for you or your children that is productive. If it doesn't provide anything other than filling time, don't watch it.

Use programming to bring your family together, not to separate them. I strongly recommend that individuals not have TVs in their own rooms. One television in a central living area will make TV a tool to bring your family together. Watching a program as a family and then having the opportunity to discuss the program helps children learn, interpret, and understand what they are watching in the context of your family's value system.

As with most things to which we expose ourselves, the age of the viewer is an important factor. Even the evening news is violent and unhealthy for young children. However, as they get older, it will be important for your children to begin to learn more about the world, and a news program can be an effective teaching tool if you watch it together and discuss the issues presented.

Movies

Pay attention to movie ratings and reviews. There are Internet web sites that rate movies for sexual content, profanity, and violence. This information will assist you in making decisions for your family. Be deliberate in your selections. Don't let your kids go to a movie because "everybody says it's great." When the movie *Titanic* was released, my nine-year-old daughter was the only child in her class who did not see it. I discovered this fact at a parent-teacher conference when her teacher told my wife and me that she was planning a classroom discussion on the movie, but my daughter was the only one who had not seen it. I saw the movie myself and it was very well done. The effects were impressive and many of the details of the actual event were captured on film. However, I think many parents have missed something. Despite its impressive effects, *Titanic* contained profanity, sexually suggestive scenes, nudity, fighting, a graphic suicide by a firearm, and other forms of death graphically portrayed. Looking at this list of potentially offensive material, it seems there was no type of objectionable material that was not included in this movie. One has to wonder why parents allow their children to view such material. Unfortunately, many parents give little thought to what their children see or they just don't care. Other parents think carefully about what their children see, but the hype of big-budget movies clouds their judgment. They don't realize what a film contains until someone points it out.

In the 1970s, a parent could be sure that if the movie was rated "G," or if Disney produced it, it would be appropriate for any age. Neither of these beliefs holds true these days. For parents of young children, it is a good idea to see the movie before you let your child watch it. For older children, at least read the reviews and know the actors, director, and producer. Consider your child's age and what may be appropriate for him or her. In summary, deciding on the role of the media in your home is just one more thing that makes parenting time-consuming and hard work.

COMPUTERS

Children who spend several hours a day with computer games are more lethargic and physically less fit than children who don't. Likewise, children with attention deficit/hyperactivity disorder (ADHD) show more aggressive and uncontrollable behaviors if they are exposed to rapidly changing media—the very type of images that are common in video games and many television programs. A study in 2000 by Stanford University, published in the *Archives of Pediatrics and Adolescent Medicine,* showed that the more television and video games elementary school children were exposed to, the more physically and verbally aggressive they were.[2] In turn, when children were exposed to less television and fewer video games, their aggressive behavior decreased.

This may seem self-evident, but it was actually a new finding. It was once thought that only children who were already aggressive were detrimentally affected by television and video games. Yet this new study presents the possibility that even nonaggressive children are more aggressive following television and video game exposure, and that reducing exposure to these media can be a treatment for aggressive behavior in both children who are already aggressive and those who are not.

As with any other area of their lives, children need supervision when using computers and video games. Don't just let them play games without knowing something about the games. Supervise what they are playing and evaluate its appropriateness given the child's age, maturity, and level of responsibility.

As mentioned in previous sections, even good things should have limits. Vitamins are good for you, but some vitamins are toxic if you ingest too much. Decide how much time each day is to be allotted to computer games. An hour a day is plenty for young children, and two hours for adolescents. Help your children find other things to substitute for computer games. Reading, playing games with other family members, talking walks together, bicycle riding, and crafts are all things you can do as a family instead of playing computer games.

The Internet

The Internet is here to stay and it can have a significant impact on our families and our children. In many ways, the Internet is a wonderful thing. With e-mail you can communicate with anyone anywhere in the world who has an e-mail address. You may also be able to communicate in real time with someone in another country through a chat room without expensive long-distance telephone bills. Through the Internet, one can have access to information from all over the world and it has been likened to the world's largest encyclopedia. As a parent, I have used the Internet to look up illnesses, medications, and other things that are of interest to me and of concern to my children. For example, one of my children has asthma. I regularly check several Internet sites that publish quality, up-to-date information on asthma. I can find out new treatments and the latest information on the illness. You can use the Internet to plan your vacations, make airline and hotel reservations, read news from a variety of news services, and even shop for groceries.

Nearly every organization has an Internet web site. Among the many organizations that maintain web sites are museums, libraries, government offices, parks departments, elementary schools, high schools, colleges, and medical facilities like the Mayo Clinic. You can research your physician's name at the secretary of your state's web site, find out if he or she has an active license, and also find out if any restrictions are on file against his or her license. Many families maintain personal web sites that relatives can visit to see current pictures of the children and catch up on the family's activities. All of this is available for free to any Internet user. Perhaps the best part about the Internet is that you can find anything you want on the Internet.

Unfortunately, the best thing about the Internet is also the worst thing—you can find anything you want. When searching the Internet, one has to invest some energy in discerning between that which is quality information and that which is not. You can be assured that *Encyclopaedia Britannica* is a respectable and credible resource, but you cannot always be assured of the credibility of the information on all Internet sites. Anyone with a computer can create and maintain an Internet web site. You have to decide the credibility of the information based largely on the host of the site. I trust what I read from the Mayo Clinic, but I don't give equal credibility to other sites that discuss medical issues unless I know something about who produces them.

Another drawback of the Internet is its breadth. You can find absolutely anything on the Internet. Parents must monitor a child's access to the Internet. Pornography, racist literature, and extremist materials are among the potential problems on the Internet. Software is available to screen such sites and make them unavailable to young users, but computer-wise children can find ways around such programs. Predators also lurk in chat rooms and have been known to arrange meetings with, and even abduct and kill, children they meet through chat rooms. Treat the computer as you would any potentially dangerous tool. Use it when you have a reason to use it. Don't let your children use it simply to "kill time," and don't let them use it unless you know what they are doing. You do not have to look over their shoulder every minute, but at least be aware they are using it, what they are doing, and how long they need to be on-line. Locating your computer in a common area of your home will make monitoring your child's activities much easier.

If you like computers and you don't use the Internet, you don't know what you are missing. It is a very powerful tool that can be an asset to your home. If you have children in school, it is a very valuable tool, but like any tool, it has to be used wisely. Like all tools, it can be both useful and destructive, depending on how responsibly it is used.

TEN THINGS TO DO WITH YOUR CHILDREN
FOR FREE

In our current culture we seem to be possessed by "bigger and better." Things that are simple and low-tech get very little attention and parents rely too heavily on hi-tech and expensive entertainment. Unfortunately, it often seems that the more money families spend, the less members see of each other. Here is a list of things you can do with your family that not only are free but also encourage interaction.

1. Visit a library. Almost every large city or town has a public library with many resources and a plenty of space. Even some very small towns have a library. Take advantage of your tax dollars at work and spend an afternoon or evening at the library, looking through books, magazines, newspapers, or browsing the Internet. There is something for everyone and every age at a library. It would be easy to spend several hours reading together or investigating some chosen topic. This encourages a vital developmental skill (reading) and keeps the family together. Make it a habit to check out books once every week or two. This will encourage your children to read and they will want to spend less time in front of the television or playing computer games.

2. Play with Legos. I know it may sound ridiculous, but Legos are safe toys that are developmentally appropriate for a wide range of ages. Playing with Legos develops creativity, a necessary part of a child's development. Legos are relatively inexpensive and one's collection can be expanded in small increments. The creative process that Legos allow is pleasurable for children of all ages as well as adults.

3. Go for a walk. It is amazing how few families walk together. When you walk together, you exercise and you can also talk with each other. Repeatedly, research has demonstrated a relationship between family closeness and how much time family members spend talking with each other. The exercise is good for everyone and fresh air is healthy even in the winter. Contrary to popular belief, cold air does not cause colds. In fact, staying in a home with stale air where germs may not be circulated out of the house for many days increases the likelihood of colds.

4. Learn about the world through field guides. Field guides are available at bookstores for under $20 each, or you can check them out at a public library. They can assist you in teaching your children about some aspect of the planet. Whether you choose to learn about birds, stars, bugs, clouds, rocks, trees, or something else, there is a field guide that can help you. Peterson's field guides and Golden's field guides are two that are usually quite good and suited to both the novice and the experienced. Field guides are often small enough to fit in your pocket and can easily be carried while on

evening walks or camping trips. While your children are out of school for the summer, dedicate those months with your family to learning about a new topic. Your family may also enjoy learning a foreign language. You can use audiotapes and books to learn words and phrases in a foreign language. Your children will enjoy the challenge.

5. Have a picnic. Many fast-food chains have play parks connected to their buildings, but the food they serve is generally unhealthy. Most cities and towns have public play parks, many that surpass any fast-food restaurant playground. While at the park your children can play on playground equipment, ride bicycles, or hike on nature trails. Take a field guide and learn about nature while you are there. Very young children will enjoy a picnic in the park just as much as they would enjoy an amusement park, and a picnic in the park is free.

6. Visit your state capitol building. State capitol buildings are public buildings and usually have no admission charge. You can tour the building on your own, visit the house and senate and even observe, if they are in session. Your representative or senator may be in the building and is often willing to take a moment to meet constituents. In my home state of Georgia, our capitol building houses a museum dedicated to Georgia's environment, agriculture, wildlife, military history, and state history. A visit to your state capitol will teach your child something about your state and its government.

7. Explore a bookstore. You can spend an entire afternoon browsing through the latest books, music, periodicals, or newspapers from around the world. A bookstore, whether large or small, will have something for every age and every taste. Many bookstores also have small cafes so you can sip a cup of coffee or have a snack while you browse. Your spending two hours in a bookstore is not a bother to the store owner. On the contrary, owners like browsers because they know the longer you stay, the more likely you are to buy a book. You may find it hard to leave without buying a book.

8. Check out a videotape from your public library. Videotapes can be checked out just like books. Movies are not first-run films, but that makes no difference. If they were good movies when they came out, they will still be good even if they have been out for a while. Libraries also have "how-to" and educational videos as well. The library in your house of worship may offer movies and videos for adults and children on religious themes that are of interest to people of your faith.

9. Do a craft or a science experiment. Craft supplies can be very expensive, but you can do many crafts, especially with younger children, with paper, crayons, and tape or glue. Science experiments can be done with simple household products like baking soda, vinegar, flour, and water. Your public

library most likely will have books on crafts and science experiments that can be exciting, safe, and entertaining. Glass etching, candle making, and other simple crafts can be fun ways to make gifts for friends and family as well as a way for your family to learn a skill together.

10. Grow a plant. Children are fascinated with how things work. When it comes to their food, unless they grow up on a farm, they do not know where the food comes from. Growing vegetables and fruits at home not only provides food for your family, it also teaches your children about the world in which they live. Even if you don't have property for farming, you can grow a plant on your kitchen counter. Plant an apple seed in a small paper cup and within days a sprout will break the surface of the soil. Even if your plant doesn't survive, your children will enjoy the experience of planting and watching something grow.

HALLOWEEN AND OTHER HOLIDAYS

For many adults, memories of Halloween, trick-or-treats, and costumes are some of their favorites. Yet because of the objections of some religious commentators, some parents have questioned whether or not to celebrate Halloween. Many religions express concern about Halloween because it has its roots in pagan rituals. Indeed, it does. Halloween dates back more than 2,000 years to the Celtic festival of Samhain in Ireland, which marked the end of both summer and the harvest season. Druids believed that on this night, souls of the dead were allowed to cross over to the living world and potentially inhabit the bodies of the living. In order to scare them away, Celts wore costumes, extinguished house fires, and sacrificed crops and animals. Around A.D. 800, Pope Boniface IV designated November 1 as All Saints' Day—a time to honor both martyrs and saints. His purpose was to replace the pagan holiday of Samhain with a holy day. The day was called All Hallows' Day. October 31 then became known as All Hallows' Eve, and eventually Halloween. During the medieval period, Christians would walk from house to house, begging for food in exchange for prayers for the deceased loved ones of the residents. Eventually, the practice of dressing in costume, asking for candy, and engaging in pranks became Halloween practices. Therefore, Halloween has its deepest roots in pagan ideology, but also Christian traditions. However, if you wish to avoid Halloween because of its pagan history, you may have to do the same thing with other holidays, because Halloween isn't the only holiday with such a history. For example, in the 1600s, the Christians of the Reformation Movement outlawed the celebration of Christmas because of its pagan history.

Christmas has its history in pagan traditions dating back more than 4,000 years, when ancient Mesopotamians celebrated the new year by honoring their god Marduk. This festival lasted 12 days. It is from this tradition that we get the concept of the 12 days of Christmas. The ancient Greeks had a similar festival to honor their god Kronos. In Scandinavia, the light of the sun would be gone for many weeks. To celebrate its return around the winter solstice, the people celebrated "Yuletide," burning the Yule log and tying fruit to trees to represent the coming spring. The Persians honored Mithras, the god of light, and Romans honored the god Saturn in a festival called Saturnalia, in which they gave presents for good luck, decorated their homes with branches, and decorated trees with candles. It wasn't until A.D. 350 that Bishop Julius I of Rome designated December 25 the official day to mark the birth of Jesus. By around A.D. 1100, Saint Nicholas was known throughout Europe and by the 1800s, Christmas was widely practiced by the nonreligious and the religious alike by decorating trees and giving gifts.

Easter also has roots in pagan traditions that can be traced back many centuries. It was originally an Anglo-Saxon festival celebrated at the vernal equinox in honor of Eastre, the goddess of the spring, who was symbolized by a rabbit. From this tradition we have the Easter Bunny. Eggs have been widely used in cultures worldwide to represent fertility gods, and Easter eggs derived from this concept. Jews who had converted to Christianity not long after the death of Jesus may well have used their Jewish holiday of Passover (Pesach or Pasch), which paralleled the time of the resurrection of Jesus, to create what became Easter. Despite the early Christian celebration of Easter, many pagan cultures still honored Eastre. Therefore, early Christian missionaries who wanted to gently convert pagans shifted the meaning of the pagan holiday, carrying with it the traditions of the pagan holiday, to its current form. Multicolored eggs symbolized the sunlight of spring and the egg came to represent the tomb and eventual rebirth of Jesus Christ. In A.D. 325, Emperor Constantine convened the Council of Nicaea to determine an exact date for Easter. It was not until after the Civil War that Easter was widely celebrated in the United States. Easter is still based on the vernal equinox, so it always falls between March 21 and April 25.

Perhaps most surprising to many is that the most important pagan holiday according to the Satanic Bible is one's own birthday. Anton LaVey, the self-proclaimed hedonist and author of the Satanic Bible, declared that if the church of Satan was to be based on hedonism, the highest holiday would be the celebration of one's own birth. Consequently, celebration of one's birthday was considered the highest "Satanic" holiday. Therefore, if one shouldn't celebrate Halloween because of its pagan roots, applying the same rule means we shouldn't celebrate Christmas, Easter, or even our own birthdays—all common holidays celebrated in many religious homes and even in places of worship.

Psychologically, there is nothing damaging about Halloween, and children love the opportunity to celebrate, dress up in a costume, and, of course, get candy. The biggest concern with celebrating Halloween involves accidents. Costumes that make it difficult for a child to see can lead to accidents, and it is not unusual for children to be struck by vehicles because their costumes made it hard for drivers to see them. Abductions, molestations, and injuries because of tainted treats are also possibilities. All of these dangers can be overcome. Trick-or-treat at a shopping mall or only at houses where you know the residents. Put safety reflectors on costumes and make sure that your child's vision is not restricted by the costume. If your religious beliefs prohibit you from celebrating Halloween, herein is the information needed to make decisions about all holidays.

WHEN YOU'VE REACHED THE END OF YOUR ROPE

Have you ever had one of those days when your patience with your children is expiring as quickly as a short fuse on a firecracker? Let me promise you that you are not alone. We all have days when we are frustrated and everything that our children do seems to get on our nerves. There are a lot of reasons for this experience, but there are a few causes that are common.

One possible reason your children get on your nerves more than normal is that they need your attention more than usual. Like the rest of us, children go through cycles. Sometimes they require more attention than at other times. Very young children require attention nearly all the time, but as they reach school age, the constant demand on your time should be easing up. Occasionally, they will feel more of a need to be held, talked to, played with, and praised. If these times occur when you are especially tired, you will experience frustration.

A second possibility is that you need time away. Many parents who are mindful of the time they are away from home feel guilty for taking time for themselves. One could certainly be too self-centered, resulting in neglect of one's children, but an occasional night out alone or an afternoon with a friend to see a movie, shop, or visit a library is good for a person's state of mind.

A third possibility is that you and your spouse need time away. One mark of a healthy marriage is that a couple still goes out together on dates. This can certainly be taken to extremes, but a weekly date is a great idea. It is easy to allow an anniversary to be the only time one spends together alone with a spouse. It is possible for a couple to live together for 15 or 20 years and never really communicate with one another because they are so busy being parents. Once the children are gone, the couple is able to talk together for the first time in years, and they realize they really don't know each other. The eighteenth year is a critical year for potential divorce for this very reason.

A final possibility is that you may not be organized. When we plan poorly, we should not expect children to take up the slack for us. If you have several things that you need to do with your children and it normally takes 45 minutes to do them, you can be sure you will be frustrated if you allow only 30 minutes for the tasks. There have been occasions when I had to get my children ready to leave the house, but I planned only enough time to get myself ready. When I was ready, it was time to leave and I found myself frustrated with my children because they were not "cooperating" and getting ready quickly enough. In fact, it was my poor planning that caused my frustration.

Certainly there are other reasons for frustration, but these few suggestions may cause these difficult days to come less often, and perhaps make them easier to bear when they do inevitably come.

CHAPTER 12

Inspiration, Motivation, and Accountability

In 1928, John B. Watson, the country's leading expert on child care at the time, published a volume titled *The Psychological Care of the Infant and Child*. In it, Watson, a behaviorist, argued that parents should never be too loving with their child because it slowed the child's ability to cope with the world. "Never hug and kiss them," he wrote. "Never let them sit in your lap. If you must, kiss them once on the forehead when they say goodnight. Shake hands with them in the morning."[1] It has taken decades to overcome his bad advice.

Since 1994, I have written a newspaper column on parenting and children's issues in *The Citizen*, a newspaper published in a metropolitan Atlanta suburb. Many of my articles have focused on practical issues in parenting. In fact, most of the topics covered in this book have been addressed in my newspaper column. However, there have been times when my sole purpose in writing my column was to encourage and inspire the reader. Other times I wished to remind the reader to take parenting seriously. This chapter includes some of my favorite articles. The recurring theme in these articles is that even though parenting is difficult, it is a wonderful journey and it is easy to miss the joy of parenting in the process. The purpose of their inclusion in this book is to provide inspiration and motivation, and, in some cases, to remind parents of the importance of their job as they struggle with the day-to-day challenges of raising children. These segments might be most effective by reading one a day, as daily thoughts, rather than reading all of them at one time. I hope you find them helpful, encouraging, and inspiring. I have edited them slightly for the context of this book, but otherwise they appear as they did when they were published.

A WALK IN THE WOODS, APRIL 2001

It was Easter Sunday. Hard rain had fallen most of the day, but the sun decided to peek through the clouds by midafternoon. My four-year-old son wanted to play outside. In order to keep him out of the mud, I went outside with him and I watched him as he worked diligently to step in every puddle yet trying to make it look like an accident each time.

As we walked, we talked about Easter, his T-ball game the day before, and his friends. He told me many important things, like how our dog likes to chew on rocks and why he would never eat a rock. He explained to me that the grass grew because the rain went into the ground and pushed it out. He also told me that when he got to be a daddy, we would be "two dads," but that I would be very old.

He took my hand and we walked quietly for a few minutes. He had to walk slowly because his feet kept slipping out of his sandals. "Benjamin," I said to him, "I really like it when you hold my hand."

Benjamin looked at me and very matter-of-factly stated, "I like that, too, Dad—when you hold my hand."

There in the dampness of the wet grass, feeling the sun on my shoulders and my son's hand snugly in my palm, I realized I was the richest man in the world. I would not trade that moment for all the money in Bill Gates's bank accounts. Benjamin was right, of course. One of these days I will be old. Equally real is the fact that one of these days he will be old, too. He won't need my hand as often.

Our day started very early. I was awake and in my office at home at 4:30 A.M. Faintly audible in the distance were the rumblings of a thunderstorm on its way and I knew it wouldn't be long before the noise of the storm awoke my children. The thunder grew louder as the storm neared, and by six o'clock a bright flash of lightning and a loud clap of thunder awoke my son in the room next to my office. He called out and I went to rescue him.

"The thunder scares me," he said. He sat in my lap, safe from the troubles of the storm. I wish I could always find it so easy to help him ease his troubles and fears, but life isn't that way. As he gets older, he will have to face some of his fears alone.

I don't think we can be reminded too often that the time we have with our children is fleeting. It seems like moments ago that I snuggled with a tiny baby in a maternity ward—our first baby, who is not so small anymore. She was so little and I was so young. Now she is an adolescent, clearly ready to move into adulthood. What a contrast to see my three children together, each at a different stage of life. I know one of these days it will be my grandchildren that I compare and I will wonder where the years went.

Like men who have walked on the moon, climbed Mt. Everest, and sledded to the North Pole, I have had experiences in my life that I can never forget—ones that have left an indelible impression on me. The really exceptional thing about my experiences, however, is that they did not require extreme courage or endurance. They only required that I notice them.

"I like that, too, Dad—when you hold my hand." Indeed, I have all I could ever want.

WHY BOTHER, OCTOBER 1994

Today I had the day off. I went to my daughter's school for a program. Afterward, I spent some time letting her show me her classroom and guide me around her school. I stayed with her for lunch. When she came home from school and we had eaten dinner, our family played kickball outside until sunset. Then we sat on our swing set, drank iced tea, and cooled down before we came in. We had a great day together. Then, without warning, she went into a tantrum over some trivial thing. As I watched her storm through the living room to her bedroom, I thought, "Why do I bother?"

Then, nearly immediately, I remembered why I bother. My daughter is only six years old. My wife and I are everything to her at this age. She is learning from me how to be a wife. She learns this by watching how I treat my wife and how my wife treats me. She is also learning how to be a parent from my wife and me. She learns this by watching how I parent her and her sister. She will likely treat her children the way we treat her. She is learning from me how to deal with stress and anger. She is learning from me how to express emotion. My daughter will grow up to be an image of my wife and me. She will have expectations in life based, in part, on the way she was raised. And, just like most of us, as she becomes an adult, she will even take on as her own some of my characteristics she always disliked.

In all my years as a counselor, without exception, every one of my clients has spent session time talking with me about issues from childhood. Clients 40 or 50 fifty years of age have shed tears over things that happened when they were children. Often these issues were directly or indirectly the result of something their parents either did or did not do.

Even as I am writing this column, I am shaping my daughter's future. Just now she came to my desk and asked me to snuggle with her. Why bother? I am, in part, shaping the way she will approach life. I am, in part, determining the type of man she will marry and the way she will see herself 50 years from now. I certainly am determining the way she will see her past.

Those times when I am too busy to talk with her, play with her, or snuggle with her will soon be gone and the tables will be reversed. The day will come when I will not be everything to her. A husband will eventually replace me as the most important man in her life. I know that one day she will be too big to sit on my lap—too busy to tell me about her day—too busy to snuggle with me—too busy to play kickball with the family after dinner.

Days like today will be remembered for the fun we had at Brooks Elementary School. They will be remembered for the fun we had at lunch. They will be remembered for the fun we had playing kickball and sitting on our swing set. Whatever it was that spawned the tantrum tonight will not be remembered. This is why I bother.

FATHER OF A FUTURE BRIDE, JULY 1996

One of my favorite movies is *Father of the Bride*. How well I can relate to the father in the movie as he sees his daughter grown, wishes he could hang on to her as a child, but knows he cannot. Perhaps it is at a daughter's wedding that all one's work as a father culminates.

How I love the sound of my daughters' little feet on the floor as they run to me when they are afraid. They are the only people in the world who think I am the smartest man on the planet. As far as they are concerned, I can fix anything and nothing is beyond my ability. How I revel in the greetings I receive as I come home each day. It seems to matter not whether I was gone for two hours or a week. My girls always greet me as if I had been gone a lifetime. I melt at the soft touch of my daughter's tiny hands on the sides of my face as I hold her in my arms and she pulls my face to hers while she tells me some important news. My wife and I delight in watching our children discover the mysteries of life that most adults take for granted—a rabbit in our yard, an interesting bug, a fascinating cloud.

My friend and colleague Robert has an agreement with his daughters. If ever they need attention and he seems too busy to be with them, they say, "Daddy, life is too short." This reminder always focuses his attention on what matters. He tells me that he will never look back on his life wishing he had watched more TV or wishing he had spent more time in the office. He knows he does not want to look back and wish he had spent more time with his children.

I know that one day I will be second place to my daughters. That is the way it should be. I don't want it to come, but it must. I want my daughters to know the joy that I have found in a loving spouse. Thinking about the days when I will come home to a quiet house, the days when I will have to wait for a letter or phone call because my daughters live far away, makes today's work of being a parent so much more bearable. I suppose that the things that drive me nuts today will be the very things that my wife and I will sit and reminisce over when our children are grown.

This lesson is especially important to us as our children are home all day long during the summer. It is all too easy to spend all my energy mediating arguments and trying to occupy their time. My work as a parent, however, is more than getting through each day. I am preparing my girls for that day when I send them out on their own—the day when I respond to the question "Who gives this woman to be wed to this man?" with "Her mother and I." I am preparing them for the days when they will see me more realistically, with all my flaws and failures. My greatest gift to them as they are children is not a toy, a trip, or anything that can be purchased. My greatest gift to them is all of me—a dad. Toys will come and go, but they will always have their dad with them even when I am gone.

A LETTER TO DADDY, JANUARY 1998

If a child could write her thoughts to her father, perhaps it would sound something like this:

Dear Daddy:

Thanks for all the great Christmas presents, but you know what? My favorite presents are those times the whole family wrestles on the floor and we tickle each other. I like piggyback rides, playing games with you, and doing puzzles. It's funny. Things like this are my favorite, but they aren't things I can take to show-and-tell. Isn't that weird? Let's do those things a lot!

I like my brother and sister, but I sometimes feel like you don't see me. I try to please you by doing things for you—drawing you a picture, making my bed, or cleaning my room. But sometimes you are so busy that you seem to forget that I'm here. I want to know that I matter as much to you as my sister and brother. Please take time every day to tell me I'm important to you and that you love me.

Sometimes I think that you like TV more than you like me. I know you say you love me, but I feel like I'm always in the way. When I feel left out, I sometimes try to get your attention by being bad. I know that if I say something mean or act up, you will pay attention to me. It is not any fun getting into trouble, but I'd rather have you paying attention to me when I'm in trouble than not paying any attention to me at all.

When you come home from work, I have so many things to tell you. I do many important things during the day. People tell me stories and exciting things happen. Just like the time that Cindy got her shoe stuck in the mud on the playground and had to wear one shoe the rest of the day. That was so funny. It made me feel so good inside when you laughed, too. I like it when you listen to my stories and act like they are important to you—when you look at my eyes when I'm talking to you. I know you are tired when you come home, but I don't understand anything about your job or what it means when you say you go to work. All I know is that you are gone from me and I miss you.

What do you think about when you see me? You tell me I look nice, especially on Sundays, but I need you to tell me I'm pretty even if I'm not dressed up. I sometimes worry that you won't like me or that I am a bad person. It helps me feel better about myself when you smile at me, tease me, take me places, and talk with me. I like it when you hug me just because I am standing near you—not because I did anything special. My favorite times are when we go for a walk or sit together in the big chair in the living room—just you and me.

I don't like it when you and Mommy argue. It scares me and I am afraid that you might leave me all alone. I always feel like somehow the fight was my fault. I want to do something to make it better, but I don't know what to do. It always makes me feel better when you and Mommy are laughing—when you include me in your joking and your games. That is when I know that I am safe.

I know you tell me I'm a big girl, but don't forget I'm only seven. I have so much to learn and I need you to teach me. Please be patient with me when I make mistakes. I don't do it on purpose or just to make you mad. I'm trying to make you proud of me.

I love you even when you make mistakes. I can't imagine having any other dad. I can't wait until I'm eight. I'll be old then. Maybe then you will understand me.

Love, Your Daughter

A LETTER TO MOMMY, FEBRUARY 1999

If a child could write a letter to her mother, it might sound something like this:

Dear Mommy:

I decided to write to you because you always seem so busy and tired. I thought that maybe you would be able to read this when I'm sleeping.

I'm glad you are home with me. I like it that you wave to me on the bus in the morning and meet me at the bus stop in the afternoon. Lots of kids miss that. I especially like it when you pick me up at school. I'm so proud of you that I want people to see that you are my mom.

Sometimes I know that I do things that make you mad, but I forget the rules you teach me. I hope that someday I'm good enough to make you proud of me. You tell me that you love me no matter what, but I feel like you will not like me if I'm bad. You probably need to remind me of the rules once in a while so I don't forget.

Isn't it fun when we aren't really doing anything in particular, but we are just at home together? You have so much to do, but I like it when we sit and read together, take a walk, or ride our bikes. I like to watch you getting ready for the day. I can't wait until I can wear makeup, high heels, and pretty dresses like you. You are the most beautiful woman I know and I hope I look as pretty as you when I grow up!

I love my sister and brother, but in secret sometimes I wish you were there just for me. I like it when you do things that show me you want to be with just me. I want to learn to cook, write checks, go shopping, and drive, just like you do. When I play house with my friends, I pretend I'm you.

I don't remember very often to tell you this, but thanks for helping me with my homework, doing all that laundry, and cleaning my bathroom. When you let me do something like the laundry or fixing dinner, I realize how much work it is and I'm glad I don't have to do it all the time. No wonder you get so tired.

Don't worry if I complain sometimes or if I seem mad at you. It never lasts very long and I sometimes even forget why I was mad. Even when you tell me I can't do things I want to do, I sometimes figure out that you know what you are doing. Maybe I'll be smart like you someday.

When I show you a picture I drew or bring my report card home, I feel so good inside when you stop what you are doing and look at it right then, like it is the most important thing in the world. I know that my pictures are not always the best and my grades sometimes aren't great, but you encourage me anyway. That makes me want to try harder.

When you tuck me in bed at night, I'm so glad you are my mom. I feel safe when I'm with you, but I am sometimes afraid I won't have you with me anymore—that you might die or go away. I like it when you hug me and tell me that you love me even when I haven't done anything special. That makes me feel good. I love you and hope you will always love me.

Love, Your Daughter

VALUABLE MINUTES, MAY 1995

A secretary telling me I had an urgent phone call from my wife interrupted my meeting. She had gone out of town with my children to visit their grandmother. As I listened, Stacey told me that Kara, my younger daughter, had a fever of unknown cause and had already narrowly escaped death. She was in the hospital emergency room and the doctors were trying to bring her fever down. That began one of the longest weeks of my life. Five times that week her fever rose above 106 degrees. Five times that week the hospital staff scrambled to save her life, and five times that week my wife and I prepared to lose our precious daughter who in only days would celebrate her first birthday. Six days later, we brought her home. The illness was never identified.

The happy ending to this story is that Kara is happy and healthy. That experience, however, will live with me for the rest of my life. In fact, it taught me a valuable lesson. We take so much for granted in many areas of our lives. It is very easy to become so possessed by the things we have to do and the troubles we have with our children that we fail to enjoy these experiences while they are occurring.

In the hospital, as we waited from hour to hour to see if Kara's temperature would rise again, we prayed that she would be all right. Fortunately, our prayers were answered. Since that time, I have tried never to take my time with my children for granted. When I am up in the middle of the night with them because they are afraid or sick, I am not so worried about how much work I have to do the next day or how tired I will be. Instead, I sit in a darkened living room in our rocking chair with them in my lap, thinking, "This is a moment I may have not had." In this context, sleep is just not that important. When my children are fighting with each other, I am happy that I have children at all. When one is grumpy, I remind myself that I would rather have a grumpy child than no child. In that context, whining is much more bearable.

When you struggle with patience with your children, try to keep their troubles in context. There will come a day when they won't want to share their troubles with you—a day when you wish they would. There will come a time when you look back on being up in the middle of the night or sitting with a frightened child in your lap with sweet reminiscence. If you think of your struggles in this context, you will find it easier to deal with your children when they push your patience.

I WAS WRONG, MAY 1996

One afternoon my older daughter noticed something at home that my wife had done that my daughter knew was an irritation to me. More than once she had heard me discussing the issue with my wife. She made a sarcastic comment about the issue and then looked at me for approval. My response to her was this: "Megan, do you know who you sound like? You sound like Daddy when he is being unkind to Mommy." Her expression changed as she realized that the comment was inappropriate. Equally important, she recognized that I was willing to criticize myself when I realized I was wrong.

I am not perfect. Anyone who knows me could tell you that, but my children will naturally perceive me as all-knowing and able to do anything simply because I am their father. (Obviously, this changes during adolescence!) As parents, my wife and I will be the most important teachers that our children will ever have. Occasionally pointing out one's own fallibility is a powerful teaching tool. A number of things are accomplished by acknowledging some of your shortcomings to your children.

First of all, my conversation with my daughter demonstrated to her that it is OK to make mistakes. As adults, we recognize that everyone makes mistakes. Because of their limited cognitive skills, however, it is easy for children to get the idea that they are the only ones who make mistakes and that if they were good enough, they would not make any mistakes. It is important that children learn that the blessing of a mistake is to learn from it and try not to make that particular one again.

Second, acknowledgment of your fallibility demonstrates how to handle making mistakes. Erring is a normal part of living and it is vital that children see how grown-ups handle goof-ups. My self-chastisement demonstrated that even though I don't have a parent telling me what to do, I am still accountable for my behavior. Having no direct supervision does not allow me to do whatever I please. Considering another person's feelings, for example, matters even if there is no one there to tell you what to do. Hopefully my daughter learned from our conversation that she must be self-monitoring and correct her mistakes when they are brought to her attention.

Third, acknowledging your mistakes teaches children how to say "I'm sorry." These words are two of the most powerful words people can use. Marriages and other relationships can be strengthened by sincere acknowledgment of responsibility. I lost my temper one day with my daughter and yelled at her. She was punished for what she had done, but my approach hurt her feelings. I went to her room and found her crying. I explained to her that what she did was wrong and that it was my job as a parent to correct her. The punishment was appropriate. However, I told her I was sorry for losing my temper. She looked at me and said, "That's OK, Daddy. I still love you." The words "I'm sorry" are not just for kids. They demonstrate our weaknesses but, in turn, these words strengthen our relationships. Obviously, there are some faults in our lives that should not be discussed with our children. However, an occasional reminder to them that we are people, too, is a healthy thing.

WHAT IS RIGHT WITH PARENTS, MARCH 1997

It is easy for writers like me to produce a commentary on what parents do wrong. But many parents do many things very well. They just need reassurance and confidence in their decisions. The parents of most of the children that I work with are well-intentioned. Even when the family is disrupted by divorce or other stressors, many, if not most, of the moms and dads I work with have their children's best interest in mind. Sometimes their mistakes are out of selfishness, but it is rare that I see a totally hedonistic parent. Perhaps the best statement regarding all the parents I have worked with over the years is that they are doing the best they can with the resources available to them.

It is for this reason that I propose three things to parents. First of all, trust yourself. If you are honest with yourself, you know if you are motivated by selfish desires or your child's best interests. If you can say to yourself that you are seeking what is best for your children, even if you make mistakes (as you will), they are usually repairable errors. Over time, the genuineness of a parent seeking to do her best shows through. You would not even be reading this book if you did not have your child's interests at heart.

At least once a week a parent says to me, "This is what I did. Is that OK?" My answer is almost always an affirmative. I have great confidence in a parent's instinct. I provide suggestions to all the parents of the children I see, but it is always their prerogative to move in some other direction. They know their children, and our collective efforts usually pay off. In some ways, I rely on them as much as they rely on me.

Second, teach yourself. Bookstores are loaded with self-help books. Some are good and some are not. However, many of the books that I've seen regarding raising children are adequate at the very least and some of them are quite exceptional. Available are books concerning discipline, divorce, adolescents, and other areas of interest to families and parents.

Third, allow yourself to be human. We all make mistakes. The mother of one of the children I see asked me this question: "Tell me honestly. Are your children perfect?" Of course they aren't. My wife and I share the same frustrations and developmental difficulties all parents face. My children have free will. My career and experience as a child therapist make it possible that I may make fewer mistakes than I otherwise would, but I certainly am not perfect and neither are my children. Part of the education of our children is for them to realize that it is normal to make mistakes. Our maturity regarding our mistakes is reflected in how we respond to them—not in never making them.

WORTH THE RISK, APRIL 1997

One of my most vivid childhood memories involves a mistake I made with my younger sister, Beverly. We lived in the Midwest, and one snowy winter we had agreed to substitute as newspaper carriers for a friend who was leaving town for a week. Her parents graciously provided us with the key to their home so we could fold the papers inside, out of the snow and cold.

One of the first afternoons of our work, we were in their living room folding papers and decided that we would see if they had any food we could eat. In our poor judgment, we looked through their refrigerator and cabinets and put together a nourishing meal of maraschino cherries and Pop Tarts. We knew what we were doing was wrong. In fact, we even went to the trouble to make sure everything was back where it started so that we would not raise suspicions. A week later, Beverly told my older sister about the incident and she told our parents.

My father told Beverly and me that when he came home from work the next day, we would go to the store, purchase a jar of cherries and a box of Pop Tarts with our own money, take them to our friend's home, and tell the parents what we had done. I'll never forget that long day at school, trying to figure out how to get out of the trip to our friend's house. I even thought about running away to join the circus.

That night my father drove us over to our friend's house. I prayed that they would not be home. Not only were they home, but they were all in the living room together when we knocked at the door. I was crying so hard when the door opened, I could not even talk. I'm sure we must have been quite a sight—two children standing in the snow on their door stoop, crying and holding Pop Tarts and maraschino cherries. My sister managed to deliver our collective confession and apology. We handed over our purchase and left.

For years, I thought that was one of the hardest things my father ever made me do. Now, however, I feel quite differently. Instead, I believe that it was probably one of the hardest things my father ever had to make *himself* make us do. It would have been much easier if he had just spanked us, lectured us, or disciplined the two of us in some other private way. As it was, he went with us to a home where he knew no one and stood behind us as we admitted that we were thieves. I realize now that he was risking his name—his reputation—to do the right thing and to teach us a valuable lesson.

The actions of our children are not independent of us as their parents. We are reflected in the way they behave. I think about my father often as I try to decide what will teach my children the best lesson. Several years ago, while I stood with my own child in front of a store manager as she admitted, "I stole this," I thought of my father and that cold winter night nearly two decades earlier. Just like my father, it would have been easier for me to ignore the behavior. Often the hardest lesson is not only hard for them but hard for us as well. The risk of my reputation was well worth it if, like me, her mistake is remembered more for the lesson rather than with shame of the behavior. Oddly, as I held her up to the manager's window so she could make her confession, I realized I also was proud of her as she faced her mistake. The truth is that the thing that defines our character is not our mistakes as much as it is our response to our mistakes.

PERFECTING THE JOB, JUNE 1997

Well-balanced and highly functioning children all have something in common. It isn't their money, nice clothes, or nice houses. These children come from both very wealthy parents and very poor ones. They live in all sorts of neighborhoods and attend all kinds of schools. They are white, black, Asian, and Latino. Some of them are very bright and some of them border on retardation. Some come from homes with both biological parents and some reside in foster care.

What these healthy children have in common is a significant adult in their lives who invests in them—invests time and energy. These adults are actively engaged in perfecting the skill of leading the child for whom they are responsible. They consider their role as parent, guardian, big brother or big sister, grandma or grandpa as a calling. They perceive it as a responsibility and they accept that responsibility—no questions asked. These parents read books, attend seminars, talk to other successful parents, and work in other ways at perfecting their roles in the lives of the children for whom they are responsible.

These successful leaders understand that leading is like a job. To get better at it, you have to work at it. The job involves things that are enjoyable as well as things that are not so pleasant. It is a package deal. One of my former students was a 40-year-old father of three from Thailand. His name was Poyon, and he worked on our maintenance crew. Every time I saw him for nearly a month one summer, he was painting something around the campus. He always seemed to be enjoying his work. I said to him one day, "Poyon, you must really love to paint." His response was "I have to." He recognized that working—no matter what the job—was his responsibility as a father and he could either complain about it or enjoy it. He chose the latter.

Not only is there a common thread in the families of healthy children, there are also common threads in dysfunctional families as well. In these families children are seen as noisemakers that are to be tolerated. Parents talk to them carelessly. They insult and humiliate their children. Sometimes these children are physically abused or neglected. Sometimes they are sexually abused. More often, however, they are simply ignored.

We live in a culture where adults are encouraged to be irresponsible. Lawyers tell us that we should "stand up for our rights" if we've been injured. It would be exceedingly rare to hear a lawyer say that his client should take responsibility for his own careless behavior. There is no financial reward for being responsible.

Some parents treat their automobiles and boats better than their own children. Are you spending more time reading pleasure books and magazines, watching TV, or working in your yard than you are mentoring your children? Do you spend equal energy perfecting your parenting skills as you do perfecting your golf or tennis game? If not, you may need to reconsider your responsibilities and priorities.

A QUESTION OF CHARACTER, SEPTEMBER 1997

While visiting Mexico a few years ago, I let a peddler talk me into buying a "silver" ring. I wore it only a few weeks until it became evident the ring was merely silver plated, and it was worthless. I paid almost nothing for the ring, but it was undoubtedly worth even less than what I paid for it. Everything I have ever owned has been that way to some extent. Even large purchases for which I saved seemed to lose their luster after a while, and they eventually became relatively unimportant.

All of my assumptions concerning families and child rearing in one way or another are based on character. A person of integrity, I believe, makes the best parent, spouse, or child. Without character, we are like that silver-plated ring—shallow and of little enduring value. We like to talk about character and integrity, but these characteristics come with a heavy price tag. The cost of character includes daily sacrifice, endurance, and self-discipline. We seem to prefer, however, to avoid the very things which develop in us wisdom, patience, and integrity, all the while pursuing with fervor the shallow rewards and shiny trinkets of our culture. We live in a society that encourages immediate gratification and hedonism. True character says, "I will give you what I know you need regardless of the cost to me." Instead, however, our culture instructs, "Get what you 'deserve' regardless of the cost to others." Things of significance are things one works for, but we have the luxury in our affluent culture to continue to pursue the path of least resistance even though we know nothing of value waits for us at the end of the path.

The auto accident in 1997 that claimed the life of Princess Diana was a tragedy, but not because Diana was a princess. It was a tragedy because three human beings lost their lives. (It is interesting that very little was said of the "tragedy" of the death of her driver and her companion.). Among the many letters to the editor that were published in papers across the country during this time, one noted the irony of the culture's response to the death of Princess Diana and, soon after, the death of Mother Teresa. "While Diana was being whisked away in her Rolls-Royce to a five-star hotel after a hard day of showing her concern and raising awareness, Mother Teresa was falling asleep holding the hand of a child who would wake up in heaven the next morning."[2] He went on to say, "Therein lies our problem. We increasingly want to *be* something without having to *become* something."[3] This is, in fact, a brutal but accurate description of what we are.

The rewards of character are internal and long-lasting. The rewards of hedonism are like shallow silver plating. A man I once knew was immensely wealthy. He worked hard for what he had earned, but somewhere along the way he decided his personal pleasures were more important than the needs of his family. He now lives like Scrooge McDuck, alone with his millions of dollars and yet has no one with whom to share them. I honestly believe one of the saddest homes I have ever visited was his lifeless, empty, $40 million mansion.

Nonstop media coverage, candlelight vigils, and unending table conversation followed the death of one whose life was characterized by infidelity, a broken marriage, a gigantic dress collection, and other excesses of wealth. The death of one whose life was characterized by self-denial and the betterment of humanity received honorable mention. We have the power to change the way we are. We simply need the will to do so.

TAG-ALONG, FEBRUARY 1998

I went to Girl Scout day camp because my older sister was a Girl Scout and my mother was a Girl Scout leader. Therefore, when summer day camp rolled around, I had to go along. They had a separate place on the campground for those of us who came with parents. We were called "tag-alongs." We had our own program, but it was run by teenagers whose job was to keep us occupied and safe for the period of time the "real" program was going on across the lake. We were extra baggage and we knew it.

There are a lot of tag-alongs these days. They are children of parents who are so busy that they drag their children along with them, forcing them into their schedules with little regard of the effect of such a relentless routine on their developing minds and bodies. We live in a time where we perceive we need certain things and we adjust our lifestyle to fit this misperception. We live under the myth that it takes two incomes in order to make ends meet, but that just is not true. I learned this lesson from one of my students when I tried to use the same argument many years ago. My student suggested that my wife and I could adjust our lifestyle to my income rather than adjusting our income to a lifestyle we wanted. He was absolutely right. We began weaning ourselves from my wife's income and over several months we eventually reached the point where she could be a stay-at-home mom. We have never regretted this decision.

Some people dismiss my argument because they do not want to deny themselves some of the luxuries to which they have grown accustomed. Only you can know for sure, but there are several things you can do to avoid treating your children like tag-alongs. First, treat your children with respect. Consider how your behavior will affect their futures and avoid subjecting your children to a series of day-care settings, baby-sitters, and social gatherings that are of interest to you but not beneficial to them.

Second, allow children to be involved in some decisions at home at a level appropriate for their ages. Where you go out to eat, where you go on vacation, and how you spend your family time are all decisions in which most children can at least minimally participate. Allowing your children to participate in decision making is empowering and also teaches them how to make decisions. Not allowing them to participate creates helplessness, and they become tag-alongs.

Third, consciously evaluate how often you are selfish in your decisions and how often you sacrifice your own wants in order to meet the needs of your children. I have never met anyone whose mother or father stayed home with them when they were younger who complained that they didn't have enough "stuff" because of it. On the contrary, they appreciated the sacrifices their families made in order to be together.

Of course you should not cater to your child's every whim and children need to be tag-alongs on occasion. It teaches them patience and also teaches them to experience fun regardless of circumstances. At Girl Scout camp, I was forced to put my personal wants away and allow my sister to be the focus of attention. It is important to learn to teach siblings to stand in the background and celebrate while another child has the limelight. Good parenting involves teaching life skills. Some of these skills involve tagging along. However, it is not in the child's best interest to live in an environment where he is always a tag-along.

NO GUARANTEES, MARCH 1998

Most parents want their children to grow up to be respectable, hard-working, and moral in their choices and behavior. It is ironic that parents who do little to cultivate these traits in their children express surprise when they find their children in trouble at school or with the law, pregnant, or using drugs. We assume a cause-effect relationship in most things in our lives, and one certainly exists between the way we engage our children and what they become. This seems so evident it is almost embarrassing to state it, but enough people have argued the point that it seems that some of them don't see the connection between their behaviors and the behaviors of their children.

It is not uncommon for parents to argue that good parenting practices "don't guarantee anything." Of course they don't, but these arguments generally come from one of two sources. The first source is the family where children have, indeed, elected to violate a lifestyle that their parents have attempted in good faith to teach. My heart goes out to this group because they have tried their best. Children have free will and can choose their own paths regardless of how hard one tries to teach them otherwise. Just as children can turn out to be decent human beings despite irresponsible parents, children can choose to be irresponsible despite the direction of responsible parents.

The second source includes parents who seek a reason to excuse the irresponsible approach to parenting. They do whatever they want with their time and resources, regardless of the impact on their children. They invest more energy in their work, toys, and recreation than they do their children, and they then blame society, circumstances, or individual choice for the situation in which their children find themselves.

It is interesting that those who say that working hard at being a good parent doesn't guarantee anything are often businessmen and -women who spend millions of corporate dollars on advertising campaigns, personnel development, and marketing research. These practices don't guarantee anything either, but they consider this good business sense. The reason that this is good business is it increases the probability of a company's success.

In the same way, good parenting doesn't guarantee success, but it increases the probability of success. A parent can work very hard at the job of raising children and yet we all know that our children could make choices that are not reflective of how they were raised. The best we can do is to train them as best we can. Training involves a *lifestyle* of mentoring children. Every event is a potential teaching tool. Every argument is a part of this training. Every evening walk or conversation in the car is a chance to teach. After 20 years of training, mentoring, and teaching your children, you have created a high probability that they will choose to live as they have been taught. This theorem holds true in every other form of education; therefore, it is logical to suppose it will hold in parenting.

Being a parent is, without a doubt, the most important job in the world. You have the chance to influence the lives of your own children more than anyone else ever could. Take it seriously.

DO WHAT YOU WANT, JULY 1999

I am amazed at the behavior people try to excuse. For many years I was a college administrator. Students would be disciplined for stealing, vandalism, and other inexcusable behaviors. Their parents came to my office, not to apologize for their child's behavior but to complain about the discipline they had received. This attitude is not limited to the college environment.

With startling regularity the media report on people who misuse the U.S. Constitution and Bill of Rights as a magic wand that gives them permission to do or say whatever they want, regardless of the harm that may be done to others by their words and actions. Our governmental leaders and even psychologists who should know better have normalized single-parent households, allowing parents to pursue their own interests at their children's expense.

People argue with my opinion of day care, movies, and other topics I've written about in the past, arguing that I blow these issues out of proportion. I've often wondered what these people, adhering to their current points of view, would write if they were in my shoes. To see what their ideas sound like all together, I've written an article from their perspectives. Here is what their position might sound like:

Don't worry about how many hours you work or how little time you spend at home. Children don't need parents in the house. They just need the things your money can buy. After all, parents are cultural inventions and kids can learn all they need about growing up from TV and their friends. Spending a few minutes once in a while with your children is sufficient. Your children would rather have possessions than loving parents at home.

Let your children watch any movie, listen to any song, or read any book they want. No matter how profane, vile, or vulgar, it has no effect on them. Allow your children to spend hours in front of the television, on the Internet, or at computer games, no matter how violent or profane the themes. Children are resilient and recognize violence, pornography, and profanity as entertainment and would never imitate these behaviors. No monitoring by parents is needed.

Carefully change the perspective on issues when your children are in trouble. Never accept that your children have done anything wrong. Find where the system has wronged them and focus all attention there. It is obvious that they are powerless and have no choice but to do the wrongs they do because of a system that is biased against them. Ensure that your children understand that their race, gender, socioeconomic status, or religious background totally incapacitates them and makes personal choice and responsibility impossible. When necessary, hire a lawyer and sue all possible parties rather than admit any responsibility or wrongdoing.

Children cannot control their sexual energies, so you should expect sexual activity from your child. Conservative groups that encourage abstinence are clearly out of touch with reality and their Puritan ideals have no place in a modern society. Sexual activity in the early teens and even younger is to be expected. Abortion is the solution to unwanted pregnancies when they occur. By the way, you don't need to be informed if your daughter has an abortion. Even though we concede that government agencies should get your permission before dispensing aspirin, it is old-fashioned to assume that you should be informed if your child wishes to have a surgical procedure like an abortion. Teach your daughter that her right to choose an abortion has nothing to do with the rights of an unborn child. Make sure you dehumanize an unborn baby by calling it "tissue." Never allow your daughter to consider that "the right to choose" occurs at the point of deciding on intercourse. Instead, teach her to do what she wants at the moment and then teach her that the consequences of her actions are unfair tragedies that are thrust upon her by conservative religious groups.

If your son rapes a woman while on a date, make sure he understands it was not his fault. Explain that sexual intercourse on a date is his right even if a woman says "no." Teach your son that if a woman dresses in a seductive way, he can treat her in any way he chooses.

Finally, and perhaps most important, encourage your children to speak and act disrespectfully to adults, especially teachers. After all, we are all equal and there is no reason adults should get any special recognition from young people.

—Signed, A Modern Parent

If we followed this absurd advice, we would raise a generation of children who would have no respect for authority and who would refuse to take responsibility. Teen pregnancy and juvenile crime would be out of control and we probably would even have children killing each other in our schools.

STICKS AND STONES, MAY 2000

When I was in grade school, there was a young boy in my third-grade class who was much larger than the rest of us. He had been held back two years, so his physical development was well beyond the other third graders in his class. Not only was he large, he was also a bully. It wasn't unusual for him to pick a fight with me after school. When that happened, my sisters would rush home and get my mother, who would come to my rescue. One day, my classmate cornered me just beyond the school yard. In desperation, I swung my metal lunchbox in an attempt to protect myself. The lunchbox hit him in the chin and I escaped. He never picked on me again.

You no doubt remember the little poem that most of us were taught in childhood that says, "Sticks and stones may break my bones, but words can never hurt me." Learning this poem was supposed to teach us that we should ignore what people say because their words have no power to harm us. While this might be a good strategy for coping with painful words, it isn't true.

Words are very powerful and, like my metal lunchbox on my classmate's chin, they can leave an indelible impression. When they are used correctly, they can encourage and strengthen egos. When they are used carelessly, they can slay the spirit of a person, leaving wounds from which one may never fully recover.

We cannot insulate ourselves from all painful words, but we can work hard to be responsible with the words we use. Simple words like "I'm proud of you" can be all the motivation a child needs to work toward a goal. A well-timed encouraging comment can be a powerful constructive force, while thoughtless criticism can be incredibly destructive.

Think carefully about how you use both praise and criticism. We are responsible to correct and modify the behavior of our children; therefore, criticism is sometimes necessary. How we do it is what makes the difference. At times your children should know that they have disappointed you. Shame and guilt are motivators for productive behavior. Just use your words carefully. Look for opportunities to praise and encourage, knowing that well-placed and thoughtful positive words can be equally powerful motivators for good behavior.

My classmate probably still carries a scar on his chin where I hit him with my lunchbox. Undoubtedly, it has faded, but he surely recalls the day when he received that wound and I would guess he might still feel bad about that humiliating experience. Likewise, painful words leave emotional scars that are vivid reminders to the recipients. Over the years, the scars may fade, but they are always there. Thoughtful use of words can prevent such wounds.

"MEAN"—AND PROUD OF IT, JUNE 2000

"You're a meanie!" That is how my three-year-old son described me when he wanted something that I would not let him have. He stomped away, certain that I was the meanest dad in the whole world. How many times do parents find themselves faced with this attitude? Unfortunately, it is not just from three-year-olds, either. Grade school children complain because they want to stay up later than we know they should. Middle school children argue that they should be allowed to go to a party without mom "nosing in" to find out where it will be. High school children are insulted that they have to bring themselves home by midnight.

Don't you wish that in some way you could convince your children that you are only trying to protect them? A mother once asked me how she could get her adolescent daughter to understand that she (the mother) got no pleasure from grounding her for violating a rule. I know what this woman wanted. She wanted to have a reasonable conversation with her 13-year-old and at the end of the conversation she wanted her daughter to say, "I see now that you only want what is best for me. I understand that I can't always see the benefit of your discipline, so I'll just accept your wisdom and hope I learn from this experience."

Obviously, there was nothing that she could say that would appease her daughter, and the response she wished for was pure fantasy. Remember your own childhood. You were so sure that your parents sat around into the wee hours of the morning, plotting ways to make your life miserable. Anytime their imaginations went dry, you were sure they called in consultants to help them devise punishments and rules for the sole purpose of making you unhappy. It is funny to think of how logical this all seemed back then.

Good parents will find their children angry with them occasionally. Doing the right thing often means doing the hard thing. Disciplining my children has the power to bring me to the edge of tears because I don't want them hating me—even though I know their "hate" won't last. How much easier it would be not to care. How much easier it would be to take the path of least resistance, to avoid the argument or confrontation, yet to take the easy route would be irresponsible. The work of being a good parent involves enduring false accusations, hateful looks, and the silent treatment.

Parenting is sort of like the stock market. It pays its dividends over many years. If you expect short-term windfalls, you will be disappointed, but diligence in parenting will produce honorable, decent human beings over time. At the small, private college where I teach, I work with more than two dozen very dedicated parents whose children are now grown. I watched them with their children when their children were young and I know how seriously they took their jobs as parents. Now that their children are grown, I see what fine people they have become and many times I have thought that I would be proud if my children grew up to be like them. Through their examples, these parents have encouraged me, and I encourage you to be patient and endure the storms, because the cost is worth it.

I AM KID 1, DECEMBER 2000

My eight-year-old daughter came running up to me, obviously full of excitement. "I got a speaking part in the Christmas play," she told me. I was so excited for her. My daughter elaborated. "Yeah," she said, "I'm Kid 1." I tried to keep from laughing. I don't know what I expected, but I know I wasn't ready for "Kid 1." I told her how happy I was for her to have been chosen. "I've already memorized my line," she told me as she quickly recited her one big line. The night of the program, I read her name listed in the printed program as "Kid 1" and watched as she flawlessly delivered her line. I was so proud.

In this play, my daughter's character didn't have a name, only "Kid 1," but it was very important to her to have been chosen. It made her feel important. As usual, it was one of my children who reminded me, although unintentionally, of the importance of my job as a parent. My children sit in my lap and look up to me for identity, purpose, and value. They get it from other places, such as participation in a play, but I am primarily responsible for communicating worth to my children. Adults can easily forget how important seemingly little things are to children and how thoughtless words can easily defeat or even destroy a child's esteem.

Most of us can remember times in our childhood when something seemed terribly important to us. How hurt we were when we tried to share it with someone who was important to us, like a parent, and yet he or she didn't seem to appreciate its significance. Even as an adult, isn't it defeating when you try to share your excitement with your spouse and he or she doesn't seem interested? We can easily take it personally, and we are adults! So much more is this true with children.

I let the facial expressions of my children tell me how important something is to them. If their faces say, "This is a big deal," then it is a big deal for me, too. Adolescents have learned to hide their feelings in order to protect themselves from discouragement, so they are harder to read. I try to put myself in their place. I ask myself, "If I were in their shoes, would it be a big deal?" If so, it is important to me even if they say it isn't to them.

People have an innate need to feel competent and worthwhile. As adults, we fill this need through our hobbies, activities, jobs, or other areas of interest. Children have not developed coping skills or objective ways to evaluate their competence. They live in a world where their competence is always open to question. They can quickly begin to doubt their competence because of a poor grade, an embarrassing episode in front of friends, or an unkind word. Likewise, their competence can be affirmed if they are picked for a part in a play, if they perform well on a test, or if a parent for no special reason says, "You are important to me."

Esteem is like a suitcase full of ideas. It is empty when we start life, and as the years go by we fill our suitcase with the comments and ideas of others regarding our self-worth. As we reach adulthood, that suitcase is reflective of our views of ourselves. Even though we cannot, and should not, protect our children from all discouragement, I want the suitcases that my children carry into adulthood to be filled with many more ego-strengthening comments than ego-defeating ones, and I work to purposefully reach that goal. Resolve to look more carefully for opportunities to build confidence in your child than you may have in the past. I know I will—my daughter was Kid 1!

COMPASSIONATE HEARTS, OCTOBER 2001

I sat at the bedside of a dear friend in a convalescent center. He was well into his eighties and I have watched his health decline over the past several years, but I remember him when he was a spry gentleman, quite active, who could easily take care of himself. Now he remains in bed most of the time, unable to get out by himself. His skin is wrinkled with age and patched with discolorations, rashes, and various sores.

I spent about 45 minutes with my friend and the entire time I was there, another resident on the same floor lay in her room and yelled over and over, "Help me, help me, help me." Her mind had long since failed to serve her properly and she could not be consoled. The halls smelled of medicine and even death. Weekly, beds there are emptied as residents pass away. I would imagine it is a frightening place to anyone who isn't accustomed to the destructive nature of our years. As a child, I visited my great-grandmother in an ancient Gothic structure, a place called "The Gorge," so named because of its location, tucked away in a forest valley. Bare light bulbs hung from the ceiling in the residents' rooms and elderly men and women lined the hallways in wheelchairs. Occasionally, they would reach out at me as I walked by. They scared me to death and so did the facility, but my mother and father insisted that my great-grandmother would want to see me. They were right, of course.

As I sat with my friend, listening to him tell stories of World War II, and I watched him drift in and out of sleep, I saw something in him that many people would miss. I did not see his gray hair or his tired and frail body. I saw my friend whom I love dearly, much as one might see a mother or father, remembering them as they used to be, and seeing far beyond the wretchedness that might frighten one who could not know any better. My compassion for my friend made it impossible for his condition to frighten me away.

My children occasionally accompany me when I visit friends in the hospital or elderly people who are unable to leave their homes. I do not force them to go, but sometimes I have to encourage them to come along. Like me when I was their ages, the foreign nature of a hospital or convalescent center with its sights, sounds, and smells, as well as the enigma of age, dying, and death, can be frightening to them. But I want my children to learn to see beyond appearances. I want them to learn to look at other people with a compassionate eye, one that sees beyond wrinkles, frailness, and sickness. If they can learn to do that, they can also learn to see beyond skin color, religious differences, and lifestyle choices. By going with me to visit the aged, like my friend, my children have the opportunity to learn from them. It is amazing that my friend, incapable of caring for himself and sometimes even finding it difficult to keep his mind focused on a simple conversation—this man who will most likely never see my children as adults—can still be their teacher.

A LESSON FROM THE AMISH, DECEMBER 2001

Is there anywhere you can go these days where you don't see someone on a cellular telephone? Recently, I actually heard someone talking on his cell phone in the stall of a public bathroom and he even told the caller where he was and what he was doing! Many people have cellular telephones and there is nothing inherently wrong with them, but maybe we could learn something from the Amish.

The Amish don't have telephones in their homes. Some of them have a telephone in a small booth (with no seat) in their yard, but not in the house. This may seem hypocritical, but much thought went into the decision as to what role telephones would play in their culture. The Amish are not opposed to telephones, but as a community they long ago decided that the telephone is a tool to be used carefully and that thoughtless use of the telephone is dangerous to individuals, families, and community. They use the telephone only when absolutely necessary.

How many of the telephone conversations while people are driving, shopping, or sitting in a theater are really necessary? Instead of interacting with family or thinking about the people around us, we are on the telephone. We have a few rules in our house about the telephone, some of which I have adopted from the Amish. My children do not have telephones in their rooms. If they need to talk on the phone, they can use one in the hallway. My children have a time limit on the phone. Ten minutes is plenty of time to do whatever business might need to be done, with the rare exception of a school project that might require more time.

Rules don't apply only to my children. I am careful with the telephone as well. I do not talk on the telephone after 8 P.M. or during a meal because those are family times. I don't talk to telemarketers. I politely say I'm not interested and I hang up. If I have a visitor at home, I may not answer the phone. I do not put a guest in second place. Isn't it irritating when you are at a business being waited on and the clerk takes a call? It is as if the customer on the telephone butts directly to the head of the line. I don't want to do that to my guests.

Cellular telephones have only exacerbated how the telephone can erode family and community. They distract us while we are driving. Because we are always reachable, cell phones make our lives busier, not easier, when most of us actually need some quiet time with friends, family, or time alone. Ironically, even though cellular phones make communication easier, they isolate us from those in our immediate vicinity. People walk through airports and down the sidewalk completely oblivious to those around them because they are so wrapped up in their telephone conversations. Cell phone users alienate those around them by discussing personal business in public places.

Because cell phones are cheap, accessible, and can make communication easier, we have failed to ask whether this convenience is good for us. Even though I know some people need cellular telephones because of their businesses, the majority of us don't "need" them; we "want" them.

Maybe the Amish are on to something in their approach to the telephone. Our lives are busy, but we could function very well without a cell phone or at least with more limited use of it. Your choice about how you use the telephone or cellular phone is your business, but at least consider how the telephone, and any other appliance, can negatively affect your family as you make your decisions.

A PARENT'S RESPONSIBILITY, MARCH 2002

A writer once complained in a letter to the editor that young people in his hometown did not have enough to do. The writer argued that one reason for the increase in arrests of young people his community had experienced was that they had no youth center or place for them to congregate. Statistics back up this person's argument. Communities that have youth centers and places for children to congregate see a decrease in some kinds of juvenile crime. However, there are at least three problems with this gentleman's argument.

First of all, his premise that there is nothing for children to do in his hometown was incorrect. On the contrary, there were many things for children to do. There were places for shopping, outdoor athletic fields, bookstores, and public libraries. There were parks, an indoor soccer center, movie theaters, batting cages, running tracks, biking and walking paths, lakes, swimming pools, a dive center, and restaurants. What the writer of this letter really meant was that there was nothing for children to do of a specific type. There was no youth center specifically. Even though I agreed with some of what the writer said, the letter sounded somewhat like my children when they look past mounds of toys, books, videotapes, computer games, the swimming pool, bicycles, pets, and so forth and tell me that there is "nothing to do" at home.

A second issue is perhaps even more important. For some reason the writer supposed that it was the city's responsibility to entertain the city's youth, but it is not the city's responsibility; rather, the responsibility to monitor a child's behavior lies with parents. The crime rate is the city's problem, but the solution begins at home, not at city hall.

Finally, there are other factors that contribute to lowered juvenile crime rates other than the presence or absence of youth centers. Children who are supervised by their parents are far less likely to engage in vandalism, sexual assault, petty crime, stealing, and the use of drugs and alcohol. Teenagers should not need 24-hour-a-day supervision, but I'm talking about parents who are actively involved in their children's lives. It is an unfortunate truth that many parents are uninterested in supervision of their own children and look to others who will take on that obligation. Other parents are interested in their children, but they are too busy with their own interests, jobs, and hobbies to take an active role in their children's lives. In either case, these parents just want their children out of the house and out of their hair.

My friend and I had a business meeting at a local restaurant one afternoon. Our meeting started in the early afternoon and continued after the local high school dismissed for the day. Between 10 and 15 young people congregated at the booth next to ours. For over an hour, they smoked cigarettes and engaged in loud and vile conversation. It was interesting that these kids could hang out for an hour or more after school, engage in unhealthy behaviors, and apparently raise no suspicions or concerns at home. It is likely that most of them did not have a parent at home.

It is unrealistic to expect children with no accountability and no supervision to make responsible choices. This mentality doesn't take place overnight.

It comes from a history in a home where parents communicate that anything goes as long as the child doesn't cause any trouble for the parent. A youth center in such cases will only give these kids a place to congregate and engage in the same behaviors they would have anywhere else. Buildings where kids can hang out do not promote a healthy community; rather, it is involved and active parents that can make a difference.

ONLY YESTERDAY, JUNE 1999

It never fails. Any time I talk with someone who has adult children, they tell me that it seemed like only yesterday when their children were small. I attended the wedding of one of my former students recently. I watched this handsome gentleman, poised and mature, as he took the hand of his bride and lit a unity candle, symbolically separating permanently from his parents and beginning a new life with his wife.

I tried to picture my son in a tuxedo marrying some beautiful young woman. He is so young, his future bride may not yet be born. I pictured my daughters in white lace, standing before the altar with their husbands-to-be. It is hard to picture my six-year-old, with her broad toothless grin and little-girl body, as a woman, ready for life apart from my wife and me. Easier, though, was picturing my soon-to-be adolescent as a bride. It is conceivable that over half of her life at home with us is past. As busy as children keep us mediating their disagreements, running to band practice, dance, baseball, and other activities, we can lose sight of what we have right now. I never expected that being a parent would be the most challenging, entertaining, frustrating, and yet fulfilling part of my life.

Driving home one night, all three of my children were playing together in the van. There was no screaming or fighting. They were so loud, but their voices were like a chorus. I wish for them a future that includes pleasant memories of their childhoods. When they are older and married and they get together and reminisce, I want to hear things like "Do you remember when Mom and Dad used to let us swim in the pool late at night?" and "Wasn't it fun when we went on long hikes with Daddy on Saturdays?" I hope my oldest will remember fondly the many days that we rode to piano lessons together, just the two of us. I want my children to remember the many lunches we had together at school and I want my son to remember the many mornings he helped me make coffee and then we walked together to the mailbox to get the newspaper. I want my younger daughter to remember our conversations every night at bedtime when we asked each other, "What was your favorite part of the day?"

Of course, their memories will include things that I did wrong—times when I lost my temper or was gone more than I wanted to be, but I want their hearts to swell with nostalgia when they think of me and the many days we had together. So many of my adult clients over the years, when they recall their childhoods, feel rage, discontent, and resentment. Their memories of home are not pleasant ones. Sometimes this is true because of cruel and selfish things that their parents did to them deliberately. Often, however, their bad feelings are the result of cruel or selfish things their parents did to them without even knowing it. They didn't think about how their behavior would affect their children in the long run. They were too busy, too distracted, and simply didn't take the time to think about it.

People often talk about various stages of a child's life as if it were something to be dreaded. I have enjoyed every stage in the past and I look forward to every stage in the future. Despite the frustrations, I wouldn't trade it for the world. We only get one chance at it with each child. Don't let it slip away.

Notes

CHAPTER 2

1. "5 Reasons for Contraceptive Failure," *Women's Health*, January 23, 2002, womenshealth.about.com/library/weekly/aa52201a.htm.

2. British Telecommunications, "Abortion Statistics," 2002, http://www.btinternet.com/ DEvans_/abstats.htm.

3. Heritage House, Inc., "Quick Facts," January 19, 2002, www.abortionfacts.com.abortion/q_facts.asp.

4. Centers for Disease Control and Prevention, "Surveillance and Research," August 14, 2001, www.cdc.gov/nccdphp/drh/surv_abort97.htm.

5. Elliot Institute, "A List of Major Physical Sequelae Related to Abortion," January 1998, www.abortion facts.com/reardon/effect_of_abortion.as preference.

6. Ellen C. Perrin et al., "Technical Report: Coparent or Second-Parent Adoption by Same-Sex Parents," *American Academy of Pediatrics On-line Version*, February 2002, www.aap.org/policy/020008t.html.

7. "Are You Ready for Another?", *Pregnancy & Baby Care*, March 3, 1999, www.ahealthyme.com/topic/7055.

CHAPTER 3

1. Eleanor E. Maccoby, "Perspectives on Gender Development," *International Journal of Behavioral Development*, 24(4), 398–406; see p. 399, December 2000.

CHAPTER 6

1. C. L. Thompson and L. B. Rudolph, *Counseling Children*, 3rd ed. (Pacific Grove CA: Brooks Cole, 1992), 509.

CHAPTER 8

1. Kaiser Family Foundation/Nickelodeon/Children Now, *Talking with Kids about Tough Issues: A National Survey of Parents and Kids* (Menlo Park, CA: Kaiser Family Foundation, March 2001).

2. A. Kinsey, W. Pomeroy, C. Martin, and P. Gebhard, *Sexual Behavior in the Human Male* (Philadelphia: W. B. Saunders, 1948), and *Sexual Behavior in the Human Female* (Philadelphia: W. B. Saunders, 1953).

3. L. J. White, D. Browning, W. J. Doherty, M. Gallagher, M. Luo, and S. Stanley, *Does Divorce Make People Happy?* (New York: Institute for American Values, 2000).

CHAPTER 9

1. American Psychiatric Association, *Diagnostic and Statistical Manual of Mental Disorders*, 4th ed., text revision (Washington, DC: American Psychiatric Association, 2000).

2. C. Neely, M. L. Shew, T. Beuhring, R. Sieving, B. C. Miller, and R. W. Blum, "Mother's Influence on the Timing of First Sex among 14- and 15-Year-Olds," *Journal of Adolescent Health*, 31 (September 2002), 256–265.

3. B. C. Miller and T. D. Olson, "Sexual Attitudes and Behavior of High School Students in Relation to Background and Contextual Factors," *Journal of Sex Research*. 24 (1988), 194–200; see 196.

4. Neely et al., "Mother's Influence."

5. D. M. Reddy, R. Fleming, and C. Swain, "Effect of Mandatory Parental Notification on Adolescent Girls' Use of Sexual Health Care Services," *Journal of the American Medical Association*, 288 (2002), 710–714.

6. Ibid.

CHAPTER 10

1. S. Farkas, J. Johnson, A. Duffett, L. Wilson, and J. Vine, *A Lot Easier Said Than Done: Parents Talk about Raising Children in Today's America* (Washington, DC: Public Agenda, 2002), 39.

2. Ibid.

CHAPTER 11

1. Madeline Levine, *Viewing Violence: How Media Violence Affects your Child's and Adolescent's Development* (New York: Doubleday, 1996), 3.

2. T. N. Robinson, M. L. Wilde, L. C. Navracruz, F. Haydel, and A. Varady, "Effects of Reducing Children's Television and Video Game Use on Aggressive Behavior," *Archives of Pediatrics and Adolescent Medicine*, 155 (2000), 17–23.

CHAPTER 12

1. John B. Watson, *The Psychological Care of the Infant and Child* (1928), as quoted in Robin Karr-Morse and Meredith S. Wiley, *Ghosts from the Nursery* (New York: Atlantic Monthly Press, 1997), 88.

2. Letter to the Editor, *Atlanta Journal/Constitution* September 22, 1997.

3. Ibid.

Bibliography

Discipline, dealing with death, attention deficit disorder, stuttering, shyness, and other problems are among the many topics for which parents seek books and articles that will help them work more effectively with their youngsters. In order to be more useful to the inquisitive parent, instead of presenting references in an alphabetical list, this bibliography is organized by topic. Readers can quickly scan the subjects and find references for the topic that interests them. No single book can include every possible topic or question a parent might have. Therefore, this bibliography includes references for material that is not discussed in this book as well as for material that elaborates on issues that are discussed in the chapters of this book.

ADOLESCENCE

Apter, Teri. *The Myth of Maturity: What Teenagers Need from Parents to Become Adults.* New York: W. W. Norton, 2001.

Dobson, James. *Preparing for Adolescence: Straight Talk to Teens and Parents.* Ventura, CA: Regal Books, 1978.

Scott, Buddy. *Relief for Hurting Parents: How to Fight for the Lives of Teenagers.* Nashville, TN: Allon Publishing, 1989.

ADOPTION

Keefer, Betsy, and Schooler, Jayne E. *Telling the Truth to Your Adopted or Foster Child: Making Sense of the Past.* Westport, CT: Greenwood Publishing Group, 2000.

Perrin, Ellen C. "Technical Report: Co-Parent or Second-Parent Adoption by Same-Sex Parents." *American Academy of Pediatrics*, 109 (February 2002), 341–344.

BOOKS TO HELP CHILDREN THROUGH THEIR PROBLEMS

Andrews, Steven, and Andry, Shepp. *How Are Babies Made?* New York: Little, Brown, 1997.

Holmes, Margaret. *A Terrible Thing Happened.* Washington, DC: Magination Press, 2000.

Quinn, Patricia O., and Stern, Judith M. *Putting on the Brakes: Young People's Guide to Understanding Attention Deficit Hyperactivity Disorder.* Washington, DC: Magination Press, 2001.

Sheppard, C. *Brave Bart: A Story for Traumatized and Grieving Children.* Grosse Pointe Woods, MI: National Institute for Trauma and Loss in Children, 2000.

Whitehouse, E., and Pudney, W. *A Volcano in My Tummy: Helping Children Handle Anger.* Gabriola Island, BC: New Society Publishers, 1996.

BREAST-FEEDING

Eisenberg, Arlene. *What to Expect the First Year.* New York: Workman, 1993.

Huggins, Kathleen. *The Nursing Mother's Companion*, 3rd ed. Summit, PA: National Book Network, 1995.

Mohrbacher, Nancy. *The Breastfeeding Answer Book.* Schaumburg, IL: La Leche League International, 1997.

Neifert, Marianne. *Dr. Mom's Guide to Breastfeeding.* New York: Plume, 1998.

Spangler, Amy. *Breastfeeding: A Parent's Guide*, rev. ed. Amy Spangler, 2000.

CONCEPTION, PREGNANCY, AND PRENATAL ISSUES

"Are You Ready for Another?" Pregnancy & Baby Care. March 3, 1999. www.ahealthyme.com/topic 7055.

British Telecommunications. "Abortion Statistics." 2002. http://www.btinternet.com/DEvans_23/abstats.htm.

Bruce, Debra Fulgham, and Thatcher, Samuel S. *Making a Baby: Everything You Need to Know to Get Pregnant.* New York: Ballantine Books, 2000.

Centers for Disease Control and Prevention. "Surveillance and Research." August 14, 2001. www.cdc.gov/nccdphp/drh/surv_abort97.htm.

Curtis, Glade B., and Schuler, Judith. *Your Pregnancy Week by Week.* Boulder, CO: Perseus, 2001.

Eliot Institute. "A List of Major Physical Sequelae Related to Abortion." January 1998. www.aborionfacts.com/reardon/effect_of_abortion. aspreference.

"5 Reasons for Contraceptive Failure." *Women's Health*. January 23, 2002. Womenshealth.about.com/library/weekly/aa052201a.htm.

Heritage House, Inc. "Quick Facts." January 19, 2002. www.abortionfacts.com/q_facts.asp.

Martin, Margaret, and Bing, Elizabeth. *Pregnancy and Childbirth: The Basic Illustrated Guide*. Boulder, CO: Perseus, 1997.

Murkoff, Heidi E., Eisenberg, Arlene, and Hathaway, Sandee. *What to Expect While You're Expecting*, 3rd ed. New York: Workman, 2002.

Otis, Tina. *The Illustrated Guide to Pregnancy and Childbirth*. Chicago: McGraw-Hill/Contemporary Books, 2000.

Reddy, D. M., Fleming, R., and Swain, C. "Effect of Mandatory Parental Notification on Adolescent Girls' Use of Sexual Health Care Services." *Journal of the American Medical Association*, 288 (2002), 710–714.

Rosenthal, Sara. *The Gynecological Sourcebook*, 3rd ed. Chicago: McGraw-Hill/Contemporary Books, 2000.

CULTURE

Bennett, William J. *The Broken Hearth: Reversing the Moral Collapse of the American Family*. New York: Random House, 2001.

Howard, Philip K. *The Collapse of the Common Good: How America's Lawsuit Culture Undermines Our Freedom*. New York: Random House, 2002.

DEVELOPMENTAL ISSUES

Brazelton, T. Berry, and Sparrow, Joshua A. *Touchpoints Three to Six: Your Child's Emotional and Behavioral Development*. Boulder, CO: Perseus, 2001.

Emde, Robert N., and Hewitt, John K. *Infancy to Early Childhood: Genetic and Environmental Influences on Developmental Change*. Cary, NC: Oxford University Press, 2001.

Kreuger, Anne. *Parenting: Guide to Your Baby's First Year*. New York: Ballantine Books, 1999.

Potter, Melody Milam, and Milan, Erin E. *Healthy Baby, Toxic World: Creating a Safe Environment for Your Baby's Critical Development*. Oakland, CA: New Harbinger Press, 1999.

DIVORCE

Christensen, Andrew, and Jacobson, Neil S. *Reconcilable Differences*. New York: Guilford Press, 1999.

Garrity, Carla B., and Baris, Mitchell A. *Caught in the Middle: Protecting the Children of High-Conflict Divorce*. San Francisco: Jossey-Bass, 1997.

Johnston, Janet R., Breunig, Karla, Garrity, Carla, and Baris, Mitchell. *Through the Eyes of Children: Healing Stories for Children of Divorce*. New York: Free Press, 1997.

Newman, Margaret. *Stepfamily Realities: How to Overcome Difficulties and Have a Happy Family*. Oakland, CA: New Harbinger Press, 1994.

Rubin, Judith. *My Mom and Dad Don't Live Together Anymore: A Drawing Book for Children of Separated and Divorced Parents*. Washington, DC: Magination Press, 2002.

Teyber, Edward. *Helping Children Cope with Divorce*, rev. ed. San Francisco: Jossey-Bass, 2001.

Thayer, Elizabeth, and Zimmermann, Jeffrey. *The Co-Parenting Survival Guide: Letting Go of Conflict after a Difficult Divorce*. Oakland, CA: New Harbinger Press, 2001.

White, L. J., Browning, D., Doherty, W. J., Gallagher, M., Luo, Y., and Stanley, S. *Does Divorce Make People Happy?* New York: Institute for American Values, 2000.

Whitehead, Barbara Dafoe. *The Divorce Culture*. New York: Alfred A. Knopf, 1996.

EMPTY NEST

Lauer, Jeanette, and Lauer, Robert. *How to Survive and Thrive in an Empty Nest: Reclaiming Your Life When Your Children Have Grown*. Oakland, CA: New Harbinger Press, 1999.

ESTEEM AND EMOTION

Cox, Maureen V. *The Child's Point of View*, 2nd ed. New York: Guilford Press, 1991.

Forward, Susan. *Toxic Parents: Overcoming Their Hurtful Legacy and Reclaiming Your Life*. New York: Bantam Books, 1989.

Goldberg, Susan. *Attachment and Development*. Cary, NC: Oxford University Press, 2000.

Greenspan, Stanley, and Greenspan, Nancy Thorndike. *First Feelings: Milestones in the Emotional Development of Your Baby and Child*. New York: Penguin Putnam, 1994.

Stern, Daniel. *Diary of a Baby: What Your Child Sees, Feels, and Experiences*. New York: Basic Books, 1990.

Wright, H. Norman. *The Power of a Parent's Words: How You Can Use Loving, Effective Communication to Increase Your Child's Self-Esteem and Reduce the Frustrations of Parenting*. Ventura, CA: Regal Books, 1991.

FATHERHOOD

Barras, Jonetta Rose. *Whatever Happened to Daddy's Little Girl?: The Impact of Fatherlessness on Black Women*. New York: Random House, 2000.

Brott, Armin A. *The New Father: A Dad's Guide to the First Year*. New York: Abbeville Press, 1997.

Brott, Armin A. *The Expectant Father: Facts, Tips, and Advice for Dads-to-Be.* New York: Abbeville Press, 2001.

GENDER AND SEXUALITY

Dobson, James. *Bringing Up Boys.* Wheaton, IL: Tyndale House, 2001.

Kindlon, Dan, and Thompson, Michael. *Raising Cain: Protecting the Emotional Lives of Boys.* New York: Ballantine Books, 2000.

Kinsey, A., Pomeroy, W., Martin, C., and Gebhard, P. *Sexual Behavior in the Human Male.* Philadelphia: W. B. Saunders, 1948.

Kinsey, A., Pomeroy, W., Martin, C., and Gebhard, P. *Sexual Behavior in the Human Female.* Philadelphia: W. B. Saunders, 1953.

Maccoby, Eleanor E. "Perspectives on Gender Development." *International Journal of Behavioral Development,* 24(4) (2000), 398–406.

McNeely, C., Shew, M., Beuhring, T., Sieving, R., Miller, B.C., and Blum, R. W. "Mother's Influence on the Timing of First Sex among 14- and 15-year-olds." *Journal of Adolescent Health,* 31 (September 2002), 256–265.

Miller, B. C., and Olson, T. D. "Sexual Attitudes and Behavior of High School Students in Relation to Background and Contextual Factors." *Journal of Sex Research,* 24 (1988), 194–200.

Thompson, Michael. *Speaking of Boys: Answers to the Most-Asked Questions about Raising Sons.* New York: Ballantine Books, 2000.

ILLNESS, DISABILITIES, DISEASE, AND DEATH

Capper, Lizanne. *That's My Child: Strategies for Parents of Children with Disabilities.* Washington, DC: Child Welfare League of America, 1996.

Chasnoff, Ira J., ed. *Your Child: A Medical Guide/The Illustrated Medical Guide and Health Advisor.* New York: Beekman House, 1987.

Neifert, Marianne, Price, Ann, and Dana, Nancy. *Dr. Mom: A Guide to Baby and Child Care.* Chicago: Signet, 1986.

Spock, Benjamin, and Rothenberg, Michael B. *Dr. Spock's Baby and Child Care.* New York: Pocket Books, 1985.

Stoppard, Miriam. *Baby and Child: A to Z Medical Handbook/Parent's Easy Reference Guide to Children's Illnesses, Symptoms, and Treatment.* New York: Perigee, 1996.

Webb, Nancy Boyd, ed. *Helping Bereaved Children: A Handbook for Practitioners,* 2nd ed. New York: Guilford Press, 2002.

Worden, William J. *Children and Grief: When a Parent Dies.* New York: Guilford Press, 2001.

Wozniak, Leigh A., and Goodheart, Carol D. *Living with Childhood Cancer: A Practical Guide to Help Families Cope.* Washington, DC: American Psychological Association, 2002.

IMAGINARY PLAYMATES

Taylor, Marjorie. *Imaginary Companions and the Children Who Create Them.* Cary, NC: Oxford University Press, 1999.

INFANCY

Dunnewold, Anne, and Sanford, Diane. *The Postpartum Survival Guide.* Oakland, CA: New Harbinger Press, 1998.

Karr-Morse, Robin, and Wiley, Meredith S. *Ghosts from the Nursery: Tracing the Roots of Violence.* New York: Atlantic Monthly Press, 1997.

Robinson, Carl. *Parents Dr. Carl Robinson's Basic Baby Care: A Guide for New Parents for the First Year.* Oakland, CA: New Harbinger Press, 1998.

INFERTILITY

Daniluk, Judith C. *The Infertility Survival Guide: Everything You Need to Know to Cope with the Challenges While Maintaining Sanity, Dignity, and Relationships.* Oakland, CA: New Harbinger Press, 2001.

Steelman, Megan V. *Thinking Pregnant: Conceiving Your New Life with a Baby.* Oakland, CA: New Harbinger Press, 2001.

LANGUAGE DEVELOPMENT

Golinkoff, Roberta Michnick, and Hirsch-Pasek, Kathy. *How Babies Talk: The Magic and Mystery of Language in the First Three Years of Life.* New York: Plume, 2000.

MARRIAGE

Arp, David H., Arp, Claudia S., Stanley, Scott M., Markman, Howard J., and Blumberg, Susan L. *Fighting for Your Empty Nest Marriage: Reinventing Your Relationship When the Kids Leave Home.* San Francisco: Jossey-Bass, 2000.

Dobson, James. *Love Must Be Enough: New Hope for Families in Crisis.* Waco, TX: Word Books, 1983.

Jordan, Pamela, Stanley, Scott M., and Markham, Howard J. *Becoming Parents: How to Strengthen Your Marriage as Your Familiy Grows.* San Francisco: Jossey-Bass, 2001.

Popenoe, David. *Life without Father: Compelling New Evidence That Fatherhood and Marriage Are Indispensable for the Good of Children and Society.* Cambridge, MA: Harvard University Press, 1999.

Waite, Linda J., and Gallagher, Maggie. *The Case for Marriage: Why Married People Are Happier, Healthier, and Better Off Financially.* New York: Random House, 2000.

MENTAL DISORDERS AND OTHER PARENTING PROBLEMS

American Psychiatric Association. *Diagnostic and Statistical Manual of Mental Disorders*, 4th ed. Washington, DC: American Psychiatric Association, 2000.

Barkley, Russell A. *Taking Charge of AHD: The Complete, Authoritative Guide for Parents*, rev. ed. New York: Guilford Press, 2000.

Fassler, David G., and Dumas, Lynne S. *"Help Me, I'm Sad": Recognizing, Treating, and Preventing Childhood and Adolescent Depression*. New York: Penguin Putnam, 1998.

Frankel, Fred. *Good Friends Are Hard to Find: Helping Your Child Find, Make, and Keep Friends*. Glendale, CA: Perspective Publishing, 1996.

Hagans, Kathryn B., and Case, Joyce. *When Your Child Has Been Molested: A Parent's Guide to Healing and Recovery*. San Francisco: Jossey-Bass, 1998.

Hawton, Keith, and Van Heeringen, Kees, eds. *The International Handbook of Suicide and Attempted Suicide*. San Francisco: Jossey-Bass, 2002.

The Hidden Feelings of Motherhood: A Guide to Coping with Stress, Depression, and Burnout. Oakland, CA: New Harbinger Press, 2001.

Kearney, Christopher A. *School Refusal Behavior in Youth: A Functional Approach to Assessment and Treatment*. Washington, DC: American Psychological Association, 2001.

Lardner, George, Jr. *The Stalking of Kristin: A Father Investigates the Murder of His Daughter*. New York: Onyx Books, 1997.

Magid, Ken, and McKelvey, Carole A. *High Risk: Children without a Conscience*. New York: Bantam Books, 1990.

McCann, Joseph T. *Stalking in Children and Adolescents: The Primitive Bond*. Washington, DC: American Psychological Association, 2001.

Ozonoff, Sally, Dawson, Geraldine, and McPartland, James. *A Parent's Guide to Asperger Syndrome and High-Functioning Autism: How to Meet the Challenges and Help Your Child Thrive*. New York: Guilford Press, 2002.

Rapoport, Judith L. *The Boy Who Couldn't Stop Washing: The Experience and Treatment of Obsessive-Compulsive Disorder*. New York: New American Library, 1997.

Shamoo, Tonia K., and Patros, Philip G. *Helping Your Child with Depression and Suicidal Thoughts*. San Francisco: Jossey-Bass, 1993.

Terr, Lenore. *Too Scared to Cry: How Trauma Affects Children and Ultimately Us All*. New York: Basic Books, 1976.

Terr, Lenore. *Unchained Memories: True Stories of Traumatic Memories, Lost and Found*. New York: Basic Books, 1994.

MISCELLANEOUS

Dobson, James, and Bauer, Gary L. *Children at Risk: The Battle for the Hearts and Minds of Our Kids*. Waco, TX: Word Books, 1990.

Thompson, C. L., and Rudolph, L. B. *Counseling Children*, 3rd ed. Pacific Grove, CA: Brooks Cole, 1992.

PARENTING SKILLS

Barber, Nigel. *Why Parents Matter: Parental Investment and Child Outcomes.* Westport, CT: Greenwood Publishing Group, 2000.

Baum, Joanne. *Respectful Parenting: From Birth through the Terrific Twos.* Washington, DC: Child Welfare League of America, 2001.

Berk, Laura. *Awakening Children's Minds: How Parents and Teachers Can Make a Difference.* Cary, NC: Oxford University Press, 2001.

Borba, Michele. *Parents Do Make a Difference: How to Raise Kids with Solid Character, Strong Minds, and Caring Hearts.* San Francisco: Jossey-Bass, 1999.

Borowski, John G., Landesman Ramey, Sharon, and Bristol-Power, Marie, eds. *Parenting and the Child's World: Influences on Academic, Intellectual, and Social-Emotional Development.* Mahwah, NJ: Lawrence Erlbaum, 2002.

Dobson, James. *Parenting Isn't for Cowards: Dealing Confidently with the Frustrations of Child-Rearing.* Waco, TX: Word Books, 1987.

Farkas, S., Johnson, J., Duffett, A., Wilson, L., and Vine, J. *A Lot Easier Said Than Done: Parents Talk about Raising Children in Today's America.* Washington, DC: Public Agenda, 2002.

Kaiser Family Foundation/Nickelodeon/Children Now. *Talking with Kids about Tough Issues: A National Survey of Parents and Kids.* Menlo Park, CA: Kaiser Family Foundation, 2001.

MacGregor, Cynthia. *Night-Night: Settle-Down Activities for Easy Bedtimes.* York Beach, ME: Conari Press, 2002.

Pillsbury, Linda Goodman, and Wetmore, Barry. *Survival Tips for Working Moms: 297 Real Tips for Real Moms.* Glendale, CA: Perspective, 1995.

PETS

Anderson, Moira K. *Coping with Sorrow on the Loss of Your Pet.* Loveland, CO: Alpine Publications, 1996.

PLAY THERAPY

Boyd-Webb, Nancy. *Play Therapy with Children in Crisis*, 2nd ed. New York: Guilford Press, 1999.

Gil, Eliana. *The Healing Power of Play: Working with Abused Children.* New York: Guilford Press, 1991.

Nemiroff, Marc A., and Annunziata, Jayne. *A Child's First Book about Play Therapy.* Washington, DC: American Psychological Association, 1990.

POTTY TRAINING

Arnold, Samuel. *No More Bedwetting: How to Help Your Child Stay Dry.* New York: John Wiley, 1997.

Frankel, Alona. *Once upon a Potty: Boy*. New York: HarperCollins Juvenile Books, 1999.

Frankel, Alona. *Once upon a Potty: Girl*. New York: HarperCollins Juvenile Books, 1999.

Mack, Alison, and Wilensky, David. *Dry All Night: The Picture Book Technique That Stops Bedwetting*. New York: Little, Brown, 1990.

STRONG-WILLED CHILDREN

Dobson, James. *The Strong-Willed Child: Birth through Adolescence*. Wheaton, IL: Tyndale House, 1978.

Forehand, Rex, and Long, Nicholas. *Parenting the Strong-Willed Child: The Clinically Proven Five-week Program for Parents of Two- to Six-Year Olds*. New York: McGraw-Hill/Contemporary Books, 2003.

TELEVISION, THE INTERNET, AND THE MEDIA

Goodman, Sherryl H., and Golib, Jan H., eds. *Children of Depressed Parents: Mechanisms of Risk and Implications for Treatment*. Washington, DC: American Psychological Association, 2002.

Levine, Madeline. *Viewing Violence: How Media Violence Affects Your Child's and Adolescent's Development*. New York: Doubleday, 1996.

Robinson, T. N., Wilde, M. L., Navracruz, L. C., Haydel, F., and Varady, A. "Effects of Reducing Children's Television and Video Game Use on Aggressive Behavior." *Archives of Pediatrics and Adolescent Medicine*, 155 (2000), 17–23.

Van Evra, Judith. *Television and Child Development*, 2nd ed. Mahwah, NJ: Lawrence Erlbaum, 1997.

Winn, Marie. *The Plug-in Drug: Television, Computers, and Family Life*. New York: Penguin, 2002.

VIOLENCE AND ABUSE

Holden, George W., Geffner, Robert A., and Jouriles, Ernest N., eds. *Children Exposed to Marital Violence: Theory, Research, and Applied Issues*. Washington, DC: American Psychological Association, 1998.

Moffatt, G. K. *Blind-Sided: Homicide Where It Is Least Expected*. Westport, CT: Praeger, 2000.

Moffatt, G. K. *A Violent Heart: Understanding Aggressive Individuals*. Westport, CT: Praeger, 2000.

Moffatt, G. K. *Wounded Innocents and Fallen Angels: Child Abuse and Child Aggression*. Westport, CT: Praeger, 2003.

Simmons, Rachel. *Odd Girl Out: The Hidden Culture of Aggression in Girls*. New York: Harcourt Brace, 2002.

Index

About the Author

GREGORY MOFFATT has been a college professor for 20 years and in private practice as a therapist specializing in child psychology since 1987. He writes a regular column for a Georgia newspaper, addressing families and children.